John Skillen is a multifaceted Martial Artist and reality borne Self Protection expert. He holds black belts in several disciplines, including Kung Fu, Kickboxing and Judo. John is a fully qualified amateur boxing coach and a former national Judo champion. John spent over twenty years working as a nightclub bouncer and is a trained bodyguard. John is an international Self Defence instructor. John weaves his writing around his family life and his own Martial Arts & Fitness Centre.

This is John's first book.

www.johnskillenmaf.com

John Skillen

EXTRA CHILLI SAUCE

A TALE OF VIOLENCE, RETRIBUTION AND SUCCESS

Copyright © John Skillen 2017

John Skillen has asserted his right under the Copyright, Designs and Patents Act 1988 to be identified as the author of this work.

All rights reserved
No part of this publication may be reproduced, stored in any retrieval system or transmitted in any form or by any means without the prior written permission of the author.

This book is a work of fiction and, except in the case of historical fact, any resemblance to actual persons, living or dead, is purely coincidental.

Dedication

For my sons Luke and Thomas, so they may see the error of my ways and stay on a true and righteous path.

Acknowledgements

Thank you to Geoff Thompson for his encouragement to put pen to paper and Peter Consterdine for his knowledge and support; Robert Higgs, Colin Stainton, Ian Jones, Paul Wooley and Dr Steve Joyce for their guidance and advice.

A special thank you to my wife Tina for her patience and understanding.

Thank you to Peter Skillen and Nick Hardy for their continued support.

Thank you to Dennis Martin; you are an inspirational combative instructor and a true warrior.

In memory of past warriors: Marios Tinentis – never forgotten; and Peter Robbins – a true gentleman.

FOREWORD BY GEOFF THOMPSON

BAFTA-WINNING WRITER, TEACHER AND MARTIAL ARTIST

It is a genuine pleasure for me to write the foreword to John Skillen's first book, Extra Chilli Sauce, not just because it is a fantastic read (and it is an amazing story), but because John is a fantastic man. The word legend is bandied around a lot these days, but with John the term really fits. When I first met him in the early 90's his reputation was formidable, he was revered, and his experience on that pavement arena was unparalleled, I don't think I have ever met a man with as much experience in violence as John Skillen. He started out as a ferocious young fighter that the town bouncers could not handle. So they gave him a job, and he ended up running club doors himself where his reputation as a knock out merchant spread fast. All the more remarkable is the fact that John was later able to transcend the world of violence and become a renowned gym owner and martial arts teacher of the highest calibre. When you meet him you can see the vast experience in his gait, it is written in every line, every gesture - every movement talks of his prolific history. When you are a man of experience you don't have to preach it, you are your own gospel. What I love about John and what makes me want to promote him to everyone with a penchant for martial arts, self defence or development of the character is that he is such a genuine man. I love him. He has a rare and delicious polarity; extreme physical prowess balanced with a genuine desire to pass on life saving skills to others. You hardly ever see that any more. It is a scene full of snakes painting legs on themselves and claiming to be dragons. What excites me about this book, and what excites me about John Skillen is that he is none of that, he doesn't need to posture, he does not need to brag or boast, he is the real thing. He is one of a kind.

It is not the heavy content of claret inducing nightclub battles that draws me to this book or to John, rather it is the transition of this man of violence into this man of words. I read an early draft of Extra Chilli when John first starting writing it some time back and loved it. It was a brutally honest, often disturbing, funny and very enlightening. The finished job is even better.

I hope you love it as much as I do. And when you meet John you will be just as impressed. Geoff Thompson

MEMORIES

They say that what we experience in our childhood shapes our life and makes us who we are. We're conditioned by those around us. As we grow we look, listen and take in information. Our senses become stimulated and we experience many emotions. Those experiences become our memories and they're filed away, billions of neurones full of information, which give us a massive biological library. There, deep within the cortex of the mind, they wait to be awoken.

It's strange how we entertain the good memories, whilst grappling with our subconscious to suppress the bad. Think hard enough about a past experience and before you can take another breath you'll be whisked back in time to relive the feelings and emotions of that experience. The tastes, smells and sounds of that past memory uncontrollably flood back: the taste of chocolate; newly picked strawberries; the smell of ground coffee; baked bread or the evil stench of stale piss and the metallic taste of blood.

The memory can play tricks with reality. The image of a loved one long since dead delivered via dreams can overcome you with joy or sadness. The memory is a wondrous array of electrical impulses recording everything we do in our lives. It can make us great or haunt us into the gutter.

Our experiences make us who we are. They mould us. Without our memories we would be nothing.

What follows are my memories, some good, some bad, some I would like to forget for ever. These are the memories that make me who I am today.

GOLDEN WORDS

"Always keep yourself fit and strong, Johnny boy. Always get the first punch in. It doesn't matter if he beats you. Let him know that he's been in a fight. You give him half a hiding whilst he gives you a good one and he won't want to fight you again."
My dad Samuel Skillen

My dad drilled 'golden words' into me as I entered manhood. That's all that was going through my mind. One phrase in particular stood out; 'Get the first punch in!' I'd thrown thousands of right hands against the heavy bag, and here I was invisible. Standing in the shadows watching, waiting to throw one more.

Circa 1984, Loughborough, my home town was addictive. I didn't know why but when I was there I didn't want to be, then when I left I wanted to return. Situated in the East Midlands on junction 23 of the M1 motorway, Loughborough is a market town within easy reach of Derby, Nottingham and Leicester and just a couple of miles from the Royal Signals army base in Woodhouse Eaves. Loughborough was a town that thrived during the hosiery boom of yesteryear. Now, however, it's better known for its university sports science and the many famous athletes who were educated here.

Back then, the town came alive at weekends. Everyone had the same idea: 'a good piss up!' There were two nightclubs in Loughborough, Adam and Eve and Sammy's formerly known as Rebecca's. Sammy's was always packed on a Saturday night. The dance floor gave the club its great atmosphere. This was the ultimate 'townie' venue and this is where we were headed with a mixed bunch of twenty-something lads.

The lads had been through loads of scraps together and had a reputation around town for kicking off if required to do so. Nobody messed with us! Everyone was aware: if you fought one, you usually fought them all. We did what we wanted, went where we wanted; we had respect!

We approached the club and made our way directly to the front bypassing the long queue and in, no questions asked. The reputation preceded the lads.

We filed in through the doors. I followed 'Bullet'. They called him Bullet because of his speed of hand and his willingness to be first in in a ruck. He was the main man, a furious fighter who was also a gentleman with a big heart. Bullet by-passed the pay desk and led the lads up the staircase.

'He pays!'

The voice froze me for a second. I turned to where the voice emanated from. I caught the piercing gaze of Regan. I stared at the six footer of Irish origin; a big man with powerfully built shoulders and hands that hung at his sides like shovels waiting to scoop any troublemakers out of the club.

Regan was the classic bouncer, old school image, dressed for the kill, dinner suit, white shirt and bow tie. He was the head doorman brought in by the owner to look after his interests. *He* made the decisions and *his* word was final. He had a fiery temper and he always looked like someone had really pissed him off. I heard he boxed and was some kind of martial artist – a 'Kendo' expert. One rumour was that he drove his car by a man who had upset him, leaned out of the window and slashed him across the back of the legs with a Samurai sword then drove off. I didn't know if there was any truth in the rumour and I didn't care. All I knew was what I'd seen for myself. I didn't take any notice of people's reputations. I took people as I found them and drew my own conclusions. I'd come to the conclusion that Regan was a bully and a dangerous one.

I broke the gaze and looked at Bullet for moral support.

'It's all right, Regan. He's with me,' Bullet said.

'He pays.'

His voice was stern and there appeared no room for negotiation. Bullet ignored Regan's comments and looked to the manager. A look was all it took!

'He's all right, Regan,' the manager said. Regan glared at me but said nothing. I followed Bullet up the staircase. The music got louder as we made our way towards the doorway to the club. I felt the anger rush through my insides. This wasn't the first time Regan had tried to force a confrontation with me. I usually ignored him but the more I ignored him, the more he had a go.

I told Bullet if Regan fucked with me again I would kill him. Bullet's reaction was to warn me off.

'Don't mess with him, John. He's a real hard fucker.' Coming from one of the hardest lads in town I took note of his advice, but I meant what I'd said.

That night went without incident. I kept out of his way and he kept out of mine, although the odd time I could feel his stare piercing the back of my head. I didn't trust him and I'd be watching my back.

A couple of weeks later, I made my way into the club in the usual fashion. This time there was no hassle. The dance floor was throbbing to the sound of Michael Jackson's 'Thriller'. I looked across the dance floor noticing one or two of the birds in the crowd that could have been extras from Jackson's video! I moved to the far end of the club and stood at the bar trying to look cool (and doing a good job of it I might add). I was also keeping well away from the dance floor. I was one of those lads who never danced. It was too un-cool and I always felt vulnerable.

I'd only been in the club for ten minutes when one of the town lads approached.

'John, your Sam's just been kicked out! That cunt Regan threw him down the stairs. Sam's outside going ballistic and he wants to see you,' he said.

Sam, who had been in the club with a couple of friends, had been ejected during a fight. When I got there Sam was angry and frustrated at the way he'd been thrown out by Regan.

Sam hadn't started the fight but admitted he was involved. Sam was prepared to walk out but Regan had other ideas. He head-locked Sam and dragged him to the top of the stairs. After a short struggle Regan launched him down two flights of stairs then forced him into the street. He could have let him walk but that wasn't Regan's style.

Sam was losing his head and wanted Regan outside. Sam wasn't alone. He was joined by his mate Swanny, a crazy skinhead who had a vile temper, especially when saturated with alcohol. I calmed them both down, bringing to their attention the situation between

Regan and myself. Besides, Regan looked a right handful and with his reputation, I didn't want my brother getting any further involved. I told Sam to go home and I would deal with the situation. Sam saw sense.

I spoke to Dave, a mate of mine who was on the door. Dave confirmed what Sam had said was true. He also added that Regan was out of order. I'd had enough of Regan taking the piss. This time he'd gone too far. I decided there and then to confront him.

I told Dave it was personal and I didn't want to involve any of the other bouncers. Dave agreed to keep out of it. He couldn't assure me about the other bouncers though. I decided to take my chance; this was a matter of honour. I went upstairs and positioned myself in a small seating area known as the speakeasy.

This area was raised above floor level, giving a nice vantage point. I stood where I could see the entrance doors that led into the club; the way Regan would enter. I'd noticed over the last couple of weeks when the panic alarm sounded the bouncers would burst through the doors and head for the fracas. Regan was always the last man through the door. The plan was to lie and wait for the panic alarm to go off, which it did several times a night. Once the bouncers had gone to the scene of the trouble, I would be left to deal with Regan one-on-one, none of this out-the-back shit. I would just steam into him and give it my best shot. I'd run through many mental scenarios in my mind. I didn't know whether I could beat Regan. I didn't even consider the outcome. This was a matter of honour.

My nerves were kept at bay. An anger simmering below boiling point. I waited. The ear piercing sound of the panic alarm forced adrenalin into my system. A cold chill shivered my spine. It was time to show this wanker the respect he deserved: Fucking none.

The bouncers burst through the double doors and headed to where the fight was taking place. I stared at the doors waiting. I didn't want to rush out too soon. I had to take him by surprise. I could feel my heart beating out a warning on my chest. 'Come on. Where are you?' I mouthed. Then he appeared. I took a quick look to see where the bouncers were. They were still in the thick of the action at the far end of the club. It was now or never. Regan's impressive frame filled the doorway. He looked how Bullet had described him earlier: a hard fucker. I took a deep breath and left the safety of the shadows.

I lowered my head and sprinted towards him. When I was in range, I fired in a right hand punch like a fast bowler delivering a cricket ball. He didn't see it coming and if he did it hadn't registered. The punch landed flush on his jaw. The forward momentum of my bodyweight and the power of the punch were enough to drive him backward and unbalance him, but it wasn't enough to knock him out. I kept forward momentum and tried to follow through with a barrage of punches. Before I could get another punch off, he encircled my body trapping my arms to my sides. He clung on like a boxer in a clinch. His grip was strong.

We reeled backwards into the ladies' toilet and crashed to the floor; his back taking the full weight of both of us. He still had a tight hold of me. I was breathing heavily and the smell of perfume and deodorant mixed with cigarette smoke hit me in the back of the throat. My lungs struggled for air as I thrashed about trying to break free of his grip. This was a bad position. I had to get my arms free. He was still stunned, but if I didn't get my arms free, he would recover and I'd be in trouble. The fear of the other bouncers joining in and me getting beat, fired me up. His grip was getting stronger crushing me; he was recovering. I let out a deep, animalistic scream and tore one of my arms free.

'Come on, you bastard!' I shouted, and drove my thumb deep into his eye socket. He yelped and released his grip. I pushed harder with the thumb and dug my nails into the side of his head drawing blood as the skin ripped. I pulled my other arm free. I now tore at his face and eyes with both hands. I was still struggling to dominate him and I needed to get to my feet. If I stayed on the ground, my energy would soon drain.

He gripped me again and held on. I roared trying to break free. My nails raked his eyelids, ferreting for his eyeballs. I grabbed both sides of his head using his hair for better grip and continually smashed his skull against the now blood-soaked floor tiles. I could smell the sickly aroma of stale beer and puke. I slipped forward into a mount position and pounded his face. Punch after punch landed. Blood spurted from his wounds. I noticed two girls cowering behind the toilet door unable to get out or move. I reached toward them and was able to grab hold of one of the girl's dresses. She reeled backward with a look of horror on her face and screamed. There was enough grip to get me to my feet. I was now standing and out of control. I couldn't stop myself. I continually booted and stamped on his face. Years of anger and frustration were in every stamp. I had to make sure he didn't get up. His head fell to one side, arms motionless beside him, his body now still. I stared at him through narrowed eyes and balled fists, hatred burning through my veins.

Then they came, like they always did. Those words; those words that were supposed to make me feel I had a right to be judge, jury and executioner.

'Don't ever fuck with my family again. Do you hear me? Do you hear me, you fucking prick?' I was breathing heavily, consumed by a rage pumping up my system. I stood over him, the victor, staring down at his lifeless frame. He was finished!

An eerie silence came next. I turned toward the girls, the only witnesses. They were now silent, staring at me, their faces locked in fear. My anger subsided and I slipped into a dream like state. Was this real? I caught sight of myself in the mirror and stared at my reflection. I lifted my hands to my face and drew my fingers down the skin, clearing the blood from my eyes. The movements of my reflection were slow and distorted. The image in the mirror stared at me through dark piercing eyes: a face contorted and made ugly by a rage. Was this me?

The sound of a man's voice brought me back to reality. I turned to see Lincoln, a friend, standing in the doorway. He looked shocked at what he saw.

'John, what ya done? You've fucking killed him!'

The words made me panic. I'd known Lincoln for years. He was cool but I didn't know how the other doormen would react to what Lincoln had seen. I had to get out of there. I'd done what had to be done. I pushed past him and ran down the stairs into the main entrance area. The door was unmanned and open. I looked outside and saw a police van was parked across the road. I walked out calmly and once out of sight, I ran home.

As soon as I was out of sight of the club the feelings of panic were replaced by those of euphoria. As I ran, I realised the euphoria of the win was blinding me to the consequences of what I'd done.

'Yes! Yes!' I chanted. I'd beaten him. Yet deep inside I sensed something was wrong.

I got back to my parents' house, and walked into a room full of shocked faces. I was breathing heavily after the run. My mother gave me a horrified look. 'My God John, what have you done?' Between breaths I told them.

'Get in the shower. Look at yourself. You're covered in blood,' she said. I paced the room like an expectant father waiting for news of a birth. I felt invincible. My dad, who had initially praised me, was now worried. 'Get in the shower Johnny boy, before the police come. Get changed, we'll tell them you've been here all night. Hurry! Get in the shower.'

I stripped off and jumped into the shower. The water ran over my bloodied skin cleansing my body. I felt a chill, even though the water was hot. I closed my eyes. The magnitude of what I'd done began to present itself like a slideshow in my mind. I could see my mirrored image, the faces of the girls screaming, reeling back in fear. I could see Lincoln's face, and hear his words, 'You've fucking killed him, John!' The words reverberated over and over again in my mind like a tune you can't get out of your head.

What had I done? I felt afraid. I tilted my head back and the water rushed onto my face. I wished it would wash away the fear, make everything OK. It didn't!

Had I killed him? Had I actually finally committed the ultimate sin? The fear welled up inside me. I felt sick and weak. I sat down in the shower, unable to stand. He couldn't be dead. It was a fair go, just me and him. Fuck! But what if he was dead? I put my hands to my face and covered my eyes. Why didn't I just leave it? Why didn't I just walk away…why? As I sat there with the water cascading over my body I began to reflect on my life.

GROWING UP

My mother gained her temperament and fighting experience after being influenced by her father Jum Olley, the son of a cockney market trader. My granddad taught her what was required in a fight. One day she came home from school crying saying that she'd been pushed around by two girls. My granddad sent her back outside telling her not to come home until she'd battled it out with the girls. She did as he said and gave them a sound thrashing. She, the eighth child in a family of fifteen, found herself sticking up for her brothers and sisters which meant fighting became part of what she had to do day-in-day-out. And although she was a fun loving character she developed a temper held back by only a thread of emotion.
It was 1957, and after leaving home, my mother took a job at the King's Head Hotel in Loughborough. There she met my father, Sammy Skillen, a Frank Sinatra look-alike with piercing blue eyes and a huge infectious smile that lit up the dreariest of places. He was an Irish Catholic from Banbridge town in County Down, a kind-hearted man who hated the politics of his own country and believed that everyone should be able to live together in peace. He was proud to be British.
It was love at first sight for my mother and father. Corny I know, but it really was. They married soon after at a small church in Lutterworth, Leicestershire where her parents lived. Shortly after their marriage they moved to Ireland and my eldest brother Joseph was born. A year later, they moved back to England and I was born in Leicester on the 15th July 1960 weighing 6lbs 15oz. Straight away I was born into confrontation. My granddad, Jum Olley, when seeing me for the first time referred to me as having a 'bull neck' an English phrase used to describe a strong-looking neck. My dad not understanding the meaning took offence to the phrase thinking it was an insult. If it wasn't for the timely intervention of my grandma Olley there'd have been a fight in the hospital! Another year later my mother gave birth to my sister Bernadette.
In 1963, one of the coldest winters on record, we made our way once again to Ireland, to a one bedroom house with a small living-room-kitchenette and very little else. The house was situated away

from the town on top of a steep hill. There were no street lamps, no running water, and very little heating.

As Bernadette and I had been born in England, my dad's family and friends hadn't celebrated the birth, so my dad was invited out with his mates for the head-wetting. He didn't want to leave my mum on her own in a strange house with three children, but they insisted he go. Before he left, he gave instructions to my mum not to open the door to anyone under any circumstance unless she was sure who it was.

Later that night my mum heard a knocking at the door and a muffled voice she didn't recognise. Mum was frightened and refused to open the door. A couple of hours passed and a neighbour came knocking frantically at the door.

'Open the door, Josie,' the man said in a broad North Irish accent.

'It's your neighbour. And if you don't open the door your husband is going to die.'

After deliberation, she finally opened the door to see her husband covered in snow and frozen to the floor with the next door neighbour trying to free him by scraping beneath his arse with a shovel. He'd got incredibly drunk and, not being used to the Irish ale, had collapsed outside after being refused entry by my mum. They eventually freed him and set about thawing him out. If the neighbour hadn't seen my dad, he'd have surely frozen to death. They both saw the funny side.

The house we lived in had no floorboards. It was mud-based and covered in lino. The floor was solid until the big thaw came. Overnight it was awash with melting snow and ice. The lino in our living room began to squelch under foot. Mum pulled it back to reveal a muddy, sodden mess. She was forced to move us upstairs because the water level began to rise and the lino had started to float.

A couple of years passed and during that time my sister Helen and brother Sam were born.

My first experience of violence happened at the tender age of five. There was always a huge open fire burning in the house and the smell of wood-smoke blended with home cooking filled the room. We had a sheepdog that lay in front of the fire chewing on a bone after a hard day chasing sticks. I was a playful five-year-old who thought it was fun to take the bone from the dog. He let out a terrible growl and grabbed me by the throat, its teeth sunk into my skin and hung from my neck narrowly missing my jugular vein. My dad rushed into the room and removed the bone throwing the dog into the door then out of it! The dog was given to the farmer to do what he was intended for, to work the land. I had a fear of dogs after that attack, one I would eventually get over.

My parents were on the housing list waiting to be re-housed in a new building project, which was replacing an old housing estate. They used the condition of the house to make a point and get one of the new properties. After a long battle with the local council, my mum and dad were allocated a house on a mainly Protestant estate called Sea Patrick, just outside of Banbridge town, Belfast. Everyone who was allocated a new house moved in but my mother was kept waiting. The only reason was my father being Catholic and being married to an English woman.

The council wouldn't release the keys and refused to give them on several occasions. My mother decided to take drastic action. She took me, my brother, two sisters and baby Sam, who was still in nappies, and left us in the council offices screaming our heads off. She'd leave us there until they handed the keys over to the new house. It was a gamble as we could have been taken into care, but it was a gamble she was prepared to take. It paid off. It wasn't long before someone came over with the keys and Mum claimed her children back. She had to fight for the right to be housed in a home fit to bring her children up. Her strong will and stubbornness paid off.

We used to go visiting family in a nearby village. To get there we had to cross a rickety old bridge in need of repair. I remember having to stay away from the edges due to the loose railings. Beneath the bridge raged a torrent of water. It was a frightening experience crossing the river, made more frightening by the news that my cousin Martin had drowned in the river at the very place we used to play together. It was a sad time.

In my memory Banbridge always appears dull and cloudy. I'm sure it wasn't. However, violent memories always come to my mind.

As we were Catholics we naturally went to a Catholic school. The teachers were harsh and strict. This style of teaching was designed to toughen up the young in order to become desensitised to the

tormenting that went on between Catholics and Protestants. My brother and me made our way to school in no particular hurry. On the way, we passed a huge factory unit with doors that opened like an aeroplane hangar. Inside, were wooden crates full of live chickens, stacked three or four high. In front of the unit was a yard the size of a small car park. There were a few men in the yard moving the crates around, coming and going in and out of the factory. I noticed a few crates stacked next to a block of wood. Standing next to the crates was a thick-set man wearing a scruffy apron. He stood with a meat cleaver in his hand, looking like a crazed psychopath in a horror film. His other hand was stuffed inside one of the crates. He called to us in his broad North Irish accent. When he had our attention, he pulled a chicken out of the crate like a magician pulling a rabbit out of a hat. With the chicken going wild, he placed its head on the block then brought the blade down like a guillotine at an execution. The man placed the chicken on the floor then let go. He bellied up with laughter as the chicken's headless body ran round and round in circles. I gasped and felt sorry for it. My brother put his hand on my shoulder.
'Come on. Let's go,' he said.
There was something sinister about the way the butcher decapitated that chicken.

My dad used to drink in a small pub a few hundred yards from where we lived. Inside the smoked-filled room, which smelt of beer and tobacco, was a small, traditional, wooden bar. A few tables and chairs were scattered round, each with its own ashtray. The floor was covered in sawdust to catch any spillages from the beer mugs or from the dogs that frequented the place. The tables were always busy, with men playing cards or dominoes and smoking pipes or roll-ups. At the end of every session, the floor would be swept and the sawdust burnt on the fire in the yard. The next day, Joe and me would sift through the cool ash looking for discarded coins dropped by the inebriated locals. When we found them, we'd take them home, clean them up and spend them at the local shop next to the pub.
Whilst sifting through the rubbish one day, we encountered a couple of Protestant youths. They lived next door to us and were bully-boys who constantly picked on us. As soon as they got in

range, they began pelting us with rotten tomatoes and calling us names. Joseph returned fire and scored a direct hit with one of the tomatoes. The youths who were around 16 years old, weren't impressed with Joseph's accuracy so he got a slapping. We ran home and told Mum. Mum lost it. Her temper overwhelmed her. With Joe and me in tow, she immediately confronted the youths. When one of the youths swore at her, she gave him a hefty slap and knocked him backward. She couldn't hold her temper and would fight like mad to defend her family. To make matters worse, the youth's parents didn't get on well with my mum either. The reason was political and religious based racism.

My mother was an English Catholic, married to an Irish Catholic, which was frowned upon by our Protestant neighbours. They tried to bond on occasions but it just wasn't to be. The feelings on religious and political matters ran high. Every year between the 1st and 12th of July, the time of the Orange Parade, the neighbours would totally ignore my mother. One year, the neighbour asked my mother to lend her an umbrella for the parade. The weather was atrocious, so she obliged and lent her the only umbrella she owned. When the woman got to the parade, she put it up and it blew inside out embarrassing the neighbour. She thought that my mum had done it on purpose and never spoke to her again.

The hatred between the two families grew. The neighbour's daughter was by far the worst. Every time she passed my mum in the street, she would call her a 'Fenian bastard', and spit on the floor in front of her regardless of whom my mother was with. The Fenians were a group of Irish rebels from the 1860s. My mother ignored the derogatory remark, until one day she finally cracked and gave the daughter a good hiding. My father kept out of what he termed 'women's troubles' and left Mum to it, which was fine if it was just women involved, but the hate was about to take a sinister turn.

The violence with the neighbours finally came to a head in my mum's kitchen. She'd had an argument in the street with her neighbour and it led to blows being exchanged in the street. My mum got the better of her and she ran into her house. My mother gave chase but was faced with a locked front door; the door had two glass panels. In her rage she put her fist through one of the panes of glass cutting her wrist in the process.

Later that day my mum was preparing dinner and I was happily playing away beside her. The back door of our house led into the kitchen. The window looked over the back yard. I remember seeing a shadowy figure flash by the window and it caught my mother's eye. 'What was that?' she asked. She ignored it and turned back to her cooking. I watched as our neighbour's husband appeared through the open door. I couldn't warn my mum. It was too late. He rushed at her. The first punch landed before she realised the man had come in. She screamed and tried to fight back, but was overwhelmed by the attack. I watched as the man battered her. I recall running to the coal shed, which was in the hallway adjacent to the kitchen.

I picked up a small hand axe used for chopping fire wood and ran at the man.

'I'll chop his legs off, Mum,' I shouted. The axe was far too heavy for a seven-year-old to wield with any effect. The man stopped hitting her, grabbed the axe from me and pushed me aside. He shouted abuse at my mum and stormed out of the kitchen with the axe in his hand. I ran and clung to her; she was sobbing.

Mum called the police and instead of making an arrest they tracked down my dad at a local pub and arrested him, even before he found out what had happened. They informed him of the incident and held him in the police cells until he had cooled off. He was warned to stay away from the neighbour or he'd be charged. The neighbour remained free and no charges were brought by the police. The police weren't very sympathetic towards Catholics.

I thought about that incident a lot growing up and I felt I'd let my mum down. I felt useless. As I got older, the feelings got worse. My mum believed that if I hadn't intervened that day, he'd have probably killed her. The sight of a seven-year-old wielding an axe and screaming had brought the man back from the brink of temporary insanity.

The trouble in Ireland got worse and although my dad loved his country, he loved his family more and saw no future in Ireland for himself or us. My dad decided to move the family back to England for good. Just before we left, my dad took revenge on the neighbour. The neighbour had just bought a new car, so in the early hours of the morning, my dad and my uncle broke into it and released the hand brake. We lived on a steep sloping road. They gave it a good shove and it rolled down the hill picking up speed as it freewheeled down. The car was wrecked. That morning we were on the ferry back to England.

SUNNY DAYS

Once back in Britain, my dad got a job on a farm in Market Bosworth, a small town in the Leicestershire countryside. We moved into the farmer's tied cottage, which was a perk of working for the farmer; rent-free as well. Unlike Ireland, my memories of the Leicestershire countryside are always sunny. We played in the fields, building dens with bales of hay. We explored the woods by day and feared them by night. I loved being in there. It was like an adventure playground. I remember being in the house one night and being called out by the farmer's son. He told us to watch the sky. Whilst we marvelled at the stars, he switched on a huge torch and the beam hit the blanket of stars. The beam paraded to and fro like a giant light sabre. I was amazed at its power.
During the day my dad worked the farm and during the night he did a night shift at a local factory. In the mornings that we weren't at school, we ran through the damson-lined lanes shouting out his name as we ran. He'd hear us and shout back. When he was close, we'd sprint towards him; it was a truly happy time for me.
At school we were the centre of attention and surrounded by children asking us to speak to them just so they could listen to our Irish accents.

The happy days on the farm came to an abrupt end. The farmer asked my dad to work for him full-time and for whatever reason my dad refused. He had to give up the tied cottage, which meant we were homeless. In order to find accommodation he could afford, dad moved us back to Loughborough, a town he knew well. Housing was hard to get, so my mother got on the council housing list and waited again. In the meantime, she hired a caravan on Swingbridge Road Caravan Site. The site was full of growing families waiting to be re-housed in council properties. The caravan was a four berth, which had to house seven of us. Whilst living in the caravan was cramped, it was also very damp. Sam, my youngest brother, was rushed into hospital diagnosed with pneumonia. His condition worsened and my parents were told he wouldn't live through the night. That night my parents prayed hard for baby Sam. In a dream my mother had a vision of her sister Rosemary who had died of cancer at the age of sixteen. Her sister gave her words of comfort and told her that Sam would pull through. Sure enough later the next day the sunshine shone through the caravan window and happiness abounded, the doctors were astounded at Sam's recovery.

In the time we were on that site, Joe and I would play along the nearby canal bank, sometimes fishing for sticklebacks. We learnt how to open and close the locks, so we'd spend hours there watching the barges and boats passing through. When it was warm, we'd play with Mum, Dad and the rest of the family, swimming and floating in the canal using giant lorry inner tubes.

Eventually we were moved to a council house on Wharncliffe Road. We spent a couple of years there and my brothers, James and Peter, were born. I was now one of seven, nine including Mum and Dad.

Joe and I would roam about the town using the canal and old steam railway routes, or walk for miles playing on the embankments, bridges and in the old steam railway station at Loughborough. One game we'd regularly play was stoning the pot connectors on the telegraph poles which lined the tracks or smashing the panes of glass in the abandoned signal boxes.

Our house seemed big after living in a small caravan and at night I'd feel scared. I think the fear was brought on by the story my mother told us. She'd say if we don't go to sleep the 9 o'clock horses would come and take us away. I'd hide under the covers awaiting their arrival. I don't think Mum realised how scared I was.

Facing school was always a problem for me; I hated it! I'd been to several different schools before I was eight years old. Maybe it was the constant moving and not being able to settle down in one school for long enough to fit in. Maybe the school in Northern Ireland had affected my idea of what school life should be like. Catholic schools were notoriously strict and some of the teaching bordered on abuse.

The most unforgettable moment of my young school life was in a class with a teacher known as Mr Varner. He was a tall, lean man with skeleton-like features. He was strict and appeared not to like children. He'd ask a question then survey the whole class daring someone to put up their hand and get the answer wrong.

It was late afternoon and I needed the toilet. I was afraid to put up my hand and ask his permission for fear of being barked at. I eventually plucked up the courage and raised my hand. Mr Varner seemed irritated that I hadn't put my hand up to answer a question and refused to allow me to go. My hand went down a lot quicker than it had gone up. My bowels rumbled and I was feeling uncomfortable. It was becoming painful to stop myself from going. I frantically waved my hand in the air but was ignored. I spoke up, much to my embarrassment.

'Please Sir, I'm desperate. I need to go to the toilet, now!' I said pleading with him.

'You'll have to wait,' came his reply. I felt my eyes begin to fill up with tears.

'But sir, I can't hold it any longer, please sir,' I begged him, fighting back the tears. Still he wouldn't let me go. The other pupils stared at me. I felt myself shrinking in the chair.

Then the unthinkable happened. As I fought to hold back the inevitable I pleaded one last time hoping to touch on his compassionate side. 'Please sir, I need to go!' I should have just gone, but I was too scared of Mr Varner to move without his permission. Besides, it was too late, the smell began to announce what I'd done.

The tears ran down my face. I dared not get out of my chair even though I felt like I wanted to run away. It felt like that same squidgy feeling when you stand in a cowpat, only this was warm and under my arse. The caring Mr Varner announced to the whole class that I'd had an accident. As if they hadn't already guessed. He felt the need to repeat this making me feel worse than I already did. The bell sounded at the end of the class; it was home time. I remained in my chair as the classroom emptied. 'You'd better go to the toilet, Skillen,' Varner said. I was wearing shorts and dared not move.

I was totally embarrassed and humiliated. The warm pile smelt disgusting. My brother Joseph, who was in a different classroom, came to help me. I was so pleased to see him. I walked out of the school with my head hung low, and my brother at my side comforting me. You can imagine what the next few years of my school life were like.

My dad was working in a well paid job as an overhead crane driver at Brush Electrical Machines, while Mum always seemed to be decorating. We'd be moved from one room to the next to make way for her. This moving around nearly cost me my life. The television was moved from the back room along the hallway to the front room. There was no electricity supply in the front room, so a cable ran from the back room to the front. The cable was still too short, so it was lengthened by twisting another length of cable together and taping it up. In the end, the cable was one foot from the floor and ran the full length of the hallway. We were given strict instructions not to go into the back room. As I was passing, I saw the back room door open and climbed over the cable and went inside. When I ran back out, the cable snapped in half at the joint. Not wanting to get caught, I picked up both cables and joined them together. The cable was live and I was flung into the air and hit the wall with a terrific bang. I don't know what saved me that day. Both my palms were burnt brown where the cables had been and I was shocked but relatively unhurt.

It was 1970 and England was playing host to hundreds of Asian families looking to start a new life. My mum and dad were told that our house at Wharncliffe Road was going to be demolished to make way for a new road. We were re-housed on the Shelthorpe Estate in a five-bedroom home with a huge garden. Shelthorpe Estate was full of big families. Some were so big they lived in two five-bedroom houses converted into one.

Fighting was a normal activity there. Any neighbourly disputes were usually sorted out with the fist. It wasn't unusual to see two mothers scrapping on the grass verge, usually mine being one of them.

I remember going through the same routine my mother went through with her dad. My older brother Joe was always scrapping. He was the one who'd be first in. If anyone threatened us we stuck together. Joe got into a fight with his mate over something trivial. After a long scrap his mate got a lucky shot in and heeled him in the face and Joseph was beat. I ran in the house and told my mum thinking she'd sort it out. I got a clip round the ear and sent back outside and told not to come back in until I had beaten the lad. I lost my temper and ran out into the street and got stuck in. We scuffled and scrapped until the lad ran off. I had stood by my brother. My mum was proud of me, and although I felt afraid and didn't want to get involved. As soon as I did, the fear left me. That had an effect on me that would last a lifetime.

There were a lot of issues with people on the estate. The lack of money being one. Whoever said, 'You've never had it so good,' didn't live in our neighbourhood!

Manor Drive was always full of children. In the summer months the streets were alive with overactive kids; a population explosion was taking place. We did all the things kids did in those days, hedge jumping, British bulldog, haystack jumping, kiss chase, and scrumping (stealing fruit from trees), which became serious when food was short. I had a good childhood there. We went through some tough times like a lot of the families did. But the good far outweighed the bad.

It was 1974. Slade, T-Rex, The Sweet and Alice Cooper were ruling the charts. Life became a little more serious at 14 years old. I got a job on the local market selling fruit and veg. If I lost one job I moved to the next stall and got another. To compensate for the low wage, I'd get my sister to come to the stall and buy some produce. I'd then stick in some extra and give her more change than was required. I never took too much, just enough. This went on for quite a while, until one of the girls that worked on the stall got suspicious and grassed me up. I denied all knowledge and they couldn't prove otherwise. I was stealing but didn't see it as that. I saw it as helping my mum provide for the family. If Dad and Mum had found out what I was doing, I'd have felt the wrath of their anger and a boot up my arse.

I decided to stay well away from the market stall tills and took a job wheeling out the stall boxes and fixing the stalls up early in the morning. Twice a week during school holidays, pushing out the heavy barrows, built up my shoulder and back muscles. I also took up a couple of paper rounds on a Sunday morning. Sprinting on my bike, racing to finish the rounds in record time built up endurance in my legs.

Money was always tight at home and things got worse when Dad lost his job. He had an argument with the foreman. The argument became heated and when he called my dad an 'Irish bastard', his answer was to knock him out. Dad said he didn't mind the Irish bit but he wasn't a bastard! My dad was forever the joker. He had a great sense of humour and always saw the funny side of life. But Dad knew in his heart he should have kept his gob shut and his hands in his pockets. Jobs were hard to come by and after being sacked for violent conduct Dad never really worked again. Like a lot of other men, he got caught in the benefits trap. Basically, he received more money in benefits than he could earn at work. He didn't see the point of work: a full week's graft for less money than he was getting on the dole.

Out of boredom he turned to drink. He'd come home pissed up night after night. He'd spend money we didn't have. Then when the drink started to wear off, he'd become aggressive and shout about his frustrations with life. He couldn't sleep and would often stay awake until three or four in the morning talking to himself and shouting abusive words to anyone who'd listen. I lost count of the times I'd go down, wake him then guide him to his room. His drunkenness brought out feelings about his father whom he loved immensely. He always blamed himself for not being at home when his father died at the untimely age of 49. He found out about his death through a letter sent to him. The letter arrived too late for him to attend the funeral.

Mum and Dad would argue late into the mornings and through anger and frustration I'd cry myself to sleep. Night after night I'd pray and ask the Lord to stop the arguing. I felt desperate at times. This period of listening to confrontation between my parents night after night affected my schoolwork and I needed help. I didn't get it, I was too proud to ask for it and it wasn't offered.

My hatred of school manifested itself. My parents couldn't afford what I needed for school so I wore hand-me-downs; second-hand clothes and grant clothes that were renewable once a year. It wasn't long before the knees were out or the arse split. I got free school meals; I felt like a scrounger.

Children can be cruel and piss-taking became the norm. I got called names like 'Trampass' or 'Scrounger', two names which I loathed. I never let on that the name-calling got to me, but it did! I bottled up the feelings. If it wasn't the other kids taking the piss, it was the teachers. Not having the right kit for the right class meant I wasn't trying. I became blacklisted as a disruptive child, 'a non-runner' as my dad used to say.

Truth was, my family life wasn't conducive to school and many days were missed skiving because I couldn't face the humiliation of attending. Not all, but most of the teachers put me down, made me feel, and in some cases told me, I was useless.

My way of dealing with the stress and torment of having the piss taken out of me was to fight. I also became a smoker huddled in the yard with the other kids. Smoking was seen as cool and although I couldn't afford a smoke, I'd hang round the yard waiting for the stub end. Some mornings I wouldn't go to school unless my mother gave me a fag. I hated the taste of cigarettes and they actually made me feel sick, but to look cool and be accepted by the gang, it had to be done. This led to me being caned on several occasions and on one occasion I got my arse slippered in front of the entire PE class! Me and a friend Simo sorted that one out. One evening whilst the PE teachers played badminton we threw all of their clothes into the shower block and switched on the showers. We laughed all the way home. Revenge was indeed sweet!

My hatred of school continued up until my expulsion at 15 years old. I was overjoyed. I also quit smoking when I left. I left with one qualification – a CSE in English – the only subject I really enjoyed, which I give credit to a teacher by the name of Mr Everly, a kind helpful man.

There was still high unemployment in Loughborough, and having poor qualifications made it almost impossible to find a good job. I became a shelf stacker at Tesco's and to bump up my money, I did contract cleaning after the store shut. I felt good when I had money in my pockets. They weren't the best-paid jobs, but it was far better than school.

The money didn't last long. I started to visit gambling arcades to play the slot machines. Week after week I'd spend my wages. I became addicted to one arm bandits, the appropriate name for a machine that draws your cash in and doesn't give it back. I felt great when I went in and incredibly depressed when I came out skint. My parents would ask where my money was going. I'd lie about where it had gone. I had to stop! I found I could for a short while, then I'd relapse and go on a spending binge and lose the lot. Occasionally I'd come out a winner. Winning fed my addiction and the inner voice. I'd then go back thinking I could do the same and beat the machine. It never happened enough to go into profit. I found out the hard way. You could never beat a machine designed to absorb cash. It was months before I got the strength of mind to stop using them. I eventually made it a rule not to go into the arcade. I began to take my dad's advice. 'No matter how much money you have in your pockets, Johnny boy, always keep yourself smart and clean and a bit of polish on yer shoes.' I kept what money I had in my pocket and when I did spend it, I spent it on clothes and looking good.

My dad's drinking habit got worse. Joseph moved away from home to find work and Mum struggled to feed us all. There were times when we had no electricity or gas because we'd been cut off. The family starved on more than one occasion. Now I was working, I chipped in where I could but Mum found it hard to cope. She worked at several cleaning jobs just to bring in the cash to keep the electricity on and some grub in the pantry.

My father oblivious to it all, would get drunk, tell jokes and move around the living room throwing punches into the air showing off his boxing skills to the rest of the family. He had a fantastic right lead and a very powerful grip. He put this down to pulling flax in the mills of Ireland. Even though my dad was a habitual drinker and at times hard to live with, I still loved him dearly and felt very protective toward him.

I was 16 years old and my confidence since leaving school had just started to grow. My parents' ability to fight through tough times and my mother's short temper were passed on to me. I was drilled into protecting my family like my mother had protected us. I had a rule. If anybody threatened my family, I took it personally and got stuck in.

It was about this time that I hit the town. It was an exciting time for me. I wanted to do all the things men did. This is the time when you're under pressure from your peers to partake in whatever it was they partook in be it good or bad. I was about to get a reputation.

ON THE TOWN

There was a gang of us that went round town together. We'd meet, walk round town, get drunk, have a laugh and try and pull a bird. A good night always ended in a scrap. I got my first knockout on a night out with the lads known as Will, Glen, Steve and Mac. These were some of the lads I grew up with on the same estate as me; ordinary lads who were gainfully employed and enjoyed the weekends on the piss.

It started when we all walked into the Unicorn pub. A tall, lean 50 something guy ran the pub. I remember him looking pale and stressed. His arms were a give-away to his sexuality. His elbows stuck to his sides, wrists raised up, fingers splayed as he shuffled and skipped around the bar. The *'piéce de resistance'* was his voice. Now I know you shouldn't take the piss but that's what lads do. He was as funny as fuck when he spoke. He sounded like he was on helium and gave a good impression of being a real shirt lifter type.

We walked into the bar pushing and laughing at each other like lion cubs at play, trying to come to some seriousness before we got to the bar. We were all under age and it was easy to get served in the Unicorn. We put on our 'I'm old-enough' typefaces, frowning to make ourselves look older. Girls wear make-up, boys frown. The landlord approached us. 'Yes, boys, can I help you?' he said. His effeminate voice was so high pitched not one of us could answer for fear of laughing. We broke down one at a time until we were one bunch of giggles. 'Now come on, boys, do you want serving or not?'

'I'll have half a lager, mate, please,' I said, making my voice deeper so that he wouldn't suspect my age or take me for one of his own.

'Yeah, we'll have the same,' Will said. He poured the lagers and placed them on the bar then shuffled off.

'You behave now, boys.'

Just behind us I could feel the presence of a big man. He was suited and booted. His hair was black and swept back revealing swarthy, weathered skin as if he'd been over exposed to the elements. He drew our attention to him.

'Do you lads always take the piss?' he asked. Will turned towards the guy and fronted him up.

'You what, mate?' Will was a good scrapper. He already had a reputation for fighting. He just wouldn't back down from anyone regardless of who they were.

'Think you're a big man do you, son?' the weathered man asked. Will stared at him.

'It's got fuck all to do with you, mate, what we do.' The weathered man stared back. Will's confident reply put the man on a war footing.

'Outside!' he said. The man made his way to the door then vanished outside. Will followed with the lads close behind. One after the other they filed out cursing as they went. Glen called back to me.

'Come on John, let's fucking 'ave 'im.' I was frozen to the bar and couldn't move. I had butterflies inside my stomach. I felt like the guy was looking at me. I felt threatened.

'I'll be out in a minute,' I replied.

'Suit yourself,' he said, and out he went.

I could see their outlines through the frosted glass, one bigger than all the rest. Fuck it! I had to go. I couldn't stay. What if he beat them all? I'd never be able to face the lads again, I thought. I finished my lager in one swallow, walked out the door and into the street.

I stared at him. 'Who the fuck does he think he is?' I said to myself. I was angry and wasn't afraid any more. The anger had taken away the sensation of fear. The lads were spread out in front of the weathered man, taunting him like a pack of school kids do in the playground. The man moved cautiously keeping distance between him and the lads, his hands raised ready like a boxer. He was looking for a shot at one of them. He had positioned himself so he could see them all, but forgot the most important area, his back. He was blind to my presence and I knew it. It was time for me to take the advantage. I ran straight at him. A buzz of adrenalin fuelled my attack. In a split second, I had landed a wild overhand right punch on to the back of his head where the nape meets the skull just behind the ear. I was surprised when he went down so easily. He stumbled forward as he fell. His hands came out in front of him breaking his initial fall. His face carried on into the tarmac. The lads were on him before he could recover. Boot after boot rained in. 'Fucking leave him. He's finished,' I shouted. The lads backed off waiting for the man to rise. Will laughed excitedly as we scarpered down the road.

'Fucking great punch, John,' Will said. We left the man lying in the road. We didn't care. I never gave it a second thought. He started it and deserved all he got. Will put his arm on my shoulder like a father congratulating a son, he said. 'You should be proud of that knock-out, John. You probably won't ever get another one.' I laughed. I was high on the excitement of being the focus of the attention. It felt good to get praise.

We continued to Saleh's Kebab House, a new type of Mediterranean food, which was fast becoming the alternative to chips. We walked in, ordered our kebabs and went into the seedy restaurant area. It was laid out with cheap-looking tables and chairs. There were far too many tables and chairs for the size of the room giving it a crowded feel. A couple of the lads went to the chip shop next door; Will and the rest went to the toilet, and I sat down waiting for the waiter to take our order. A youth sitting in the row of tables opposite stared at me with glassy eyes. Still in fight mode I challenged him. 'What you looking at?'

The lad jumped up from his seat, his eyes turned from glassy to aggressive. He was up for it. Will appeared in the room just as I double tapped the youth with two straight lefts. The lad was driven back into his seat by the force of the blows. Blood appeared on his lips. He took the punches well, and didn't go out. He couldn't quite get up either. Another youth rushed in through the doorway. Will stepped in.

'Leave it, it's between them two.' The kid stopped dead in his tracks, frozen by the aggressive instructions.

The youth whom I'd cracked said, 'Leave it. I'm OK! That was a fucking good punch. Are you a boxer?' the lad asked in a well-spoken manner.

Will spun the bullshit, 'Yeah, he's an ABA champ so don't fuck him about.'

I wanted to tell Will to shut up. I was no amateur boxer. All I'd done for the last year or so was hammer an old army kit bag filled with rags and paper, which hung from a tree in the back garden. My only tuition was from my dad and watching the old black and white boxing films. The posh lad apologised for the way he looked at me. We shook hands. Then I detected a hint of sarcasm in his voice and a subliminal challenge.

'You'll have to come and have a game of rugger some time,' he said as he walked out. Cheeky fucker I thought.

The rest of the lads came in from the chip shop. Will once again sang my praises. Winning two scraps in one night boosted my confidence. These were two exams I hadn't failed.

ONE OF THE LADS

*"It's easier to cope with a bad conscience
than with a bad reputation."*
Friedrich Nietzsche

Everyone knows everyone in a town like Loughborough. Reputations built on violence are made or wiped out before the back of the head hits the pavement. Loughborough was full of lads up for a scrap. The Shelly lads, named after the Shelthorpe Estate, drank in the Bull's Head and the Hunter's Moon, the two big estate pubs. Also, there were the Sharpley Road lads who drank in the Blackbird. The lads had their differences, and at times fought amongst themselves, but eventually blended together.
There would be regular visits to football matches. Other pubs in other towns. There would always be a scrap, either with the locals, rival fans or the bouncers. Hit and run tactics always applied. The mix of lads were all within a couple of years of each other, but were all individuals. When they got together, there could be up to 50 hard-core lads walking the town. When they went into a pub they filled it, and when they left they emptied it. The crowds followed the lads from pub to pub just to witness the action.
It was 1976, the hottest summer on record. 'Young hearts run free', 'Disco Inferno' hijacked the charts and 'Disco Duck' was the dance floor filler. Ice cold lager was the drink of the day, perhaps with a lemonade top or a dash of lime to kill the sharp continental taste. We headed for Rebecca's nightclub. Will was a cunt when he drank. He did some crazy things when the beer took effect. We were in Saleh's one night when he decided it was a good idea to nick a whole roll of kebab meat, complete with giant skewer out of the freezer. Before I could tell him to put it back, he was climbing through the toilet window dragging the giant kebab skewer with him.
'Come on!' he shouted. I didn't know what he was going to do with it. I was puzzled, but knowing what Saleh's temperament was like, I wasn't going to stay behind and face the infamous kebab knife. Peer pressure forced me to clamber through the window, and grab one end of the kebab skewer. It was too heavy to run with.

Saleh was alerted to the noise and gave chase. Will did his usual trick and sprinted off leaving me with the kebab skewer. I dropped it and ran after him. I could hear Turkish Saleh shouting abuse at us as we ran off laughing.

Another idiosyncrasy of Will's was to 'TWOCK' a motor; Take without the owner's consent. He'd nicked loads and had never been caught. We'd been drinking all day, and were both pissed. We made our way home through a delivery road at the back of Boots the Chemist in Loughborough town centre. Will moved to the side of a car for a piss, while I pissed up a nearby wall. I noticed him fumbling against the car door and within seconds, he was inside. It was a Ford Zephyr. He wound down the window.

'Come on. Get in,' he said.

I refused. He started the engine. Will was a dab hand with cars.

'Fucking 'ell, Will! Get out of the car,' I said.

Will laughed as he revved up the engine, teasing me with its sound. I resisted the temptation. As he teased me a car entered the alleyway approaching in the opposite direction. Will revved the engine and shouted again.

'Come on, get in someone will see you.' I had a choice: I could walk off and leave him to it or jump in the car. Although I wanted to I couldn't leave. We were mates. We'd been through a lot together. I felt like I owed him. I jumped into the car.

'Listen, Will. Let's fucking leave it. Let's go,' I said trying to talk sense into him. The car approached driving slowly. It was a Ford Escort mark two, the car of the CID plainclothes coppers known to us as Cunts In Disguise. The silhouettes of two plainclothes coppers stood out in the dimly lit alleyway. In seconds they would be bumper to bumper with us. Before Will could drive off, the CID put on their full beam and sped toward us. I instinctively covered my face, giving the game away. Will accelerated and went to drive away. The Escort manoeuvred and blocked his path. The two officers were out of their car at the same time as us. I saw Will throw a barrage of punches temporarily dropping one of the coppers and he was gone. I had my hands full. I was in a neck-hold and struggling to get out. I eventually struggled free forcing the officer against the car. I turned and ran into the other copper who had come to assist his mate. I felt the weight of both men as they wrestled me to the floor. I almost got free. I now had two officers locking both my arms.

'You're in big trouble now, Skillen – assaulting a police officer, stealing a car.' I kept my gob shut.

I was held in the cells till the early hours, then taken in for questioning. The police made a huge error. In their excitement, they assumed I was over 18 years old. They didn't ask me my age before they interviewed me. I was only 16 and therefore a minor. They had broken their own law that a minor can only be questioned in front of a responsible adult, namely a parent. They took fingerprints and decided to charge me, until they realised how old I was. They had to let me go without charge. Just as I was walking out of the cells with a big grin on my face, one of the officers gave me a stern warning which stuck firmly in my mind.

'We'll get you, Skillen. Eventually, we'll get you!' The words spun around in my head.

'Fuck you!' was all the reply I could think of.

I'd had a lucky escape. I'd kept my mouth shut as to Will's identity. We had an important rule: don't grass. If we got arrested we said nothing and took the consequences of our actions on the chin. Will's antics carried on, but now I knew when to slip away.

There was one time I never lightfooted it, and that was when we fought. We had another rule: stick together. If we stuck together we couldn't be beaten. It made good sense but wasn't always possible.

The lads at the front of the queue at Rebecca's weren't impressed at Will's attempt to gain entry before them. One of the older lads barged into Will.

'What's your fucking game? There's a queue here.' Will didn't take kindly to being barged and without warning whacked him. The lad hit the deck unconscious. Steve, one of the other lads with us, jumped straight in and whacked the first lad within range. Then we were all fighting. The fight spread into the nightclub doorway, the foyer and on to the pavement. I landed a right hook flush on the jaw of a tall, well built youth. He fell onto the steps unconscious. I continued throwing punches. His mate got it next; down he went too. A third lad came at me from the side. He missed the mark with a big punch, which sent him off balance and on to my right hook.

He joined the other two on the steps of the club. I'd floored three in a matter of seconds, witnessed by scores of people. I didn't know it at the time, but they were brothers, good scrappers and a few years older than I was. I wasn't the only one scrapping. The whole front of the queue was at it. Will was pasting a lad in the doorway; Steve was inside the foyer with Glen and Mac fighting like fuck. Glen and Steve were grappling with two guys. I heard an almighty roar as another gang of lads came running down the street towards the club, shouting, 'Get them! Fucking get them!' By 'them' they meant us. We were already outnumbered and doing all right, but it was time to shoot off. I grabbed Will.

'Let's go. It's the Sharpley lads.' Glen and Mac pulled back and nipped into the alleyway quickly followed by Will and me. Steve who was a gobby fucker and never listened to a word we said, stayed put. With the reputation the Sharpley lads had, we weren't going to stick around.

We waited for Steve not realising he was still in the thick of it. He appeared battered and bruised a couple of minutes later. Steve got a right kicking but in his own words he never went down. We laughed and joked and took the piss like lads do. We made a tactical retreat and a soft-shoe shuffle back to Shelthorpe.

The knockouts outside the club boosted my reputation. My name circulated around town. It also circulated in the police briefing room; I had arrived on the street-fighting scene.

FOOTBALL CRAZY

Eventually the lads of the town came together. The Loughborough lads rivalled the gangs of Leicester City's Kop, namely the Longstop Crew. Loughborough had one of the biggest gangs in the Kop. I wasn't into football. I disliked it because I was told without doubt by my old PE teacher, Mr Lynch, I was useless at it! A great comment from a man who'd failed to do his job and teach me how to be a good sportsman or athlete. He'd single-handedly put me off football and school sport for good. Something the teacher hadn't ruined for me was boxing; it was more my scene. I loved watching it and although I couldn't afford to go to shows, I'd watch it whenever I could on TV.

There was an older lad I remember from school, a kid called Johnny Moreland, a good, light heavyweight boxer from Loughborough who trained at Checketts Road Gym in Leicester. His name would crop up in conversations from time to time. Whilst we fought in the streets, che fought in the ring. Everybody seemed to be into fighting. If you were good at it, you were like a hero. After a good scrap there would always be a discussion. Phrases like, 'Did you see his head explode when I jumped on it?' Each person had their own version. They would bull themselves up looking for recognition from their peers. I loved the praise. I can't remember being particularly good at anything to get praise for, so when I got it for fighting, I loved it. I revelled at being the first one in.

It wasn't always roses. I remember arranging a night out in Nottingham the week after my 17th birthday. I'd arranged to meet a girl and her friends at the Palais de Danse nightclub. She told me what a good club it was and how easy it was to get into. I wasn't going to go, fearing the knock-back from the bouncers, but after talking with Mac, we both decided to take a chance. At the last minute we were in a taxi and on our way. We couldn't afford the taxi fare to the club so we got dropped off at the Broadmarsh Bus Station. We'd been given directions and followed them. We were both pissed and hadn't really listened to the directions. We realised we were lost. It wasn't long before we encountered a gang of lads making their way toward us. Mac, who was a little less streetwise than myself due to the excessive amount of lager he'd drunk, decided in his wisdom to ask for directions. He was excited about going to the club and forgot about the intense rivalry between Nottingham Forest and Leicester City fans.

'Here mate, can you tell us where the Palais nightclub is?' Mac asked. He walked toward the lads as he spoke. I tried to call Mac back without alerting the lads to my desire not to talk with them; it was too late. I cringed as I heard one of the gang ask the words.

'Why, where you from?' It was a phrase I'd used myself on a few occasions just before a kick off. Mac gave the reply I knew they wanted. Instead of saying Nottingham, Mac proudly replied Loughborough. That was all they needed. 'Leicester lads aye.'

Mac protested his innocence of football. I shouted, 'Run!' Mac didn't need any direction. He was already in motion. I was sprinting faster than a good sprinter trying to break a world record. Mac sped past me and into the distance. I was tiring and the Forest lads were gaining on me. I stopped dead in my tracks. Mac looked behind and stopped.

'Keep running, you twat!' he shouted.

'Fuck 'em, Mac, I ain't running from these wankers.'

Running made me feel like a coward. I turned and sprinted toward the Forest fans shouting, 'Come on, you fuckers!' and they did, I was on a collision course with seven nutters. As soon as I was in range, I jumped into the air, boot first and landed in the middle of them. I cracked the first one and started swinging wild hooks, each one narrowly missing its target. I wasn't the only one missing. The blows that did connect were weak. I carried on swinging as the lads who now surrounded me rained in knuckles and boots. I became overwhelmed. There were too just too many of them. I hung on though. I didn't want to go to ground. If I did, they'd kick bits out of me. I screamed obscenities trying to keep my anger and aggression fired up. I felt my hair being grabbed and a highly polished brogue hit me flush in the middle of my face; my nose exploded with a searing pain. My eyes filled with water blurring my vision. It was all one way traffic now. All I could do was hang on. Blow after blow struck my arms, but I didn't go down. I hung on and pulled a youth in close to shield my face. I felt my shirt get yanked over my head, then I was free. I heard the familiar sound of running feet. I straightened my shirt. I looked up at the gang of lads and declared myself a winner. 'Run, you fucking wankers!' I shouted. They disappeared into the night chanting, 'Forest! Forest!' having satisfied their lust for violence.

I turned to see where Mac was. He was further up the road sensibly watching from a distance. Why didn't he come back? I thought.

'Cheers, Mac,' I said as I got closer to him. Mac stared at me, a bewildered look on his face. 'You should have come back. If we'd have stuck together we'd have beat them!' I said.

Mac told me I was fucking crazy. I was pissed off with him, but we had a club to visit and a fat, bloody nose wasn't going to put me off.

The club was just a few yards up from where we were heading. We got to the club doorway, then realised I was covered in blood. If Mac had kept his gob shut instead of asking for directions we'd have walked right into the club. Now we'd probably get refused entry. I put Mac's denim jacket on to cover the bloodied shirt and approached the bouncers. The bouncers stood there with big grins on their faces, looking as cool as fuck, immaculately dressed in classic 'James Bond' style dinner suits pointing their fingers like guns. Their timing was impeccable as they mimed the opening line to 'Ma Baker' by Boney M.

'Put your hands in the air and give me all your money,' they said in unison, then the tune kicked in. I stood perfectly still as that moment became impressed on my memory.

'Well are you coming in, lads?' We walked into the light of the foyer. 'Been scrapping have you, lads?' one asked.

'Yeah, a gang of Forest fans jumped us.'

'Did you win?'

Mac spoke up.

'Yeah he did, seven on to one and he didn't go down.' Well at least he gave me the glory, I thought.

'Do the buttons up on your jacket. You won, you're in. Now clean the blood off your nose and keep it clean,' he said. Despite the aggro we had a good laugh in the club.

I'd learnt something that night. Never rely on anyone in a fight but yourself. Also, doing what I did was sheer madness. If you can escape, escape. The cemetery is full of dead heroes. There was another thing, having hair long enough to grab hold of gives an advantage to your attacker.

When the lads were told of the fight, they wanted to head for Nottingham to search them out. I didn't have a clue who they were, and if we'd have gone, we'd have been scrapping with whoever we bumped into. Besides, I had it down as a victory. I did good even though my nose got broken and I sported a black eye. I declined the offer and put the whole affair down to experience.

The reputation of the lads, as individuals and as a gang, was growing. There was always talk of who was the hardest in town. The main thing was not to back down from anyone, no matter how much the odds were stacked against you and always get the first punch in, which my dad had drilled into me.

On the way round the circuit of pubs we visited, we had to pass a Chinese restaurant. It was one of Loughborough's finer places to eat and was usually very busy. The window of the restaurant was open to public view. As we passed by, a couple of the lads couldn't resist the temptation of pulling faces and blowing up their cheeks like a puffer fish, by placing their lips on the glass and blowing or mooning (showing their arses) to all in the restaurant, or even, pretending to piss against the window as if lined up facing a urinal in a toilet. This went on for a few weeks. The Chinese generally ignored it. The one thing that did get them angry was the crack of the arse against the glass window. This infuriated them. But they still ignored the lads. The more they ignored it, the more we did it.

It came to a head with the Chinese one night, when a couple of us lads went into the restaurant and helped ourselves to food from people dining. The Chinese went crazy and were ready for us. They ran us out into the street. One of the lads dropped a Chinese waiter. It's hard to get a waiter's attention, but that night we got more attention than we wanted. The Chinese poured out of the restaurant clutching meat cleavers, oriental cooking knives and weird looking coshes, screaming some foreign rhetoric. I'd never seen so many Chinese chefs in one restaurant. I didn't have a clue what they were saying and I wasn't going to stick around to ask. I moved swiftly on my toes keeping my distance.

I couldn't help laughing. The Chinese looked and sounded comical, but I could tell by their body language they meant business. One Chinese was almost stepping on a lad's heels as he swung his meat cleaver, narrowly missing the lad's back. The lad made off like a chicken escaping a fox. It was a crazy night and a miracle no one was seriously injured. It was the first time I'd seen some of the lads on the back foot.

The restaurant antics stopped after that kick-off. To us it was just a laugh. The Chinese saw it as disrespectful and an inconvenience to their livelihood.

The games we played were dangerous, cruel and uncaring. We didn't give a toss. We were just lads having a laugh at someone else's expense. Something to brag about to impress our peers or beef up a boring night out.

The lads were barred from several pubs at a time, but it didn't stop them going where they wanted. One particular pub was the Saracen's Head. A scruffy, run-down, townie pub, with a great atmosphere. It was dark and dingy and you could smell the toilets before you entered the pub. There was a disco on most weeks and without fail, there would be a scrap. The landlord would bar the lads then let them back in a few weekends later. He probably realised his takings had dropped. When the lads were barred, they would wind the landlord up by walking inside the pub and staying there until the police came to kick us out. Then it would be a standoff with the police and the dogs.

The Loughborough lads became as one. Occasionally there would be infighting usually when there was no common enemy to fight. I had many brushes with the law, and the odd snap on the arse by the local police dog. I was a cocky fucker. We all were! Every weekend my liberty was at stake. It was only a matter of time before I fucked up.

BAD MANNERS

*"Always use your manners.
Manners don't cost anything."*
My mum

After a good piss up, there's nothing better than fish and chips. We headed for the chip shop in the Rushes next to Saleh's Kebab Shop for a bite to eat. I got to the door and was about to enter. My path was blocked by one of three men. They were all well over the six foot mark. They were laughing and joking with each other. I entered the chip shop.
'Excuse me, mate,' I said as I tried to squeeze by into the queue. One of the men peered down at me and exclaimed in a posh voice.
'Why, what have you done?' He turned to his mates and all three erupted into laughter. I hated people laughing at me. I felt humiliated especially after trying to be civil. The quip was funny, but it was said at my expense. If it'd been said amongst friends we'd all be laughing. I realised he was taking the piss. The red mist shrouded my vision. I felt intense anger well up inside me. I countered his verbals.
'It's not what I've done, it's what I'm going to do if you don't fuck off out of the way!'
The laughter stopped. A serious look veiled the man's face. 'It's only a laugh, mate!' I squared up to him.
'A fucking laugh, well I don't find it funny!' I didn't take my eyes off him. He was one question away from being banged out. Mac kept silent, his eyes piercing those of our antagonists.
'If it was only a laugh, then you won't mind apologising?' I said trying to stand as tall as the man in front of me. Before the posh man could answer, one of the other two men made a comment I didn't catch. Mac had. It was enough to kick it off. This time, Mac didn't run. He smacked the biggest lad from the side and we were scrapping. They were up for it and we were wrestled out of the chip shop and into the street. They were giving as good as they got whilst we grappled. But as soon as I broke free, I connected with the jawbone of one of the lads with a cracking right hand punch; he went down like a puppet with his strings cut. His mate landed next

to him sprawled out face down. I laid the boot in making sure they didn't get up again. Mac finished off his man by stamping on his head. All three were unconscious. We didn't have time to celebrate the victory; a passing patrol car spotted us. Mac shouted a warning and we were gone. The cop car accelerated, passed us, and then screeched to a halt. After a brief struggle, we were cuffed, arrested and on our way to the nick.

We were both charged with two counts of actual bodily harm and released on bail. This time the police didn't screw up. Both of our parents were informed and present when questioned. I thought back to the words of the CID officer who cocked up last time, 'We'll get you eventually, Skillen!'
He was right! His smile said it all.

The court date came round quickly. We were both found guilty. It turned out the three men were students studying at Oxford and Cambridge. They were visiting Loughborough University for a rugby match, hence the good grappling skills. If we'd taken a kicking we wouldn't have gone to the law. We'd have taken the beating like men. But they weren't like us. They turned up in court dressed in Tony Blair suits, complete with waistcoats, looking and sounding like members of parliament, and telling as many lies.

What chance did two cocky teenagers from the council estate have? We were both sentenced to three months in a detention centre, which was harsh considering it was our first offence. The trouble was, the courts knew of our reputation; it preceded our appearance in the dock.

SHORT – SHARP – SHOCK

North Sea Camp Detention Centre; one of the government's youth prisons. It was originally opened as a borstal in 1935 by the then Governor of Stafford Prison. From there he marched the prisoners and staff who would establish the site in Freiston, Lincolnshire. It changed to a detention centre in 1960. It was to become one of the country's toughest youth prisons.

The beak ordered us to be taken down. I felt like jumping over the dock and punching the shit out of the magistrate, but the jelly feeling in my legs prevented me from attempting it. Instead, I settled for a hard stare. Mac giggled nervously then a deep red flush fell across his face highlighting his scruffy ginger hair. He became silent.

I was led to a cell which resembled a toilet without fixtures and fittings. It even smelt like one. The door was slammed shut by a police officer with a satisfied look upon his face. He too was silent. The walls in the cell were scrawled on with names of previous inmates, and neat little phrases adorned the walls. (Don't let the bastards grind you down – Harry is a grass – ACAB – All Coppers Are Bastards.) I felt kind of numb standing in the cell. A mixture of confusion and excitement. This was my first offence and they'd sent me down. The hatred for the so-called system simmered inside me. I could hear muffled voices, but I couldn't comprehend what they were saying. I could only imagine they were pleased with the result. I stared at the phrase on the wall: 'Don't let the bastards grind you down.' I had to put on a tough exterior, even though I felt choked up. I bit my lip and set my mind, 'Fuck 'em! What could they do, kill me?' I mouthed.

After about 30 minutes of what felt like 30 days of incarceration, Mac and I reunited in the back of a police van, cuffed and taken to the local police station ready for the move to North Sea Camp.
The gutted feeling left me when I saw Mac's smiling face. He'd been held in the cell next to mine. I suspect he felt the same way as I did, but we looked at each other and sniggered. I remembered

Mac at school sniggering in the same fashion outside the headmaster's office just prior to getting a caning. Everything was a joke to Mac! I suppose it was his way of handling the situation.

'You won't be laughing soon, McConnell,' said the young, fresh-faced copper assigned to deliver us to the camp. He turned to his colleague, whispered something in his ear and laughed. They knew something we didn't.

Detention Centre was the government's 'short–sharp–shock' establishment designed to shock inmates into not re-offending. A few of the Loughborough lads had already had a dose of this and both Mac and I were well aware of how hard the camp was. The journey to North Sea Camp was a long one. It was over 70 miles from Loughborough. I usually got car sick on long journeys, so the sick feeling I already had couldn't get any worse.

Mac and I sat in the back of the police van. It was a sombre affair. I couldn't think of anything to say. My mind was busy wondering what was ahead. The horror stories I'd heard from the lads that had already sampled the delights of DC had come to the forefront of my mind. I wasn't looking forward to it! The coppers who were escorting us to the camp appeared as though they loved every moment of the journey. The young, cocky copper kept sticking his face against the grille separating us from them, and with a big game show host type of smile would say, 'Not long now, boys'. He'd say it that often, he sounded like Bruce Forsyth. Through the grille he actually looked like him. He loved every minute of it.

SHOCK TREATMENT

Shock: A sudden and disturbing effect on the emotions
Oxford dictionary

We arrived at Freiston and made our way up a long tarmac road, past some houses and into North Sea Camp. It was October 11th 1977 and this was to be my home for the next three months. There was a big sign that read 'HMP North Sea Camp.' The sick feeling was now accompanied by huge butterflies bashing wings together deep in the pit of my stomach. I'd be out in two months with good behaviour. I stepped out of the van. I was glad to get my feet on solid ground. I took a deep breath to clear the nausea I was experiencing and scanned the area. It reminded me of an army camp I'd seen in one of those old movies about conscription or nowadays, Bad Lads' Army. The air smelt fresh with an earthy aroma and a hint of rotting cabbage. I felt a distinct chill in my bones.

I noticed a youth with close-cropped hair dressed in black trousers, a grey shirt, red tie and sporting a beige jacket pass us by. He looked a complete dick marching along with one hand behind his back carrying a plastic mug.
The coppers, still with that satisfied look upon their faces, led us through a door and into a corridor. It sparkled and smelt of disinfectant and carbolic soap. At the far end of the corridor was another youth. He was dressed in faded blue dungarees over a grey knitted jumper. He was kneeling down as if praying to some god. As soon as he saw us he put both hands on a wooden brush and started frantically scrubbing back and forth, stopping every few seconds to rub the brush against a large block of coal tar, a greenish yellow soap. He looked in our direction, nodded his head then carried on scrubbing.
Mac and I were still handcuffed. We were ushered into an office and the handcuffs were released. I rubbed my wrists.
'All yours,' the copper said smiling. He leaned over to the screw and mouthed something in his ear. The screw turned his gaze

toward me. The game show host uttered one last catchphrase before he left.

'See ya in a few months, lads. Enjoy your stay.' He and his mate left like a comedy duo leaving the stage looking back for one last wave. Fucking tosser, I thought.

'Name?' the screw asked.

'Skillen!' I replied just as abruptly.

As soon as the words had left my mouth, he whipped in a slap, which landed on my left cheekbone. Before I could retaliate, he surged forward, grabbed me by the throat and rammed my head against the office wall behind me. He pushed his face into mine. I could smell his foul breath.

'You call me "sir" when you answer me, do you understand?' I stayed silent and killed him with a stare. He repeated it, this time underlining what he'd said with pure aggression and a staccato voice that made me take note of every word he spoke.

'Do you fucking understand me, son?'

'Yes, sir!' I said. Talk about shock. He squeezed my throat so hard, I felt the veins in my head grow bigger. Whatever the copper had said to him had really pissed him off.

The guy holding my throat was six feet tall with the military stature of a drill sergeant. His colleague, a six-foot-five man with a frown as big as a ravine, stood beside him in threatening silence, observing our every move.

'You're a cocky fucker aren't you, Skillen?' he said, his grip tightening.

'No, sir!'

'Are you fucking arguing with me, Skillen?'

'No, sir.'

'You better not or your feet won't touch the fucking ground. Do you understand me, Skillen?'

I understood him all right. He was a cunt and I was close to telling him so, but there was an even bigger cunt standing next to him, so I decided to play the game. 'Yes, sir, I understand!' He let go of my throat and directed his attention to Mac.

'Same applies to you, McConnell.' Mac's nervous smile beamed across his face. He gave a smart, tight-lipped reply.

'Yes, sir!'

The screw got closer to Mac's face and said, 'Are you fucking laughing at me?' Mac's sunburnt complexion drained from his face, making his ginger hair appear orange.

'No, sir!'

These guys meant business. I stood perfectly still, not daring to move or make a facial expression for fear of upsetting them. The screw made his way over to the desk and sat down. He told us a few rules and regulations. He made a point of telling us, if we didn't play the game we'd do the whole three months.

We were given a release date of 11th December. If we got the remission we'd be out before Christmas. We were marched from office to office: the governor, the doctor, and the stores where we were issued with uniforms, then taken to a unit known as the induction block.

There we were to be assessed for the next two weeks before being sent to one of four cell blocks, which were like army billets. These were known as houses.

RUDE AWAKENING

The induction unit housed around 50 lads, split into two dormitories. Most of the lads I spoke to were in for fighting or some other public order offence. The dormitories were clean and spacious. The single beds lined either side of the room; each had a set of blankets neatly boxed within a bedspread or top blanket. Each bed space had a cupboard next to it. Inside the cupboard was the con's personal kit. Everything I saw was neat, tidy and clean. It was obvious from the tidy layout; this establishment was run along military lines.

I was shown to my bed space, given a cupboard and a nine-inch, plastic measuring strip. Next we were herded off to the DC barber. The cons filed out one after the other looking like skinheads without the sharp clothes and the Doc Martens. The day was drawing to a close. It was 9.00 p.m., and time for lights out. I fell asleep rubbing my shaven head wondering what the next day held in store for me.
It was early morning when the bright lights forced me under the covers. That was my first mistake. The cover was ripped from my grip. I sat up to recover the blankets, ready to scrap with whoever it was that had the balls to fuck me about. That was my second mistake. I was met with a challenging stare that dared me to say one word out of order.
'Hands off cocks! On with socks!' the screw bellowed, with his eyeballs bulging. The blankets were strewn over the end of the bed. The whole room was alive with activity. 'Breakfast in five minutes,' yelled the screw.
'You'd better get a move on, mate. They don't fuck about in here!' said a passing con. I wiped the blears from my eyes and took the advice. I noticed he was carrying his razor and towel. I grabbed my towel and followed my adviser. He walked into the corridor collecting a blade for his razor from a strip of webbing designed to house the blades; each blade was in a numbered section cut into the webbing. You had to take it, shave, and return it. If it didn't get returned, it was a serious offence and days would be added to your sentence.

The wash room was frantic. I got my horse-hair shaving brush and rubbed it into the stick of white shaving soap. I'd seen my dad doing this many times. I lathered my face with soap and began to shave. 'Get that razor higher, Skillen. Get them sideburns off and get a move on,' said the screw. I took the sideburns off, but that was all there was. I hadn't shaved before.

The first rule I learnt in there was, don't fuck the screws about. The second rule was, you shaved every day whether you needed to or not.

I returned to the dorm and one of the lads was still in bed hiding his head under the covers. I was just in time to witness the screw's idea of a rude awakening. He got both sides of the mattress and launched the lad from his bed. He landed with a thump on the floor. The kid started to rise. The screw grabbed him by the ear lobe and lifted him up onto his tiptoes then ran him out of the dorm screaming abuse at him. Nobody dared comment. This was far from a laughing matter. I joined the rest of the dorm standing at the end of the bed; knife, fork and spoon inside my mug and held neatly behind my back; the other hand at my side and my gob firmly shut. I just wanted to do my time and get out of this place. A lump formed in the back of my throat; I wanted to go home.

The daily routine unfolded. We lined up, marched through the dormitory, across the yard and into the dining hall. It looked like a typical school hall. Instead of miserable-looking dinner ladies, the servery was manned by several cons, in gleaming white chef uniforms. They stood behind different trays of steaming food, awaiting the orders to serve.

We were lined up behind tables and were ordered to sit down at exactly the same time. The dining hall was silent, until the food was served, then the clatter of cutlery, metal trays and murmuring of voices filled the air. I was starving and cleared my metal tray.

We had to stand up at the same time and march back to the dormitory. I noticed quite a few of the cons on my table hadn't eaten. I hadn't bothered to ask why. I would soon find out!

THE GYM

As we got back, we were directed to the gym. The gym was the most feared place of all. You didn't fuck around in the gym. The screws were ex-military PTIs. I thought the screws who brought us here were strict, but these guys made them appear as angels. We dressed in oversize shorts, vests and black school pumps. The shorts resembled the idiot shorts I'd been forced to wear at school. The only difference here: we were all idiots.

The circuit training was the hardest. No matter how fit you thought you were, it was designed to fuck you up. It involved running around a fixed circuit of weight-training, callisthenics and plyometric exercises. The circuit included press-ups, burpees, sit-ups, and mixed in were various weight-training exercises: curls, military press, and bench press. The circuit was set around the outside of the gym. Rope and frame climbing were added part of the way round. The exercises were put into order of difficulty to cope with all fitness levels: 10 reps, 15 reps and 20 reps. The reps were assigned colours, white, red and the most feared, black.
The screws demanded a high work-rate and would push you to the point of blowing your breakfast over the person nearest to you. It happened more than once. I now knew why some cons left their early morning meal. I learnt not to eat much breakfast, if anything at all. Failure in the gym wasn't an option. I saw lads crying because it was too difficult. The screws showed no mercy. Me, I just got my head down and got stuck in. Most of the lads hated training with a passion. They'd try anything to get out of it. The gym screws showed no respect for those cons.
I loved the gym and the discipline that went with it. Don't get me wrong. It was fucking tough, but after a session I felt so good I wanted more. The regime was harsh and the gym remained a feared place.
After the gym it was showers, then back in dungarees for cleaning duties. The morning march was repeated at dinner time. The food was tasteless: meat, vegetables and watery gravy, followed by a hard sponge-type pudding known as duff. The duff was served with custard that tasted almost the same as the gravy and had the

same consistency. I noticed most people on the other tables cleaned their plates. On the induction table, it was a different scene. Food was played around with and pushed to one side. My plate was empty.

We were marched back again to do more cleaning: scrubbing, polishing, sweeping and mopping. Once the cleaning was done, it was into the yard for drill practice. This wasn't a problem for me. A stint in the army cadets had cured my timing. After, it was back to the gym for a second helping. We'd play British bulldog, pirates or murder ball. Two days a week we'd learn how to lift weights. We were pushed until nausea and jelly legs set in. Then it was back to the dorms for a small amount of free time, where we were allowed to write letters home to our families then prepare for inspections. The dormitory had to be kept spotlessly clean. I had to learn how to layout my kit for army style inspections. The kit was laid out to exact specifications. Shirts, jumpers, and trousers had to be neatly measured to nine inches wide, folded and stacked. The blankets had to be precisely boxed inside the top bedspread cover. Inspections could happen at any time of day. Each piece of kit had to be laid out and presented in a certain way. If it was wrong, you paid the price. There was no room for error.

Once prepared, we got ready for lights out. We had to wear stripy, prison issue pyjama jacket and trousers. I thought the lad I saw in the yard when I arrived looked like a dickhead. Well I felt like one wearing those pyjamas. Teeth had to be cleaned with a hard-bristled toothbrush, which made my gums bleed and a horrible green powder they called tooth cleaner. It had a clinical taste that reminded me of the stuff you rinse your mouth with at the dentist. It was fucking awful! Then we'd await inspection before lights out at 9.00 p.m. The day was full and after the manic and exhausting routine the quiet of the night was not welcome.

SLEEPLESS NIGHTS

The thoughts of home and loved ones, kept at bay by the pace of the day, would creep in by night. The lump that first appeared in my throat on incarceration would return. I'd only ever been away from home once before. It was during the annual army cadets' summer camp. I was just fourteen at the time. I remember the initiation ceremony – being woken up at night by a gang of older cadet squaddies and having my balls blacked with boot polish! Then I was unceremoniously dumped into a freezing cold shower to scrub my balls clean. Not nice! I suffered terrible homesickness, but I stuck it out. It was tough and I could have gone home anytime; here I had no choice.
It was the second night. I was tired but unlike the first I couldn't sleep. I could hear coughing, whispering and what sounded like muffled crying. I think that was the lad opposite me. He didn't look old enough to be in here. The atmosphere in the dormitory was tense. I lay in bed unable to sleep, wondering what tomorrow would bring.

Waking up in the mornings was a major shock to the system. I'd lie there dreaming wonderful things, then the lights, accompanied by the bellowing of the screw, would shock me awake. I loved the comical, piss-taking phrases they came out with, 'Stop wanking. Hands off cocks. On with socks. I'm your mother now, lads.' I would jump out of bed, heart pounding and fly into DC routine mode. Those who didn't move felt the wrath of the screws and were yanked or tipped out of bed while still asleep.
The cons twho'd been there a while moved sharply. Not daring to stand still, towels covering their morning glory, they made their way to the shower block for the three S's: a shit, shower and shave. The new cons, not yet accustomed to the lights, tried to get with the programme fully aware of the price they'd pay if their captors caught them shirking. Everyone was shouted at, bullied and intimidated from morning till night.
Towards the end of the first two weeks, things started to come together for me. I could lay out my kit, bail my blankets, piss all

over the circuit and weight-training routines and march like a veteran soldier.

There was one other thing I'd figured out. Most of the lads were covered in a shaving rash from shaving too often. I had a simple solution. The razors were screwed together and the blades were fixed inside. I shaved without putting the blade in and as I didn't have anything to shave off, no one was any the wiser. It was simple but effective, the art of shaving without shaving! The routine soon caught on and the shaving rashes diminished. It was the induction block's closely kept secret and our way of fucking off the system.

I was ready to be moved onto the blocks. I found out I'd be put into 'LL' block. Mac, who was in the dorm opposite, would accompany me. I'd met and made some new friends and together, we waited nervously for the move.

GINGER NUT

Moving to LL block was like having your mortgage suddenly paid off. I almost felt free. The first night of inspection changed any thoughts I had of it being easier than induction. It was more like receiving a tax demand you weren't expecting and couldn't afford to pay. Inspections felt worse than standing in front of the magistrate waiting for sentencing. I stood to attention, keeping a solemn face. I didn't want to smile or talk.

The screw known as Mr Casey made his way into the dormitory. This dorm sparkled. Everyone's kit was immaculately laid out. The cons were lined up at the ends of their beds, staring forward not wanting to catch the eye of the feared Mr Casey. Mr Casey stood in the doorway and I could see his face in my peripheral vision. I felt he was staring at me, even though he faced forward. I dared a glance, which went unnoticed. This guy looked more like a villain than a screw. His ginger locks highlighted the deep red complexion that was present, like he'd been in the sun too long. I noticed an uncanny resemblance to my friend Mac.
'What you smirking at, boy?' screamed Casey. I straightened up and looked forward. His scream startled me. I felt intimidated. His voice was raspy, loud and grated on my teeth like a file grating metal. His opening phrase was delivered in such a way it would scare you still. 'You, boy! What are you looking at?'
'Nothing, sir.'
Without looking, I recognised the voice; it was Mac, his nervous laugh getting him noticed. I could hear the quiver in his voice as he tried to fight back laughter.
'Wipe that smile off your face, boy, before I wipe it off for you.' The sound of a loud fart that echoed around the dormitory drew Casey's attention away from Mac. Casey wasn't impressed by the impromptu sound. He exploded into a rage and looked like a weightlifter going for his best lift. The veins in his head appeared to be nearly at bursting point.
'Who was that? Who did that? Was it you?' he asked looking in the direction of a fat lad.

No sir.' Casey headed for the lad's bed, which was laid out immaculately with his kit. Casey snatched the top blanket like a magician trying to do the tablecloth trick and failing miserably. The kit flew into the air and landed with a clatter. Casey's rage continued. I winced and bowed my head so not to catch his eye. Bedcover after bedcover became airborne. I felt like joining in when mine took off.

Casey stormed out of the dormitory shouting, 'Inspection in five minutes.' They were the last words he rasped before vanishing into the corridor.

'Fucking 'ell!' the fat lad said in a real Lincolnshire accent. He sounded like a farmer. Those who needed to put their kit back in order and waited nervously for Casey to return.

He never came back that night. Instead, we were treated to the company of the night watchman known as Basher Brown. The night-watchman's job was to keep order in the dorms during lights out. This particular guy was firm, carried a stick and wore a flat cap. He walked the full length of the dorm checking every bed.

'Right, who's been upsetting Mr Casey?' he said as he quickly inspected the layout of the kits. Nobody spoke. Basher was a bit of a joker and you didn't know when he was being serious or not.

'Was it you, lad?' he got close and stared into a youth's eyes.

'No sir.'

'What's that on my forehead?' he asked. When the lad looked at the night-watchman's head, he butted the youth then walked off saying, 'Got to be sharper than that, lad.' The dorm erupted like a comedy show crowd just getting the punch line, until Basher Brown cast his gaze over the room. 'Right, fun's over. Kit away and lights out in one minute.' He too vanished into the corridor.

Discipline was the key to earning remission. But, if you fucked the screws or night watchmen about, you could kiss any chance of an early release goodbye. If you continually conformed to the rules and regulations you were issued with a coloured tie. The ties ascended in order, yellow the first tie, then green (required for early release) and red (the trustees' tie). This meant you were a trusted con. You could wander around the detention centre grounds unaccompanied. If you wanted early release the green tie was the minimum requirement. Eight weeks on a twelve-week sentence. The tie was easier to lose than to gain, especially with nutters like Casey around. The screws were extremely strict.

The experienced cons on LL block, helped us, the new inductees, to settle in. When you have a common enemy, there's rarely any in-fighting unless it's a personality clash or leadership battle. Violence sorts the latter out. If you can scrap, you're safe. Violence was the only thing the cons truly understood.

WORK PARTY

The camp was built on reclaimed land from the harsh North Sea by building dykes to keep back the flow of sea water. It was built by cons for cons. One of the main jobs on offer was known as the marsh party. It was no party. The marsh was a feared place in winter. The lads were marched off like soldiers going to war. If you were lucky enough to avoid it, you'd either work in the kitchens, down on the farm or on what was known as the garden party. I was allocated to work on the farm, which compared to the marsh, was indeed a party. I was led to believe it was a doddle, but this was DC and that word's not in their dictionary. In fact, no matter where you worked, life in DC was tough.

The mist hung low in the air. It was a patchy cold mist that gave the camp an eerie feel. At the edge of the camp, the mist was thick. I held my hand out in front of my face and watched it disappear. My hair (what was left of it) was wet with the moisture. My nose tingled, dripped and was becoming sore from the constant rubbing away of snot. It was cold, I mean fucking cold. I was hungry even though I'd just eaten breakfast. There would be no more food until midday.
We were ordered into the back of a waiting tractor and off we went in the direction of the marsh.
'Where we going, sir?' I asked.
'You'll find out when you get there.'
Wanker, I thought. I pulled up my collar, drew my head into my shoulders and sunk lower into the trailer. The tractor chugged on. I felt every bump rattle my spine. We made our way along the track that led to the marsh. The temperature dropped as we got into open land and closer to the sea.
We pulled up beside what looked like marshland.
'Right, everyone out,' the screw shouted. I looked out across the open land. It was surrounded by mud banks, which I assumed were dykes. Through the patches of heavy rolling mist, I could make out what looked like rows of potato crops. This was a solitary-looking place, cold, damp and almost barren. It made sense. Potatoes would be the easiest and best crop to grow in these conditions.

Plastic wire baskets were neatly stacked at the side of the road. I felt my stomach turn over. Not potato picking! Fucking back-breaking, knee-numbing, potato picking, I thought. The screw jumped out of the tractor, grabbed a handful of sticks and walked into the field. He stuck a stick in the ground, paced out a few yards then stuck in another. These were known as stints, and each con was given one. Once the soil was tilled and the potatoes were churned out of the ground, we'd start to pick them.
'Right you lot, grab a basket,' ordered the screw. The cons looked with disbelief. I grabbed mine and made my way to one of the stints. One of the tractors moved into position and started to till the soil, leaving a trail of spuds behind it.

I loved the smell of freshly tilled soil. I took a deep breath and filled my lungs. The smell reminded me of the trips to the farm with my mum and the other mothers of Shelthorpe. They'd meet at the end of the street, early in the morning during October. They'd sneak into the back of the farmer's transit van and be whisked away to pick spuds. All the mothers were claiming benefits and this little earner helped bring in a few extra quid before Christmas. The work was back-breakingly hard. It was the first time I'd earned any money of my own. At 14 years old, it enabled me to buy my first record, a double A side of Alice Cooper's 'School's Out' and 'I Wanna Be Elected'. The smell of the soil was really the only compensation to this job. I felt a tinge of sadness and wished for those days back.

I started delving into the soil, picking out spud after spud and dropping them into the basket held between my bent knees. I shouted to Mac who was in the stint in front of me. '
Come on, Mac. Don't let the bastards grind you down!' I started singing the first few lines of 'School's Out' at the top of my voice until the screw told me to button it.

The faster I worked the warmer I got. I wasn't going to let the bastards get to me. Trouble was, the warmer I got the more I'd sweat. The sweat got cold beneath my clothing, dropping my body temperature. I was colder now than before.

I'd picked for what felt like hours. The flesh on my fingernails was torn and bloody. I hadn't noticed how sore they were. The cold anaesthetised them to the pain. Mud was ingrained in my skin and it was painful to straighten out my hands.

The feelings of hunger combined with the cold brought on a feeling of depression. I wished I hadn't gone to that fucking chippy. It seemed ironic, me picking potatoes after being caught fighting in a chip shop.

The mist had cleared for a while, but was now beginning to thicken and envelop our surroundings. I'd lost sight of Mac even though he was working only a few yards ahead. The screw decided to call a halt to the picking and ordered us back into the trailer.

The ride back was a gloomy affair; nobody spoke. I thought about jumping over the side and vanishing into the mist. I'd heard stories of lads absconding and getting lost in the marsh, only to get caught and get a fucking good hiding from the screws. I decided to sink lower into my coat and continued feeling sorry for myself.

Spud bashing was hard on an empty stomach. I always felt cold and hungry. So much so, that I'd taken to eating raw potatoes. I felt like I'd picked enough spuds to keep Britain in chips for life. After a couple of weeks of that, I was transferred to the garden party.

The garden party was seen as an easy job by comparison. In and around the camp the sun shone. It was still freezing, but without the damp and mist. Mac and I got tasked with cutting down foliage on the perimeter of the camp: a nice little cushy number, which involved using a scythe (a curved blade about two feet long with a wooden handle). It was held in one hand and a stick in the other to prevent the blade following through and slicing your leg. We burned what we cut down. After the morning mists cleared, the low winter sun broke through and with the heat of the fires we lit, made it feel like spring.

FAST FOOD

The food in DC was horrible. It had a texture and flavour I hadn't tasted before. I'd been through some tough times on the estate back home; I'd starved on many occasions. I'd eaten all sorts of dodgy food, but nothing like DC food. It made school dinners look and taste like *haute cuisine*. The added ingredients introduced by the cons shall be left to your own imagination. But that night after the freezing day in the field, it tasted fantastic. I scoffed it like a ravenous wolf ripping at its prey. Even though I had an extra piece of duff hidden beneath my metal tray, it still wasn't enough to cure my hunger. Like the rest of the lads, I watched and waited ready to pounce on anyone's leftovers. I lived for meal times. I was always famished.

Now being lads that got hungry quickly and with the shortage of food, we had to find a way of supplementing our diet. I'd noticed a shed full of the potatoes we'd picked stored in the farmyard. The DC was self-sufficient and the farm produced its own grub. I was chewing on a raw potato I'd pinched from the shed, when an apple fell on my head. I confided in Mac, my partner in crime. He had a word with one or two lads to see if they were interested in purchasing extra food. The idea of supplying freshly baked potatoes to our fellow cons was born.
We decided to produce our own baked potatoes using the potatoes from the farm store, cooked in the hot ashes at the base of the foliage we were tasked to burn. It was risky. If we got caught we'd lose time, but a full belly was more important to me.
We'd be lighting the fires for a few days, so we started taking orders. We'd collect the spuds in the morning, hide them inside our clothing and once we got to where we were working, we hid them in the undergrowth until we were ready to cook them. It worked a treat! We ate baked spuds till we were full. Then, what we didn't eat, we traded with the other cons for portions of DC food, mainly duff from the dining hall, which was easy to hide as an evening snack. Duff was a heavy sponge bread, a type of cake flavoured with essence and food colour. A lot of lads detested it and so the treat of a baked spud was a welcome change.

One of the lads on the garden party would pass by, pick up the spuds and deliver them to some of the lads on the farm to keep them quiet. One lad from the farm exchanged fresh tomatoes lifted from the greenhouse. The kitchen cons supplied us with small pats of butter in return for the odd favour, like writing a letter or reading one in confidence. We ate like kings, for a while.

Mac and I were having a discussion about an up-and-coming weekend visit. He was telling me how he was going to get some fags dropped at the gate by his mum. A drop was a way of smuggling in contraband. Mac had arranged for a trustee to pick up the ciggies at the cost of a couple of spuds and a favour. We were so engrossed with the conversation, we didn't spot the screw until he was a couple of feet away. Mac uttered the words that were going through my mind as the screw spoke.
'Shit! Fuck!' he said.
'Everything all right, boys?' the screw asked. I looked at Mac and gestured toward the fire. Mac picked up a handful of foliage and covered the potatoes, which were about ready to be lifted out. I could see Mac's worried expression change to a look of relief as the spuds disappeared under the foliage.
'Yes sir, everything's fine,' I replied.
'Oh dear, look at the fire, McConnell. You'll put it out dumping all that foliage on there at once. Where's the flame?' he asked. He moved toward the fire. 'A good fire should always have a strong flame to cut through the damp in the grass or all you'll create is smoke.'
'Sorry sir,' Mac replied.
'Come out of the way, lad.' The screw was irritated by Mac's obvious lack of understanding. 'I'll show you how to get a fire going.'
I stole another look at Mac. His trademark nervous smile was beginning to crack into laughter. I looked at Mac and, like a schoolteacher, put my finger to my mouth and gestured to him to be quiet. We'd be spending the rest of our time on the marsh if the screw knew we were taking the piss out of him. I stood back trying to sound interested then moved in.

'Oh I see, sir.' The more interested I became, the more he wanted to show off his expertise. He removed the foliage carefully and placed it to one side. He got a stick and started to open the hot ash, moving it away bit by bit.

'He's fucking rumbled us,' I mouthed to Mac. Mac turned pale.

'I'll do it, sir,' Mac said. The tops of the potatoes were now visible; we were about to be rumbled. I pulled up the corners of my mouth and drew breath between my teeth. I could see myself marching out to sea in the freezing winter weather.

'Sir,' I said, about to ask a question.

'What, boy?'

'My scythe needs sharpening, sir.' I was trying to distract him, so he didn't spot the potatoes.

'In a minute, lad. Let me get this fire sorted.' The screw knelt down, grabbed a handful of foliage and held it next to the ashes. I felt myself blowing as he blew at the ashes. Light, you fucker, please light, I thought. Another blow and whoosh, the dry grass sparked and lit. He blew again creating a smokescreen across the top of the ash. The smell of the burning grass was pleasurable compared to what could have been the smell of the marsh.

'You make it look easy, sir,' I said paying him lip service. The foliage caught quickly. Flames leapt high.

'Go on then, son. Pile it on.'

'Thanks, sir,' Mac said through a tight-lipped smile.

'That's okay, son. Looks like you're making good progress here. We'll move you down to the greenhouses tomorrow now I know I can trust you both.'

'Thank you, sir,' we both said in unison. The screw left. We laughed as we dug out the last of our potatoes. After nearly getting caught we retired from the fast food business. It was too hot to handle.

GREENHOUSE BLUES

Each day is like a year, a year whose days are long
Oscar Wilde

Mid November and North Sea Camp was feeling the effects of the freezing sea winds. We were on parade army style, all of the cons from each house neatly lined up awaiting the order to go to work. The screws were dressed in their civvies but couldn't hide their obvious military experience.

'Dead Eyes', as he was known due to his dark and sinister stare, scowled at the rows of cons daring one to catch his gaze. He was a very serious-looking character, solidly built with huge shoulders and a frame to suit. Speech was not his forte. A silent Mary Shelley monster without the scars.
The sun was shining. The usual dampness and smell of rotting cabbages was replaced with the smell of clean fresh sea air with a hint of earthiness blowing in from the marshland that skirted the camp's perimeter. The freezing air bit into my nostrils burning as it flowed into my lungs. The marsh was a harsh place to be. I didn't meet a single guy that came anywhere close to liking the job on the marsh. I watched Dead Eyes lead away the marsh party, a fitting place for a screw of his demeanour. I felt sorry for the lads as they marched off, but not sorry enough to exchange my cushy little number on the farm's garden party.

I'd been tasked with cleaning out the greenhouses and getting them ready for the next crop. The greenhouse was huge compared to the average garden variety. The low winter sun shone through the glass, warming the air making me forget it was winter. The air inside was warm and smelt like drying rain after a summer deluge. The warm damp aroma of soil bought back childhood memories. I thought about my granddad, Jum Olley, in his greenhouse and was whisked back in time. I would watch him plant, prune and trim his way round the tiny foliage-filled space, the smell of tomatoes, cucumbers and lettuce enticing the taste buds.

The shattering sound of a jet fighter rattled the panes of glass on the huge greenhouse interrupting my train of thought. I looked skyward to catch a glimpse of the pilot as he manoeuvred into low flight. The deafening sound wave, which came seconds after the plane, rattled the glass more intensely. Then in the distance, I could hear its shells booming in on its target out at sea.

I was left on my own for most of the day. The lip service I paid to the screw made him feel like he could trust me. The greenhouse was indeed a cushy little number, but with too much time on my hands, the thoughts of freedom and the amount of time I had left made me feel depressed. Maybe the screw had me sussed. After all I was doing hard time.

HOGWASH DAY

Sport in DC was compulsory: weight training, rugby, circuit training and the infamous boundary run. The boundary run was a long-distance run around the boundary of the camp. No matter what the weather, the run always took place. This was the closest I got to experiencing the bastard cold of the marsh. We set off at a steady pace. In the standard, prison- issue gym fashion: shorts, plimsolls, vests we were forced to brave the winds that swept across the open fields that was once sea. Most of the course ran along the dykes, huge man-made embankments built to keep the sea out of the reclaimed land.

It was a vicious affair with no escape from the elements. The training gear I wore gave no protection from the extreme cold. The wind forced the rain to bite into my skin. It was difficult to see where I was going. I forged onward, running as fast as I could. The quicker the run was completed, the less time spent in the elements. Even though the weather was against us, I enjoyed the freedom of running. Mac set the pace. He was a superb runner. I tried to keep up with him, but his determination and desire to win kept him firmly in the lead. He won every boundary run we did. My best was third place, only achieved by keeping up with the wiry Mac. I was proud of that achievement.

The sports field was where you could let off some steam or exact revenge on someone that had pissed you off and usually get away with it. If you wanted to give somebody a dig you did it on the rugby field.
The two teams lined up a few yards apart. One of the lads in our team kicked the ball toward the opposing side. We charged forward chasing the ball like ancient soldiers going into battle. I was on the left wing. The ball fell into a group of three cons. One of them grabbed the ball. I dived into the middle and got both of my hands wrapped around the ball. I felt one of the cons dig me hard in the chest as I went in.
'Cunt,' I said turning toward the con. The con stood in front of me angered by my statement. 'What's your fucking problem?' I said.

Before I could say another word, his hand was around my neck. His steely grip tightened around my throat. I could feel his nails ripping into my larynx. He pushed his face close to mine. I couldn't help thinking how ugly he was. His head was shaped like a box with a little crop of hair on his skull. He'd obviously upset the DC barber. His eyes were so close together they formed part of his nose. If he had horns coming out of his flared back nostrils, he'd have looked like a warthog.

It was clear this game was not alien to him.

I knocked his hand away with the palm of my right hand like a boxer parrying a punch. He stepped back. His body looked solid and thickset like his brain. He'd have looked better if he'd have been taller.

'You're fucking dead!' the warthog blurted out in a harsh northern accent.

'Come on then, you bastard,' I shouted, countering his verbal attack. I splayed my arms inviting him to come forward. He growled but didn't take the step. A circle of cons formed around us. Before he could move, the screw intervened.

'Break it up. I'm in charge on this field. If anybody wants to fight they can fight me.' The screw stared at the warthog and then at me waiting for a reaction. The warthog stood his ground, his stare piercing mine, then he broke off the gaze and looked toward the screw. I never took my eyes off him.

'I'll see you later!' was the warthog's last word as he ran back down the field.

'You ain't fucking good enough,' I replied.

The whistle blew shortly after the confrontation with the warthog. It was time for dinner.

I left the situation with the warthog. If he wanted a go, he could have one anytime he wanted. I doubted he would. He didn't have the bottle. Besides, there were easier victims for him to hassle.

The warthog was always picking on someone, usually someone who looked like a soft touch. Most cons avoided him or ignored him. They didn't want to risk losing time for fighting. When he realised this, the bullying got worse. He became an irritant and had to be taught a lesson. So I got together with Mac and a few of the kitchen lads and decided to do just that. The warthog was in the same dormitory as us, so we set a plan in motion. The plan would be executed just after lights out and after the visit of the night-watchman.

Just before lights out I started the ball rolling, teasing him up. 'You want to watch it picking on people all of the time. It's going to backfire on you. No fucker likes you. You're a bully boy.' He grunted and stared at me. I stared back, then added, 'You might frighten some of the dicks in here, but you don't scare me!' He looked away, mumbled something and climbed into his bed.

The lads in the dorm had already decided what they were going to do. We had warned everybody in the house to keep quiet. The warthog's reputation ensured the house silence. It was time to teach the bully a lesson. The lights went out at 9.00 p.m. sharp. We waited until the night-watchman had been on his rounds and the hog was dozing. It was quiet, apart from the odd cough and fart accompanied by a muffled giggle. After a while I heard the shuffling of blankets. I looked around the dorm. The lads were on the move, tip-toeing toward his bed. I joined in. I could hear the warthog snoring as we got close to him. One of the lads held a blanket at the side of the hog's bed and threw it across him. Another of the lads grabbed it and pulled it down hard pinning the hog to the bed. The warthog woke; it was too late for him to react. The rest of us punched and hammered his body. The only sound I could hear was the thud of the punches as they landed and the muffled screams of the hog as he struggled to move. All the shots were to the body; we couldn't afford to cause facial injuries. That would mean too many questions and time lost. The whole house would be in the shit. One of the lads announced that he'd get more of the same unless he changed his bullying ways. We swiftly got back into bed.
I could hear him moaning as he lay beneath his blankets. The warthog didn't know who had beaten him, so he couldn't grass. In the morning he hung his head low and kept himself to himself. His usual angry personality softened. I never heard of the hog bullying anyone after the visit. In fact, he turned out to be a decent lad. I suppose we all need a wake-up call at some point and that was his.

DC was tough all the way through the sentence and the screws didn't relent. They kept their distance. Being civil or nice wasn't part of a DC screw's make up. New kids were arriving all the time, the short–sharp–shock had to continue and it was relentless.

Any chance we got to take the piss we did. Mac and myself got our green ties at the same time and nearly lost them on several occasions. If the cons knew you were worried about losing time, they would prey on you, winding you up over the least thing. If you cracked and started scrapping it would be lost bird.

Mac was always playing the joker. On the last night, we were lined up for inspection, standing to attention at the bottom of the bed, kit laid out in perfect order, pyjamas on, clean shaven and looking good. Just before the screw walked in, Mac who was in the bed next to mine, called to me in a hushed voice. 'John,' he said gesturing toward the floor. I held back a smile that was becoming laughter. Mac was standing perfectly still, hands at his sides military fashion. The cunt had his dick, including ginger pubes, hanging out of his pyjamas. He maintained a serious look on his face. And, before Mac could put away his tool, the screw walked in. The rest of the lads spotted Mac's idea of a giggle. The screw came in and eyeballed everyone in the room before he made his way down the rows of beds to make his inspection. The lads fought back laughter. Mac kept his hook shaped dick out the whole time and the screw was the only one who didn't notice. When the screw left, the whole dorm erupted into hysterical laughter. Mac knew how to take the piss!

Mac and me were to be released the next day. If he'd been caught taking the piss, he would have lost time, but that was Mac, anything to get one up on the screws.

I'd had good and bad times in DC. Mac and I were incarcerated together and remained together throughout the sentence. DC was Mac's only sentence. He never went to prison again. Eventually he became a Territorial Army PT instructor and later sold gold for a living earning himself the nickname 'Gold Mac'; his humour brightened many of my days.

RICE PAPER

I was released from DC on the December the 11th, just in time for Christmas. My short–sharp–shock was over and I was as strong and as fit as a good athlete. I did eight weeks of a 12-week sentence. It felt good to be out. The air smelt different. Everything was more colourful after the drab surroundings of North Sea Camp. After release from detention centre, I was put on licence. That meant if I committed a crime within a one-year period, I would be recalled to Detention Centre for a second term, usually six months depending of course on the seriousness of the crime. For a young man with an attitude, this was like trying to walk on rice paper without breaking it.

Had I learnt anything? Yes, sure I did! I learnt you can't trust anyone and that coppers and screws all piss in the same pot. My hate for anything authoritative was underlined and set in stone. I'd also learnt more about violence and had become a more deceitful bastard. The trouble was: I had no respect for law and order. I hated the coppers. I didn't have any respect for them whatsoever.

At home I felt comfortable in my own bed, but I couldn't sleep. I was too buzzed up and excited at being free. It was nice just to lie there and not be turfed out by some miserable twat. I eventually got up, got dressed and went through the DC routine, partly before I realised what I was doing. I had become conditioned to that way of life. I couldn't wait to get down town and show my face and see what I'd missed.

I walked into the Saracen's Head about 12.30 p.m. and ordered half of lager. 'Staying Alive' by the Bee Gees was playing on the jukebox. I heard a familiar voice.
'I'll get that, Johnny. How yer doing mate? When did you get out?' said Guff. Guff was one of the lads.
'Yesterday, mate.'
'I bet you're fucking glad you're out for Christmas!'
'Too right, mate. Where is everybody?'

'Dunno mate! I've been at work this morning, cash in hand.' He pushed his hand down to his side and pointing his fingers behind him made a cupping action with it. This was the hand gesture for a tax-free fiddle. His head was crowned with a little woolly hat hiding his baldness and the many scars caused by dropping the nut (head-butting) – his favourite move when aggro reared its head. He'd just walked off the building site still covered in cement dust.

The lager tasted sharp against the back of my throat. I sank it in one. 'Get him another one,' Guff said. The landlord obliged. I took my time on the second half even though I felt like sinking it. It didn't seem right that I was in the pub. I felt a sense of guilt. The beer soon changed that. I thought I'd get drunk really quickly, but due to the excitement of being free, I couldn't feel the effects. Last orders came and Guff decided we'd go over to the India Club, a members' club for Asians, where you could drink all day if you were a member or a member's guest. Neither of us was, but it was a scam the Asians ran to get money into the tills. The India Clubs as they were known, were always playing host to the local lads. The atmosphere was thick with smoke and felt sinister. It was common for fights to erupt over gambling or spilt beer. It didn't need much to kick it off.

Guff knocked on the door. It opened slightly. 'It's Guff mate. Are we all right for a late one, Sugar?' The bouncer shut the door then opened it again.
'Come in, man,' he said. Sugar was a bodybuilder; his arms were as big as balloons hanging just inside the doorway. I think he was from the Caribbean Islands originally. He was about five foot eight with a massive chest. He was a powerful looking bloke. He dealt with the problems in the India Club. He looked at me suspiciously.
'Is he old enough?'
'Yeah he's all right. It's John Skillen. He's just got out of DC.' Sugar stood aside and let us in.

The smoke hit me in the eyes. They stung and started to water, then it got me in the throat drying it out. I could taste it in my mouth. The India Club was at the top of a flight of stairs. It was about the size of a big living room with a small bar along one side of the room and a few tables and chairs dotted around. A window looked out over the street. There were a few men in there that looked like they hadn't been home for a couple of days.

'What the fuck are we doing here?' I said to Guff.

'It's all right! We'll have a drink then shoot off and get ready for an early start tonight.'

I'd forgotten about the 6.00 p.m. start with the lads. I leant against the bar and ordered Guff and me a couple of lagers. Just opposite, the guys who were playing cards started to arm wrestle each other. Arm wrestling was a popular pub sport amongst the lads. Sometimes a broken glass would be placed where the hand would eventually fall, the loser either bottling it before it hit the glass or getting a nick on the hand. Most bottled it. One guy was slamming down arms as quick as he could grip them. He beat everyone on the table. The victories had gone to his head. He surveyed the club in the same manner a peacock parades his feathers looking for a mate, only this guy was looking for another victim.

He caught my gaze. 'You want a go, kid?' I didn't like being called kid.

'No you're all right, mate,' I said. Guff laughed.

'Come on, John. You'll thrash him.'

'No it's all right, Guff. I'm not in the mood.'

'What's up? You scared?' said the wrestler trying to wind me up. Guff butted in.

'He ain't scared of anybody! Come on, John. Show him!' Guff stood by all of the lads. To him the lads were the tops, unbeatable. I wasn't happy about the situation. I knew where it was heading. But, fuck it! I got up to a cheer. I sat down opposite the peacock and set myself in a good position. We both put our elbows on the table, then put our forearms together and the most important, the grip.

Guff held our hands in position then said, 'Ready,' and let go of the joined hands. The peacock went for it straight away pushing my arm down toward the table. He twisted his hand at the wrist in a kind of half circle changing direction. Our knuckles turned white as we gripped. 'Come on, John,' I heard Guff say. I stared the cock down and forced his hand back. Keeping up the momentum, I slammed it down hard onto the table.

'Bastard!' he exclaimed. Guff cheered.

'My boy beat you,' he said laughing.

'Again, come on again?' The wrestler was agitated by the loss. 'Best of three,' he said. We went again. Guff let go of the grips. This time I slammed him immediately. The wrestler was furious.
'You fucking cheated!' He sounded like one of those card-playing gunslingers from the Wild West. 'Come on!' he said. 'Let's go again.' I heard one of the men he was with tell him to leave it. 'No, fuck him. What's wrong? Scared of me beating you?' The cock was starting to become a cunt. I stood up. Guff stepped forward blocking the lad's exit from behind the table. He got up. 'You're a fucking chicken.' It was my second day out of DC. I was on licence for a year. If it kicked off now I was in danger of getting nicked. I kept cool and ignored his taunts. I could take him anytime. I looked at his glass on the table. He hadn't made a move for it, but he looked the type. He mouthed off again. Guff told him to calm down. 'I want you,' he shouted pointing his finger. I sat down on a stool at the bar and took a sip from my lager glass. I stared at him, then blew him a kiss and laughed. This had the effect of sending him over the top. The huge figure of the bouncer appeared, moving swiftly and coolly he slammed his hand down on the cock's shoulder and pulled him from behind the table. He put his other hand on his neck and dragged, then turned and pushed him towards the exit. Shouts of protest from the wrestler were ignored by the bouncer. They disappeared round onto the staircase. I'd come close to a scrap and I could almost smell that marsh.

Christmas came and went without incident and spring was now upon us. Friday was lads' night out. We'd meet up, cruise the circuit of pubs and then end up in one of the town's two nightclubs, most of the time visiting both. The weekends were fantastic. I was now well and truly one of the lads, Cock-o-the-walk. I didn't want to go back inside but I wouldn't back down from a scrap either. I saw it like this. If anyone thought I'd back down because I was worried about going back inside, they would chance their arm and have a go. I feared no one.

The lads were always up for a scrap. It was part of the night out. We didn't look for trouble. It just happened. A lot of the scraps were territorial. If we caught a gang of out-of-towners or football hooligans pissing on our patch, then we'd get together, no questions asked. We'd find where they were and pile in. We didn't give a fuck about the law or anyone else for that matter. We saw it as our right to protect the town, our town.

In 1978 football hooliganism was rife. Every weekend during the season football fans would scrap it out. Villages, towns and cities would become battlegrounds. Without a doubt, football hooligans were the worst type of offenders. They would invade the town without warning. Usually one or two coaches would drive into Loughborough off the M1 motorway, which is five minutes' drive from the town centre. The police were often caught by surprise and the first they knew would be when some landlord rang them to report a kick-off in a bar. The town was short of police officers because their hours were used up policing football matches. And this was the era when the landlords and landladies policed their own venues. Pubs didn't have bouncers. Some had the odd stool sitter who would help out the landlord for a pint or two. Other than that most were out on a limb.

Loughborough was surrounded by major football grounds: Leicester City, Nottingham Forest, Notts County and Derby County. Others close by were Birmingham, Stoke and Coventry. Hooligan teams passing Loughborough on their way back up north or heading down south would often call into the town via the motorway or through the train station pausing on their way back home. They'd make their way into the town centre and go on the piss causing havoc and intimidating and terrorising people, people who didn't want trouble – until of course they met up with the lads.

The scraps were brutal affairs. Knuckles and boots would flail in. There were many knockouts and bodies littered the streets. I can't ever remember the lads losing a scrap. I'm sure they took a few digs, but never lost. Most of the football hooligans were arrogant bastards, a few tough lads interspersed with a shed load of wankers. Nevertheless they were always up for a scrap.

There was another form of violence in vogue at this time: student bashing. Students were attacked on a regular basis. Some of the town lads despised the way they dressed and called them 'scoobies'. The fact they were in the town was enough to breed hate. Students had never bothered me before DC but after being sent down for scrapping with them, after they had started it, made me feel hate towards them. I saw them as part of the system that I hated. It wasn't an individual thing as I didn't even know them; it was just hatred for students in general and their attitude to our town. The hatred fermented in the pit of my stomach. The students were seen as an easy target and attacks were regular – so much so, that the university advised them to go around in groups. To me and a few others they were just another gang.

Me and a couple of lads got together midweek and practised boxing in my mother's spare room at Manor Drive. The sparring was full on heavy stuff – very little skill though – more like army milling to test ourselves out. After the midweek sparring sessions, we'd hang out around the town. As the gangs of students made their way downtown, we would lie in wait down one of the student routes until a large gang came by. Then we'd jump a few. I didn't agree with the gang mentality of kicking the shit out of a solitary student. We gave them a chance, unlike the court gave me. I'd send the younger lads in first. They would walk through the middle of the gang and bang a few shoulders. As soon as they got a reaction, they would start whacking anyone who was in the way. The only rule was: don't hit the girls. Sometimes I'd wait across the road watching and give the younger lads marks out of ten. It was just a laugh. If the lads got into trouble, I'd steam in and help them out. It must be said, that some of the students were more game than some of the football hooligans I'd encountered.

For me, student bashing was a short-lived affair. I learnt a lesson I wouldn't forget. It was during one of the *mêlées*. We hit a gang that fought back hard. During the fight, I threw an uppercut, which hit someone in the mouth. The guy reeled back and hit the deck. I felt a searing pain and realised a tooth had stuck in my knuckle. The knuckles split open and pissed with blood. The lad was up and on his way, none the worse for his experience. I, on the other hand, suffered for weeks. The knuckle became infected and the hand blew up like an inflated rubber glove. The wound that had been stitched had to be re-opened and cleaned out. I was on antibiotics to kill the infection. I thought twice about entering into a battle for a while. Attacking students because of the wankers that got me sent down was wrong but it gave me a release to the anger I felt toward them.

I was still on licence from DC and that night we narrowly missed getting arrested. I stayed away from the student population. Student bashing continued in the town on and off over the years. I would hear stories about students being bashed. One lad got three years accused of glassing a student. He served somebody else's time for that crime. He was innocent. The guy that actually did it got off completely free.

The town was alive with youths. The student population was growing year after year. They had the midweek scene and the townies had the weekends. The divide eventually closed and the students became an important part of the town and over the years, I would make some very good friends.

BIG MICK

When I wasn't running around town fighting and taking the piss, I would be at home listening to music, mainly Northern, Stax and Atlantic Soul sounds, or messing around with Lambretta and Vespa scooters. Scooters were my second love, training being the first. In the winter months, my mother allowed us to use a redundant downstairs room as a garage to repair or do up old scooters. We'd wheel in a scooter through the front door and into the back room, strip it down, find the fault, repair it and get it back on the road. This went on for some time, until I started one of the scooters up in the room. We'd done all sorts in that room: paint spraying, stripping, rebuilding, but starting up the engine while *Coronation Street* was on was one step too far. After an argument with my mother, which got out of hand, she lifted a broom and broke the handle across my back. We were kicked out into the garden, spanners and all.

Training for me was how I kept the edge. I knew I could be fighting at anytime. In fact, I wanted to fight. I loved it, every minute of it! I would run for three miles across the fields to Quorn, a small, nearby village, and on the way, stop at the railway bridge between Quorn and Loughborough and hill sprint. The routine was ten times up the steepest part of the hill, then jog back down backwards to recover. This was a routine suggested by my dad and one he used to do as a young amateur boxer in Ireland. I made the sprints harder by adding in press-ups and sit-ups at the start and finish of each run. I also ran in heavy steel toecap boots to add resistance. When I returned home, I'd hit an old army kit bag, which was filled with soil, rags and paper and hung from a tree. I would punch the bag for as many rounds as time permitted, which being young was loads. Fifteen to twenty three-minute rounds was normal.

One night on the way back from one of the sprint sessions, I met a guy by the name of Big Mick. Mick was one of those guys with his morals firmly in place, morals that not all agreed with, especially the law. His width and depth made up for his lack of height, but his five foot, ten inch frame would fill any doorway. I always believed that if Mick had taken up wrestling, he'd have been a champ. He had a low centre of mass, ideal for wrestling, but Mick wasn't into competitive fighting. He was an out and out brawler. Besides with a punch like Mick had, wrestling wasn't necessary. He was both tough and powerful. His pet hate was drug dealers, so much so, that he'd hunt them down and either move them on or play mind games with them. Mick asked me if I'd train with him in his back yard. I agreed to meet him after my hill sprinting session.

Mick had a made a huge punch bag and hung it from the washing line pole, which only took the weight because of its concrete construction. I belted the bag. It was a real beauty.
'What do you think, John?' Mick asked.
'I'll tell you after we've trained,' I replied with a smile. Mick and I punched for three-minute rounds, alternating after each round. Whilst one of us punched, the other held the bag and shouted phrases of encouragement to keep the puncher motivated. When either of us felt like quitting, the shouts would get louder, spurring the other on.
'Hit the fucker!' Mick would shout as I slowed down. He held the bag steady and continued shouting at me, 'Knock the cunt out.' Then he'd let it swing, shouting to hit it as it came toward me.

Mick's visualisation technique was spot on. 'There's two of them. Hit him and him!' We'd butt the bag, elbow it and shoulder it, drive it back then pummel it till fatigue set in. Once fatigue set in, name-calling began in the form of insults. This had the desired effect of clicking on the aggression; I found it easy to get angry. The insults fired me up.

I found Mick to be a naturally aggressive person and at times it felt dangerous to wind him up. We needed the tormenting to help us get through the three minutes at the pace we worked at; it was hard going. This type of bag-work drained the energy levels and three minutes recovery between rounds was welcome. After our workouts, Mick would retire to a hot bath. Whilst in there, he would consume two whole chickens and four pints of real ale, all supplied by his wife, Bev. She too could scrap, but that's another story.

Mick had a temper and was an intimidating guy. He wouldn't intimidate on purpose. It was just the way he was. He wouldn't back down to anyone either. There were many stories circulating around about Mick and one story sums him up. He broke his back once in a car crash and was confined to a wheelchair. He still got out and about and, whilst in the local boozer, a scrap started. Mick got stuck in punching from his wheelchair. Although Mick was intimidating to look at, he was a real nice guy. If you needed a favour or help, as long as you were a decent lad, Mick would never turn you away. I learnt a few things from Mick, the main one being, when the going gets tough, keep going!

Like Mick, I wasn't training to box; I was training to keep an edge for the street. And training with Mick gave me that edge. Now although I don't see Mick very often, when we do meet up we always talk about those times.

I remember one workout on a Friday night before I hit the town. I'd done the usual three-mile run including the three sets of ten sprints. We'd done 20 rounds on the bag and to finish off, we did the last three just on the straight left, not jabbing like boxers do, but full on straight lefts as hard as we could. We alternated the rounds. I went for three minutes, then Mick went while I held the bag for him. I felt the pump in my arms after the third round, a solid feeling especially in the forearm, like the muscle was going to break out of the skin. After the rounds, I went home feeling fantastic then I got ready for the night on the town: smart shirt, neat trousers and a pair of Doc Marten non-slip Airwair shoes. Just before I left, I put a sliver of black boot polish along the rim of the highly polished toecap and threw a few punches into mid air. I looked smart, felt smart, and if anybody started I would fight smart and they would know they had been in a fight.

COMING UP TO SCRATCH

In the old, bare-knuckle boxing matches, two lines were drawn in the dirt. These were known as scratch lines. A round was counted when one boxer went to ground; the fight would only resume when the grounded fighter came up to scratch.
Old saying

I'd arranged to meet Guff in the Three Nuns. I arrived just after 6 00 p.m. An early start. I surveyed the pub as I walked in. I always did this to check who was in there and to weigh up any potential threat. I couldn't see Guff, so I made my way round the bar and into the back room. The smell excited my senses. I could feel it was going to be a good night. I got a whiff of my Old Spice aftershave. I felt fresh, clean and fit after my session at Mick's and was in a buoyant mood. I awaited service at the bar and the arrival of Guff. I positioned myself so I could see clearly around me. I noticed a huge lump of a lad sitting close to the bar. He stared at me and grimaced as my gaze passed him by. I didn't know the guy, I'd seen him around a few times, but had no idea who he was and why he was trying to intimidate me. Maybe he'd had a bad day? I decided to ignore him and turned my attention to the other side of the bar.
The bar was unmanned. As I waited, I noticed Guff in the lounge playing the bandit and shouted through. Guff raced round. 'How you doing, mate?' Guff always sounded like a cockney, even though he was an out and out midlander. Whilst Guff chatted away, the bulky kid who looked like a roadie for a rock band continually stared at us. Guff who was constantly scanning whilst he spoke, noticed the lad and caught his eye. The roadie immediately challenged him.
'What you looking at?' Guff smiled playing down the comment.
'What do you mean, what am I looking at?' The roadie stood up, all six feet two inches of him. He was chubby but well built with a huge barrel chest.

'Do you want a fucking go?' he said to Guff. Guff looked surprised but stayed cool and turned to front the roadie up. Before Guff could say anything, I butted in.

'Hey don't fucking talk to him like that. If you want a fucking go, we'll go outside, me and you and sort it one on one!' The roadie switched his gaze to meet mine. The front was the test most would back down from at this point, but using the front was a dangerous ploy if you aren't prepared to back it up. I was.

'Yeah, well come on then. Let's go!' the roadie replied. What happened next was like a comedy sketch. We both started arguing who was going to take him outside.

Guff said, 'It's all right, John. I'll take him outside. You got to be careful. You're still on licence. And he's not worth getting nicked for.'

'No Guff, I'm doing it! He's been screwing me out since I walked in.' The roadie looked from one of us to the other slightly confused that we were arguing. 'Fuck it, Guff.' I pushed by Guff and looked directly at the roadie. 'Outside!' I said gesturing to the doorway leading to the back yard. The kid stood back to let me go first. I kept my distance. 'No, after you,' I said in a posh voice taking the piss. The roadie wasn't bothered about going outside, even though there were two of us. I felt no fear, only confidence as I followed him outside.

Normally if I got the chance, I would crack him one on the back of his head as he walked out in front of me, but this kid was switched on, he walked out like a crab. The roadie was too cool. I had to rile him up, get him close to losing it, so he would make a mistake. We faced off in the yard. I watched him squint and the sun burnt into the back of my neck. I wondered how many times over the years this yard had been used as a ring. I looked toward Guff. 'Guff, stay out of it, this is between me and fatso!' I said trying to anger the roadie.

The kid took the bait. 'I'm not fat!' he growled. He was right, he was just big!

'Come on, fatso. Let's see how good you are.'

He raised his arms and made himself tall like a bear about to wrestle. Then like the action of a heavy bag swinging, made a rushing move toward me. He dropped his head. I lunged forward and caught him with a straight left on the right eyebrow. Unable to remain on his feet, he sat down. He tried to get up. 'Come on, fatso. Get up.' He got angrier at my comment and managed to stand up. As soon as he was upright and moving forward, I drove two straight lefts one after the other into his face. Again his head dropped and he hit the floor. Both eyebrows opened like zips and the blood streamed down into his eyes making him squeeze them shut. He tried to rise once more. Guff shouted to him to stay down. He ignored good advice. As he started to rise, I caught him square in the face with the toecap of my air wear shoe. It left a black polish mark, which looked like a Nike tick down the side of his face.

'Stay down!' Guff shouted at the kid. The roadie looked at me blinking uncontrollably as he tried to see through the blood that was seeping into his eye sockets. I leant down toward him. And said into his face, 'Don't ever fuck with me again!' We left the yard by the side gate, leaving the roadie to contemplate his future.

Guff was ecstatic. 'That's one of the best one to ones I've seen,' he said. And Guff had seen a few. To me it felt easy. The straight left, I'd been practising at Mick's, landed with perfect timing and accuracy. It was a conditioned response to the man's attack that required no thought. I still wonder to this day why the guy wanted to fight me. I saw him a few times after the scrap and he'd just nod in a respectful way and I'd nod back. He deserved my respect. We had a fair go and he never grassed me up. I beat him because I had an edge. If you talk the talk you should prepare yourself to walk the walk. Guff repeated the tale throughout the night to whomever he met, bolstering my reputation further.

FAMILY TIES

It had been a quiet night round town. I'd had a few beers and left the Saracen's Head and headed for the Adam and Eve nightclub. I was laughing and joking with a couple of the lads when I was approached by a mate of mine known as Mozz. He had that serious look on his face. I sensed something was wrong and knew by his look there had been trouble. Then it came, the words that brought my blood to boiling point.
'Your sister's been in a fight and Rory got involved. She had words with him and there was a bit of pushing and shoving. Your sister lost it and Rory whacked her.'
'You fucking what? Where is the cunt?' I asked. I couldn't believe what I was hearing. That disrespectful wanker. 'What do you mean he whacked her?'
'He beat her up, John.'
'Where is he now?'
'He's gone. Your sister's over there in tears.'
I made my way over to where my sister Bernadette was. I was surprised he'd hit her. He knew she was my sister. I could only assume he had no respect for women and none for me. I felt it was his way of causing a confrontation with me. I jogged over to confirm Mozz's story with my sister.

Rory was a bouncer and fancied himself as a bit of a hard man. He surrounded himself with lads that looked up to him. Lads that would back him up in a crisis. I saw Bernadette crying hysterically mainly due to her temper. 'Bernadette, what's up?' I asked.
'That bastard's just hit me,' she shouted. Bernadette pointed in the direction of Rory, who was now making his way toward the chip shop in the Rushes.
'Come with me. Show me who it was,' I said. I had to be sure I got the right person. I didn't know Rory, but I knew of his reputation and had seen him around town a few times. The anger was getting stronger as I got closer to the chip shop.
'That's him over there,' she said pointing her finger.

Rory had just pushed in front of the chip shop queue and was surrounded by his mates. I pushed through them and stood inside the chip shop, then confronted him.

'I want a fucking word with you!' I said. He gave me an arrogant look and peered above me toward the chip shop assistant as if I wasn't there. Rory was built like an athlete of African descent. I repeated the phrase. 'I want a fucking word with you!' The second phrase finally got his attention. He looked at me then grunted.

'What's up?' he asked with an air of arrogance.

'Why have you just hit my sister?' I stood directly in front of him with about a foot of space between us. He was seconds from being banged out! The question was to prime him for the first shot. The answer would be irrelevant to the outcome of the conversation.

'She fucking deserved it!' was his reply. I should have hit him as soon as he opened his mouth. But I couldn't believe his arrogance. He moved backward and positioned himself in the doorway. His mates had backed off out on to the pavement. I was now facing him square on. I made a statement so everyone in earshot understood what this was about.

'No fucker hits my sister and gets away with it!'

'What you gonna do about it? Do you want a gang fight? Your lads against mine?' he said. I stared at the prick for a second. 'Gang fight! This isn't the fucking playground. Your lads against mine!' They weren't my lads as he put it. They were my mates, but I knew what he meant.

'This is between me and you. It's fuck all to do with anybody else.' I stared at him looking for his reaction. I wanted him to feel alone. He made no move. I lined him up. Got my distance. He didn't seem to notice. He was going to get it no matter what. I needed to get the first one in. I set him up with another question.

'You'd better apologise to her now!' I said, switching my gaze to the side and behind him, as if I was looking toward my sister. The daft prick fell for it. He turned for a split second to see what I had looked at. That was enough time for me to send a peach of a right-hander directly on to his jaw. The right-hander was my lead into an explosion of hooks, left hook, right hook; the forward momentum of the punches carried me forward and I almost fell over him as he crashed to the floor. I tumbled over his legs. The first punch put him to sleep on his feet and the second and third sealed his fate. I was now outside on the pavement. I rushed forward then felt someone's arm's encircle mine from behind, trying to prevent me from getting to Rory.

'Leave it out, John. He's had enough!' I couldn't see who had grabbed me. I shrugged the hands off.

'Get your fucking hands off me!' I shouted. I broke free from the grip which was trapping me into a bad situation. I didn't look to see who it was. I was blinded by the red mist of anger that forced its way into my physical being. I could see only Rory. He was all that I focused on. I started to kick and stamp wildly on his head and body, finishing by repeatedly stamping on his face. I was like a wild animal fighting for its territory. Blood leaked from every facial orifice. I looked down at him. 'No bastard hits my sister and gets away with it!' I surveyed the crowd trying to catch the eye of any other fucker that wanted a go. The challenge never came. I felt my anger subside. I lifted my head and looked around. The shroud of red mist had cleared, I felt calm. As my anger finally diminished, I felt like I hadn't been there, like it wasn't me for the time I was fighting. The pats on the back ended the surreal emotion I was feeling. I felt no remorse. I told my sister to go home.

Mozz walked over, placed a whisky bottle in my hand.

'Here, John you deserve it,' he said. I took a slug from the whisky bottle and the nasty taste burnt my throat. I looked across at Rory lying motionless on the pavement.

Mozz grabbed at my shoulder. 'Come on, John, let's fuck off before the pigs come.' Mozz had two birds with him and I tagged along. I knew the coppers would be involved and if I went home I would be locked up for the night. The cheap whisky didn't help matters. I got so drunk I could hardly see.

The last thing I remember was the room spinning frantically out of control, some bird trying to undo my trousers and Mozz in fits of laughter.

I awoke with a sparkle of sunlight in my eye from the nearby curtain. The night was soon forgotten amid the throes of a fucking bad hangover. Empty beer bottles littered the room. I was alone. I stood up and felt a booming headache shroud my skull. I was in a strange house with a bad hangover. I made my way to the front door and quietly slipped out into the early morning sunlight. I nicked a bottle of milk from next-door's doorstep. The streets were deserted except for a lone cyclist who looked like he was on his way to work, and a milkman whose electric float sounded ten times louder than they usually do. I inhaled a breath of fresh air and opened my newly acquired contraband. I took a big swallow, not giving a thought to the neighbours' needs. I suddenly felt sick as I recalled the fight with Rory. He'd looked in a bad way when I'd left him and there were stacks of witnesses. Fuck it! It had to be done.

I was arrested later that week and charged with grievous bodily harm. I was expecting a second helping of North Sea Camp, so when the court case came up, I said my goodbyes and prepared for a six-month stint.
Rory didn't come across well in court. He was known to the police and the magistrates' court is a police court.
His injuries were read out. Shattered jaw, broken nose, cuts and bruises. My solicitor put forward my reasons why I did what I did and the court looked on it in my favour. I was guilty and admitted it, but with extenuating circumstances; Rory had provoked the fight by hitting my sister. I received a fine and was bound over to keep the peace for a year. I had to pay compensation, but was allowed to go free from the court. I smiled at Rory as I left the court house. His gaze fell to the floor.
He knew he was in the wrong and he'd think twice about hitting a woman again.

THE MODS AND ROCKERS

Looking smart and travelling to see new, up and coming bands was cool. One of the bands the lads followed was Paul Weller's The Jam. They were gigging all over Britain inspiring a Mod-type musical revolution, stepping out of the shadow of the punk era. We hated punks, all that spitting and slam dancing. It was horrible. There was another scene building momentum a monster left over from the late '60s, the rock idol. These giants and their spin offs were followed by the biker gangs. The music was extremely loud and heavy. The bikers resided in the back rooms of pubs usually off the town circuits. We despised the filthy look the leather and cut-off denims, the bikes, the grease. They were known to us as grebs or grebos. We didn't sit well together. Brawls were serious business.

Quadrophenia, a new film, was being screened at our local cinema. This film about '60s Mod culture, based on a rock opera written by The Who, a former Mod band known as the High Numbers, was about to fuel a new wave of modernism. The irony of the movie was The Who were now known as being a biker band. Shortly after the film there was a youth culture explosion; lads and girls were bodding around on reconditioned '60s Italian scooters wearing ex-army parkas, 501 Levi jeans and desert boots. It was an exciting time for youth culture. Those that didn't suit the mod thing were either punks, bikers, skinheads, townies or scoobies. Others preferred the cool, northern soul underground circuit. There was something for everyone.
The call was that the film *Quadrophenia* started the new wave Mod scene off. Not true. It had never really gone away. But the movie did bring the Mod scene to the attention of thousands of bored youths looking for a direction.

I can't remember why we went to war with the grebs. Something had cracked off with one of the lads. There had been a battle here before which ended in a few lads getting three and six month DC sentences. Feelings ran high and revenge was on the agenda. We headed for the Volunteer pub in the town centre. As we passed through several pubs on the circuit our numbers swelled until we were close to sixty hard core lads from in and around Loughborough. We weren't alone. As the walk to the Volunteer gathered pace word spread and youths tagged along. Some wore ex-army parkas the uniform of the Mod. We stopped opposite the Volunteer. I decided to be the one to go into the pub and check out their numbers. A couple of the lads accompanied me just in case it kicked off when we walked in. We stood at the bar feeling uneasy. We had a quick half of beer and scanned the many faces now screwing us out! They were ready for us. I could sense it. We went back outside. The crowd was huge and not a copper in sight. They started to chant, 'Mods, Mods, Mods.' This chanting incited the lads and gave a clear indication to the grebs that we were about to attack.

The main core of lads was grouped outside the motor factor's shop opposite the pub. We started to move forward toward the doors. The chanting in the background echoed throughout the street. We got halfway and stopped. A group of grebos appeared in the alleyway. They were wearing silver crash helmets and carrying pickaxe handles. They lined up in formation like Roman soldiers and spread out in front of the pub. I heard an almighty crash and turned to see the motor factor's plate glass window explode. Dozens of cans of oil which had been neatly stacked against the window now littered the streets. I grabbed one and pulled back the strip like I was pulling the pin out of a grenade and launched it into the ranks of grebs. 'Get the bastards.' The noise was incredible. We charged at the same time as they did under a hail of oil cans. The whole area became one mass brawl. Temporary steel street posts used for the market days were ripped out of their holdings. They flew through the air landing with a clatter. Scuffles were everywhere. I was now in the thick of the action with no one to hit! The grebs had pulled back into the pub yard and were regrouping. A car came speeding towards us attempting to clear us from the front of the pub. I jumped clear. One of the lads rammed a street post through the windscreen. The whole scene was sheer madness. Blue flashing lights and coppers arriving at the scene triggered the sprint through town. We charged through the centre and headed toward the precinct. Plate glass windows were exploding all around me. Chants of 'Mods, Mods, Mods,' rang out. I turned into the precinct just as a cop car skidded to a halt. A youth in front of me jumped high and side-kicked a plate glass window. The glass shattered and hit me as I sprinted by. I exited the precinct and ran toward the Rushes and ducked quietly into Saleh's kebab shop. The counter was unmanned. Unseen, I slipped through the toilet window and into an alleyway, where I would wait for the riot to end. I could hear the chanting still going on; the distant echo of far away voices.

I didn't get nicked that night. In fact I don't think anyone did. And to think I couldn't remember throwing a punch in anger, everything else but not a punch. The whole riot was like the scene from *Quadrophenia* without the scooters and bikes. The Mod thing grew and riots were commonplace in our fair land. Wherever there was a scooter rally or a gig, violence was ever present. I was addicted to the thrill of a good brawl. Every bloody minute of it!

STICKING TOGETHER

Although I hung around with the Loughborough lads I had my own identity. I was John Skillen, ex-con, known to the police and known in the town as a scrapper. There were mixed views as to my reputation. Some would say I was a hooligan, to others I was a kind of hero. I liked the last tag; helping out someone who was in trouble was a common occurrence. If I saw someone getting bullied or picked on, I would jump in and help them out. If we were in a scrap, I would back up any of the lads even if they didn't need backing up. I lost count of the times I'd jumped in to save someone from getting a kicking.

I wasn't alone either. My best mate known as Spider had the same trait. He was as strong as they come. He had a great physique due to his weight training regime and all natural. He was nicknamed Spiderman by the lads for saving a young boy, who could have drowned in the local canal. The name Spiderman was shortened to Spider and the name stuck. Some say the nickname came from the way he splayed his arms and moved his feet when he danced to the Two-Tone sounds of the Specials, Madness and The Selecter, making him appear like he had several legs especially with the lights strobing. If there was a scrap, Spider was right there beside me. Our friendship grew strong due to the mutual respect we had for each other.

I remember leaving Rebecca's nightclub one night. Spider was in a right state having consumed enough alcohol to last him the week. When Spider had a drink, he was on fire, a true party animal. One night he ran over the top of a police car and kicked the blue light off the top, and many a plate glass window was met by his youthful fury. Drink sent Spider crazy. I coaxed him toward a taxi. Spider's anger erupted when approached by a lad he knew. The lad's face was a bloody mess.
'What's up with you?' he demanded to know off the lad.
'I've just been hammered by those squaddies over there,' he said. Spider looked across the street to see a group of seven squaddies, soldiers from the nearby Garat's Hay Barracks on town leave.

Spider shouted to the lads inbetween retching in the gutter. 'Fucking wankers!' Spider exclaimed. The squaddies laughed, which was not wise considering Spider's emotional state. We were well out-numbered as usual. I told Spider to leave it. But it was too late. He retched one more time then sprinted towards the squaddies. No matter how pissed he was, Spider could sprint like a rugby player on his way to scoring a try for England. He was amongst them before I could move. The only way to beat this lot was to stick together. I sprinted toward the scrap that had broken out. Spider was bent forward and in a bad situation. His jumper had been pulled over his head and fists were flaying him from all sides. I scanned for the coppers as I ran in. The first one went down from a right hand punch to the side of the head. The second fell on top of him as the left landed. I steamed forward into one of the others, forcing him back against the glass window. He went down from another right hand punch. I turned and exchanged punches with a fourth youth. The first punch missed, but the second knocked him unconscious. With the others dealt with, Spider gained ground on the squaddies he was scrapping with.

I bowled one more over with a cracking punch to the nape of the neck and he fell unconscious his head narrowly missing the street bench. The other two legged it. Spider gave chase to the last two squaddies standing. The chase ended in a doorway. Spider had one of the squaddies cornered. The other one got away. He forced the lad through the glass window of the doorway and continued to stamp over him. I didn't give chase; I was too concerned with getting Spider off the youth in the doorway before the coppers showed up.

'Come on, Spider. Let's go. The coppers are coming!' This brought him back to his senses.

The adrenalin he'd felt during the brawl had completely sobered him up. Spider realised what he was doing. We skipped across the road and headed for a taxi. The two lads who'd had the hassle with the squaddies appeared and began sticking the boot into the unconscious lad. We called them off as we passed in the taxi. What I didn't realise at the time was, that the whole situation was witnessed by a group of reputable lads from Leicester and word spread of the multiple knockouts.

Spider often lost it. He was full of anger. He had reason to be. He had been deserted by his father and mother as a young child and brought up by his lovely grandma. At that time, Spider didn't know who his father was and often talked about meeting him. It would be a couple of years later before he got his explanation and the anger he felt eased

REFLECTIONS

The mirror behind the bar gave me a full view of all around me without me having to turn around, I could watch people unseen. Looking into the mirror stirred my memory.

I remembered a man by the name of Johnny Griffin, an old-school Loughborough legend who was always in and out of prison and was regularly the talk of the town. The first time I saw him he was wearing jeans and a waistcoat which revealed his muscular tattooed body. The waistcoat appeared too tight due to the stocky frame beneath it. Johnny was, as some put it, a hard man. He hung around with lads much younger than himself and he had a Fagin-like quality about him; the pied piper of Loughborough. The younger lads looked up to him and he was feared. He was a crafty streetwise guy who hit first and didn't stick around to ask any questions. I learnt a valuable lesson off Johnny one night in the Golden Fleece pub.

The pub was heaving with the youth of the town and it was a struggle to get to the bar. I noticed Johnny standing with his back to the crowd, not a good position for a man that is supposed to be streetwise. Always have your back to the wall and know how to get out in a hurry. The Fleece was renowned for erupting into a free-for-all brawl and this particular night you could cut through the atmosphere. It would be easy to whack someone from behind especially if they weren't paying attention. The way he stood he'd left himself wide open to attack. I inspected Johnny with a hard stare. I was curious as to what made this guy tough. My stare was interrupted by a firm hard-sounding voice and my stare met with a pair of ice-cold eyes.

'I'm watching you, son. You know I'm the Griff and I'm always watching. Your Sammy Skillen's lad aren't you? How's your dad?' Within a second he had mentally disarmed me. I was taken aback. This crafty bastard was watching his own back through the mirrors behind the bar.

'He's all right, Johnny,' I said. Johnny's stare was intimidating, his ability to deceive excellent. He'd turned a possible confrontation into a friendly chat.

'Mirrors son, always use the mirrors.' It felt weird talking to him through the mirror. He continued. 'You can see everything from any angle and mirrors are all around us.'
I'd taken good advice that night and over the years perfected the use of the reflection.

Now I was watching the pub crowd behind me through the mirror having taken the Griff's lesson into my repertoire. As I ordered my drink something caught my eye. A lad to my right had taken hold of the handle of his empty pint glass. He held it so tight his fist turned white. The dimple glass was a bastard of a glass. When broken it left the holder with the perfect pub weapon: a glass duster. His face was contorted with hate. He was transfixed to my image. I recognised one of the lads, a scumbag from a nearby town. He leant over to his mate and made a comment I couldn't hear. I could only guess as to their intentions. They both now stared at the side of my head which reinforced what I'd already guessed. Attack was imminent and they were about to go for it! But they hadn't spotted themselves being scrutinised through the mirrors.
The lad twitched and launched the glass toward my face. I reacted, spun right and ducked under the lad's shoulder. My timing was perfect, the glass whizzed past my face and into a nearby pillar. I sprung upwards and launched a barrage of fists decking one of the lads, who immediately jumped back up to be met by a forward driving muscle mass in the form of Spider who had been watching from a short distance away. I changed my attention to the glass merchant who ran for the open door. I surged forward spun him round and unleashed another barrage of hook punches.
Every punch hit its target. The glass merchant fell to the floor unconscious. I dragged his limp body into the hallway, booted him and coolly returned into the pub.

The landlady was arguing with her husband about the scrap and wanted us to leave, but nobody had the bottle to tell us. We finished our drinks and left in our own time. An ambulance arrived as we walked out. The lad who had attempted to rip open my face with the glass was coming out of unconsciousness.
'You fucking animal,' screeched a girl standing over the youth.

I ignored her and approached the glass merchant. The crowd listened to what I had to say.

'If you ever fuck with me again I'll kill ya.' On that phrase I stamped on his face a couple of times.

I looked around the crowd. No one wanted to catch my eye. The girl turned away after giving me a look of disgust. I wondered how sympathetic she would have been if he had been successful and shredded my face.

I figured I owed Johnny Griffin. If it wasn't for the lesson on mirrors it could have been me in the ambulance, or worse a coffin! I never saw the glass merchant again and the police were never involved.

Glasses are a nightmare. The damage they can do with one strike can be far worse than being slashed with a blade. A slash can be treated by casualty far easier than a ripped and shredded wound. The glass that was aimed at my face ended up hitting a pillar in the middle of the pub narrowly missing a couple youths. It left a two-inch deep dent in the plasterwork.

WELL, WELL, WELL

The police were always out to nick someone and we were the intended targets. Violence was the norm for me and I was desensitised to the horror of it. To me having a scrap was as normal as taking a piss. At the weekends the coppers were on edge and would herd a group of lads from one part of the town to another, usually the Loughborough lads. They never forgot faces or names. Due to me having a big mouth and the fact I'd wound a few coppers up, my card was well and truly marked. I wasn't the only lad in the town whose card was marked by the local constabulary. Most of the lads had been harassed or nicked at some point. Some had learnt how to walk away or keep their mouths shut. Others would probably never learn.

As I was passing Sammy's nightclub I nipped in to have a quick chat with one of the lads on the door. Andy who was out with me that night waited on the cinema steps keeping out of the cold wind. I'd seen the van screech to a halt as I came out of Sammy's doorway. They pulled up and jumped out of the van and made a direct line to where Andy was standing. 'Well, well, well', I heard the copper say. I always thought they said, 'Hello, hello, hello'. He was a long coated leather-gloved type of copper as arrogant as a German SS officer.
'Skinheads back in fashion,' he said. And pushed Andy back against the wall. Andy stared at him; I could see it wouldn't take much for Andy to flip. His Irish blood that he inherited from his father influenced the 'don't push it too far' look on his face. Andy kept his gob shut and his hands in his pockets. The copper pushed Andy again. This time he hit the wall hard. Andy looked pissed off but didn't bite the bait and stared at the floor. I couldn't stand by and watch Andy get set up. Who the fucking hell did this copper think he was winding people up just so he could get a nicking? I intervened.
'Oi leave him alone,' I said as I ascended the cinema steps. I felt an excited lump form in my throat as I neared the copper. 'Go on, Andy. Get going. He can't nick you. You haven't done anything. I'm a witness to that.'

'Well, well, well, if it ain't Skillen,' the copper said. I really wished this guy would get another phrase. I think I preferred 'hello, hello, hello'.

'What are you picking on him for?' I asked. The copper turned his attention toward me and away from Andy. Another copper stood slightly back from his colleague with a cheesy grin on his face.

'What's it got to do with you, Skillen?' He walked closer to me as he spoke. I had my back to the cinema doors and both coppers were now facing me. Their van with the back door slightly open sat with its engine running directly opposite hiding us from general view.

'He's my mate and besides he's only sixteen.' I saw the cogs begin to turn. Juveniles the coppers hate them – too much hassle, paperwork, dealing with the parents. They can't be doing with it.

'You're a wise guy ain't you, Skillen.' He moved closer. He was now in my space. 'Think you're a hard man do you?' I said nothing and stared at him. 'What's up Skillen? Scared? I thought you were one of the lads. A hard man.' This cunt was really pushing my buttons. He pushed his face close enough for me to smell his coffee breath. I knew this copper wanted to nail me. His voice deepened, his face contorted. He prodded me with both hands digging his leather-clad fingers deep into my chest. This had an irritating effect of making me feel a surge of hate. I wanted to bang him out. But I didn't want to be drawn into his little game. My dad had warned me many times. 'Never hit a copper, son.' He splayed his fingers and hit me again.

'Come on, hard man.' I felt his fingertips almost pierce my flesh. My anger began to rise, forcing out words I didn't need to say.

'I'll fucking show you how hard I am if you do that again.' He hit me a third time and forced me into the cinema doors. I felt a searing pain between my shoulder blades. I rebounded off the door frame and smashed the copper with a right hand punch, which sent him sprawling to his knees. I instinctively followed through booting him and stamping anywhere I could. The van doors burst open. I was wrestled to the floor. My arms and legs were encircled.

'Get the bastard down,' I heard one shout.

'Fucking cuff him,' said another.

'Get the cuffs on him now. You've really done it now, Skillen.' I felt a knee pressing down on my spine. The pain was excruciating.

'Fuck you,' I snarled. My anger flared. They struggled to restrain me. My rage had taken over. I started to kick out in all directions.
'Get his legs,' one shouted. I felt sick. Silver sparks flashed in my eyes as the blows landed on the back of my neck and head. I could feel hard metal cutting into my skull. It felt like some bastard was hitting me with their cuffs on their fists.
'Come on, you bastards,' I shouted. Firing up my aggression, which blocked out the pain I continued to struggle wildly. These wankers were going to have to fight hard to get me in the van. They managed to get the cuffs on. I felt more pain as the cuffs tightened around my wrists. They dragged me into the back of the police van and pushed me face down. The bodyweight of the officers made it difficult for me to breathe. Some lard-arse was sitting on my back. I shouted abuse and tried to break free. My face was unceremoniously rammed into the floor of the van. A foot was pressed against the side of my jaw. A pair of hands were holding down my head, which was still ringing from the handcuff blows. Both of my arms were pinned behind my back and both legs were being held. I was well and truly trussed up like a Christmas turkey waiting to be stuffed.
'Wait till we get you down the nick. You're really going to fucking get it.'
'Fuck you!' I grimaced as the boot on my cheek pressed down harder. 'It will take more than just you fuckers,' I said as the boot eased off. I had nothing to lose now. I might as well go for it. Pressure was applied to my arms and wrists. They locked me up tighter. I screamed out as the pain seared up my arms. I'd done something I was always told not to do, hit a copper and now I had to suffer the consequences.
I'd really fucked it this time. The van roared down the street. The coppers continued their abuse. 'Hitting a policeman. You're going down for this. They'll throw the fucking key away.
'Fuck off, pig,' was my reply. The blows rained down on my head. I tried to see the face of the copper that was whacking me with the cuffs. The first chance I got I would give him a fucker as well. I couldn't turn round far enough to see who it was.
'That's enough. Leave him alone,' one of the coppers said. It sounded like a woman. They eased of slightly. Just then there was a loud bang and the scraping of metal. In their haste to get me to

the cells the van hit something in the road. It sounded like he had hit the kerb or the wall as he turned into the station yard. The vibration passed through my jaw. The van stopped and the doors opened.
'Get him up,' one copper said.
'Watch him,' said another. I was surrounded and at that moment I was being treated like Public Enemy No.1. The cuffs tightened as I was dragged to my feet. The pain was again excruciating. I winced as the copper that I had hit grabbed me by the throat and pushed his face close to mine.
'Look what you've fucking done to my face,' he said.
'Leave it out. Let's get him inside,' another said. I could smell the leather from his gloves. I knew what I would be smelling next. The pissy damp smell of a cell.

'Right, calm down, you lot,' the desk sergeant said. I was burning with anger. I'd been set up, forced into hitting the copper. He wasn't bothered about a smack in the mouth. He'd got what he wanted, me nicked. Where Andy refused to take the bait I became the dumb fish and got netted. I'd fallen for their tactics.
'Name?' the desk sergeant asked. I used my favourite phrase.
'Fuck you.'
'Now come, on son. You'll only make it worse for yourself.' More stupid tactics. They'd obviously formed a very low opinion of me and who could blame them after me falling for the wind him up and nick him routine. I was already up shit creek without a boat never mind a paddle. There was no point in being a conformist.
'You know my fucking name.'
'Okay. Address?'
'Just fucking lock me up.' The pain in my wrists was getting worse as the adrenalin that anaesthetised the pain wore off. It was time to bring my own tactics into play. 'Loosen these cuffs and I'll tell you what you want to hear.' The sergeant nodded in the direction of his colleagues. The cuffs were slackened just enough to ease the pain. I gave them my name and address. My anger had now eased off. They emptied my pockets, stripped off my brogue shoes and silver neck chain. I looked around at the faces of the coppers. None would hold my gaze. They looked seriously on edge and full of fear.

Pointing to the paperwork he was completing, the desk sergeant said, 'Sign here, here, and here.'

'What – with my fucking teeth?' I replied twisting my back toward him to show him the evidence of why I couldn't sign.

He realised that I was still cuffed and therefore could not sign. He also realised I'd just made him look like a complete dick in front of his subordinates. The sergeant's attitude changed from one of being fair; to fuck you, lock him up. I was pinned hard against the desk. I watched as he wrote refused to sign. He glared at me and with a smile, he said, 'Didn't your daddy ever tell you, never hit a copper.'

'Screw you,' I growled and I spat at the sergeant missing him due to the fact that my mouth was too dry for anything to come out but air. I stared at the sergeant as I was dragged to the cell.

Two coppers stood by the open cell door. 'Here we go,' I thought. I glanced back to see four coppers behind me. I was still cuffed and I'd heard about some of the recent beatings they'd dished out. I prepared myself for a kicking. I felt the pressure from the sudden surge of body weight as the coppers pushed me into the cell, ramming my face into the smooth flooring. I could feel the cold and taste the dirt as I my face was forced further into the cell floor. I was in a bad position. It was time to keep my gob shut. The cuffs were released. I quickly covered up expecting a beating. It didn't happen. Instead the cell door slammed shut and the door locked. I heard a muffled chattering then an eerie silence. I lay there cold and sore. I was alone. The fear hit me making me shiver. Fuck me! I was really going to get it now. I countered the feelings of fear. Fuck it! He'd started it, I'd warned him, he fucking deserved it, but who would believe me with only coppers as witnesses.

The cell stank like they always did but this one was the worst I'd been in: no mattress, no lights, the toilet was completely blocked with shit and almost overflowing, the smell making me heave. I felt spew beginning to rise up from my stomach. The smell lingered heavy in the air. I couldn't shut the toilet lid as it wasn't designed with one. The smell reminded me of the outside toilets I had to use as a kid with torn up newspaper hanging on a strip of wire to wipe your arse on, the toilet itself an open wooden box with a bucket beneath to catch the shit.

I sat on the boards beneath the dimpled glass blocks which formed the window of the cell. I stretched out on the boards my body aching from the blows I'd taken during the arrest. I sat up and pulled my knees up into my chest encircling my legs with my arms waiting for them to come. I knew they would. They weren't finished with me yet. I read the scratches on the cell wall: if you can't do the time, don't do the crime; couldn't give a fuck, Tony from Barrow; Rocky is a grass. One stood out more than the rest – 'ACAB' – All Coppers are Bastards. They weren't, but at that moment in time I certainly thought they were.

The cell door hatch slid back. The SS copper peered through complete with cut across his nose. He looked like he'd done a round with Tyson.
'Look what you've done to my nose.' He sounded like he had a cold. 'You'd better not sleep tonight, Skillen.' His eyes were angry and pierced mine. I stared at him showing no emotion. Underneath I was bricking it.

I felt my eyes droop then open again, I was drifting off to sleep. I had to stay awake. I was like a sleepy child trying to keep his eyes open. I must have slept for a moment. That's what they were waiting for. It was the sound of the key turning slowly in the lock which woke me. I froze not daring to move. The lock continued to turn. They were making a real effort not to wake me. I felt my heart begin to pound. I felt a shiver of cold. Fuck 'em I thought. Even though I was ready for them, I jumped as they burst into the cell. It was dark, then darker still as the blanket encircled my head. I knew what was coming. There must have been at least six of them. They punched kicked and stamped on my legs, arms and body. I crawled into the foetal position and covered my head as the blows rained in on me. They attacked in silence. I felt like fighting back but took their justice. I shouted abuse at them to show I didn't care.
'Come on, you bastards. Give it to me. Come on, come on,' I screamed. The blanket and my arms cushioned the blows to my head. My jaw ached and pain once again ripped through my body. I lay still for a second. I felt like I had a bad dose of the flu every joint ached. I waited for the door to shut and the footsteps to

disappear. Then I jumped to my feet. And gave them some more abuse. 'Is that the best you've got, you fucking wankers?' I laughed like a crazy man.

'You're going down, Skillen,' were the last words I heard. They sounded happy as they walked away, happy they'd given some back. I wasn't worried about the beating. You give some, you take some. I felt a minor victory as I turned back toward the cell bench and realised that they had left the blanket behind. I curled up and tried to sleep awaking every time I heard a sound.

Daylight shone through the dimples of the cell window. I'd got used to the smell of the shit from the toilet. I lay there thinking of a way out of the mess I was in. After a while I realised there wasn't one. I was glad I wasn't too pissed the night before or I would have felt a lot worse.

'Do you want breakfast?' I heard a copper say. I didn't bother looking at the door. I lay, hands behind my head, staring at the ceiling.

'Fuck off,' I said.

'Have it your way,' came the reply and the hatch shut. I drifted off again. I was awoken by the sound of the hatch opening.

'Tea,' the officer said in a piss-taking fashion. I really wanted one. I hadn't had a drink of any sort since my arrest, which was at least eight hours ago. And who knows what was in it? I had visions of them laughing and dancing around the mug pissing in it, cursing me like those witches in Macbeth. I declined the offer.

Later that afternoon I was charged, finger printed, photographed and taken to a special court where I was placed under a police bail curfew and given a court date for a committal to crown court. The police didn't oppose bail. Instead they insisted that I sign on at the police station at a certain time each day. I couldn't go out between the hours of 7.00 p.m. and 7.00 a.m. and had to reside at my home address. It was a shit situation but better than being remanded in prison. At least I was still enjoying the fruits of freedom.

The court case came round quickly and was pointless as it was a foregone conclusion. I listened whilst every copper that gave evidence on oath committed perjury. Like Billy Liar they told lie-after-lie-after-lie. They were pushing the evidence to get me the longest sentence they could. It was obvious they had written their statements out together by comparing notes. And who could blame them? I'd hit one of their own. I pleaded guilty in the crown court dock hoping to get a lighter sentence. I couldn't deny the fact I had banged out a copper. The government should have instant sentences for criminals that plead guilty. It would save a lot of time and money having to take them to court and the con could get on with his sentence.

The judge was vicious in his summing up due to the statement of the copper, which read: Skillen replied, 'I'm only nineteen but I'm hard.' I hadn't said this phrase, but the judge jumped on it, creating a newspaper headline. He said, 'Skillen, you're not a hard man. You're a stupid man. A very stupid man. And you can be a very dangerous man. In order to protect the public, I sentence you to two years of borstal training.' I was expecting borstal so it didn't come as a shock. All I could think of were the courtroom jokes we used to laugh about in DC.

Judge says to man,
'Have you been up before me before?'
The man replied,
'Why what time did you get up?' or
'I sentence you to five years.'
The man replies,
'I can do that standing on me head.'
The judge replies,
'Well here's another five to get you back on your feet.' I smiled to myself as the judge finished off.
'I hope that during your time in borstal you will reflect upon your actions. Take him down.' The smile on my face was replaced with a frown and a lump in my throat that threatened to choke me. Cunt, I thought. Fucking cunts.

As I walked to the police van all that kept going through my mind was my dad's voice. 'Never hit a copper, son.' I knew I was guilty and accepted that, but so were they.

I acted in self-defence but I'd had no chance to prove it.

BORSTAL BOY

It was 1979. Dexy's Midnight Runners' 'Geno' topped the charts and the clubs were booming. Me, I arrived at Welford Road Prison, was taken into the processing cells, ordered to be stripped naked and told to get into a bath. I sat naked in two inches of very hot, cloudy water. I felt humiliated. There was so much disinfectant in it the smell lingered in my nostrils for days. I was given a set of clothes; blue jeans similar to what Elvis wore in jailhouse rock, only this particular pair would have fitted him better in later years. The shirt I was given had two buttons missing. I couldn't be bothered to complain. Truth was, I still had a lump in my throat as big as an apple and felt it difficult to talk. I had to put on a hard exterior. As far as I knew this place was another DC. I kept my gob shut – exactly what I should have done the night I hit the copper.

I was eventually assessed, categorised a violent risk and shipped over to Glen Parva Borstal in Leicester. Glen Parva had a reputation for being a tough place to do your time. So close to home yet so far away.

It was a totally different regime to DC. The screws were more relaxed. I found the un-uniformed screws to be very civilised, nothing like the short–sharp–shock nutters of North Sea Camp. But these guys could be just as ruthless if you fucked them around. I was given an interview where the screws laid down the law, a kind of letting you know who the boss was and what was expected from you whilst you were there. They also gave me an overview of the other trainees as we were known.

I got changed into the usual designer prison wear, took my plastic cutlery and mug and went into the unit, the unit which housed around 30 lads incarcerated for various crimes from burglary to arson. They looked a dodgy bunch. I approached the table and could sense the chitchat. I was the new boy, but all these guys knew about me was what was printed in the pages of the Leicester Mercury. I put my mug and cutlery on the table and went to the toilet: first mistake. After visiting the toilet I returned to the table to find that my new mug and cutlery had been replaced with a scratched up mug, broken knife and a fork with a prong missing. The spoon had bite marks on it. The red mist began to form just like it did before I dropped the copper. I hated anyone taking the piss. I exploded into aggressive verbal.

'Right, you fucking wankers, I'm gonna go back into the toilet and when I come back out my mug, knife, fork and spoon better be back on the table or I will fuck you all up.' I scanned the table. The screws looked on but didn't intervene. The room went silent. I meant what I'd said. All eyes were now on me. If things didn't materialise I'd have no choice but to check every mug, knife, spoon and fork and whoever had taken them would have to take the consequences no matter what. If I failed this test I would be the target for more shit. I turned to walk away and then smiled to myself when I heard the clatter of knives and forks and a plastic mug roll up the table. The atmosphere in the room changed and the chitchat restarted.

'There's no need to be like that. It's only a joke, mate. We're all in the same boat in here,' a con said.

'Don't fuck me around. I'm not one of your Joeys,' I said. I'd made my entrance. They knew one thing: if I was crazy enough to whack a copper I ain't gonna think twice about whacking another con. All I had to do was maintain my reputation and my time would be easier.

SWORD OF DAMOCLES

Borstal training was supposed to rehabilitate you, give you an education in respect and behaviour and prepare you for a better life. At least that's what I was told. The original concept, put together by the Gladstone committee in 1895, was for delinquent boys aged between 16 and 21. The idea was to reform boys by getting them used to regular work, education, discipline, respect for authority and obedience, leading to good character formation. The boys were to be regulated into good habits, regular meals, exercise, toilet training and early morning showers – a lot of which is really common sense, unless of course you're a delinquent boy aged between 16 and 21.

For me the worst part of borstal training was the bang up: the lack of freedom to do what I wanted to do. One thing I learnt very early on was that there is nothing as precious as freedom. The sentence I had received was two years maximum but I could be out in six months and one day with good behaviour.
The six months and one day was seen as the magical figure. Six months and a breakfast and then I'd be out. But the magical figure was out of reach for most. Very few attained the required level of behaviour.
The first few months of your sentence you were assessed and eventually given a release date. One fuck-up meant you would lose that date and then have to be re-assessed for another release date. It was like having a sword dangling on a thread over your head, a thread that could break at anytime. I wanted out as soon as possible. Even early release meant that I'd spend 24 weeks of incarceration mixing with burglars, robbers, muggers, buggers, rapists, arsonists, thieves and violent nutters.
I figured I would miss 24 Friday nights out with the lads, 24 Saturday nights on the pull, 24 weeks of lost pay and no job when I got out. It seemed like a lifetime living in a confined space with over 30 other inmates.

The same faces, day in, day out and hard time. Violent confrontations were the norm in these institutions. Arguments, bullying, intimidation and theft. You had to maintain an overtly violent nature to ensure survival. I was practising daily with the toughest of tough young men. Some of these guys were on their second or third sentence and staying aware made you feel on edge all of the time. You couldn't trust anyone. And although there were other Loughborough lads in at the same time as me, they were kept in different units in various parts of the borstal. I was on my own, simple as that.

Sport was a major pastime in borstal. I got to try out most sports, an opportunity I didn't get at school. The gym was where it was at for me. I felt good after a workout, the harder the better. There was another game we played regularly, one I tried in DC; murder ball. In this game you could whack who you wanted and there would be no repercussions from the screws. It gave you a chance to let off steam, get rid of some of the pent-up aggression and anger.
The idea of the game was to get a medicine ball, which weighed about five kilos from one end of the gym to the other. Two mats were placed at each end. The object of the game was to get the medicine ball from your mat to your opponent's mat, whilst everyone including your own team mates fought for the ball. On the way anything goes: punching, kicking, grappling. It was every man for himself. If you got the ball the lads fought ferociously to get it off you. It was murder.
I would play many sports in borstal: badminton, basketball, volley ball, weight training, circuit training, running, cricket, rounders, rugby and the classic con games: table tennis, chess and darts. My favourite was power lifting, but my introduction began with five-a-side football.

I wasn't a very skilful player but my sheer aggression made up for my lack of on-the-ball skills. Getting stuck in, ramming bodies into walls and making a real nuisance of myself was my forte, much to the detriment of one huge Rastafarian.
He looked like a cross between the Dutch soccer ace, Ruud Gullit, and the reggae master, Bob Marley, only with bigger shoulders and longer hair. His arrogance matched his aggression and he was one

nasty piece of work. He had a sweet skill on the ball and was very fast and nimble for a big lad. He practically pirouetted around the gym like Billy Elliott. His feet balanced on the ball when he twisted and pivoted and turned. It was a pleasure to watch. Trouble was, he was on the opposition. In hard DC style was the only chance I would have of stopping him.

I chopped away at his legs every time we met then steamed into him fully committed and took the ball from his feet. No skill, just blatant cheek. I passed it on and we scored. The Rasta was furious. Walking me into the gym wall he pushed his face into mine. I stared him down almost laughing to show I didn't give a fuck about him. The screws jumped in and gave him a warning. Then we were off again.

The ball bounced off the wall and he was on it racing to goal. I curled my leg around him from behind and took his legs away from him. The ball rolled on into the goalie's hands. The Rasta threatened me with a look. I ignored him and carried on. A kid ran past me. 'Watch the Rasta, mate he's a nutter,' he said.

The Rasta was on the ball again coming down the left wing. I powered across and slammed him into the wall. This time he turned and headed straight for me with killer in his eyes. The screws surrounded us both. After a minute of the usual 'I'm gonna fuck you up' rhetoric the Rasta calmed down. I could tell it wasn't forgotten. I smiled at him trying to ease the situation. After all it was only a game. This infuriated him more.

The game was brought to its conclusion by the loud voices of the screws. I made my way into the changing rooms keeping one eye on my newfound friend. I sat down and started to get changed. My shorts were halfway down my legs revealing a bare arse. The Rasta headed straight for me. The fire in his eyes was burning brightly.

I'd figured out during the match that the Rasta's communication skills were poor, so there was no point in talking to him. I quickly pulled up my shorts and as soon as he blurted out his Anglo Jamaican blurb I cracked his jaw with a solid right hander. A screw instantly pinned me back against the wall.

'Leave it, Skillen.'

The gangly Rasta was pinned almost simultaneously. He spat out the words 'Bumba clot, blood-clot, cha-man.' I didn't have a clue what he was on about but due to the circumstances I took it as an insult.

'Fuck you, anytime,' I said. I stared him down until he broke off the stare. The screw led me to one side.

'Next time hit the black bastard properly,' he said. I didn't like the racist comment. The kid's colour or creed had nothing to do with the fact he was a cunt, but at least I wouldn't be put on report. The PT screws never took any action. What happened in the gym stayed in the gym. The Rasta approached trying to intimidate me.

'I will see you soon, man,' he said, the fire in his eyes now doused. He walked off with arrogance in his stride.

Later that day I was staring out of the unit window when the Rasta appeared with a screw. He was outside the unit clearing up shit parcels, (literally parcels of shit thrown out of the cell windows by the cons so they didn't have to endure the smell in a confined space). The Rasta came toward the window and stared through at me.

'I'm gonna fuck you up tonight, man. Watch your back. That was a lucky punch you got me with. Next time you won't be so lucky,' he said. As he went to walk away my voice stopped him.

'I told you before, big man. Anytime. And remember I've got a few more lucky punches waiting for you.'

'I will see you tonight before the class, man.' He walked off taunting me. I wasn't lucky as he put it, I was first and in the world I was in, being first is everything.

The confrontation was witnessed by Ben, one of the cons. Ben was either laughing or angry about something and this pissed him off. He took it as a threat against the unit.

'Fuck him, Skillen. We're with you. We'll make sure no one else joins in,' he said. It was great the unit sticking together, but I didn't need the attention. I just wanted easy time, but I'd have to fight the Rasta that night before the classes and put an end to the confrontation and keep my reputation intact.

Just before the unit left for the nightly walk to the classes I was pulled over by one of the screws.

'Make sure you do the job right this time, Skillen, and when you've done don't hang around.' I was surprised at his comments: a screw condoning violence? Were they all racists or had this kid committed some heinous crime?

Ben had got a crew together, all ready to back me up if required. We almost ran down the corridor to the junction where the units interlinked like a crossroads. The word was out. The lads were tense as we got closer to the meeting with the Rasta and his mates. This could easily turn into a riot. Each corner I turned I expected to be fighting. We hadn't passed one screw on the way. It was like they'd stayed home. They weren't the only ones. The Rasta did as well. He never showed, much to the dismay of the rebellious Ben who was itching for a scrap. I spoke to a friend from Loughborough in the corridor. 'Give a message to the Rasta for me. Tell him Skillen said anytime he wants a scrap he knows where I am and I ain't going anywhere for a while.' The message was passed on. I never saw the Rasta again after that. Some say he was shipped out. Some say he was released. I didn't know whether or not he had been released but I did know one thing: he wasn't liked.

There were daily confrontations that never came to blows. Lads would use the excuse that they didn't want to lose time for fighting and I used that against them. We were all in the classic Sword of Damocles situation.

STIR CRAZY

I had a lot of laughs in borstal, usually at the expense of others. Piss-taking was the normal thing to do; it's laddism at its peak. But if you're doing something to someone and they don't like it, or it's making them feel uncomfortable, it's bullying. One con had the piss taken out of him every day of his borstal life until it almost sent him to a mental institution.

This lad's downfall was his personality: he didn't have one. He spoke in a very boring monotone voice and it was hard to listen to him without switching off. He obviously gained a complex and thought himself uninteresting and this caused him to remain silent for long periods, much to the delight of the cons. When he did finally speak he was an easy target. His soft demeanour sent out signals to the other cons. He may as well have had 'Kick me when I'm down' printed on his back. He was in for stealing cars but many doubted the authenticity of his claim and accused him of being a nonce (sexual offender).

I didn't like the way people picked on him but he actually deserved what he got because of the way he behaved. He made himself a target and could be an annoying fuck.

I was in the shower after football training and was already pissed off and hungry. The kid pushed in front of me and took the free shower that I was about to enter. It was stupid moves like that that got him into trouble. I challenged him and when he refused to move I dropped the nut on him. His eye split open and pissed blood. I panicked and ordered him out of the shower.

'Get out there and tell the screw you slipped in the shower and banged your head,' I said. He threatened to grass so I throated him and scared him into doing what I'd said. The screw didn't believe him but couldn't prove it. After dinner I started to feel bad about butting the kid. There was no real need for me to whack him, but when you have a pack of animals behind you baying for blood you have to make a stand or you're seen as weak and become a victim yourself. He was weak and getting weaker.

I befriended him and put up with his boring conversation. I started to stick up for him on occasions if I thought the other cons were going too far. But it was too late for him. He was too far gone and on his way to a breakdown. He became dangerously quiet and developed a strange stare. He never smiled.

I'd lent the kid some books which he hadn't returned. One was a manual on amateur boxing by David James, the England boxing coach. We were banged up awaiting lights out when I heard a shout coming from outside my open cell window. We had small mirrors in our cells. I got mine and held it out of the window so that I could see below to the cell beneath me. I could see the kid's face in his mirror and hear his voice.

'Sling a line down, John. I've finished that book,' he said. (A line was lengths of cord pulled from the bedspreads and knotted together to create one long line. Lines could be swung from cell window to cell window or lowered down with items attached, used during long lock-up periods or to pass contraband or information.)

I went to my mattress, pulled the line from inside the lining where I hid it and lowered it down to him. He tied the book onto the line and I pulled it back up. For the first time in days he was chatty. Why couldn't he have waited until tomorrow I thought? I went to bed and slept. I was probably only asleep for an hour when I was awoken by the sound of shouting emanating from the corridors through the cell door.

'He's fucking just hanging there, someone help him. Get the night-watchman.' The voice was frantic.

I went to my window and looked down. I could see what looked like the shadow of a man hanging from a rope, the silhouette highlighted by the light from the cell window and projected on the ground below.

'Fucking get him down,' someone shouted. The kid had tied his sheets to the cell window and was dying only a few feet from me and there was nothing I could do. I joined in the ranting and ran around the cell banging on the door and walls to wake the other cons.

We needed to make as much noise as possible to get the screws' attention. I banged the door as hard as I could and everybody began to join in. The noise was deafening. I looked out of the window and could see six screws sprinting up the outside corridor leading to the unit. The shadows darted in all directions across the lawned area outside of his cell as they released him from his improvised rope. They rushed him to hospital where thankfully he survived. He never came back on the unit. I heard that later on he'd slashed his wrists whilst on suicide watch in another attempt to either end his life or get some attention so that he could be helped out of the situation he was in.

Borstal turned many a lad toward suicidal tendencies and there were many reasons: depression, boredom, guilt or being found out that they were nonces – child molesters or rapists – or from just being weak on issues that if they had proper support would prevent an unnecessary death.

I sat in the visitor's block waiting to go back to my cell after having a visit from my family. Visits in prison are just another wind up. You could do without them. It was nice to know that people cared but having to return to your cell after being reminded of home was a bastard. I was depressed. I'd eaten too much chocolate and drunk too much tea. I was feeling bloated and emotionally drained. I was opposite a tall, strong-looking lad with swarthy, tattooed skin. His eyes were filled with tears, tears that he didn't want to let go of. His face was contorted with pain. His fists balled tightly together and rested on his thighs. If he was anymore tense he'd shatter like a car windscreen in a smash up. Normally I would have spoken to him, try to help him ease his pain but I felt like shit myself and in no mood for talking.

He stood up and began to pace the room, I'd seen animals do this in the zoo and he had that same trapped look about him. He started to growl like he was winding himself up, his face more contorted than before. The screw picked up on the kid's actions.

'Sit down,' the screw ordered. He either ignored the screw or he was so out of his mind he hadn't heard him. He paced defiantly towards the locked door, let go an almighty roar and punched his fist through the reinforced wire and glass window that formed part of the security door. His anger and aggression had given him the immense strength required to punch through the toughened glass.

Blood spurted out intermittently like a water fountain as he withdrew his arm, ripping and slicing the skin. The screw hit the panic alarm and dived on the kid who leapt about screaming and crying. Flesh hung from the bone and the blood from the gaping wound covered his arm. The screw clamped one of the wounds with his hand to stem the flow of blood. I sat still desensitised to this type of rage. I'd seen it too often. Within seconds we were whisked away. The lad, he was still pinned to the floor screaming and kicking. I found out later that his girlfriend had dumped him for someone else and decided it was the right thing to come to visit him and tell him face to face. She walked in, dumped him and then walked straight back out again. He was left to deal with the problem on his own and obviously couldn't. At least she had the bottle to tell him to his face. Most just do it by post.

The lad was stitched up in more ways than one. His arm was fucked as well as his relationship. He got on with his time. What else could he do?

BOYS WILL BE BOYS

After a few months in borstal I was assigned community service. I would be working for the old folk of Wigston in Leicestershire. Gardening was the main job and four of us were assigned to the gardens. We were allowed to leave the borstal and trusted to return at a certain time. This we did on the dot. It wasn't long before we were allowed out on day visits into Leicester, but we weren't allowed to go out of Leicester. If we did and we got caught, time would be lost. But the temptation was too great. It was a half hour run back to Loughborough where I'd shoot back for an hour, see friends and family, have a laugh then shoot back making sure I was on time.

I finally got a release date. I would be out in less than six weeks and it was a dangerous time. Once the lads knew your release date jealousy reared its head. The community service continued and I was let out on my own. I could have escaped at any time, but escape was not on my list of things to do. I was moved off the gardens to work at the Fosse Day Centre helping to look after the mentally disabled. It opened my eyes to another side of life. I often left the centre with a tear in my eye. Mixing with those less fortunate made me feel like I was doing something worthwhile and made me realise that there is always someone out there worse off than yourself. I learnt many things whilst at the centre, one of them being that the most important thing in your life is your health and vitality. When you've got those you have everything. There was one more thing: compassion.

As I was now a trusted member of the unit I got told that I would be moving from a single cell into a dormitory. Instead of sitting or lying around I got to interact with the lads in the dorm. We were all nearing the end of our sentences and got on well together. Being in the dorm was like being in a smaller version of *Big Brother*: different personalities getting along with each other (well most of the time anyway). I always found myself being a kind of a peacemaker. We were all close to release but everybody knew my thoughts on scrapping and nobody would chance it. Me? I would still fight no matter what.

This attitude towards violence stopped a lot of confrontations before they became full blown scraps. If two guys were having a go at each other I would intervene most of the time. It only took a phrase or two.

All of the lads in the dorm were as fit as a good athlete. We didn't smoke, drink or take drugs; we took part in several different sports and activities and ate four meals a day. It was no wonder the borstal was heaving: most of the lads lived like kings compared to what they got on the outside. It was like an extreme adventure holiday. It was tough. But for me and a few others, if you could walk the walk and talk the talk, it was a good tough.

Tony was a half-cast Jamaican ponce. He'd always fluff his hair up into the classic '70's Afro and was immaculately clean. He'd sprinkle talcum powder over his bed sheets to take away the smell of the prison laundry before he got into it. This the lads found strange 'Why do you do that?' one of them asked.

'Do what?' Tony said as if it was normal to sprinkle your bed sheets with talc.

'Put talc in your bed. One of these days you're gonna wake up white,' he said. Tony ignored the comment and laughed.

'Fuck it,' Tony said. 'I'm out of talc. I need a drop more powder. I can't sleep without it.'

He sounded like a junky needing a fix. 'Have you got some, John?' he asked.

Before I could answer Ben appeared in the bathroom door.

''Ere, Tony, have some of mine,' Ben said. Tony walked toward Ben and was hit with a puff of talc. As Ben erupted into laughter Tony stopped dead and stood perfectly still. Ben had hit him square in the chest with the talc and Tony was now completely white, matching his prison y-fronts, the only item of clothing he was wearing.

One of the other cons shouted Tony's name and threw him a bottle of talc. Tony caught it and fired at Ben, missing by a couple of feet and hitting one of the other lads.

'Wanker!' the lad said, then delved into his bedside cupboard producing a bottle of talc. I was already laughing at the scenario that was unfolding before me when two shots of talc exploded all over me within a couple of seconds of each other. The air became heavy with talcum powder. I managed to grab my talc and returned fire. The talcum powder fight raged well and truly out of hand. When the talc ran out and the laughter subsided I looked around the room. Beds, cupboards, windows and the floor were all covered in a thick layer of talc dust. My jaws ached with laughter; this was the best therapy I had had in ages. I almost forgot I was inside. The sight of the lads standing completely white was a surreal sight indeed. We became still like shop dummies waiting to be dressed, arms splayed in disbelief, heads bowed. The silence was broken by Ben.

'Hey Tony, I told you you'd turn white one day.' Tony hurled the talc bottle at Ben as the rest of us laughed out loud.

'Fucking hell, lads. We'd better get this place cleaned up. Look at it. We're going to be in real shit if the screws see this mess. We'll lose bird,' I said. Reality kicked in. Ben turned on Tony:

'It's all your fault, Tony.'

'Why my fault?'

'Putting talc in your bed.'

'Fuck off, nonce,' was Tony's only reply.

The noise of the key turning in the lock and the cheerful voice of the screw shouting, 'Morning lads,' awoke me. My mouth felt as dry as a camel's arse. My nose itched and my eyes felt full of blears. I sat up like Dracula getting out of his coffin. Little did I know I looked as pale as him. I looked around at the rest of the lads and the dorm.

'Fucking get up, lads. Look!' I shouted as I jumped out of my bed. The dormitory was covered in a sheet of pure white talcum powder looking like virgin snow. The lads' faces told me what I already knew: we were fucked! The cell door pushed open wide

'Morning, lads, I trust you slept well.' The screw trod on virgin snow leaving giant footprints behind him. The lights had now come on and he could see clearly the mess we had created. It didn't seem to register with him at first. After all, we were his most trusted trainees. Then his expression changed from bright and happy to a scowl reminiscent of a DC screw. He didn't say anything, he didn't have to: his body language and the cell door slamming was a good indicator of how he felt. A few seconds later another screw appeared.

'Get it cleaned up now!' he growled. And the door slammed again.

The talcum powder fight cost us dearly though it was a good laugh at the time. We lost association time: that meant no TV, table tennis etc. and were put on report. Oh, and much to Tony's dismay we were banned from having talc. One picture remains firmly in my mind: the sight of Tony with a white Afro. Every time I see or smell talc I'm whisked back in time to that moment. Priceless.

Borstal training was finally withdrawn as a punishment under the 1982 rehabilitation of offenders act. It was deemed a failure, but did it work? Could it work again? That remains to be seen. I will say one thing though: seeds take time to come to fruition. They need nurturing, feeding and positivity to help them break through the soil and grow strong, rather than being left to dry out, fester, rot and die.

GO SOUTH, YOUNG MAN, GO SOUTH

Being released from borstal was fantastic for about a week, then the novelty started to wear off. I was bored after having my life structured for me for the last seven and a half months. I felt lost. I was lost. I had these incredible feelings of guilt, not about what I'd done because I had paid my price with my liberty, but about my life. I felt cheated. Nothing ever seemed to work out for me. Whilst I was inside both my brothers, Sam and James, had been taken into council care. My mum and dad had tried in vain to get them out but failed. I blamed myself for not being there for them.
After a few weeks Sam was released. I'd been to visit them both with my mum and dad and told them to play the game and they would get out quicker. They were both violent and difficult to control (the original reason they were taken into care in the first place). Sam was released because he showed an attitude change; an old prison trick – play up for a few weeks then ease down and they think they have beaten you. But James had been kept on in a secure unit and they refused to allow him to leave saying he was violent and disruptive and a danger. It was the era of pin down and stories of abuse would eventually surface out of the care system which would rattle the nerves of government-run offices. I worried continually about James and even considered busting him out as we waited for his release.

My father was drinking more now than ever, spending money which was meant for the house. My mum was holding down several cleaning jobs just to feed the family and pay the bills. I couldn't find any work in Loughborough mainly due to the fact I had a criminal record and a reputation for kicking off. I got a few jobs here and there, backhanders and was signing on the dole which made me feel like a beggar. It was getting to me. I had to leave Loughborough and start again.

My sister Bernadette had moved to work down south at Butlins holiday camp. I rang her and told her of my predicament. She didn't hesitate in inviting me down south.

Once I got down south Bernadette got me some digs in Bognor Regis with her Nigerian boyfriend Ike. This was a new beginning for me. I felt good about myself for the first time in ages. There was a plus to being in borstal: I was the fittest I'd ever been; my abdominal muscles showed through my T-shirt. I was self-sufficient, clean-shaven, well groomed and my communication skills had improved.

Ike resided in a second floor Victorian terrace with four big rooms and another two on the next level. Ike lived there with several other Nigerian students, all in England to take advantage of the education system. All were from wealthy Nigerian families.

Ike was an amicable man but very serious. I liked him even though our cultures were miles apart. The flat that I stayed in was luxury compared to what I had been used to back home in Shelthorpe.

The door opened, in walked the Nigerians with a couple of girls in tow. They'd all been on a night out celebrating with a visiting family member and had decided to carry on the party, much to my irritation. Ike didn't seem to care especially when he saw the cans of special brew. We'd been watching *Enter the Dragon*, featuring martial arts legend Bruce Lee. Two of the Nigerian lads spotted the movie and immediately circled each other and imitated the cat-like calls of Bruce Lee, only their voices were too deep and instead of sounding like a cat they sounded like a cow mooing!

They were both well pissed and it wasn't long before they were falling into the furniture. They calmed down when Ike set the stereo too loud and the heavy funk bass sounds drowned out the mooing. The bass pounded my ears and the movie became just a visual as the audio of the stereo took precedence. The music was too heavy for me. I preferred the sweet sounds of soul but it was a lot better than two Nigerian Bruce Lee impersonators.

I left the Nigerians to what looked like tribal dancing and went for a piss. I was just coming out of the toilet zipping up my trousers when the front door burst open and smashed against the wall. It startled me at first. A man entered. At first I thought he was a friend of one of the Nigerians and late for the party. It soon dawned on me that he wasn't, when the angry stocky guy pushed one of the Nigerians aside sending his special brew can into the air. The solid-looking, white guy stormed into the living room.

'Turn that fucking shit off, you fucking black bastard. I'm trying to get some sleep,' he said. I didn't like the way he burst into the house or the racist comment. These guys had been good to me. It was hard but I held back my feelings and observed. I was here for a new start and I didn't want any trouble. The music stopped. I could hear the soundtrack of the movie.

'Calm down, man, it's off,' Ike said.

'It better fucking stay off,' the racist said. I glared at him as he turned to walk back out of the flat. The feelings inside me were too strong to hold myself back any longer. The guy was angry and ready for a fight and he had some bottle coming in to the flat. The Nigerian lads were big lads and he was way out-numbered. His aggression had stunned the lads. Not me though. I knew his type. The racist went to manoeuvre past me.

I challenged him. 'Oi, dickhead!' he turned and put his back to the wall and faced me off. I positioned myself within punching range. 'Who you calling a black bastard? You fucking wanker, who do you think you are coming in here acting like a cunt? Fuck off out.' I gestured toward the door with a nod of my head. Then said, 'Turn the music back on, Ike.' I kept my gaze fixed on his. The racist man glared at Ike.

Ike stayed put.

'Keep out of this. It's none of your business,' the racist said.

'Well I'm making it my business.' At that the man rounded off his shoulders and surged forward meeting my straight left balled fist which caught him square on the chin just below his bottom lip. His head was forced back by the blow and the back of his head smashed into the wall. His body stiffened and he fell forward. My right uppercut lifted him back up. I jumped back ready to boot him to bits but there was no need. He crashed to the floor unconscious. The Nigerians stayed silent as I leaned over the man's unconscious body.

'Fucking wanker!' I exclaimed.

The movie soundtrack was all that could be heard. I looked at the screen through the open door. Bruce Lee let out a yelp as he flayed his nunchaka.

The Nigerians erupted. 'Bruce Lee, Bruce Lee' they chanted. The pats on my back rocked my body. I felt like a hero. These were big lads scared by the sheer aggression of the angry racist neighbour. I grabbed the body and dragged it down the metal fire escape, which served as the entrance and dumped it in the gutter – a fitting resting place for a racist prick. Ike protested.
'You can't leave him there.'
'Fuck him,' I said.
The incident ended the party. At least now I'd get some sleep. I thought.

Early the next morning there was a knock at the door. Ike opened it. I positioned myself behind Ike and out of sight just in case it was the Old Bill. I listened.
'I don't want any trouble, Ike, I've come to apologise. I was out of order last night,' he said.
Ike responded by accepting the apology telling the man to forget it. He had one more question – his real reason for being on the doorstep so early.
'Who hit me?' His tone changed when he realised Ike was being amicable and he sounded aggressive, I intervened. I moved into full view and faced him as I had done the night before.
'I did. Why?' I said challenging him. He put his hands up and showed his palms. I was cautious at this point.
'No trouble, mate. I'm sorry about what happened. I was pissed. I deserved it.' He leaned forward and put his hand out to shake mine, at the same time staying well out of punching range. I tapped his hand but didn't take the full shake just in case he tried to pull me down the staircase. I accepted the man's apology and told him if he'd have asked nicely the lads would have turned the music down. I later found out the reason for the Nigerians' silence: the guy had a reputation as being a local hard man.
It was my last day at the Nigerians' place. I thanked them for their hospitality. It was time for me to move on.

BEDSIT LAND

I'd found a job and a bedsit which I moved into with a sports bag and a baseball bat. The bedsit was a pokey little shit-hole of a place with worn carpets, a shared toilet and shower room with a trickle of water, which ran cold in seconds. But at least I'd have my privacy, something the Nigerians didn't get much of.

A couple of days later I started my new job at the local supermarket as a trainee assistant manager, basically a glorified shelf stacker. I hadn't told them I'd been in DC and borstal; I think it may have changed their perception of me. The money was OK but I had high overheads and struggled to pay the rent on the bedsit. The bedsit was meant for two so I had to pay the double rent. My mum suggested that my dad come down south, get a job and lodge with me, helping me to pay my way and at the same time help my dad cut down on his booze and help save his marriage (which was well and truly like his drinks: on the rocks). Well, not exactly true. Part of the reason was that if they could fake a break up of their marriage my mum would get all types of grants and her rent would be written off as she would become a single parent, a con that was quickly coming into vogue. I agreed to help.

My dad arrived in Bognor an hour later than he should have done. I found him in a bar, pissed and lost, but very happy. My dad found work immediately in a hotel on the sea front as a night porter. I worked days, he worked nights. It worked well for a while, but we still struggled for money. It was mid October and the two bar electric fire we had in the bedsit ate the electricity. On the nights off we went to Bognor Regis boxing club where my dad watched and gave me advice as I trained for my first amateur fight.
I was impressed with the boxing club. It was clean, had plenty of equipment and was very busy. I noticed one guy who was punching a bag stuck on the gym wall. He had positioned himself on the angle so the corner of the wall was pointing at his centre line, then he'd whack a big left hook into the pad. No boxing style, hands down at his sides then whack. He was fast and the brick wall

vibrated when he hit it. His name was Red, a Scottish guy who worked as a bouncer at a local back-street nightclub. My dad and I went to visit him one night after he invited my dad down for a drink. The club was a smoked-filled heavy music venue known as the Blues Club. I felt more intimidated in there than when I first walked into the boxing club. There were some rough looking characters and I realised why Red was whacking the bag like he was. Red was a cool Clint Eastwood type character who could hit hard with both hands.

I spent most of my spare time training in the gym, running and sprinting the breakers on the beach. It was rare for me to go out. I wanted to keep a low profile and didn't mix with anyone socially. The fight I'd had a few weeks previously at the Nigerians' place had reminded me of the reason I'd left Loughborough; to stay out of trouble.

The staff at the store invited me out on a works party. I really didn't feel like going, the reason being I'd sussed out that the manager, who was married, was knocking off one of his staff, who was also married, and they were using the front of a staff party so they could spend time together. They were now trying to pull me into their circle of deceit by pairing me off with one of the girls who had a fiancé! I had met and chatted regularly to their respective partners at the store. I wanted no part of their little game. It made me feel very awkward. Nevertheless I went.

We visited the local nightclub on Bognor's famous pier, famous for an event called 'the Birdman' where people dress up in weird and wonderful outfits and jump off the pier in a feeble attempt to fly. The nightclub was a cheesy downmarket affair in dire need of a makeover. It reminded me of a council estate social club and not a particularly good one either. I'd also had enough of watching the deceitful antics of the manager and his knock off. The bird who was stalking me was beginning to get better looking as the beers went down and it was time to make an exit before the inevitable happened. I faked a visit to the toilet and vanished through the main door to the sound of 'I'm gonna run away from you' by the Tams. The smell of the onions enticed me over to the hotdog stand.

Nearby I noticed three lads pushing and shoving at each other in playful fight. I ignored their antics and ordered a giant hotdog.

'Onions, love?' asked the sleek, over-tanned blonde. The onions smelt delicious. I declined knowing they gave me heartburn, I settled for ketchup instead.

'Cheers, love,' I said and turned to walk toward the taxi rank. My path was blocked by one of the playful youths. He had a serious look on his face. I was in no mood for shit. I moved the dog into my left hand, licked my lips and wiped them with the back of my hand. As I pulled my hand off my lips I let rip with a right hand punch. The kid flew back and landed on his arse unconscious from the force of the blow. I spun round to face his mates who were glued to the floor. 'Do you fucking want some?' I said almost barking like a savage dog. The lads stood firm.

'No trouble, mate,' one of the lads said.

'Well fuck off then and take that cunt with you.' I walked off tucking into my hotdog as I went, occasionally looking over my shoulder. Up to this point I was doing a good job of keeping a low profile but the mix of booze and a bad night had raised it somewhat. I jumped into a waiting taxi and it sped off in the direction of bedsit land.

GLOVED UP

My boxing training was going well. I'd signed for Bognor Boys' Club and was due to have my first amateur fight. Red gave me some sound advice. 'Get in there and knock him out. If it's close and it goes to points you could get stitched up,' Red said. 'You can't argue with a knockout, John.' Good advice I thought.

At the venue I was nervous, very nervous. It wasn't so much the fight but the crowd I was about to face. I was going into the unknown. Being on stage was something I hadn't done before. I was always shy of the school play scenario and never really got picked to do anything in front of an audience. The ring looked a scary place. The only stage I had ever been on was at school when I got to play an animal at a Christmas play. I hated every minute of it. The idea of going into the ring and making a fool of myself made me quiver. My dad loved boxing but he didn't look like he was going to enjoy this bout; he looked worried for me.
The ring, lit up by overhead lights, stood out in the smoky, dark atmosphere of the venue. The venue was packed with people surrounding the ring. The adrenalin was turning my legs heavy with a jelly-like feeling. My mouth was completely dry. I felt drained. I looked at my dad. He squeezed his fist at me. 'Go on, Johnny boy. You can do it.' He held his fists high and clenched them gripping the air. I took a deep breath and felt the nerves grab at my chest. The sensation in my legs increased. It felt like they did after a good beach sprinting session. I climbed the steps at the ringside, ducked under the ropes and I was in the ring. The first in.
I stood tall. My coach removed my robe and I jumped up and down on my toes. I bashed my gloves together. There was no turning back now: this was it. I watched my opponent climb into the ring. He looked bigger and heavier than me. I was billed as middleweight and weighed eleven stone four, but felt smaller. He was tall and strong looking and very smartly turned out. We were beckoned to the centre of the ring by the ref, given instructions and then we were parted. I never looked at the kid I just stared at the ref. The smoke hung heavy over the ring. I felt sick in the pit of my stomach. I took a deep breath as the bell sounded for the first

round. The smoke burned my throat. I moved into the centre of the ring and threw a combination of straight punches. The first right hand connected. The rest followed through hitting the target. I felt a blow on the head and we exchanged a flurry of punches. I surged forward using both hands left, right, left, right. I just kept punching. I couldn't hear a sound. It was like I was boxing in a vacuum. We clashed and tied up. The ref pushed us apart. He had a quick look at my opponent. 'Box on,' he shouted. I threw a couple of straight lefts catching him on his forehead. I threw another right hand and pressed forward my attack. He backed up and then leant forward as his legs buckled and he stumbled almost going down. He looked in pain. The ref jumped between us and stood in front of my opponent waving his arms frantically in the air. He turned to me directed me to go to my corner. I looked to the corner. My coach looked tense. He waved me over as he climbed into the ring. 'It's over. He's stopped it. You've won.' The referee stopped the fight in less than 60 seconds, TKO.

I looked down to where my dad had been standing. I heard his voice shout 'That's my boy!' He was standing by the ring apron with both thumbs in the air. To see his smiling face you would have thought that I'd won a world title. The referee held my hand high. My opponent's eye was badly cut. We shook hands and went our separate ways. I felt uncomfortable in the ring. I hated the smell of the smoke. But it was over quickly and I did get a nice trophy. I wondered if I could have gone the full three rounds feeling like I did. I was sure glad I'd done the sprinting. If I hadn't I think the adrenalin would have stopped me.

A couple of weeks later I had another match. This time the nerves weren't so bad and I actually enjoyed the build up. I fought a guy from the Royal Navy who was land based at Portsmouth. Being land based meant that he got regular training. He was a fabulous boxer, tall, lean and his footwork was very good. I chased him for three rounds. He back pedalled most of the time catching me with jab after jab. The last round I caught him on the ropes and let a cluster of punches go. I caught him on the jaw and he was going. I continued my attack only to be thwarted by the bell. I waited for the decision which I already knew. I lost on a unanimous points decision. Even though I lost I enjoyed the fight and felt like a winner. A couple of seasons later the kid went on to fight in the

ABA English finals. My dad who enjoyed the fight immensely said after 'his jab was in your mouth so often, son, I bet you thought it was a lollipop.' He had a way with words, my dad.

A couple of weeks later we decided to move back to Loughborough. I'd had enough of trying to scrape a living. I worked hard, but I was still skint. I would be far better off on the dole.

OFF THE RAILS

Back in Loughborough I joined the dole queue, which was a long one. I remember Thatcher's idea for shortening the dole queue: make them stand closer together. Well I didn't want to get close to this lot; the 'Gun Convoy' as it was known was in town. These hippie-type travellers were encamped on the edge of Loughborough in a place known as Tickow Lane. These travellers usually followed the outdoor hippie festival circuit. They were signing on to get money and weren't after work; they were a lawless bunch. One of the guys that was reputed to have led them was a Loughborough lad known as Shaky.

Shaky had a rep with the old Loughborough crew as a streetwise scrapper. I considered joining up and vanishing; that lasted for about a minute. They stunk, were dirty and went against everything that I stood for. We had one thing in common though: we both hated authority. The Gun Convoy would later become famous for an epic battle against the police known as the Battle of the Beanfield.

I kept my distance in the queue. These guys wouldn't be around long once winter broke and the festival season began. They'd disappear into the night. Like me they had no career prospects even though a lot of them were educated and from good families. They were just a scruffy bunch of rebellious hippies and musicians that were allegedly peddling drugs and guns and having a ball of a time doing it. I felt I was no better but at least I was clean and smart.
The Gun Convoy crew were made to go to the back of the queue leaving me at the front beside my brother Sam. Sam stood in silence with a serious look on his face. Neither of us wanted to be here but we needed the money. As I was about to sign on the dotted line the Gun Convoy surged forward pushing the queue as a show of arrogance. In my temper I grabbed the counter and forced the full queue backwards. I spun round and threw down a challenge.
'Who fucking wants a go?' I scanned the group looking for a worthy adversary. Not one was willing to take up the challenge. In

fact they all stood in perfect position. I turned and gave a wink to the girl on the counter signed on the dotted line and left. They were an intimidating bunch if you allowed them to be.

I did a few short-term, unskilled jobs on the building site and got backhanded tax-free cash for my labours. The pay was poor but it topped up the dole money and it was enough to keep me in booze and clothes and pay my way at home. Signing on the dole made me feel like a beggar. It demoralised me. I hated signing on.

Drugs were becoming more popular in Loughborough due to their accessibility. I couldn't go out without somebody offering me a wrap of speed or a toke on a joint. The film *Quadrophenia* and the resurgence of the scooter scene with its all night northern soul gigs gave rise to more usage. I'd tried speed in pill form known as 'Bluey's' back in '76 whilst attending a northern soul all-nighter. They were horrible things; all they did was make me yawn and feel like everyone was watching me.

There was a seedy side to Loughborough that I glimpsed into. There was a place we nicknamed the 'Devil's Kitchen', a block of bedsits a few minutes from the town centre and just around the corner from the police station. Drugs were sold there regularly.

The place smelt of weed and body odour and the pungent smell of burning joss sticks. It was scruffy and looked derelict. All types of drugs could be found there from the softest to the hardest. The drugs were bought through contacts on the Gun Convoy and at free festivals. Two men in particular (both Loughborough men who shall remain nameless) were responsible for the sale of heroin in the surrounding areas. The place got its nickname because of the wild parties, violence and the drug taking. No one complained because whoever lived there was involved in some way. A friend of mine had his skull cracked open by a notorious family over some kind of dealings; they hammered his head in with claw hammers while he slept. He was a tough fucker though and survived. Mind you, he had one hell of a hangover!

Drugs had become part of Loughborough's subculture and I felt myself being drawn into it. I had fuck all to do in my life – I was bored and boredom is the killer. I was on the piss from Thursday through till Sunday. I still trained regularly but my heart wasn't in it and the effects of partying and training were leading to burn out.

It was mentioned to me that I could make good money from selling drugs. Amphetamines were class B drugs considered by most to be a soft social drug: a weekend snifter to get you high so you could have a laugh. The pressure to indulge was strong. If you were out with a group of friends and hadn't had any you became an outcast from the circle.

I never got into the drug thing in a big way. Drugs cost money and all the money I had went on a pint or new clothes. I could have made money selling drugs. But I sure wasn't going to start dealing. There was a lesson on the horizon that would ensure I never dealt in drugs or tried them again. A lesson that could have cost me my life.

BUSTED

The street was deserted. I waited across from the Golden Fleece pub in Loughborough town centre. Music emanated from the open door and through the window I could make out the silhouette of my brother Joseph and his mate. The meet had been arranged by my brother. The guy he was meeting had supplied him with a sample of drugs and had said he could get my brother a bigger consignment from a nearby pharmaceutical company at a knock-down price. My brother asked me to watch his back in case anything went wrong during the meeting. I'd questioned him about going ahead with the deal but all he could see was the money and I would get a cut for helping him out.

I was nervous about the whole situation, something didn't feel right and I was suspicious that my brother was being set up. I noticed two cars parked a distance apart facing each other. I thought I could see someone sitting in one of the vehicles but my brother came out of the bar with a serious look on his face, looked across to where I was standing and waved me away. He started to walk off at a quick pace. Then within a split second he was attacked and pushed against the pub wall by two men who had followed him out of the pub. I sprinted across the road and shouted.
'Get your fucking hands off him,' pushing one aside and grabbing the other one by the throat. My brother was gone, sprinting down the street like a handbag thief. A radio squawked into the night air confirming what I'd thought: a set up. One of the men shouted down it as he gave chase.
'I'm in pursuit. One male heading toward library,' he said.
Fucking drug squad! I had to think fast.
'Take your hands off me. You're under arrest for assaulting a police officer,' the officer said.
'Hang on a minute. I didn't know you were a police officer. I just saw you attacking that man and came to his aid.'
'You what?'
'I didn't know you were a copper.' He stared at me for a second.

'Ask the lad. I'll go with you and you can ask him. I don't know him.' The copper fell for it.

'Okay, come with me.' We ran to where a group of coppers had my brother cornered. They were applying the cuffs and my brother was shitting himself. He knew he was in deep dirt.

I shouted to him, 'I don't know you, do I, mate? Do you know me? You don't, do you? Tell 'em!' I hoped he'd click on to what I was trying to do. I had to get out of this situation: the first batch of drugs was hidden in my mother's house. Without a doubt the police would raid the house and if the drugs were found my brother and the rest of the family would be in serious trouble. My brother stared at me for a second.

'Who is he?' asked the copper.

'I don't know him. I've never seen him before,' he said.

'All right. On your way,' the copper said. I left the scene to the sound of my brother struggling with the coppers and walked casually away. It was hard to leave my brother but I knew he'd know where I was going.

I burst through the doors of my mother's house and ran upstairs. The house was full: neighbours drinking tea, friends of my brother's drinking cans and both my parents laughing and joking.

'What the hell is going on, John?'

'Never mind,' I shouted. 'I'll tell you later.'

I stormed up the staircase. I had to get the drugs out of the house before the drug squad came. I ripped up the carpet and pulled up the loose floorboards in my brother's room. Beneath them lay a biscuit tin full of plastic bags of powder. Also under the staircase was a plastic bag with thousands of empty capsules inside, which were to be filled by my brother and sold onto the northern soul scene. I grabbed the lot and ran downstairs into the garden. I couldn't be sure they wouldn't check the backyard, so I leapt over into the neighbour's garden and buried the lot in the newly-dug potato patch. I skipped back into the house safe in the knowledge there was no evidence in the house.

Mum and Dad were a bit taken aback but not really that surprised.

I explained that I had got rid of my brother's hoard and the house was clean. I also briefed them on the fact that the house would be busted that night and thoroughly searched. I also knew they would wait until the early hours to strike.

As I lay in bed unable to sleep I heard a rustling in the backyard and the sound of a radio in the distance. I got up and went to the curtain. I was still dressed knowing they were coming. The whole house knew. We almost got the kettle on in anticipation. Further down the street there were unmarked police cars that stood out like an un-circumcised prick at a Jewish wedding. But I still reeled back in shock at the sound of the door being bashed in and the shouts of the police. I felt sorry for them trying to smash their way in and opened the front door just as the back door busted open.
'What the fuck's going on? You only had to knock,' I said.
'Police! Don't move,' an officer shouted.
'We have reason to believe there are drugs on these premises and have a search warrant.' My mum ran at the front two coppers.
'Fucking get out of my house,' she screamed. The whole place went up. The brothers grabbed the coppers to stop them arresting my mum. I was dragged to the floor not resisting, shouting at the others to calm down. My shouts were unheard as the house was overrun by coppers and plain clothes drug squad. It must have cost a fortune to put this raid on.
I was ordered out of the house and arrested on suspicion of being in possession of class A drugs and in receipt of stolen goods. I stayed cool; I knew they had no evidence. I also knew my brother wouldn't talk. I smiled at the copper as he opened the van door. The curtains in Manor Drive were lit up and faces peered through the gaps. People were at their gates. I sat in the van and could hear this almighty roar.
'Get your fucking hands of me, you bastards.' Four coppers were struggling to get my mum in the van.
'Calm down, Mum. It's all right,' I said. My mum shrugged off the coppers and sat in the van. It was quite surreal sitting handcuffed next to my mother. We looked at each other and giggled. 'Now you know what it's like being arrested, Mum,' I said.
My dad and my sister were the only ones not arrested. My dad, the ever-crafty Irishman, faked a heart attack and my sister was allowed to remain with him and be present when the police searched the property.

We were taken to Loughborough Police Station and locked up. After a very short time we were unlocked.

'You're free to go, collect your property,' the copper said.

'You what? After all that we're free to go? Who's going to pay for my back door?' Mum said.

'Hold on, Mrs Skillen. You're staying a little longer,' the copper said.

'Why can't she go?' I asked.

'Well she can, John, but she's being charged with obstructing a police officer in the execution of his duty,' the copper said. My mum was the only one to be charged. On the way out I met the drug squad officer who had let me go at the scene of my brother's arrest.

'Very clever, Skillen. Think you're smart don't you? We'll get you in the end.' I leant forward and ever so politely said into his ear a '70s cop-show phrase which really hit home.

'Fuck you, pig!' I walked home relieved to be free of any charge.

The drugs tin and plastic bag remained in the neighbour's garden for a few weeks. Spring was upon us. There was a scooter rally approaching at Great Yarmouth and we had decided to go on a weekend bender for a laugh. We were all skint so in order to make a few quid me and another of my brothers decided it would be a good idea to dig up the pills and make the capsules up. We waited until the house was empty. We didn't want Mum to know what was going on. She would have gone crazy. She put up with enough things going on as it was, but drugs she despised.

We filled about five hundred capsules; enough to finance our weekend trip and flushed the rest down the toilet. After filling the capsules we sat and counted them. As I counted I heard a strange noise like a whispering sound coming from the landing area at the top of the staircase.

'What's that?' I asked my brother.

'What?' His eyes were bulging. 'What is it, John?' I could feel my heart racing in my chest, then it started pounding almost pushing my ribcage apart. I could see my heart beating through my skin.

'Look', I said to my brother. 'Look at my heart. It's going crazy. What am I going to do?' I started sweating profusely. I could see an expression of fear across my brother's face.
'My heart's pounding too, John. It's the pills!'
'We haven't taken any of the pills. It's the dust! We were breathing in the dust. We're overdosing. We're going to die,' I said. Just then the bedroom door opened. I jumped back on to my bed. It was my mum. I felt like a small boy.
'Help us, Mum. I think we've overdosed on those pills.' I showed her the pills. 'Feel my pulse. My heart. Feel it.' She looked scared. I was finding it hard to breathe. I felt a rage coming over me. I wanted to run. Instead I paced around the bedroom. At one point the wall looked like it was melting.
'Help me, Mum. What are we going to do?' I was like a child; very afraid and my eyes felt as wide as my mouth. My skin felt thick but soft to the touch as if I could push my finger through my skin. My mum rang the ambulance. 'Don't tell them what's caused it, Mum. They could call the coppers,' I said. The ambulance was there in minutes.

My brother who was in the same state as me walked into the ambulance. I told them we'd had some speed. They talked us down and said we were suffering from extreme paranoia. I heard my brother ask if he was going to die. The ambulance man never replied. When we arrived at hospital we were thoroughly checked over and told to wait in separate rooms. I refused and joined my brother. Everyone was sniggering at us and watching what we were doing, or so we thought. In fact there was very little wrong with us other than the effects of the stimulant we had taken. It wasn't as we thought: amphetamine sulphate. It was a diuretic substance used for slimming which had the same side effects of amphetamine only more severe and uncomfortable. The substance also had a psychedelic tripping effect causing hallucinations. People's faces became distorted, almost devil-like. We sat staring into space for a while. It was the worst feeling I've ever had in my life. We had experienced one giant panic attack. As the effects wore off we decided to skip further treatment.
'Let's get out of here before the coppers come,' I said. My brother agreed and we sneaked out of the hospital and made our way

home. We laughed about it afterwards. If we had continued to fill the capsules instead of ditching the gear down the toilet we would have been close to being in a coma or worse; dead.

FAIR COP

If you can't do the time, don't do the crime.
Scribbled on a prison wall

Inbetween scooter rallies with the Wildcats Scooter Club and the weekends on the piss, I would spend midweek, yes you guessed it, on the piss. One night I had been at the Forest Gate pub: a meeting place for a few of the scooter lads. I was hammered with booze. My old friend Spider accompanied me and we walked home planning the forthcoming weekend. When we got to my house we were starving and the cupboards were bare, so I decided to shoot down to the chip shop. It was a good walk to the chippy so out came the scooter.

Spider jumped on the back and away we went; no helmets, no lights and pissed as farts. I must have broken every traffic law I could think of on the way downtown. The first chip shop was closed. What we didn't realise due to being so pissed was that it was so late all the chip shops were closed.
I whizzed across the road and onto a one-way street going the wrong way. The SX225 Lambretta scooter was fast, but not fast enough not to be spotted by a police car going in the opposite direction. I pulled the accelerator back and sped off. The chase was on, but it didn't last long. With the combined weight of Spider and myself the scooter was too difficult to manoeuvre. The police car forced me into the side of the kerb. I loved my scoot and rather than damage it I pulled over.
The coppers jumped out with a look of disbelief on their faces 'Do you realise you rode down a one way street the wrong way with no headlights on and no crash helmet?'
All I could say was, 'We were only going for some chips.' On that I was ordered into the police car and asked to blow into his bag. 'Why are your chips too hot?' I said. The copper didn't take too kindly to my piss taking and asked me again to blow into his bag. I refused for no other reason than I was being a cunt! I was arrested and taken to Loughborough Police Station for refusing to give a specimen of breath.

I also refused a blood test, was eventually charged with failing to give a specimen of breath and several traffic offences and released. When the case got to court I was banned for eighteen months, given three months' prison sentence and taken to Welford Road Prison in Leicester. It was the first time I'd been a real con and it didn't bother me. I was used to the system having spent seven and half months in borstal and it was short lived. Two weeks later I was out on appeal with my sentence reduced to a suspension. The scooter had to go. I was back out having treated the whole situation as one big joke. The only lesson I'd learnt; Jamie Oliver *is* right. Too many chips are bad for you!

FULL ENGLISH

Boredom and low self-esteem coupled with frustration at not having a good job, the lack of qualifications, a criminal record and the constant hounding by the police, (who would often drive slowly by me and stare out of the car and give me the finger, trying to wind me up) meant I was on the piss more than I'd ever been.

My boxing training and sprint conditioning continued, along with heavy weights three times a week with Spider. But training in the week and pissing it up the wall each weekend, meant I was burning the candle wax one end in the week then the other at weekends.

I awoke to the aroma of freshly cooked bacon: a smell that could make my mouth water whilst I was still asleep. I loved a nice full English breakfast or a nice bacon sarny with a cup of hot sweet tea in the morning, but not this morning. My mouth felt so dry my lips were hard to part. My teeth felt furry and I couldn't work out whether it was my tongue or teeth that had become like the furry dice of a cheesy mark one Ford Cortina. The inside of my head pounded the sound of a pneumatic drill from the inside out. The light beaming through the partially drawn curtains made me squint. I felt incredibly sick. My dry mouth suddenly became watery. My stomach rolled over like I'd just come over a big roll on the roller coaster. I jumped out of my bed with my hand over my mouth. I ran downstairs and into the toilet. The bare floor tiles felt cold on my feet, which was refreshing. I retched, splattering my feet and the tiles with the remnants of the previous night's piss up. I could smell kebab meat through the stench of stale lager and an optic rack full of spirits.
I hated being sick. I remember as a kid I'd cry while my mother soothed my head and rubbed my stomach. I stood up straight and instantly broke into a sweat. I heard my brother Sam's voice behind me. 'Come on. I think you need a hair of the dog that bit you,' he said. I tried to laugh and make small the fact I felt like shit. I laughed then lurched forward making the sound of a dog. Nothing came up this time. The retching continued as I showered.

I gave the bacon sandwich a miss and headed for the pub. Sam, me and Spider were having a laugh about the night before as we approached the recce: a scruffy council play area about the size of two football pitches surrounded by council houses on both sides, with a road encircling it like a moat encircles a castle. I spotted a familiar figure and one not so familiar. One of them was a rival of Sam's, an old friend turned enemy; Frankie was headed straight for us. Sam spotted Frankie too and immediately altered his course to one of confrontation. Sam and Frankie hated each other. Frankie was a nutter. It was rumoured around the estate that Frankie had beaten up his dad and threatened his own mother. He was a rebel and dressed like one with scruffy jeans and leather jacket to finish off his greasy look. A sheath knife was always strapped to his side: he was a crazy fucker. Sam closed in on Frankie.

I wasn't in the mood for this confrontation. I felt like what covered most of the recce; dog shit!

'Leave it, Sam, another time. Come on. Let's go,' I said.

Frankie was a big lad and outweighed Sam by at least two stone. But Sam's aggression more than made up for his size.

'Come on Sam,' I pleaded again. 'We don't need this.' What I meant was, I didn't need it.

Frankie and Sam got close and faced off. Frankie opened his mouth to speak but no words came out due to Sam's right hand landing on his jaw. Frankie grabbed Sam in a clinch and down they went hitting the ground with a thud. They rolled from side to side gripping each other tightly like a courting couple – only this couple were dodging punches as they tried to reach each other's head.

They were making noises that sounded like the snarling of fighting dogs. I leant forward to break it up.

'Stay out of it.' The Scouser's voice was full of menace. It was enough to get my attention.

I looked at the stocky Scouser; he was virtually unknown to me but he had a reputation that preceded him. He was a tough lad and had done some form of ju-jitsu – a Japanese form of all-in fighting.

'It's between them two. Stay out of it,' he said. He had a point, it was a fair go. I stood back and watched, keeping one eye on my new friend.

Like two bull terriers they tore into each other. They were breathing hard and tiring quickly, one momentarily getting the better of the other. Then it would suddenly change as they bucked, rolled and ravaged each other. It was painful to watch my own brother fighting and not being able to join in. I knew Sam wouldn't want me to, but I felt the urge. The Scouser had psyched me out. I shouldn't have taken any notice of him and should've broken it up. I continued to watch as the older, bigger fighter tried to get control of Sam. Sam's fire and determination kept Frankie from dominating. I knew Sam could turn it around. One good solid punch could change everything. I just hoped it was Sam who got that punch in and not Frankie. Frankie got himself into a dominant position on top of Sam. Sam wrapped his legs around Frankie's body. Frankie grabbed both of Sam's arms and pinned them. Sam struggled to free his arms. I held myself back. I wanted to jump in. I waited.

'Come on, Sam,' I shouted. Frankie finally got a grip on Sam's throat pressing his head into the ground from above. Sam struggled to release the grip. I went cold as I noticed Frankie reach for the eight-inch sheath knife strapped to his side. He gestured toward the clasp fumbling to free the blade as Sam struggled to get free of his grip. I felt a fear wash over me. Adrenalin raced through my veins, speeding me up. This was going terribly wrong. I ran forward and drove my right boot toward Frankie's head catching him high up on the forehead. He reeled backwards letting go of Sam. Sam jumped to his feet and stood over Frankie. Frankie was still stunned from the kick. I forgot about the Scouser. I didn't see him until his face was in mine and his grip was firmly locked in on my jacket lapels. He pulled both hands in tight choking me for a second. I was cold in his grip unable to move or say anything. The grip was strong. He twisted his hands, pulled the grip in tighter and me closer.

'I'll fucking have you, Johnny lad,' the Scouser said, his course accent sounded intimidating. Our noses touched. He was that close. I reacted to the closeness.

'Get your fucking hands off me,' I demanded. I twisted my body to the right and tore his hands away breaking his grip. He backed off. I'd been close to passing out in his grip. I'd felt dizzy but tried to show no fear. I remembered where we were, in full view of everyone. I looked around. People were watching. It wouldn't be long before the coppers arrived.

Sam and Frankie were still stalking each other. Frankie had one hand on his knife, which thankfully was still sheathed. He was still stunned from the kick.

Sam kept his distance. The anger in them both appeared to have subsided. The hate match had no conclusion and there would be no shaking of the hand after this one. I didn't want to risk the chance of losing a fight to the Scouser. I bluffed it out.

'Come on, Sam. Let's go. The coppers will be here in a minute.' The mention of the Old Bill was enough to bring everyone to their senses. Sam laid down the standard threat.

'Anytime, Frankie, anytime.' Frankie kept quiet but never took his eyes off Sam. The Scouser laughed.

'And I'll have you, Johnny lad, anytime.' I walked on, mad with myself for not laying into the Scouser at the point when he grabbed me. I'd been caught off guard. I didn't expect him to attack me and it was obvious he didn't care about my reputation. I couldn't help thinking that he'd beat me. Mentally he'd thrashed me and I knew that he would let everyone on the estate know about it.

Scouse and his brother's reputation for dishing out violence on the estate were growing and people were becoming afraid of them. If you crossed them their party piece was to kick in your front door in the wee small hours and batter you to pulp with claw hammers. Nice blokes. They loved their cars and motorbikes and could be seen regularly roaring down the road; no helmets, no insurance or tax and no sense. They were always covered in grease and looked for the most part dirty and intimidating. Shortly after the altercation on the recce, I started to hear rumours that Scouse had beaten me in a fight. He was spreading the rumour to enhance his own reputation and it was working to the detriment of mine. It had to be sorted. Scouse was a bully and he would become worse if I left the situation as it was. The animal had to be tamed.

About a week later my brother James came to see me. He told me that Scouse had been bragging about the fight on the recce. He'd cornered James and threatened him then told him to tell me not to fuck with him again or he'd wipe the floor with me. It was time to put a plan together, nothing too intricate. Next time I saw Scouse I would knock him out and stamp all over him.

To add fuel to the fire I met an old friend of mine: Mike. He had a very serious head wound, both eyes were blackened and his face badly swollen.

Mike, a handy lad who could look after himself, told me that he'd had a disagreement with Scouse. Scouse and his brothers paid him a visit and played the congas on his head with a set of claw hammers in front of his wife and children. I reassured him as much as I could without revealing my plan and told him not to worry as Scouse was going to get what was long overdue. 'What goes around comes around,' I said.

'Be careful, John. They're fucking animals.' I laughed and winked at him before I walked off. I'd lay off the beer and up my training. Next time we met I'd be ready. By now Scouse was revelling in his newfound glory making him arrogant and careless. I wasn't going to go out of my way to find Scouse. He would show up and when he did, I would do what I should have done in the first place: deal with it when it's in your face.

PAY BACK

Friday night. It was a lads' night out, but getting pissed was off my agenda. Me and Lefty (a great lad always ready to back you up in a scrap) made our way out of Sophie's Bar. It was one of those warm, sunny evenings and there was a real buzz about town. Taxis were dropping off groups of smartly dressed girls and lads. The smell of perfume lingered with the smell of the fish market that had not long since closed. We crossed the road opposite the Town Hall heading for the Nelson pub still deep in conversation. I stopped talking to Lefty when I saw Scouse walking arm in arm with his girlfriend. He spotted me. The arrogant bastard almost mocking me, called out my name.
'Aye, Johnny lad,' he said with a big piss taking grin on his face. He turned to his girlfriend and said something to her. She then gave me a look that would put down even the most confident of men.
I recognised her from the local dole office. She was one of the counter assistants. What a choice. He was probably using her to help him fiddle the dole. He'd shouted at me as if he'd known me all his life like we were friends. I could sense his confidence. I was on fire with rage burning inside of me.
'Hang on a minute, Scouse. Can I have a quick word with you?' I kept smiling so he wouldn't suspect what was about to happen. Scouse stopped where he was. He hadn't sussed me. The arrogant bastard still had a hold of his girlfriend's hand. I darted towards him, approaching as if I had something real important to tell him. The smile on my face hid my true intent. It was time to teach this cunt some respect and let him know he couldn't kick the shit out of people and get away with it. Besides, I had to give him a proper hiding so there was no chance of a comeback. As I got closer I thought about nothing but the plan of attack. He let go of his girlfriend's hand and turned to face me.

He now had his back to the Town Hall bench. He continued smiling as if I was no threat to him. His smile vanished as the first punch landed high on his left cheekbone. I'd so much wanted to knock him out with the first punch. But I was too eager. Too tense.

The punch rocked him but didn't knock him out; instead it paved the way for a barrage of punches. He covered up as punches landed one after the other. I was alternating the punches from right to left continuously. He took most of them on the arms and body.

'You've done me, Johnny lad,' he cried out.

I hadn't even come close to doing him. He could take a shot and I wasn't going to give him the opportunity of recovery. If I'd have been more relaxed I would have done him in one. He was a tough bastard but getting the first shot in didn't guarantee me a win. I switched my punches and hammered his head and body raining in blow after blow. Tunnel vision had now set in. I couldn't hear a sound due to the effects of the adrenalin powering my body forward. It was me and him. I pounded away. The pent up anger and frustration of the last couple of months fuelled my attack. His body crumpled. I would have carried on the attack if the weight of the lads pulling me hadn't stopped my onslaught. I heard a voice.

'He's finished. He's out cold. Leave it, John.' I shrugged whoever it was that was holding me off and turned in their direction. I nearly lashed out but the sight of a friendly face brought me back to my senses. I looked around at the crowd that had gathered. I was still angry, still raging. I wanted to carry on and give him some more. His girlfriend looked at me with hate in her eyes. His blood-splattered body was strewn awkwardly across the bench. Calm was descending over me. I realised I'd done him. It was then that I noticed that his jacket was caught on the bench preventing him from falling to the ground. If he'd fallen I would have stamped him a couple of times and walked off. Instead he got a worse beating. I took it that a higher force kept him upright so he got the beating he deserved. Lefty announced his disgust at me for not letting him know what was happening. But I'd needed to sort the problem myself, one on one, the way he'd wanted it!

I took Scouse completely by surprise: the best way to enter into conflict. One thought went through my head. 'What goes around truly comes around.'

A few weeks later I'd heard a rumour that Scouse had got a few lads together and were going to jump me. I was training hard and ready for any eventuality. One night whilst I was crossing the road on to the recce I spotted a car driving slowly past me. I spotted Scouse sitting in the front passenger seat. I knew most of the lads in the car. They could scrap in a gang, but alone a different ball game. I dropped my bag onto the grass and stood hands by my side and stared into the car. I was hungry and during these bouts of hunger I got very aggressive to the point of being overtly nasty. They looked across at me and appeared to be arguing amongst themselves. Then the car drove off at speed. They had bottled it. I guess the only way Scouse could get his own back, would be to piss against the wind.

Scouse spread the rumour that he'd got his injuries after being involved in a car accident. But word travels fast in a town like Loughborough. The truth was out there. The attacks and intimidation on the estate stopped and people started to stand up to the gang's bullying tactics. The last attack I heard of was when one of the brothers hammered a copper's skull in with a claw hammer and got ten years for his trouble.

Frankie, Sam's adversary, got a hefty sentence for using his sheath knife to stab a police dog in the same incident. Scouse kept a low profile in his bedsit in Devil's Kitchen, a fitting place for him.
I'd learnt a few things. There's a time for talk and a time to act. I wasn't going to confuse the two. Getting pissed is fun, but for every piss up there's a hangover following. I'd also learnt something else: always expect your opponent to be carrying a weapon.

AFTER HOURS

My weekend piss ups continued after drinking up time, which at this time was 10.30 p.m. midweek and 11.00 p.m. at weekends except Sunday. The only way to carry on drinking in Loughborough at this time was to either buy beer and go home, get a lock in at a pub or go to a notorious late night café known as 'Greasy Don's' on Ashby Road. Don served food all night long and if you were eating then you were able to purchase a drink with your meal. I don't think what Don was doing was legal from a licensing point of view but he didn't seem to care and neither did we.

Don wore a white butcher's coat and rushed about the café talking to himself adding up the bills in his head. He always knew how much you owed him and if you didn't pay you were 'out on yer arse' and barred. Don's was one of those rare places where you could drink into the wee hours. If you kept spending, he'd stay open.
Don didn't take any messing. I remember going in Don's one night with a drinking partner and friend of mine Sean. I was well pissed and out for a laugh. I put the squeeze on Don, doing the pretend gangster thing.
'Don. I want free booze and food tonight and remember, Don. I know where you live.'
Sean stood beside me holding back laughter as Don replied.
'Yes, my friend, John Skillen, and I know where you live too, so you pay or you don't eat.' Don knew everyone there was to know and wasn't one to be intimidated. I laughed away my pretend gangster image.
'Come on, Ronnie. Let's go eat,' Sean said. Don took no shit from anyone no matter who they were.
This particular night the café was busy. I walked in well pissed and holding a chair I'd nicked from a friend's pub above my head; I was showing off and nicked it for a laugh.
'Don, where can I put this chair?' Don looked at me and said nothing for a moment.
'Can I leave it in the kitchen?'

'No, my friend. You can leave it outside.'
'But Don it's not mine. I borrowed it from a friend,' I said.
'Then, my friend, if you don't want to leave it outside, take it back where you got it from.' Then he dashed off rearranging chairs to fit us all in together. The lads chuckled to themselves and filed inside whilst I took the chair outside.

I followed the group inside to the dining area. There were about eight of us, five lads and three girls. I noticed in the corner behind the doorway, a group of about ten lads from a nearby town. One of the lads at the table, a well known scrapper started screwing me out and staring at me. It was a two way thing really so I decided to have a bit of fun. It was going to kick off no matter what. Better sooner than later.
'What's up, lads? I asked 'You gotta a fucking problem,' I said.
There was a nervous silence. One of the youths burst out of his seat and threw a plate in our direction. I mirrored his actions, grabbed the first thing within reach and hurled it back. They were game lads. You'd have thought I'd fired a starting gun the way they came out of the blocks. The whole restaurant went up: tables, chairs, knives, forks even spoons became airborne. People who didn't want to be involved ducked under their tables. In the *mêlée* that followed I noticed Don hiding behind his counter. He'd grabbed his till off the top and was cuddling it. Within seconds the restaurant looked like a tornado had ripped through it. After the hurling of the furniture we clashed. My brother Sam and Bullet surged forward with me and Tac in support. We forced the gang to flee the restaurant door. In situations like these I hit anyone who's in my way and I don't stop. I hit anyone and use anything to win because I know that's what the opposition will do. You have to be as bad as them for the time they are being bad to you and you have to keep the forward momentum. I followed the lads as they ran through the kitchen. The last one out of the door got cracked over the head with a giant ketchup bottle. The bottle broke smothering him in tomato sauce. I followed the gang out of the kitchen and into the street.
In the street I was immediately confronted by two youths. I lashed out catching the bigger one of the two on the jaw and down he went, right in full view of an arriving police van. I was still raging

at the opposition when the coppers pounced on me. I was immediately placed under arrest.

I refused to leave and was restrained. The coppers were struggling to get me to ground; I was still heavily under the influence and didn't care a fuck about what I was doing. A crowd had gathered and I wasn't going to go easily. I had a reputation to protect. The rest of the opposition and the Loughborough crew had sensibly melted into the night. I was the only one arrested.
I turned my attention to the chair. 'I will get in the van when I have my property.' I was pissed and couldn't give a toss. I was coming the cunt with the police. They checked with Don who told them I had it with me when I arrived at the restaurant. They requested that Don press charges. He refused. The police decided to play along with my game and took the chair into custody with me. I thought by telling the police it was my chair I would piss them off having to carry it round there, then have to process it causing them some extra paper work. The things you do when you're bladdered – showing off and trying to be the centre of attention!

The police took me and my chair to the station. They tried to charge me with stealing it but I gave them the name of the pub where the chair was from. They checked with the landlord Brian and he told them that I had just borrowed it. The chair was processed as my property along with some small change and a couple of notes. I was kept in a cell to sleep off my drunken stupor until 6.00 a.m. then released. I couldn't deny the crime: the police saw it with their own eyes. But this was one prank that backfired when I found myself walking home at six in the morning having to carry my charge sheet and a chair which weighed a lot heavier now I was sober. I felt a twat. I was a twat!

My solicitor did a good job when the story came out in court and the fact Don hadn't pressed charges kept me out of prison. I think the magistrates actually felt sorry for me and during the hearing I detected the odd smile on the lips of the usually serious magistrates. I was fined a large sum of money and made to serve 100 hours' community service. I took the chair back to its rightful owner. A laugh is a laugh but fucking around like I did nearly cost me my liberty again. I deserved what I got. I started the fight. Then again if I hadn't started it somebody else would have. First in last out.

COMMUNITY SERVICE OR TAKE A CHANCE

I did my 100 hours of community service working at the local council run leisure centre. What more could I ask for? I loved my training and this environment suited me just fine. For the first time I'd found a place where I was actually happy. The management and staff were brilliant. I completed my weekly service with a smile on my face. My duties at the centre were general cleaning and assisting members of staff. The bonus was, I got to train for free. Getting community service was a let off for me. It sent me the wrong message. I got cocky. Every time I saw a cop car they would slow down and stare at me. I would stand still and stare back. I realised they were out to get me. I didn't want to go back inside, but the attitude I had developed left no room for niceties. I had a reputation for not backing down to anyone no matter who they were. Violence either followed me around or I walked into it.

I had no idea until I walked into the Green Man that it was full of football fans. The Green Man was situated next to Loughborough's main shopping precinct, a cellar pub down two flights of stairs and through the door into the bar. It was an open space with alcoves and fake pillars. Pictures of Warwick Castle adorned the alcoves. The bar was to the left and the toilets at the rear surrounded by tables and chairs. It was bright but due to its low ceiling and only two ways out, it felt claustrophobic. It was unusually smoky for the time of night. Then I spotted the reason: the toilet area was completely surrounded by around 30 lads. They were all on pints and didn't look in a hurry to leave. The way they had positioned themselves left them no exit behind them. They were in essence trapped, a bad move I thought. If you're in a strange town in a gang then you need to know where the exits are unless of course you don't give a fuck.

As I approached the bar my sister came toward me. She appeared distressed. I knew then there had been some kind of confrontation. I spotted a youth at the far end of the bar moving from girl to girl. My eyes flitted from him to his mates. I wasn't happy about them being in the pub: they had already overstayed their welcome. The youth clocked my sister talking to me. He stared across the room at me. I stared back. He dropped his gaze and scuttled back to the safety of his crew. Piss-taking laughter echoed across the room as he reached the rest of the football fans.

I was with my brother Sam and Spider. They were ready for action. All it took was a word from me. 'Leave it, lads. We're a little outnumbered. The lads will be in soon. Just stay cool.' My sister Helen told me that one of the gang had threatened a lad at the bar and insulted Helen and her friends by grabbing at their backsides. Helen was clearly upset. I told her to calm down and we would deal with the situation when a few of the lads arrived.

Some of the football fans were getting agitated. They were a hardcore mix of 18 to 30s. I didn't want it to kick off. The pub was just starting to fill up. I could feel myself being pressurised into doing something. I felt I had to. I decided enough was enough. I couldn't stand my ground any longer. It was a matter of honour. I wasn't going to let that cunt upset my sister and get away with it. He had to be told regardless of the consequences. I told Sam and Spider to stay put. I decided to keep it between him and me. As I walked off I noticed Mick, one of the lads, walk in and join Sam.

I made my way over to where the dickhead was standing. It was my turn to take centre stage. He was about six two with blond hair and a big dopey smile on his face. He held a pint mug in his hand. His knuckles were wrapped around the empty glass. As I approached he sat down positioning himself between two tables. He knew I was coming for him. I couldn't get close enough to him due his positioning and had to address him across one of the tables in earshot of his crew. I would have preferred to take him to one side and have a quiet word. Instead I would have to address him in front of his crew. I couldn't give a fuck about the rest of them. He had to be told. I knew it could kick it off there and then. I wanted to show these fuckers we weren't intimidated by their presence. These were hardcore hooligans. He would stir the shit, kick it off then the rest would run riot, then vanish. Tonight was different. I faced the show off after passing my gaze around the rest of the gang. I felt a nervous twitch on my upper lip. I held back the feelings of anger. I wanted to bang the lad out in front of his so called mates but he was well out of range. Before I spoke Sam and Mick walked past me and into the toilet. I noticed the toilet door stay slightly ajar. I fixed my stare firmly on the kid. 'Oi mate, you see that girl over there?' I said. The kid looked over to where Helen was standing then back at me.

'That's my sister. If you fuck around with her again I'll rip your fucking head off. Do you understand?' I felt the full stare of the gang piercing my psyche. I kept my eyes on the kid waiting for a response. I felt a wave of adrenalin roll up through my stomach and into my chest tightening it. I was tense.

'I'm sorry, mate. I didn't mean any harm,' he said. Then he looked around at his mates. A cocky grin appeared on his face then he laughed trying to make a joke of it. Nobody said a word and nobody joined in the laughter. I felt a rise in tension. I could see tension on their faces. I paused for a second then walked away. Things were going well up to that point. If we stayed cool they'd drink up and leave.

My sister wasn't happy: she'd been insulted and demanded action. I tried to keep her calm but it wasn't working. The fans were getting more agitated, shuffling their chairs like they were positioning themselves for a kick off, but didn't really know whether to go for it or not. I noticed most of them had finished their drinks. They were waiting for one or two to drink up then leave in a group together.

They might throw a few insults back at me on the way out but they'd leave with face intact. I felt goose bumps on my skin, the hair on my arms felt like it was standing up. Earlier in the night one of the lads had a wrap of speed. I'd joined in and had a dip or two, it was strong stuff. I'd had a bad experience with gear before and had sworn I'd never touch it again but I thought, what the hell, it's just a dab. With the adrenalin flowing the powder started to work. It was known as whiz and it was used to buzz up the night. The effects were very much the same as an adrenalin rush. I started to feel edgy. Just as I thought the football hooligans were going to leave, in walked Swanny, a friend of my brother Sam's. Swanny was a scrapper who had no idea what he'd just walked into. I knew what his reaction would be if he got any shit. As he walked toward the gang his face changed. He knew immediately the gang were out-of-towners. He went to walk through the crowd and one of the lads tripped him up on the way past. Whether it was intentional or not I don't know but a couple of the gang laughed. Swanny turned red.

'What's your fucking problem, dickhead?' I heard him shout. I moved between him and the gang. They were seasoned. I could tell they wanted it.

I turned to Swanny and whispered, 'Leave it!' into his ear. Swanny couldn't hold himself back and he hurled his glass into the crowd. The gang exploded into action. A hail of glasses rained in towards me and Swanny. One of them hit me flush in the face smashing against the bridge of my nose. My eyes watered. I felt myself rise up above the action as if I was staring down at it. Glasses were flying in both directions. I didn't have time to put my hand to my face. I went ballistic, fired up by the belief I was badly cut from the glass. I hurled a nearby table into the gang, followed by chairs and glasses. The same came back at me. I pushed Swanny to one side and dropped one of the lads with a right hand catching him on the forehead. He went down amidst the crowd. I backed off as the gang let out a mighty roar and surged forward.

'Come on, you bastards,' I screamed letting go of another chair. They forced me back toward the entrance door. In front of me was Ada, another lad who had just arrived and had walked into the battle. I ran into him and pushed him through the entrance door and up the two flights of stairs with the hooligans on my tail. I stopped at the top of the staircase. Ada had a small barstool in his hand. 'Give it here,' I said. 'Hold the fucking door open. When I say run, we run.'

'You're fucking mad. I'm off. Let's go,' Ada said.

The gang were now in front of me on the staircase and were trying to get out the way they had come in. I had it blocked off. I stood my ground. I knew they could only come up the staircase two in a row. I teased them with the stool like a lion tamer. 'Come on then, you fucking wankers.'

I bounced up and down splaying my arms, stool in one hand, glass in the other. 'Come on,' I screamed.

I could see that at any moment they were going to go for it, the big charge. They were crazed with angry hate in their eyes. The effects of the adrenalin and the speed hit me hard. I felt a sensation in my groin like I'd partially ejaculated. I didn't have time to analyse it or enjoy it, I was in a very bad situation. The gang knew the coppers would soon arrive. They wanted out.

'Get the skin-headed bastard,' were the words I heard as they charged toward me. They only had one way out: through me. I sent the stool and the glass flying into the midst of them and shouted to Ada.

'Fucking go.' I didn't have to persuade him. He was gone. I followed and so did the hooligans. They were out for blood, my blood. And I was now alone.

I sprinted across the market place with the gang in pursuit. The increase in adrenalin fuelled my fire and determination to get where I needed to be. I needed an equaliser of some sort. I found myself heading toward Sammy's nightclub. I turned into the doorway and banged frantically on the door.

'Open the fucking door.' I was raging. The club wasn't yet open for business and the doormen were surprised to see me in such a state.

'Give me a fucking tool. A bat now, I need a fucking bat.' Before I'd finished what I was saying the doors rattled from the weight of the football hooligans running into it. Dave my mate shouted out, 'Give him a tool.' One of the lads gave me a rounder's bat, about two feet long, a tool designed for hitting. I turned toward the door. One of the door lads blocked my path.

'Open the fucking door.' I stood bat in hand ready to charge out.

'Let him out,' Dave shouted.

'No, they'll fucking kill him,' the bouncer said.

'Let him out.' Dave knew I meant business. The doorman moved out of the way. I was crazed. I couldn't stop myself. I didn't want to stop. I wanted to destroy the lot of them.

Dave opened the door and I charged into the hooligans, followed by Dave in support. They scattered when they saw me bat in hand racing toward them at full throttle. I blitzed anyone in my path. One went down from a blow to the side of the skull, then another got it on the back of the head. I gave chase. I felt no fear, just mad fucking anger raging through me. I was now on a rampage, a blood lust. I coshed two more as I caught up with them in a shop doorway. I carried on forward. It wasn't hard to recognise them.

Their accents were a giveaway. I caught another two in a doorway. I put the bat behind my back.

'Gotta problem, mate?' I asked. As they answered I let rip with the cosh. One went down unconscious from the blow. The other fell down on one knee and covered his head as he caught the cosh on his arms. I laid the boot in and finished him off. He reeled backward. I kept on the move the adrenalin and amphetamine fuelled high forcing me into battle. I'd made my way to the lights at the end of the market place and spotted two lads about to cross the road. I stared at them waiting for a reaction. They ran. I gave chase wielding my cosh and shouting, 'Run, you fucking wankers.' I chased them to the Casablanca pub opposite the Green Man. The bouncers, who knew me, blocked my path. 'Leave it, John,' one said.

'Fucking get them out here,' I paced the pavement back and forth thinking out my next move. As one bouncer explained his reasons for not letting me in the other vanished inside the pub.

'They're not with the football fans, John. They only just left here. They're local.' I was about to force my way into the pub, when Neil a friend of mine came out with the other bouncer.

'John what's up, mate?' It was a good move by the doormen. The friendly face of Neil calmed me down. The effects of my adrenalized state began to wear off. With no enemy around I saw little point to what I was doing.

'Fucking hell, Neil. I've just had a right go.' Neil reassured me.

'Those two lads weren't there, John. They have only just left here five minutes ago.' Neil calmed me down. I ditched the cosh and tidied myself up.

'Neil, is it bad, my face?' I said referring to the glassing I took in the brawl.

'What do you mean? Your face is clean.'

I started to tell Neil the story as we walked around looking for strays. We eventually found their coach parked outside the local library, opposite Queens Park. It was a full 52 seater. We decided to leave well alone. They were on their way out of town and there was no point in stirring the hornets' nest again and getting arrested, especially after I had already reaped vengeance.

As the town had come alive with cop vans I nipped into Sammy's with Neil to keep a low profile. I started to feel remorse for what I'd done. At the time I believed I'd been scarred for life by the glass causing my anger to rage uncontrollably, but I was lucky.

The fear of being arrested hit home. I thanked Dave for the use of his cosh and drifted into the club. As soon as the music hit my ears I felt safe. I felt cool as fuck as I wandered in, until I became aware of the wet patch in my undies! A few more beers took away the embarrassment of the moment.

When the football gangs came to Loughborough they got what they wanted: a good scrap. Out of all of the clashes we had with visiting football hooligans I can't remember them scoring a single win. They weren't in our league. Oh they kicked in a few easy prey when trashing empty pubs and running through the streets chanting the name of their team. But when it came to the real scrapping they would drop into the town off the motorway coming back from a match and cause fucking mayhem. Often we'd plan the attack and hit them from two sides or wait outside a pub and when they came out triumphant, we'd lay fuck into them.
Violence was never far from my life experience. It was like I was attracting it in. I was lucky I hadn't been arrested; far more lucky I wasn't lying in the gutter battered or worse; dead. Running riot through the streets with a bat is not what I'd call a good night out. For weeks I considered the different consequences of my actions. A sentence in itself.

COWARD

Domestic violence accounts for nearly a quarter of all recorded violent crime.
One hundred and sixty seven women are raped everyday in the UK.
Source: Amnesty UK

My sister Helen was a beautiful girl with a wonderful smile. When she walked into the room it was as if someone had turned on a bright light. She had an infectious laugh and always cheered me up. Helen fell in love with an old school friend of mine: he shall be known as Trevor Darnell. Though when I say friend, I mean associate. He was no friend. He was a bully at six foot four with a large frame and Neanderthal looking head, and a horrible person, a racist thug that picked on anyone he knew he could beat.
At school I would follow him around. I was 14 years old and I revered him for one reason: I feared him. He knew and he made sure I knew it. Eventually Trevor was expelled from school and became institutionalised serving time in care homes, borstal and prison. His skinhead image was a perfect platform to vent his racist views on life. That was the last I saw of him until he met my sister Helen. I had forgotten what he was like: a bullying, arrogant animal.
He knew of my reputation and at times tested it but he was careful how far he went. I could sense fear and insecurity in him. I decided to give him the benefit of the doubt which ate away at me, but I loved my sister and she was happy in her relationship with him.
Helen settled down with her new man in a council house on the other side of town. It wasn't long before they were a family of four after Helen gave birth to two beautiful little girls about 18 months apart. All seemed to be well.
I started to spot things going wrong in their relationship, but I didn't interfere. Interfering in relationships can backfire and you end up being the one in the wrong. And both parties turn against you. One night whilst watching TV an argument broke out and Trevor threatened to punch my sister's face in, in front of the whole family. This showed his true arrogance and his lack of

respect. I butted in and warned him off. He kept his gob shut then stared at my sister. I could see real fear in my sister's eyes, a fear that made me go cold. Later that evening I spoke to Helen and she assured me everything was OK in the relationship. I told her that if he ever hit her she was to tell me. Her answer was, 'He wouldn't dare hit me.' But my intuition told me another story.

I kept out of the situation and promised to myself that I would do the necessary if I found out he was hurting her, whether she liked it or not. Sometimes you have to take actions regardless of the consequences.

It was a Sunday afternoon. I was disturbed by the sound of crying children and a blazing row going on between Helen and Trevor. I made my way into the kitchen. The two girls were standing in front of my sister as if trying to protect her. It reminded me of the time I witnessed my own mother getting a beating. That was bad enough coming from a stranger, but these girls were witnessing their own father threatening their mother.

The frightened faces and the tears of the children, his own flesh and blood, didn't faze him. His abuse continued. He hadn't noticed me walk into the kitchen. I listened and watched standing only a couple of feet behind him. I flinched and sucked in a breath as the punch landed sending Helen hurtling back against the wall. The girls, who were still holding on to her, fell with her as she bore the full weight of his blow. At 15 stone I was surprised that he hadn't knocked her unconscious. I felt a shockwave ripple through my body, a kind of electric shock. I felt panic, then extreme anger. The rush of anger moved me into range fast. I exploded with an overhand right and he crashed to the floor piled up like shit should be. I instinctively went to follow through with a stamp kick to the side of his head. The leg was raised, but the girls' frightened expressions stopped me. It took several minutes for him to come round. I could easily have dissected his face with several well placed kicks but I wasn't like him. I had compassion. They were very young girls and they didn't need to see their uncle crushing their father's skull.

Instead when he rose I offered him outside. He was game. He picked up a length of wood the size of a cricket bat. Holding it with two hands, he took a wild swing like a child trying to play cricket and hit thin air. I taunted him in an attempt to get him to drop his weapon. He was keeping me at bay until he recovered from the effects of the punch. I felt like rushing him but the stakes were now too high. If I got it wrong I would be sealing my own fate. I continued taunting him.

'Come on, tough guy. I thought you were supposed to be a hard man. Afraid I'll beat you without that tool? Throw the tool down. Let's do this out the front in the street. I want everyone to see you get what you fucking deserve.' I turned and walked into the street. The statement had the desired effect. He threw the wood down behind him and followed me. It was a match fight. He raised his hands like a bare knuckle fighter. I ran at him and booted him in the groin. He backed off hands still held high.

'Come on, twat,' I exclaimed. He was beat. I could see it in his eyes. There was no fight left in him. He backed off and laughed nervously.

'Come on, John. We're mates. We go back a long way.' Still backing off he reached out his hand to me gesturing for me to shake: the oldest trick in the book. I take the hand he pulls me in and sucker punches me. He must think I'm stupid. I thought. I kept my distance and laid down a warning.

'If you lay one hand on my sister again I will fucking batter you. Do you understand me?' I looked at him hard, staring into his eyes. I was once afraid of this man. He now realised I wasn't a weak 14-year-old. I wasn't afraid of him now. But I was afraid of losing. If I lost to him my family honour would be severely dinted and my sister's life a living hell.

'John, I love your sister. I won't hit her again, I promise. I lost my cool. I shouldn't have done it. I'm sorry. Come on. I'll apologise to her.' I was too wrapped up in the glory to notice deceit in his eyes. He'd hit her. I'd hit him. An eye for an eye. I let it go after telling him to go in and apologise to her. I followed him in and took satisfaction after listening to the apology. But there was something in the way he apologised to Helen that made me feel uneasy.

He gave Helen the lovey-dovey routine, putting his arms around her and petting the children, reassuring her he would not hit her again. A few days had passed and things were back to normal. I remembered a phrase he used to say anytime anyone disagreed with what he said or did: 'She'll get it!'

I never took what he said seriously and assumed he was joking. The phrase kept replaying itself in my mind.

In order for Helen and Trevor to spend a night out together to rekindle the relationship my mum offered to baby-sit. Helen wasn't too keen on going out but Trevor insisted. Later that night Helen came back to the house to pick the kids up and they left together a happy family.

Later that night I awoke sweating. I felt incredibly afraid, so afraid I didn't want to pull the covers off my face. I always remember as a kid being afraid of the dark. The slightest flicker of light or shadow would have me clutching the covers tightly over my face. It was a bad feeling. I lay staring at the ceiling trying to figure out what it was that made me feel so afraid.
I heard my brother James's voice saying to my mum, 'There is an old lady coming up the stairs,' he said. I thought James was having some kind of waking dream or he'd taken something he shouldn't have. I heard a faint groaning sound coming from downstairs and jumped out of bed, then ran out onto the landing. Rippling chills passed through my spine and into my shoulder blades. My skin goosed, still feeling the fear of my sudden awakening.
'Who are you?' I asked like I was confronting a ghost. The lady didn't seem real.
'John, it's me. It's Helen.' I was unable to move.
'What the fuck?' I said. Her face was bruised and bloodied beyond recognition, her eyes were closed, her lips swollen and split. She was covered in dry blood. Her hair was matted and looked like someone had been twisting it around. Every time she took a step she winced in pain. My suspicions about the relationship being wrong was now staring me in the face. He'd been abusing her and now he'd let us all know. She confirmed it was him. The rest of the house awoke, disbelief on their faces. Then anger erupted.
My mother threw her arms around her. Helen sobbed a painful moan. It was a macabre sound. The shivers in my shoulders had gone to my legs, making them feel hollow, then the rage followed making me cry out. I felt immense pain. I exploded into an uncontrollable rage.

'Where is he?' I shouted. I ran in circles back and forth. I wanted to punch and kick everything in sight. 'Fuck 'im. He's dead,' I screamed. I felt out of control.

'Come on. Let's go. Let's fucking do him now, tonight,' my brother Sam said. James concurred. They were already dressed. I shouted at Helen.

'Where is he? Where is the bastard?' Through cracked and bleeding lips she told me.

'He's in the house. He's got the girls, John. Be careful, don't let him hurt the girls.' Helen became hysterical.

'Please stay here, John. Don't go. Get the police. Let them get the girls out.'

'Fuck the law. Let's go, lads. I will fucking kill him if he hurts them,' I said. My head was in bits. I couldn't stop myself from parading around like a wild animal trapped in a cage trying to find a way out.

'No John, don't,' I heard her cry as we ran out of the house. I felt like crying.

I was breaking down. I had to keep it together. This was intense anger and it threatened to destroy me. How could this cunt do this to my sister? I wanted to go, yet stay to protect Helen. Sam and James decided for me.

'Come on John. Stop fucking about. We have to go. We have to do him now,' one said. They were calm they knew what had to be done.

We made our way across town and positioned ourselves so we could see both ends of the street and the house. Sam and James's anger was bringing them to near tears. I held them back. I felt scared. My mind was in emotional turmoil. I was scared what we would do to the bastard. And the old fear plagued my mind. I was looking for excuses not to go into the house. My inner voice threw negatives at me. I was scared of getting arrested.

'Let's go now, John,' Sam said. James pushed for the same.

'Come on let's fuck him up. What are we waiting for?'

'No, the coppers are just waiting for us to do that, then they'll nick us all.' The police had the house under surveillance. In a way they were protecting him. I felt angry with myself. I couldn't decide whether it was fear that stopped me from attacking him or whether

I was making a correct decision. I shivered. It was dark, damp and misty. I felt useless glued to the floor. I hated the moment I was in.

Darnell appeared at his front door just as a police van pulled up next to the police car. 'There's the bastard,' Sam said.
I grabbed Sam as he surged forward. 'No leave it,' I said.
Darnell had armed himself with a baseball bat held high on his right side. He was spooked. He vanished into his entry then came back into his house. He was expecting a visit. I wanted so much to go in, there and then, but I knew I was right in walking away. Nevertheless I still felt ashamed and incomplete in doing it. I pulled the lads out. They couldn't understand why I didn't want to go across to the house. I knew why. A man who beats a defenceless woman is no man and destroying more lives was too easy. I would bide my time for justice. Besides I needed to be with my family to protect them. I couldn't do that from a prison cell. If we'd have gone in there, we would have surely murdered him, without a doubt. And then all of our lives would have been fucked and even from the grave he would have been causing more pain and heartache.

It took the police hours before they would go in and make sure the children were safe. They had seen my sister just after she had escaped from the house where Darnell had imprisoned and tortured her. She escaped by climbing out through the living room window after Darnell forced her downstairs to make him tea. She spotted a police car which was patrolling the area and ran to it thinking she was safe. They picked her up and questioned her about her injuries and when they realised it was her common law husband that had attacked her they classed it as a 'domestic'. They kicked her out of the car saying they could not get involved. She panicked when the police car left and ran around the block and stopped the car once again and pleaded with the officers to take her to her mum's house and safety. They let her inside the car then asked her where she lived and on finding out her name and that she was a Skillen kicked her out of the car again leaving her to walk two miles on her own in shock and bleeding badly. The police eventually arrested Darnell and he was charged with grievous bodily harm, a serious sexual offence including rape, a number of other sexual offences and false imprisonment. He was remanded in custody in Welford Road Prison.

AFTERMATH

A couple of weeks had passed and Darnell's older brother, a man with a tough reputation, gave a message to my dad: drop the charges or take the consequences. My dad was from the old school and took no shit. He stood strong and with the backup of his family pressed ahead with the charges. He didn't give a toss about Darnell's brother. I worried about a comeback.

There was no need to worry. I returned home later that night to the smell of petrol. I could smell it as I walked down the street. Sam and James had heard a rumour and were preparing for a possible visit. They had got together with a few of their mates and were happily practising throwing Molotov cocktails (petrol bombs) in the yard. They made them by half filling a glass milk bottle with petrol and sticking a petrol soaked rag in the top with just enough rag hanging out to light. When thrown, they hit the ground and exploded. They had neat little piles of bottles grouped together within throwing distance of the road.
'If they come tonight, John, they'll fucking fry. They're going to get it. We are going to roast the fuckers in their cars.' The situation was tense. They meant what they said. If they came I wouldn't be able to stop them. Every time a car came down the road the lads were ready to bomb it. They stayed awake all night with a bonfire blazing in the background.
Well at least Helen's safe, I thought. I didn't stop the lads. This was a kind of release for their anger. I knew Darnell's mob wouldn't come. They didn't have the bottle but there was always a chance they might show. And Darnell's older brother wouldn't risk his 'sugar pedestal' reputation.

The next few days were quiet. Darnell was now alone except for a few hangers on who licked arse for a living. The rumours of him committing sexual offences and beating a woman left him isolated from anyone with decent morals. I spread the word that I was going after Darnell through a few chosen friends of his.

I met one of his best mates in the court house. Somebody had told me he was in court expecting to get sent down. He would be going to the same prison.

I knew this lad from school. He too had a reputation for instantaneous violence (usually on lesser people). He was up in court for robbery and burglary. I nipped into the court house, immediately challenged him and he bottled it. Scrapping in the court house is not a good idea but he had to be told and I was prepared to go it, toe to toe, there and then.

I told him to tell Darnell I would be waiting for him when he got out. Whilst I was confronting Darnell's mate, I had an idea too ridiculous to even contemplate, but contemplate it I did. I thought about getting myself deliberately sent to prison so I could exact revenge on Darnell. In there it would be just me and him and this time there would be no let off. In the meantime, everything was left to the law of the land to exact justice for what he'd done to Helen.

ICE COLD REVENGE

A few weeks had passed and Helen was getting over her physical wounds. The mental trauma would take years to get over. Coming to terms with what happened to her wouldn't be easy: she had been badly assaulted by someone she thought she loved and trusted. The smile that lit up the room had dulled to a frown and her pain and anguish and the thought of going into court to give evidence paled her complexion.
I blamed myself for what happened. If I'd kept out of the situation in the kitchen this would probably never have happened or if I had battered him properly in the kitchen he wouldn't have come back. I hated myself. I had to get revenge. I had to do something to right the wrong.
I was due to appear in court to answer a charge of driving whilst disqualified, driving without insurance and failing to produce my documents. The offences were committed a few weeks previously. Going to court on motoring charges was a petty offence. A slapped wrist or a fine. I was already paying off a fine for other motoring offences, so I was likely to get a fine and community service. It was unlikely I'd get sent down: a possibility but not likely, depending on my attitude in court.
I'd lain in bed the night before trying to make a decision. There was no hesitation on my part. The answer was easy. I had to do it.
I hated the inside of the courtroom. The smell of wood polish and leather mingled in the air. I noticed a lad sitting at the back in the public viewing seats wearing a pastel coloured shirt with a tie that looked too tight for him.
I wanted to advise him to take the tie back to where he had bought it from and get a bigger one, but I didn't think he'd get the joke so I didn't bother. His tattoos stood out on either side of his neck like military insignia, his hair probably grown for the occasion. He was waiting to appear himself.
The usual feelings of guilt that I felt when inside a court room were non-existent. I knew I was going down this time. I would make sure of it.
I hadn't discussed what I was about to do with anybody else. I knew that Darnell was in Welford Road on remand awaiting trial. I

also knew that I would be taken there for at least a couple of weeks. It would be easier for me to let the law deal with the matter, but the easiest thing is not always the best thing. I had to confront Darnell.

The door behind the magistrates' bench opened and in they filed: a Cluedo look-alike Colonel, a geriatric male who looked old enough to be dead and a woman who seemed to be wearing the Queen's clothes, including hairdo. All that was missing was the pearl necklace and the corgis.
'All rise.' Everybody including the lad in the shirt and tie rose. They stood there as if the national anthem was about to play. I remained defiantly seated; it was piss-magistrate-off time. The court clerk gestured over his glasses, indicating for me to rise by wafting a sheet of paper as if he was flicking the 'V' sign at me. My solicitor gestured also. I rose. The magistrates in turn gave me a stern look. I smiled cockily as the prosecution outlined the case.
My solicitor had his say putting my case forward apologetically. I was guilty. There was no doubt of that and I had pleaded guilty. My solicitor was playing down the case and doing a good job too. Even I started to wonder why this case had even come to court. My solicitor was trying to get me a non-custodial sentence, difficult considering they were repeat offences. The Colonel appeared annoyed by my attitude and interrupted the silence.
'Have you anything to say to the court, Mr Skillen?' I pondered for a second thinking about my answer.
'Yeah. Get on with it. I'm guilty. If you're going to sentence me get on with it.'
The magistrate straightened up in his chair sporting an expression of surprise then anger. The tattooed lad in the public stand sat bolt upright. A smile appeared on his face and he loosened his tie.
'Mr Skillen, you do realise that you are in danger of a custodial sentence today?' said the magistrate.
'So what? If you're going to do it, do it. I ain't got all day.'
I'd always dreamt of talking to a magistrate or a judge this way before but never dared. It would be funny if the situation wasn't so tragic.
You can't fuck with the courts. They hold your life in their hands. If they can't get you one way they will get you in another. I needed

to get in to prison to exact my revenge but I couldn't push it too far. I might end up with too much bird. The magistrates stood up, shuffled some papers and left through the same door they had entered, like a child who had been sent to bed.

I stood and watched the last one file out. My mouth was dry, palms sweating. I rubbed my hands down my trouser leg to clear the sweat. Had I done enough or too much? My solicitor came over to me looking a bit concerned.

'Listen, John, if you carry on like this you're going down. Apologise to the court when they come back out. I will smooth it over.'

'What am I likely to get if they do sentence me?'

'Three months, maybe six if you get contempt of court,' he said.

I remained standing as they re-entered.

'All stand,' the clerk said. My brief remained standing.

'My client has something to say to the court. He wishes to apologise for his attitude.' The magistrate looked relieved at the solicitor's gesture.

'Is that right, Mr Skillen? Have you something to say to the court?'

I felt a swirl of nerves in my stomach then gave the answer that would seal my fate.

'No, get on with it.'

'If you address the court like that again, Mr Skillen, I will hold you in contempt.'

I smiled. This infuriated the magistrate. The tattooed lad's tie was now off. He sat there with a big grin, shirt buttons undone. The magistrates looked puzzled at my behaviour. The clerk and the magistrate had words barely audible to the court, probably checking what sentence was legally appropriate. The magistrate looked at me and said, 'Skillen, your attitude towards law and order and authority needs to change. You're guilty of driving whilst disqualified. I sentence you to three months in prison. Perhaps you will take this time to adjust your attitude. Take him down.'

'Thank you,' were the last words the Colonel heard as he and his colleagues stormed out of the courtroom.

As I left I heard the tattooed lad cry, 'Nice one, mate. Fuck the system!' My next stop would be Welford Road Prison.

HUNTING THE BEAST

Prison was easy for Darnell. He was institutionalised. He knew the system and treated prison like a vacation. But, like a rainstorm ruins most holidays, I was about to ruin his and make his bird a whole lot harder than he'd ever had it. It was time to hunt the beast.

There was a turn of a key in the lock and the cell door opened. The light from the landing made me squint. The silence was broken by mumbling and the shout of 'slop out!' The aromas of the prison breakfast found their way through the smell of piss and shit and reminded me of a service station takeaway first thing in the morning. Prison food always smelt better than it looked. A tasteless tray partially filled with un-nutritious crap.
The landing was full of cons dressed in blue jeans and stripy blue and white shirts. Some wore grey jumpers with a coloured neck band and all wore the same imitation leather shoes which appear to be made from compressed paper. A guy brushed past me almost knocking my piss pot out of my hand.
'Sorry, mate,' he said. His hair was black with grey running through it and his face worried looking and unshaven. I was in no mood for hobbits.
'Watch where you're fucking going,' I said.
'Sorry, mate,' he said again. My gaze followed him as he weaved his way through the lines of cons, apologising as he went along. He reminded me of the rabbit in *Alice in Wonderland*. 'Oh dear, oh dear. I shall be too late!' All that was missing was the waistcoat, watch and big ears. He finally disappeared in to the slop-out area, a bit like a rabbit hole only this hole wasn't for rabbits but for the previous night's piss and shit to be emptied into.
I stared at every cell door as I walked along keeping myself close to the railing which ran alongside the balcony. I'd seen cons taken out many times after unlocking. Tea time seemed favourite, but under the circumstances I wasn't taking any chances. I remember one guy walking back from getting his tea, tray in hand walking cockily along the landing. I noticed a youth standing in a doorway of a cell. When he passed the doorway the kid rammed the con's

own tray up into his face. The force of the tray and the surprise of the ambush attack dropped him to the floor. The youth then stamped and kicked the kid until he himself was grounded by the screws. The only thing that saved the kid from a serious beating was the prison issue paper shoes. And if the prison food had've been hot, it never was, he'd have been badly burnt by what the menu had described as Irish stew. I'm sure the Irish Trading Standards Department, if there is such a thing, would like to have commented on what they called Irish stew. Everybody was instantly banged up.

The slop-out area smelt so bad I wished I'd been ambushed on the way. The smell made me feel queasy as it penetrated my nasal passages. I noticed the hobbit sitting with a smile on his face perched like a bird on the toilet rim. The worried look was replaced with one of relief. As I took a piss in the urinal next to the toilet, the hobbit spoke.
'Sorry about earlier, mate, but I'd been bursting since five this morning and the turtle's head was popping out. The lads wouldn't let me take a shit in the cell so I had to cling on to it until slop out.'
Too much information I thought. I scowled at him. I found it hard to hold the scowl. He looked comical perched on the rim of the toilet bowl: dignity is not at the top of the prison list of 'must haves' for cons.

I decided it was time for me to leave him to it when he bent forward to wipe his arse on the prison issue toilet paper. Prison toilet paper had a strong smell of disinfectant to it, and it resembled tracing paper with the same qualities. Horrible stuff. The smell of the disinfectant clings to your fingers alerting everyone to the fact you've have had a shit and even the soap doesn't get rid of the smell.

I settled into prison life quickly. My focus was on letting people know what Darnell had done to my sister. I needed to isolate him from anyone he had become mates with. He was a regular in here and knew a lot of the regular cons. I didn't want to be fighting more people than I had to.

I spoke to an old friend, Rob, who always seemed to be inside. He was like a character from Slade prison: the prison in the popular TV comedy *Porridge*. Rob found out for me where Darnell was banged up. My plan was to confront him as soon as possible.

He was on the remand wing on the ground floor, two landings below mine. And the only time the remands were allowed to mix with the regular cons was when the prison showed a film at the weekends.
The landings ran either side of the Victorian building connected by bridges and staircases which enabled access to each landing. In the middle, thick wire mesh was stretched across from landing to landing like a circus acrobats' safety net. This net was to prevent depressed cons from jumping to their deaths or throwing screws or other cons over the railings. The screws were positioned on the bridges and stairways during unlock, supervising the movement of the prisoners. Rob accompanied me to the top of the stairway which led to Darnell's' cell. I made my way to the top of the staircase and looked down past two landings. I could see a group of cons to the left of the staircase playing pool. I couldn't mistake his laugh. It was a cruel piss-taking laugh which suited the environment he was in. I went cold when I saw him. That same old feeling rippled through my body. I wanted to run down and jump him there and then. All that separated me from the beast was a screw positioned on the first floor between the two staircases.

As I walked down the first flight of stairs the screw had his back to me talking to some old lag who looked about ready to croak it. I got down unnoticed. Darnell's laugh irritated me. It got louder as I got closer. I imagined he was laughing about what he did to my sister. I felt anger race through me. The butterflies in my stomach made me feel sick. I twitched and wobbled my shoulders and was forced to take a deep breath. I breathed out slowly releasing the air and felt better for it. I caught the eye of a con close to Darnell and gestured to the con with my finger toward the beast. The lad got the idea and poked him on the shoulder and pointed up to me. The beast turned and looked up. I was about twenty feet away from him. I saw his body sag. It was like his knees buckled. The fear of seeing me hit him hard. I'd seen enough lads shit themselves to know it when I saw it. Almost instantaneously his face paled. It took on a misty, milky colour. I mouthed the words 'You're fucking dead,' and gave him the cold stare. The only thing that stopped me from going down there was the sound of the screw's voice. I so much wanted to go down there and beat him like he beat my sister. But I dare not move. My fear was stronger than my desire for revenge. I felt like I felt outside Helen's house that night when he attacked her. I was afraid that Darnell had sensed my fear, like I sensed his. He knew I wouldn't go down there. He knew he was safe.

The screw's voice interrupted my thoughts again. 'You, where are you going?' Darnell mouthed at me to come down the stairs; he had to maintain a hard image, that's what he was known for inside. I couldn't help myself.

'When you come up here you're fucking dead,' I shouted. Darnell mouthed again, daring me to step down. He ran his finger across his own throat then pointed the same finger at me, a threat of death. My fear had gone as soon as I'd spoken aloud. All I felt now was confidence.

'Back on your landing, son.'

I ignored the screw and continued to stare down at my prey. Darnell broke the stare first, another sign that he was bottling it. I was truly the hunter.

'Now, son!' the screw demanded.

'Sorry, boss.' I laughed to ease the feelings of adrenalin and let the screw think there was no real problem. The screw peered down the staircase to catch Darnell making threatening gestures. 'Fucking nonce,' I said as I made my way back up the staircase.

Rob met me on the landing. 'Well done, John,' Rob said with disapproval in his voice. 'The screws know you and Darnell have a problem,' he said. 'They'll ship him out and you won't get a chance to get at him!'

'Fuck 'em,' I replied. But Rob was right I had to bide my time.

Later that day I was taken out of the association area and led off to the prison landing office. 'Come in, Skillen,' the screw said with a soft but commanding Irish accent. He was smartly dressed in dark pressed trousers, highly polished shoes and gleaming white shirt. He was tall, tanned and lean with hair as white as his shirt. There was an aura of confidence about him, an aura that can only be gained after years of experience. I recognised him from previous visits. The cons called him Chalky. He was the officer in charge of the wing: a fair screw, strict, but fair.

'Skillen, we're fully aware of the situation and your reason for being in here. I'm warning you not to do anything stupid. I'm sure you understand what I'm trying to say to you.'
I felt my eyes well up with tears of anger. A lump the size of an egg appeared in my throat threatening to choke me. I held the feelings back by dropping my head and balling both fists tightly together. I found it hard to talk but I was compelled to by my feelings of anger. I knew I was saying the wrong thing but I couldn't help myself.
'When he comes up onto the landings or I get to him before that, I will fucking kill him. I'm not going to let that bastard get away with what he did.'
The screw stayed silent. I realised I should have kept my gob shut. What if they shipped me out? All this would have been a waste of time.
'I understand how you feel, Skillen. I really do. Let the law take its course. Don't do anything stupid. If it was my sister I would feel the same way.'
I looked into his eyes. He was sincere.
'You can go.' I left the office after thanking the screw.
I felt humiliated that I'd nearly broken down in front of him, but the pressure I'd put on myself was driving me insane. I wasn't thinking rationally. I should have listened to Rob. I'd blown it. I was still undeterred but I'd lost the element of surprise and the screws would be watching me closely.
I would figure out a way of getting to him no matter what. I decided to keep a low profile, make out to the screws that I had calmed down. I stayed in my cell as much as I could. I read book after book, played chess and draughts, anything to keep my mind off Darnell. I knew he would be suffering. He'd be watching every doorway, the stairs, the landings. I took solace in the fact that I was making him feel the fear. I knew his court case was drawing close. The thought of knowing I was waiting for him would be keeping him awake at night. The added fear of a confrontation with me

would add to his anguish. I now knew where the beast was. All I had to do was lay a trap and wait for my chance to exact revenge.

TRIAL AND ERROR

Time passed by without incident. It was the day before the court case. I was fearful for my sister. I knew she would have to give evidence with Darnell sitting in the court dock.

Whilst I was in prison the rest of the family stood by Helen. My brothers, with my old mate Spider, kept their ears to the ground in case of comebacks from Darnell family. At any sign of trouble he'd be there with a few of the lads. Time had dragged up until now. The start of the trial seemed to set my mind and focus it on what I had to do.

A couple of days later Rob found out that the court case was over and Darnell had been sentenced. He would be up on the landings sometime that night. I would do what I planned to do the very next day, as soon as the opportunity presented itself. I just hoped he wouldn't be shipped out that night to another nick.
I'd been keeping myself fit by doing press-ups on the cell floor. I upturned the single bed and did pull-ups by hanging from the railing. I performed bench press by lying underneath the bed while Rob sat on it and sit-ups by the hundred. The battle with Darnell was going to change from the mental to the physical. He would now pay for what he'd done to my sister. All I had to do was figure out how I was going to get to him. I knew it would have to be immediately before he settled in on the landing and before he got shipped out to his usual haunt, Stafford Prison.
I was fidgety. The cell walls felt like they were closing in on me. I had constant butterflies. I kept sucking in large breaths of air which seemed to temporarily stop the wavy feelings in my stomach. I felt drained. Rob tried to console me using humour. If you cut Rob in two he would read 'crook' all the way through, but to me he was a godsend, I owed him big time. He would chat to me about anything just to keep the thought of Darnell the demon out of my head.
It was dark outside. We'd had supper: a tasteless giant rock cake and plastic mug full of scalding tea. I forced it down. It was difficult to eat not due to the fucking horrible taste, I'd got used to that, but the adrenalin being constantly trickled into my system.

Time was ticking away slowly again. Morning seemed a long way off. I prepared myself for a long night.

I lay on my bunk running scenarios through my mind. In every scenario I set in my mind, I saw myself the victor, finishing him off by stamping all over him. Losing wasn't an option. Every time I heard a clank of the keys, I would jump up from my bunk and press my ear to the cell door listening, trying to figure out if it was Darnell returning from court. I had to find out where he would be situated as it was possible he was planning to jump me. I had to be sharp at slop-out.

Just as I felt myself drifting off to sleep the clanking of keys awoke me. They sounded close by, then closer still. I jumped out of bed. I was fully awake in an instant. I was puzzled. It was long after lights out. I listened to the levers turning in the lock; Rob lifted his head and squinted, turning away from the beam of light that pierced the dark of the cell.

'What's going on, Rob?'

'I don't know,' he said looking puzzled. The door opened wider. I could see the silhouette of a prison officer but couldn't make out who it was.

'Skillen,' he whispered, which made the situation feel sinister. I went to the door. 'Skillen, come out here.' I stepped out warily, shading my eyes from the light and checking both sides of the doorway expecting to see someone else. An eerie silence gave the impression that the whole prison had been emptied and I was the only one left. The situation was almost dreamlike. I felt uneasy. My unease evaporated and was replaced with a feeling of confidence when I heard what the officer had to say.

'Skillen, this conversation never took place, do you understand?' I felt like a character in one of the thriller books I'd been reading.

'Yes, boss,' I said. I felt relief then excitement. My mouth watered. The screw continued.

'I was in court today with your friend Trevor Darnell. I didn't like what I heard and I didn't like the sentence he got. He deserved years not months. I've just locked him up in that cell,' he pointed across the landing. 'You get one chance to sort him out. In the morning we'll open him up, then you. Then we'll leave you to it. It'll just be you and him. You have to be ready. You'll only get a couple of minutes. Do what you've got to do and remember; this conversation hasn't taken place.'

I was feeling a mix of emotions. Here was a screw, a turn-key that history's cons called the lowest form of life, a man accused of taking away your liberty, dignity and pride who was now helping me, a con! The hate of their system and the screws left me at that moment. I realised they were just the same as the rest of us, compassionate and caring. Oh I knew there were cunts doing the job, but there are cunts in all walks of life. If you're respectful to them, they in return are respectful to you.

I thanked him.

'Don't thank me. Just do what you've got to do.' He pulled the cell door quietly shut and locked it. Rob was exasperated by what he had heard.

'I've never known that to happen,' he kept saying. 'Opening up after lights out is unheard of.'

The pressure was off. For the first time since being sent here I felt good about myself.

I knew now this was the right thing to do. 'Why didn't they just throw me in a cell with him right now, Rob?'

Rob being the resident expert on prison life gave me his spiel.

'Heads would roll if they did, John. They're responsible for the health and safety of every prisoner regardless of what they've done. This way it's just an unfortunate mistake that you two met on the landing. They had no way of knowing you were going to attack him.'

THE FIGHT

I didn't sleep at all after that, not what you'd call proper sleep. It was a kind of waking sleep almost like cat napping. My eyes felt sore around the inside of the lids. I rose early and got dressed. I'd have to wait about an hour before slop-out. I paced up and down the cell like a sentry on guard duty. I was taking in gulps of breath trying to keep myself calm. My mind was being bombarded with all kinds of thoughts. Different scenarios appeared in my mind's eye then faded as another thought pushed the last one out. There was just one thought I focused on: giving him pain, making him pay for what he did to Helen.

The rattle of keys, the lock turning. This was it. They were actually doing it: giving me a chance to exact revenge. I remembered what the screw said. I'd have to be quick. I felt a rush of excitement as the door was left ajar. I opened it fully and slipped out into the recess of the doorway. Rob whispered, 'Fucking kill him, John.' I looked to his cell. He was already out and walking across the bridge between the landings, piss pot in hand.

If I went too soon he might run, then I'd lose my chance. I needed that element of surprise. I waited for him to turn toward the slop-out area so that his back was to me. 'Ugly cunt,' were the last words I remember thinking as I blasted out of the doorway like a rampaging dog. When I was in range I shouted, 'Hey bastard.' I wanted him to turn, if my timing was right I'd hit him directly on the jaw. I let go an almighty right hand as he spun round. The punch thudded into the top side of his skull. His head always looked too big for his body so it was hard to miss, but the knockout I wanted so bad hadn't materialised. I was too tense causing me to lose power in the punch. I continued the forward momentum of the attack; the piss pot he was holding went skyward and spewed its contents over the tiled landing floor. His huge Neanderthal head shot forward taking his body with it. I lashed out punches as I scrambled after him. We were inside the slop-out area now wrestling in piss. He yelped as I yanked back his head and grabbed at his face. I tried to get to my feet but I couldn't get a grip on the piss soaked floor. The stench of piss was strong but I could still smell his fear more. I was growling like a wild-man; if he was hitting me I wasn't feeling it. I grabbed the sides of his head with my hands and dug my thumbs into his eyes. Simultaneously he'd forced his thumb into the corner of my cheek like a fish hook. Instead of ripping out, he pushed his thumb deep up into my gums between the cheek and outside teeth, separating my cheek from my face bone. I felt the skin tearing. I could taste the piss on his hands. I dug my thumbs deep into his eye sockets. One in particular went deeper. I tried to scoop his eyeball from its socket. I wanted at that point to blind the bastard. The thumb inside my mouth weakened off; he was more concerned with protecting his eyes. He screamed as I raked into his head with my fingers. I leaned back releasing the thumb from the corner of my mouth. I flicked my teeth over the thumb and began severing the thumb with my teeth. I could feel the bone on the edge of my teeth through the skin. I now had him and I wasn't going to let go. Like a dog I tore and shook my head from side to side as I bit down hard. He pulled back and tore his thumb from my mouth. I could taste the metallic tang of blood. I could hear nothing but his squeals and my own growls.

As I tore into him I became aware of legs around us; a crowd of cons had formed. I felt myself getting the edge. I felt his eyeball in my thumb; it was almost out. I wanted it out. He turned his head away from my thumb. I managed to crawl on top of him. If I could just get upright I would punch him to bits. I started pounded his face and body. Then I felt myself being lifted high into the air and I was upright. I began stamping on Darnell, the paper shoes cushioning the blows. A screw dived onto Darnell and covered his head with his arms preventing me from getting a stamp on his head.
As I stamped I shouted, 'You ever fuck with my family again I will fucking kill you, you fucking nonce.' The cons in earshot would now know why we were fighting and that Darnell was a sexual offender (the most hated of cons).

Darnell didn't try to get up; he was finished, no fight left in him. The cons bayed for blood: 'Fucking kill him,' I heard one shout.
I also heard the words, 'Leave it, Skillen!' I turned to see the screw that had lifted me up standing by. He never tried to restrain me. He moved into position between Darnell and me.

I left, making my way through the crowd of cons that parted like Moses parting the waves. I felt pats on my shoulder as I went. 'Good job, mate,' one said. I skipped down the landing and into the breakfast queue and tidied my pissy blood-soaked clothes. I stood next to Rob trying to blend in.

'Nice one, John. Fucking nice one. Get in here,' he said pulling me into the queue. I stood next to the wall on the far side of Rob. Two cons hid me from view.

'Brilliant, John. He never had a chance. You done him easily.'

I felt good for the first time in months. Even though I felt good about myself I still had feelings of anger. I hadn't done enough. I hadn't one visual mark on me. Piss had soaked my back and legs and I had a cut on the inside of my mouth. Other than that not a mark. I watched the screws walking the beast away, head bowed, one hand on his eye as if he was holding it in place. He looked a sorry mess. 'Fucking nonce,' I heard someone shout. The message had got through.

I didn't know whether the screws would come for me or not. I waited in the queue trying to look innocent which wasn't difficult considering where I was. Nevertheless Chalky appeared with two other screws.

'Come on, Skillen. I could have signed my own name when I heard it was you,' he said.

I took that as him letting me know that he'd sanctioned the turning of the blind eye.

I walked along, a screw either side of me. I began to feel a sense of well-being. I held my head high, I felt proud. The immense anger was still within myself for letting the situation go on for so long. I thought about Sam and James and how they must have felt not being able to take action because of me. But it wasn't over.

SOLITARY

I was taken into the block, a minimalist area set aside for the riotous nutters that frequent these establishments. The cell was about twelve feet by four feet with no furniture inside. It was immaculately clean. The brickwork was painted an off-white. A window too high to see out of was the only feature in this drab, cold-looking room. In the corner of the cell was a cardboard corner unit, a small cardboard table and chair made from the same material and a plastic piss-pot.

I spent a few lonely hours in the cell before being taken before the governor. I was given orders on how to behave in front of him. Before the governor came into the office I found out from the screw that Darnell was pressing charges against me for assault. Cheeky bastard. I thought. He's not only a nonce but also a grass. I was flanked by four of the biggest screws I'd ever seen. They formed a box formation around me as if I was a cop killer, instead of a nonce beater. They were there in case I decided to have a pop at the governor. Little did I realise that Darnell would be brought in to the office at the same time to identify me as his attacker.

When the beast entered the office I wanted to turn around and lay into him there and then. But I knew I wouldn't get the chance; if I made any kind of move I would be restrained in an instant. Under other circumstances I may have just gone for it regardless but the screws had helped me exact revenge. I owed them respect. I kept cool. Darnell grassed me up making a formal identification and was taken straight back out again. The governor read the charges out and then asked me my plea.
'Guilty. I did it and when I see him again I will do the same thing again,' I said.
'No you won't, Skillen, because we will make certain you won't.'

The governor sounded serious. I had no beef with him. I didn't even know him. I decided to keep my gob shut.

'You are guilty of attacking another prisoner. I am fully aware of the circumstances in which this situation came about. Nevertheless you can't take the law into your own hands. You will spend the next seven days in solitary confinement. Seven days' loss of privileges, seven days' loss of earnings, seven days' loss of remission, seven days' all-round.'

And well worth it considering Darnell got the same after a screw gave evidence that he'd been threatening me. It really was a slapped wrist for me. I'd indicated to the governor that I would attack Darnell again. Either me or Darnell would be shipped out. If it was Darnell he'd probably be shipped out on rule 43; the code for anyone placed in protective custody (usually sexual offenders), making sure that where he went next they would get a clue as to why he was incarcerated. It wouldn't bother him: he'd been bragging about what he'd done to other cons. The man is evil personified.

While I was banged up in solitary confinement, I kept a door-side vigil. I wanted to get a look at Darnell before he left. I needed to see his injuries, to see that he was suffering. I'd already cost him another seven day sentence. I spoke to the screw that came to the door. 'All right, boss. Which cell is he in?'

'Two away from you. You did a good job, son,' he said as he slammed the door shut.

I peered out of the cell door and caught a fleeting glimpse of Darnell, a sorry-looking bastard. His hand and eye was heavily bandaged. His lips and cheek were swollen and his head was bowed. He looked a worried and shameful man. I smiled through my anger; he would have to live with what he'd done for the rest of his life.

It was boring being in solitary confinement. At least I had a single cell, something most cons dreamed of. It was cleaner than the regular cells; the food was hotter and better quality (mind you I dread to think what the added ingredients were). I was brought up in a big family and enjoyed the company of others. I was lonely and would have to spend the next ten weeks lurking around prison killing time.

I kept myself busy whilst in solitary by doing press-ups and sit-ups. I counted how many bricks were in the cell and wondered who actually built the place. Seven boring days later with pecks and abs to die for, I was released back on to the landings. There'd be no rematch with the nonce, not yet anyway. I was informed that he had been shipped out to Stafford Prison and I would be serving my time here in Welford Road. I'd done three weeks, which with the extra week added on meant I had six weeks left to do. Or so I'd thought.

When I got to my cell I opened my mail. I had a letter telling me that I was having a visit from my social worker. That very day he informed me that I was due to appear in court the next morning to attend an appeal which my solicitor had put in on my behalf. I was surprised it had come through so quickly. I attended court the next day and was released by the appeal judge. He stated that the case was a minor one and a custodial sentence was too severe. I was ecstatic. I walked out of the courtroom head held high. I was free!

Getting myself sent down to exact revenge was stupid. It could easily have backfired. I had tunnel vision. All I could see was me and him. I forgot about the rest of my family. I was too concerned with my own pride. I'm glad I did it though. I sent him a clear message for the future. Stay away from my family.

Helen recovered from her ordeal, well as much as you can after the pain she had to put up with. The mental scars remain but she hides them well. She's happily married now with two more beautiful children, a hard working, loving and caring husband, her knight in shining armour and light years away from the kind of demon Darnell is.
As for Darnell, he never got anywhere near the sentence he deserved. The judge of the day looked upon the case as a 'domestic'. A fucking 'domestic'! There is something wrong with a legal system that says it's OK to beat and abuse people as long as they're your spouse. A crime is a crime. Mental and physical abuse towards your partner should carry a hefty sentence.

I will never get that vision of my sister out of my head. Still there's another vision clear in my mind, that of Trevor Darnell and the sorrowful look of defeat on his face. He was released about 18 months after his trial. The demon had done his time and on his release stayed well away from Helen. Shortly after his release, Sam and James bumped into him in a café in Loughborough. They jumped him there and then. They gave him another thrashing he wouldn't forget. He's been in and out of prison ever since: armed robberies, aggravated burglary, serious assault.

Prison and his conscience (I'm sure he's got one) have taken their toll. I saw him recently. What I saw was a sorry excuse for a human. The hard drug-dealing he's involved in led to a body shrivelled and prematurely aged by the abuse of those hard drugs; a body paying the price for his crimes with a life sentence of addiction and a future of incarceration. Almost a fitting end!

HOLÀ, BEER SWILLING BRITS

I was back in circulation and had pushed the thoughts of Helen's predicament to the back of my mind. Summer was coming and along with it a feel-good factor. The holiday season was almost upon us, I loved this time of the year. Loughborough's nightlife was booming; most young people were well into the 18 to 30 type party night out. This was due to the yearly Spanish holiday catching on. Gangs of lads and girls from around Britain would head for Magaluf, the party capital of Spain or one of many of the other popular resorts. Copious amounts of alcohol were drunk. The Loughborough lads were no different. Money was scraped together or grafted for and saved and we were off.

I remember being in Magaluf one year. We were in the British bar which was located on the old strip: a row of bars stacked three high all wanting the business of the young European tourists (especially the crazy beer-swilling Brits). It was big business for the bar owners and they had to take as much money as they could during the holiday season to see them through the quiet of winter.
The place was absolutely manic; the Spanish police weren't used to the behaviour of drunken Brits and their idea of policing the affair was to threaten you at gun point or gas and cosh anyone who was out of order. In a lot of situations it was like trying to put a fire out using petrol. These bars were packed with British party animals all intent on one thing, getting completely wrecked in the biggest party in the world**.** There was always something cracking off, sometimes literally!
Big Kev loved his bangers (no not sausages but I'm sure he liked those as well) and Spanish bangers were far more powerful than the English banger you have on Guy Fawkes Night. I was in the toilet singing along to 'Club Tropicana' by Wham which was blasting out of a nearby speaker. As I was having a piss, Kev appeared next to me with a mischievous grin on his face. The toilet itself was packed out, pissed up lads falling about gurgling at each other. I'd barely finished my piss when I saw big Kev throw a fizzing banger into the sink. My heart skipped a beat; I'd seen these fuckers go off before and this one was a biggie.

I sprinted toward the doorway but wasn't quick enough. I stopped and covered my ears then the sound wave hit me in the face. 'Fucking 'ell,' I exclaimed. The sink fell from the wall. I skipped out of there pretty sharpish and into the next bar not wanting to take the rap for the knackered sink. Kev was a dangerous man with a banger in his hand. My ears were ringing for an hour afterward. Kev? He just laughed.

Another time we were staying in an apartment block above a parade of shops. The apartments were the worst I'd ever stayed in. The lads had got together and done a group booking; it was a cheap deal issued by a friend or was that ex-friend? We soon found out why. But hey, we were young. Who cares when you hardly use the place? It's just somewhere to crash and sleep off the booze. Most of the time it was light when we went to bed, so the cockroaches and mosquitoes were back in hiding. We probably got on average two to three hours' sleep a night. Most of the kipping was done on the beach (if you dared kip at all). Once asleep you were at the mercy of the lads. Many a strange photo you couldn't remember being taken would appear in the pub back home.

Next door to the apartment was a gang of Scottish lads who were way over the top. We were bad enough, but in a cool way. This bunch were just a set of wankers playing loud music at siesta time, the very time the lads liked to get a couple of hours' kip before they got changed to go out. The Scottish made one mistake; we could put up with the loud noise. We all liked to party, but threatening one of the lads was a major error regardless of where we were. It was time for a house call.

There was always a quiet time in the Scottish camp. We knew they'd be crashed out around five after returning from the beach. They were usually dead to the world, sleeping off the day's booze. That was the time we decided to pay them a visit. The door was unceremoniously booted in by one of the lads and in we filed. Bodies and empty whisky bottles were strewn everywhere. We each took a room and launched knuckles and boots into our unsuspecting sleeping foe. Anyone we came across got a beating. The Scottish lads didn't have a chance. The surprise attack had the desired effect. The law was laid down and we filed back out again.

We never heard much from them after that. They calmed right down. Oh they still got pissed as farts and danced until the wee small hours.

A couple of days later, big Kev threw one of his bangers off the balcony – he was aiming for the busy street below to cause panic and mayhem like he always did when he got bored. The banger landed on the roof of the shop below which was made of corrugated tin. The banger exploded, ripping a gaping hole in the tin roof. The police were close by. At first it was funny, then not so funny as the police started to make their way to where the banger could have come from.

We lay in bed with the covers over our heads pretending to be asleep. Our neighbours, the Scottish were pissed and kicking up a bit of a party. A couple of them had gone out onto the balcony to see what the commotion was about. They seemed unaware the coppers were on their way up to the block. We could only imagine what was happening when we heard the angry Spanish voices and the screams of the Scottish lads as they were beaten, arrested and taken away. All big Kev could say was, 'oops!'

We were always getting into some scrap or other. When the beer's in and you're with such a big crowd of lads it's inevitable something is going to kick off.

We were on our way to a club on the strip, situated behind a large parade of shops. We approached the bouncer on the door and were questioned. He wanted to know how many there were of us. The lads started arguing with him saying that 'he wasn't in fucking England so butt out.' I ignored the bouncer and went to walk in. He made the mistake of putting his hand on my chest. I knocked away his hand and throated him against the wall. I pushed my face into his:

'If you want a fucking go you can have a fucking go,' I said.

The bouncer shit himself. He was bigger than me but I'd made him lose his bottle with pure aggression and a fucking good grip. I rammed him away when he squeaked out an apology. The other doormen who were Spanish stood their ground but didn't interfere. The Spanish boss sacked him on the spot and offered me his job. I declined. Why would I want to be a fucking bouncer? Bullet, who always made good sense, said, 'You should've taken the job, John.

You'd make a good doorman. You could have lived out here with all the sea, sand and birds you ever wanted.' I laughed and carried on into the club.

There were many holidays in the sun. In my memories they all seem to meld into one big party. Whether we were in Spain or Greece we were always getting pissed, partying and scrapping.

The parties carried on after the holidays in the same mad style but people had jobs to go to and it was never quite the same. I'd left home and got a bedsit in a shared house located in a student area of town. I shared a room with my brother Sam and a house full of characters that resembled the *Young Ones* from the TV comedy. There was a drug doing its rounds at the time known as acid: a hippie, arty drug which when taken was supposed to make you see things, weird hallucinations or make your emotions change.

Magic Mushrooms; small brown mushrooms, usually found on cricket pitches, were also popular. They too altered the mind state. Most of the hippie characters disappeared at the weekend; they knew the townie entourage would appear and sure enough we'd pile in after the clubs had shut down and we'd carry on drinking into the small hours.

The cellar door was ajar. I noticed someone in the meter cupboard. 'What's your fucking game?' I said.
A lad who had tagged along for the party after the club had shut was trying to break into and rob the electric meter. We weren't too pissed off about it as one of the hippie crew had already beat him to it some days before. I called a few of the lads to the scene. Laughing we decided to lock him in there for the night. As the booze took its effect the party atmosphere changed, people were crashed out in every room. I don't know how it started but an argument was raging in the kitchen. I walked into the middle of it to see my brother Sam wielding a sword and a few of the lads standing well back. He was suffering alcohol induced rage or someone had spiked his drink. No one could get through to him with the verbals. The sword: a Japanese ninja style, samurai sword

that he kept beside his bed in case of aggro, was held firmly in his right hand. The blade was live.

'Sam, put the sword down,' I said.

'No fucking way. You're all going to get it.'

His eyes were on fire with rage. Sam was a fiery fucker at the best of times but this was madness and not at all in character. I suppose that's what made it more frightening.

He started swinging it wildly chopping off light switches, slashing chairs. He had completely lost his head. I picked up a chair. The rest of the lads backed well off and left me to deal with my brother.

'Sam, put the fucking sword down,' I demanded.

He wouldn't listen. It was like he was somewhere else. He was going through a broken relationship at the time and his head was already fucked up.

'Fucking stay away from me,' he said raising the sword over his shoulder like a baseball bat. I was within striking range. If he brought the blade down I'd be finished.

I knew he wouldn't strike me under ordinary circumstances but if his drink had been spiked with acid or some other drug he might not be seeing me as his brother. For all I knew I could be some fellow samurai on the battlefield. If anyone walked in the room right now he might slice him with it. I grabbed a nearby chair and whilst swinging it around my head I pretended to lose it: 'Come on then. If we're going to smash the place up let's do it right now.' I threw the heavy chair toward the huge Victorian bay window and it exploded sending glass and wood splinters flying around the room. 'Come on!' I shouted as I grabbed another and smashed it into the table. I went crazy kicking things around the room. Sam let out a big scream like a karate man breaking wood. He smashed the sword repeatedly into the table splintering more wood into the air; he grabbed another chair and with one big swing it followed my chair through the bay window taking out what was left of the frame. The curtains were sucked out and fluttered in the wind. Sam's anger rage mellowed when he saw what he'd done. He lowered his sword. I approached him slowly and took the blade from his hand. I put my arm around him. He shrugged me off and vanished into the toilet. I took the sword upstairs and hid it. The party was over. If you ever want to end a party quick this was the way to do it! It was a close call: a dangerous weapon in the wrong hands. The sword scared most of the people away. The rest were too drunk to notice but followed the crowd. Those of us who were left eventually crashed out. We awoke the next morning to a bomb site, a massive headache and the realisation that we would be homeless in a few hours. The landlord was due in to check over the house and collect the rent which just so happened to be overdue.

We had a mad tidy up. The damage caused by the sword wasn't as bad as the damage caused by the chairs going through the Victorian bay window. We sat awaiting the landlord trying to figure out a convincing story to get us out of the shit. The last thing I needed was a criminal damage charge. I was still on a suspended sentence after my appeal. We waited for the landlord trying to think of an excuse.

We had just decided on a story when there was a knocking sound coming from the cellar. We all looked at each other then burst out laughing. It was the meter robber from the night before who was still locked in. I opened the door and he squinted when the light hit his eyes. He rubbed his hand through his hair and bid me good morning. He looked well hungover. He started to apologise for attempting to rob the meter as he made his way to the front door and outside to freedom. I was dumbfounded as I watched him walk away. The room full of hangover piss-heads were still in hysterics.

The landlord arrived that morning to pick up a rent cheque. He coughed a pretend cough. 'Well, John? What happened here?' After a tongue-in-cheek discussion and a few white lies we left the shocked landlord surveying the damage, terminating our contract before he terminated it for us. It was back home. I never thanked the landlord for his understanding nature but I was very thankful the police weren't called. The Victorian bedsit was closed down and sold on.

ADDICTION

My life was going nowhere. I flitted from house party to house party. From bar to bar. All I had in my life was booze and violence. When the booze was in so was the violence. Some people saw me as a troublemaker, others as a bully, some a saviour. Whatever it was, wherever I went people would look at me. When I walked into a bar there would be whispers. My reputation was set in stone.
I would scrap without thought of the consequences and that made me dangerous. I felt the fear like everybody else but my uncontrolled anger and aggression would quickly block it out. I got so used to the buzz of the violence that I actually enjoyed the feelings of euphoria that came with overcoming the fear. I got excited at the thought of a brawl, not fearful. I was confident, arrogant and aggressive. Trouble seemed to find me wherever I went. I was so full of anger I hated authority: the police, social services, in fact the whole system and everything it stood for and nobody could tell me different. I knew I had an over-protective nature when it came to my family. If anybody hurt them or even insulted them I took it personally. Even if they had already sorted it I had to get involved. I had become frustrated with life. Peer pressure kept me a prisoner. I felt like I had to be a certain way. I had to live up to my reputation.

I had clarity of mind now. I knew why I couldn't walk away from a fight. I knew why I couldn't back down. I was at a point in my life that frightened me. Was this it? Was this all I was capable of, instantaneous violence? It seemed that I was like a heroin addict or alcoholic only my addiction was real violence.

CHANGE YOUR WAYS

The sound of the door banging brought me back from the recollections of my past. I sat in the shower, a cold chill running through my bones, my past having flashed before my eyes as if I was dying. That's what was needed a change, a new life, but how?
I didn't regret what I'd done to Jimmy Regan. If I hadn't have done it to him sooner or later he would have done it to me on his terms.
The door banged again: 'Are you all right, Johnny boy?' my dad asked.
The water from the shower gradually got colder. I stood up and washed myself down with the Imperial Leather soap – the only luxury in this damp-ridden room. I felt like I'd been in there for an eternity.
'Yeah, Dad, I'm all right. I'll be out in a minute.'
I heard my dad mumble something to my mum. They were worried about me. I felt sad for them. They had tried their best with their children. I know my dad had given up on his own situation, but both of them stood by me no matter what I'd done in my life. I loved them both dearly and I know they loved me. They tried their best under the circumstances they were in. Me? I'd given up and I had no reason other than I felt sorry for myself. And I was scared of change; I mean, how *do* you turn your life around? It's hard to be good but nevertheless, things had to change.

Fortunately for me and his family, Regan hadn't died. He suffered blackouts and spent a week in hospital licking his wounds. To save face (no pun intended) he told the police and everyone else that during the fight I'd used a glass on him.
I couldn't prove I hadn't used a glass and was arrested and charged with section 18: malicious wounding with intent. I would have been charged with section 18 anyway due to the injuries, but I didn't want my name connected with the use of a glass. Using a glass was seen as a coward's way out. If you can't use your fists then using a tool is stupidity, because sooner or later you will get caught on the back foot without one and then you're in the shit. Far better to know and practise how to defend yourself unarmed.

I appeared at magistrates' court and pleaded not guilty. I was released on bail awaiting a committal hearing. Section 18 was too serious a charge for the magistrates to deal with. With my previous record I faced anything from five to seven years, depending on what mood the judge was in on the day of sentencing. People who used glasses as a weapon were usually made examples of. The committal hearing at the magistrates came round quickly. They set me a date to appear at crown court and I was bailed on a crown court warrant to appear a few weeks later.

NEW RECRUIT

I couldn't face five years in prison. The thought of being banged up for 23 hours a day repulsed me. I needed time to think. I needed to be away from the life that was tearing me apart. I decided to go on the run. Trouble was I didn't have anywhere to run to. Spider suggested jokingly that I join the French Foreign Legion. We'd always joked that one day we would. It played on my mind. An old friend Johnny Moreland, whose pet subject among others was the legion, told me to go to any gendarmerie (police) office in France and tell them you want to join up. To be sure I was going to the right place I checked with the French Embassy. They told me the same thing. Police stations, no matter which country they were in, set alarm bells ringing in my head. I decided to cut out the middleman and go directly to the legion.
I headed for the Fort du Nugent in the suburbs of Paris. I hadn't a clue where it was.
I would make my way to Paris and find the fort.

I got a bag together with a few things. I was still questioning what I was about to do: five years in prison or five in the Legion with a new identity when I came out? I knew the Legion took in people from many walks of life regardless of their background. I was cool and confident and decided it was the right thing to do.

The day came to board the ferry and make my way to France, a place I'd never been to.
I knew a few of the landmarks from films and books but I couldn't speak the language.
I boarded the ferry at Newhaven on my way to Dieppe. I arrived in Dieppe and made my way to the motorway. Thoughts of turning back plagued my mind but that wasn't an option. I hitchhiked along the motorway. I didn't realise it was illegal and could have been arrested at any time. The French were very obliging and it wasn't long before I was nearing Paris. I arrived in Paris in an old, battered Renault driven by an old man who reminded me of a wartime French resistance fighter complete with beret. The van clunked its way through its gears. And eventually we arrived on

the outskirts of Paris. The journey had been silent but scenic. He dropped me off, smiled revealing teeth like burnt matchsticks and pointed his finger in what I believed to be the general direction of Paris city centre. I headed for the Arc de Triomphe so I had a landmark reference. From there I got directions from the tourist information office and made my way to the fort.

The streets near the fort were lined with buildings and trees. As I got closer I started to feel apprehensive. Did I really want to do this? The answer came into my head. Where else could I go? I was bolloxed. (Irish slang meaning: in a troublesome situation, ruined, broken or screwed up.)

I had to do it. I was already in breach of a crown court warrant. And because I had failed to go to court, another charge would be added to the section 18, which would mean a longer sentence. I had made things worse for myself. There was no turning back now.

I spotted the gates of the fort. It looked out of place in the middle of this leafy suburb. I walked by it and stopped. I was afraid to take the step toward the gate. I forced myself forward. My heart pounded. I walked closer to the doors. I paused, turned back round and walked off the way I'd come. I took a breath and let it out slowly.

'Fucking 'ell. Come on, John. Fuck it. You can do it,' I said out loud.

What I was doing was far better than five years inside. At least I'd be someone in the Legion and I'm choosing my own destiny. I turned back and made my way to the gate, banged the door and waited. I felt like running off like I did when I was a kid playing red knocker, (a game whereby we would run down a street, knock on every door then hide and watch the fun as the neighbours all popped their heads out). I heard footsteps, then the lock go. I stood my ground. The door in the gate opened, an armed legionnaire about five feet nine and well built looked me up and down. He was holding a short machine gun. He raised his chin without saying a word as if to ask what I wanted. I thought it was obvious. I could hardly get my words out.

'I want to join the legion.'

'What?' he said

'I want to join the legion,' repeating the phrase a bit louder. He looked me up and down again.
'Anglais?' he asked. His tone of voice was deep and aggressive.
'Yes English,' I said.
'Wait there.'
The door banged shut. I felt uneasy standing waiting for his return but I had to see this through to its conclusion. After a couple of minutes the door opened again. He barely caught my eye.
'Come back tomorrow.'
Before I could protest the door slammed shut. Fuck. Now what?
I hadn't expected this. It was cold and wet and I was hungry. I'd left my bag with a few things in including passport and money in a locker in the train station just in case. I had a thin blue Adidas sport jacket on and was freezing. It was around midnight; I had to find somewhere to sleep until morning.

I found a phone booth on a quiet street and crawled inside it. I raised my feet off the floor and dozed off, waking every time I heard a noise. It began to rain, the type of misty irritating rain that soaks you through very quickly. I had to abandon my refuge when a noisy group of French men and women arrived gesturing to use the telephone. I made my way over the road to a block of flats, and waited until someone left the building then nipped inside the security door. I went underneath the stairwell and lay on the concrete floor. I felt very lonely and depressed and cursed at my life.

The stairwell turned out to be a non-starter. An old French woman appeared on the staircase and started shouting at me. I deciphered her body language as displeasure my presence.
I legged it saying sorry as many times as I could until I was out of the door.
I walked until I came to a nearby allotment surrounded by a hedge. I jumped the gate and found a small clearing beneath the hedge which was sheltered from the rain and the wind that had now picked up. I was still very cold and covered myself with a newspaper I'd picked up just like a tramp would. It was surprisingly warm and the bonus was the rain had stopped. I was sheltered and hidden. I drifted off to sleep.

I awoke at first light and realised I was attracting a bit of attention from passers-by. I got out of the allotment and headed for a café bar using my nose as a tracking device. It worked! I found a little café and asked for a coffee. I only had a few English coins and offered them to the man behind the counter. He uttered something in French and then turned away from me. I turned to leave. 'Monsieur,' he said.

He gestured with his hand for me to take the coffee. I smiled. I was grateful.

I drank the coffee in silence then left. I thanked my saviour. The coffee gave me the boost I needed. I felt a sense of urgency now. I didn't know whether it was the caffeine or my determination. I left the smell of fresh coffee and baked bread behind me and headed back to the fort. This time I went straight to the door and knocked. The sound echoed in the street. When the door opened it was the same legionnaire. This time he greeted me with a soft smile which didn't quite suit his image.

Inside he told me to sit and wait. I obeyed. I felt like I'd been sitting for ages when I heard the main door bang twice in quick succession. The legionnaire opened the door. 'German,' he said and beckoned in a tall, well built man with long crop of blond, scruffy hair. It was clear he was another recruit. After what seemed like hours of waiting another legionnaire appeared and indicated to us to follow him. He took us through another doorway into a parade ground. The atmosphere of the place reminded me of North Sea Camp except the entry to this place was a little more civilised.

We were led into a block and taken up a flight of stairs into a room and left on our own. We both looked at each other but remained silent. I wondered about the lad sat opposite me. What was his story? Why was he here? He was probably thinking the same about me. The room was airy, spotlessly clean and smelt of polish. The door opened again and three men filed in. It was getting crowded. It seemed I wasn't the only one turned away last night looking at the state of these guys. They all remained silent. It was obvious that they didn't know each other as they took seats apart.

It wasn't long before the room was full with 15 men. It was like a Salvation Army soup kitchen in winter. There were some worried looks on all of the faces and the stress levels were high. Not one word was spoken until the 16th member joined us.

'Fucking 'ell. It's quiet in here,' he said.
A big burly lad walked in. He looked agitated and well pissed off. He had an army squaddie look about him as he approached the vacant seat next to mine. There was something different about him compared to the others. He was very confident.
'All right to sit here, mate?'
'Yeah, no problem,' I said.
'Fucking hell. English! I thought they'd be all krauts or froggies. The name's Dave'
Before I could ask he began to tell me why he was there.
'I'm only here because of my fucking mates, if you can call them mates. Fucking wankers. I'm in the British army, tank regiment. We got pissed last night and decided to join up for the crack. I came in first. They should have followed, but as you can see they didn't. Fucking wankers. It was all just a joke to start with but you know what? I really want in now. Fuck the others.' He appeared very serious about the whole situation. He continued his reasoning for joining up. 'I worked with the Legion before. They're fucking shit hot. I've spent seven years in the British army. I'm married with two kids and I'm fucking bored of it all. My wife will go fucking nuts when she finds out I've joined up. Fuck it! If you want something bad enough you have to be selfish don't you? It's not always about them is it?'
He rattled on like he was a word junkie and talking was his fix, I feared he'd overdose on his own vocabulary. The information just flowed out. A legionnaire entering the room silenced him.
'Follow me,' he said. Everyone did as instructed. He led us into a room which resembled a classroom. One at a time we went into another room and signed the papers to say that we were committed to the Legion for five years (the minimum stay). I signed my papers and went back to the classroom. After signing I felt kind of safe. Later that day we were taken to another room and lined up outside it. We waited for a good ten minutes, then the queue started to shuffle along and the German guy three in front of me vanished behind the door.
I heard a click and a whirring sound which I recognised. Ten seconds later or so, the tall, well-built German appeared, head bowed, a wry smile across his face, rubbing his shaven head. He looked up, said something in German and laughed a hearty laugh

exposing a huge set of choppers. He would make a fortune doing toothpaste ads if he wasn't so ugly. The laughter became infectious. It broke the ice. Tears rolled down the face of a chap standing next to me.
'Where you from?' Dave asked.
'Loughborough.'
'Oh yeah, I know Loughborough. There's a royal signals' base near there.'
'Yeah that's right, at Old Woodhouse. Sorry, mate. I didn't give you my name. I'm John Skillen.'
'What you doing here?'
Before I could answer the question the door opened, and out came another clean shaven recruit. Dave went in and straight back out. Then it was my turn. When I walked into the room the first thing I noticed was clumps of hair surrounding a dining chair. There was a legionnaire holding a set of clippers. 'S'assoir.' I looked at him wondering what it was he'd just said to me. 'S'assoir.' He pulled the chair round and stood with both hands on the back of it. I sat down. 'Anglais?'
'Yes English.'
I stared at the wooden box which contained his kit. Beside the box was a barber's brush and scissors. He vanished out of my peripheral vision which made me feel uneasy. I felt like I was in the hands of Sweeney Todd the murderous barber. Within seconds of the blade running across my skull, I was sheared.
'Boule zero anglais. You like?'
I didn't understand him but I got the gist. I just did what the German did and rubbed my hand across my head. Fuck me it was gone. My pride and joy.
I walked out slightly embarrassed but smiling. It reminded me of my first haircut in detention centre; the difference being this cut was shorter and I chose to be here.
I got friendly with Dave, the ex-squaddie from England. He really wanted to get into the legion. He had a passion about it – a passion you could hear in his voice when he spoke. Even though he was married with two children he'd decided to try his hardest to become a legionnaire.

I spent about nine days in Paris, Fort de Nugent, scrubbing, mopping, cleaning and marching with long spells of boredom waiting to be told what and when to do things. The discipline was pretty much like detention centre or borstal. At one point we were taken to an army depot inside Paris for medical check-ups in cloth covered army trucks. We were kitted out in tracksuits and plimsolls most of the time. The day came when 30 of us were taken to the stores and kitted out with uniforms, boots and green berets. We were ordered to dress and were informed that we would be taken to Aubagne, a Legion base close to Marseilles in the south of France for pre-selection: a series of medical and background checks to find out whether you were suitable for the Legion or not.

There was an air of excitement in the dormitories. We were taken out on to the parade ground where an officer stood in front of us and gave us instructions in French and then English.
'You're being taken to Aubagne. We will be travelling overnight to Marseilles and will be going to the train station in five minutes.'
The level of excitement rose. Recruits mumbled to each other. A nervous shuffle ruffled the ranks.
We boarded the trucks that would take us to the station and left for Gare du Sud. I felt proud to be wearing the uniform of a recruit and wondered if I'd eventually become a legionnaire and wear the revered képi blanc (the legion's famous white hat). My only worry was the crown court warrant. Lads had been talking about the Legion working closely with Interpol and any undesirables were flagged up and binned.
We pulled up across the road from the station. The legionnaire accompanying us got out. We followed and lined up in two ranks.
'You will march across the road. Do not stop for traffic. Keep your eyes forward and march. You are not yet legionaries but you represent the legion. If anybody gets in your way push them aside or walk through them. Do you understand?'
'Yes, chef,' was the reply. Dave looked at me through the corner of his vision and mouthed:
'See! They're fucking mad. I love these fucking guys.'
If anyone of this group was going to get in it was Dave. We set off; the legionnaire chef walked proudly in front of us. Our arms were

splayed out wide as we marched in the style of the legion. The legionnaire marched through the traffic. Cars and vans jolted as they hit the brakes. Hooters started to sound off but the traffic stopped until the last recruit had passed through. Then the frenzied Parisians skidded off into the hectic roads of Paris. The legion's presence had been more effective than any traffic light.

We marched into the station. I felt brilliant. My nose was greeted by the smell of diesel fuel, coffee and croissant. The station was packed with commuters. Trains were coming and going as we headed for the far end of the station and a waiting train. A French voice echoed over the tannoy. I couldn't help smiling to myself. Here I was on my way to Marseilles with the legion; the stuff of dreams. We boarded the train, about ten to a cabin and settled down for a long overnight journey.

After we had settled, the cabin door opened and in walked the legionnaire who had guided us across the busy road. Like a surrogate father he took on a serious frown.

Almost whispering he said, 'Men, if you really want to get into the Legion you have to really want it. I think you should all be allowed in, but today it's different than before. Now you have to have something to give to the legion. If they tell you, you cannot join or you are no good to them tell them how much you want to get in. Tell them you really want to be a part of the best army in the world.'

I looked around the cabin. Everyone was engrossed in the legionnaire's instructions. They all wanted in and looked desperate. Looking at them I doubted they had anything to offer the Legion other than their lives. Me included.

I slept to the rhythm of the train wheels hitting the joints on the rails and awoke to the sound of the train jerking into a station. Morning was breaking. The platform we stopped at became alive with trolleys and salesmen frantically selling sandwiches, coffee, croissants and wine. They peddled their wares through the open windows of the train. The coffee smelt delicious. The train pulled off again. A short while later the cabin door opened.

'Next stop Marseilles,' said the legionnaire.

We got our stuff together. Butterflies were playing games inside my stomach. I breathed deeply easing the feeling, only to find them fluttering around again. It wasn't long before we were in a truck and winding our way through the narrow streets of Marseilles towards Aubagne.

It was an uncomfortable ride and I was glad to be stationary. I'd felt sick for the last mile or so. We were ordered out of the trucks and ushered into a building which looked like a small, cheaply-made industrial unit. It looked out of place surrounded by lush green trees and mountains.

The inside of the building smelt of boot polish. Two men were placing neat piles of kit on top of a counter. They were shouting to each other in what sounded like French as they laid out the kit. I asked one of the English speaking French recruits what they were saying. The Frenchie looked at me shrugged his shoulders, looked puzzled and said, 'It's not French, I do not know what he's saying.' I picked up a pile of kit hoping I was doing the right thing. 'Get changed,' came an order in what can only be described as heavy, deep-voiced English with a French twang. It was an accent I'd not heard before and I'd come across most in prison. We made our way out of the hut and into a gravel yard, the colour of Cotswold stone. I looked around taking in my new surroundings wondering how many people had done the same before me.

There was a large building to my left surrounded by huge concrete blocks lying at its base. They looked like seating areas. To my right a large wooden climbing frame, a long log supported at each side by wooden poles. A couple of ropes hung from the log. The air was warm. I could feel the heat of the sun pressing against my face. It was like a hot summer's day and it was still early morning. I wondered what would happen next. What was the routine? How would I cope with the language barrier? Could I make it through the checks? I felt very alert. I scanned everywhere taking in as much information as I could, trying to familiarise myself with my new surroundings.

Four of us were led into the large building which was full of three-storey, bunk beds. The room had that just polished smell mingled in with body odour and sweaty socks. I chose a bunk and placed my kit in the cupboard at the end of the bed. It wasn't long before the room was full of potential legionaries. After a short while we were taken to a room and sat inside. The room was adorned with photos and pictures of different theatres of war and old-fashioned legionnaires in wonderful uniforms. I passed a sign which read: 'The ambition to be the best'.

It struck a chord with me. I repeated the phrase a few times so I'd remember it. There was another sign, 'Legio patria nostra' which meant 'The Legion is my home'. I hoped it would be.

On the second day I was taken with a group of recruits and herded into a medical room for a check up. I watched as needles on the end of test tube type fitments were dug into veins with the delicacy of a farmer inoculating cattle. I cringed as the recipient of the needle cringed. We were ushered through like a human conveyor belt. Each male nurse I was pushed in front of asked me the same questions: name, date of birth, where I was from. Each one recorded my details and scribbled comments on to their paperwork.

I approached a tall, well built, black guy who looked like a boxer or wrestler.

'You English?' he asked.

'Yes. I'm from Loughborough near Leicester.'

'Yeah I know Loughborough, been through there a couple of times. I used to live in Lincolnshire for a while, North Sea Camp. Ever heard of it?' I opened up straight away without thinking.

'Yeah. I spent a couple of winter months there in '77.' As I spoke I realised I should have listened and not talked. Now he knew I'd been inside.

'Yeah, well I did six months no remission,' he said. 'Fucking small world. What you come here for?' he asked.

I remembered what the legionnaire said on the train. 'It's something I really want to do, a dream of mine.' I tried to sound passionate about the Legion.

'I've been in for years. You'll love it', he said. He picked up what looked like a metal tube with a sharp point on the end and said, 'Arm.'

I lifted my arm out flat and straight and winced as the needle pierced my skin and dug into a vein. It stung. I watched the tube fill with blood. Once it was full he withdrew the needle with the same care as he had dug it in, rubbed the vein and placed a lump of cotton wool over it.

I moved on, more questions, then mouth and teeth inspected. The next nurse ordered me to drop my pants. I was asked a few questions about which sexual diseases I'd had. ('None' was the answer just in case you were wondering!) We then sat in the same office block as the day before.

I studied the photos and pictures that adorned the walls. It seemed every room we went into was covered in pictures or inspirational quotes. It was obvious the Legion was very proud of its heritage. Some were campaign photos showing pictures of legionnaires in Mayote, Ghana, Djibouti, Algeria and Vietnam: some of the theatres of war that the Legion had been involved in. I sat for what seemed like hours before being led into an office where I was confronted by another legionnaire.

He shuffled the papers laid out in front of him. 'Name?'

'Skillen, chef,' I answered.

'It's okay, John. You can relax now. I just want to ask you a few questions.'

He spoke in a soft voice not unlike a Gestapo officer in one of the old war movies as I had imagined. I was waiting for them to bring in the torture equipment. It never came. Instead the officer just stared at his papers for a while then lifted his head and asked me a random question about my life.

I'd been tipped off that the Legion interrogated you by making you feel comfortable so you opened up to them. The questions were interspersed with long bouts of silence, then another question would be asked. I decided to tell him the truth. The legionnaire asked me why I wanted to join up. If I was honest the real reason I was there was because I had nowhere else to go. He asked me about my family. As I was telling him I felt sad. I was a cunt the way I'd treated my parents. He knew I'd been in prison – the medical officer gleaned that information in a second.

I was flush hot in my face. I was used to being questioned by the coppers but this was different. I wanted to be part of the Legion, to do something worthwhile, to start again. I had given him a window into my previous history. I didn't mention scrapping or drugs or all of my prison history. I didn't lie. I just skirted around the facts.

After about an hour I stood and was about to leave.

'Oh just one more thing.' He asked me a question in French and pointed to a chart on the wall.

'Fuck me, a drugs chart.' I hadn't noticed it until he pointed it out. The poster contained pictures of every street drug known to man with neat illustrations of piles of powders, pills and resins. I didn't understand exactly what he'd asked me but I had an idea. He looked at me with a suspicious eye as if trying to see inside of my head.
'Which of these drugs have you taken before?' He caught me unaware. I felt like a young kid caught skiving or smoking by his parents. Fuck it, I thought. I had taken speed before and I'd tried cannabis resin which was fucking sickening as I wasn't a smoker. Both were soft: class B drugs. I pointed to the white powder. I also pointed to the cannabis. The cannabis he seemed to ignore, but the white powder sent him ballistic. I didn't think it would be a problem. He picked up the phone and barked down it in French. Another legionnaire entered the room and I was rushed back down to the medical officer. The tall wrestler type looked pissed off.
'He says you have a drugs' problem. What have you told him you have taken? Your blood's clear. You have no traces of drugs in your system.'
'That's because I don't do drugs I've tried them a few times.'
'What have you tried?'
'Speed, blow. I had half an acid tab once'
'When you pointed to the poster you told him you had taken heroin.' I went cold.
'I've never touched the stuff, it's a fucking mind killer.' I'd fucked it. That was me out.
'Don't worry I'll explain it to him. Go back up.'
I was asked back inside the office.

The legionnaire talked to me for another hour asking more questions about my family life. He wanted to know about my brothers, my sisters, my parents, everything. He finished by asking me why I didn't join the Legion when I was eighteen. I paused, and right there-and-then I wished I had.

I filled in form after form and undertook various cleaning duties whilst waiting for the news of whether I was in or out. It was frustrating not knowing where my life was going, especially as I had decided what it was I wanted to do for the next five years. I

realised that I had for the first time in my life made a choice and followed it through. Being in the company of other nationalities and listening to some of their stories about how tough their lives had been to date, made me realise that my life wasn't as bad as some. It is true: there is always someone worse off than yourself.
That night before I could take a seat for dinner I heard my name being called out.
'John, John Skillen.' It was a voice spoken in a Loughborough accent.
'Fuck me,' I thought. I can't go anywhere without being known. It was a weird feeling hearing my name.
'John,' he called again.
'Fuck me. How are you, mate,' he asked.
'Not bad, mate. How are you? When did you join up?' I asked.
'A couple of days ago at a gendarmerie office in Marseilles. I heard you were here. The rumour's all over town.'
'News travels fast,' was all I could say. If he knew then the police would know. I hoped the romantic image of the Legion giving anonymity to new recruits was true.

When we weren't filling in forms we cleaned. One particular day a group of us were taken to an old fort in Marseilles that was being renovated into a holiday rest and recuperation centre for holidaying legionnaires. It was situated on the coastline of Marseilles with an impressive panoramic view of the sea and harbour. We spent the day cleaning floors in the various rooms that had been redecorated and took our breaks in the hot sun. During break we were shown what looked like an old wine store made of sandstone blocks. It had an arched ceiling and a cold stone bench running along one side of the room. There were no windows in the room. We were allowed in to cool off. On the wall, names were scrawled in the sandstone with dates, one from 1750, another from 1940. It reminded me of a prison cell. The coldness of the room chilled my bones and made me feel uneasy.

A couple of days later we were bundled into a line of trucks unaware of our destination.
The trucks drove through the beautiful Provence countryside, passing fields of bright yellow sunflowers and seas of purple

lavender. There was a harvest smell in the air and the intermittent sound of cicadas clicking their heels together blended with the humdrum sound of the truck. It was exciting not knowing where I was going.

We arrived at Domain Captain Danjou: the home for veterans and injured legionnaires. Reality struck home. The legionnaires here were different to the others I'd seen. I'd thought of heroes dying for the képi, but here the wounded, limbless, scarred and disfigured gave me the true story of warfare. Soldiers die. Some live on, mentally scarred or with horrific injuries. What I witnessed before me were true heroes, not actors on a wide screen but real people who had endured the hardship and horror of battle and survived. I felt sad for the first time since I'd left home. This was no army of conscripts or young men looking for a skill to use when they rejoined Civvy Street These were warriors. I remembered a phrase I'd heard an old soldier once say. 'I joined the army when they needed me not when they fed me.'

I noticed a couple of legionnaires sitting in wheelchairs. They were smiling and laughing and looking out over the rolling hills and fields of Provence. I paused for a moment. They were both amputees. I thought about my own life. I was a waste of my own space. A non-achiever. I so much wanted to be accepted by the Legion so I could show my worth, even if it meant losing a limb or dying in the process.

LEGION PISS-HEAD

New recruits were arriving every day filling the beds recently vacated. Every time I got called to the office I expected to be kicked out. I'd set my heart on joining the Legion even though I had witnessed some strange goings on. We were marching around the camp en route to the salle de manger, when we were stopped at the roadside and made to wait while the officer in charge went into a nearby building. A legionnaire appeared at the side of us looking very angry and paralytic drunk. He was cursing and shouting at the lines of recruits in a language I didn't understand. The officer returned and the uttered some words to the legionnaire and he waddled off, singing in a deep voice. His behaviour towards the recruits was not what I expected from the one of the world's finest soldiers. We marched on.

One evening after dinner a drunken legionnaire approached our table shouting. I understood more by his body language than the verbal. The legionnaire got angrier when we didn't respond to his rhetoric. He yanked one of the recruits out of his chair and headed toward the kitchen servery, He then beckoned the rest of the table to follow him. The guy was incredibly angry and I couldn't understand why he was bordering on violence. I watched him carefully; if he was going to go for it I would get in first. I wanted in the Legion but not at the cost of this twat taking the piss.

He moved forward and cornered me. I felt anger begin to rise. Frustration set in. One step closer and I would whack him with a right hook, which was hanging at my side and only a split second from his chin. The legionnaire switched his attention to another recruit next to me: a tall, swarthy, French guy. He pulled him into the kitchen. I picked up the phrase which I understood, 'Fais la vaisselle.' (Wash up!)

He pushed me towards two huge sinks full of greasy, metal pots. I put my hands into the freezing water. I tried to explain using broken French and English that the water was too cold to wash the pots and there was no washing up liquid. He got the message and after his next outburst, I got the message too. 'Fucking clean them in cold water.' He sounded like Schwarzenegger and acted like the angry chef, Gordon Ramsay; he threw a saucepan across the length of the kitchen which clattered on the tiled floor and then returned to his bottle.

I quickly set about the task. It took me about an hour to clean them. My hands were raw and crinkled. The rest of the lads scrubbed and cleaned until the kitchen was spotless. At the end of the job the big legionnaire reappeared. He smiled, then belly laughing he passed around small bottles of French beer.

'Drink,' he said. The bottles were dripping with condensation and freezing cold. We were under the impression we were not allowed to drink but he insisted that we drank the beer. It tasted good and the legionnaire seemed to praise our efforts. This type of outburst was common. It was hard to know whether they were serious or not. Violence never seemed far away. After all these were tough men. But it never usually came to blows, just a few choice words and angry stares.

Dave, the tank regiment guy and me were the only two left out of the original 30 that arrived from Paris. I'd seen at least 400 men come and go in a matter of days. I never knew whether they were binned or left of their own accord. One day they were there, the next they were gone. It was no good trying to get friendly with anyone.

After breakfast I was summoned to the office with a group of ten others. I was given a number and was photographed holding it across my chest like a mug-shot. At this point I felt I might be in. My gut feeling told me different.

One day we were marched onto the parade ground. I stood in silence and watched in awe as legionaries marched in immaculate uniforms wearing the white képi. Some wore beards and the full regalia of the Legion. It was a fascinating sight; at one end of the parade ground was the monument 'aux morts' which was brought from the Legion's former HQ at Sidi-bel-abbi and rebuilt at Aubagne. It is a bronze globe of the world flanked by four bronze legionnaires. I felt very proud to stand on parade with the most famous army in the world. We were marched off shortly after. The ceremony carried on. I never got to know exactly what the parade was for. I went to bed that night wondering what it would be like to be a fully-fledged legionnaire.

I looked forward to Castlenaudry, the next phase of joining the Legion. I'd heard some horror stories about the infamous training camp, such as the legionnaire who broke his leg on an assault course and was made to carry on. There were stories about recruits being shot whilst training. It should have put me off but it didn't.

NON, JE NE REGRETTE RIEN

"I have no regrets."
Edith Piaf

The following morning I was awoken earlier than usual by a legionnaire I hadn't met before and told to stay silent. I joined a puzzled looking group of recruits who were lined up in the same hut that we'd arrived in. I was ordered to hand in my kit in exchange for my civvies. I was asked to sign a sheet of paper and was told that I was being released from my five-year contract with the Legion. Binned! I was handed an envelope containing the wages I had earned whilst I was there, and given a rail warrant ticket back to Paris.

I felt like someone had stuck a knife in me and ripped out my insides. I felt unwanted and lonely. This was the lowest I had ever felt in my life. If the Legion wouldn't take me in I must be pretty damn worthless. I got no reason given as to why I was binned. I was well and truly pissed off.

An hour later at Marseilles train station I felt my mind rolling and rolling like a chess player trying to figure out his next move. I looked around at the other guys. They had that 'binned' look about them too. I knew how they felt. They needed a leader. They needed hope for a future. It came in the guise of a stocky Peruvian who was always bragging about his cocaine dealings. He was spouting off about joining the Spanish Legion.

I listened to the Peruvian guy who had the former recruits mesmerised with his talk of forming a drugs cartel.
'If we don't get into the Spanish Legion, we'll rob a few places. I know some banks that will be easy to rob. With some money and my contacts we'll be able to buy coke.'
He bragged about his contacts and the price he could get a kilo of coke for. I'd had enough of the mini gangster and his ramblings!
The Legion rejects were so mesmerised I was able to slip into the hustle and bustle of Marseilles train station un-noticed.

With my rail ticket held firmly in my hand I began to look for the train back to Paris. As I walked to the platform the gutted feeling returned when a legionnaire in full uniform passed me. He looked cool as fuck. As I admired the uniform of the legionnaire, I was interrupted by the approach of a smart looking gentleman sporting a goatee beard. He looked around sixty.
'Are you English?' he spoke with a South African accent.
'Yes,' I replied. I was taken aback by his cool approach.
'We're looking for a few guys who might be interested in some work in South Africa.'
'What type of work?'
He looked around nervously. 'Looking after the interests of a few farmers there. Plenty of work for white guys like you.'
I assumed he thought I was a legionnaire. I declined his offer and walked away. I'd had enough of fantasy. For me it was back to reality. Back to real life. Time to stop running away. As I boarded my train a man tugged my jacket.
'Fucking wankers, the Legion. They fucking binned us and let a load of fucking idiots in.'
He was an angry fucker and I took an instant dislike to him, mainly because of the way he insulted the Legion.

There is a famous song adopted by the Legion sung by Edith Piaf who was known as 'The Little Sparrow'. The song is entitled, 'Je Ne Regrette a Rien' (I have no regrets). I certainly didn't. I was thankful that I had somewhere to go. The Legion may not have wanted my services, but they fed and clothed me for one month and paid me for the privilege. My respect for the Legion remained intact. I took one last look out into the train station and uttered 'bon voyage' under my breath.
'Here have a swig of this,' the angry fucker said. He pulled a bottle of whisky from his bag and insisted I had a swig. I pulled the bottle to my lips and pretended to drink to keep him quiet. He finished the whisky then demanded he buy me a drink.
We sat in the train bar and beer after beer was followed by chasers. I matched him drink for drink, but what he didn't realise was that every chaser I took from him I ditched in a nearby bin then pretended to gulp it down. He was well and truly pissed. I noticed he had a few quid in his wallet which was dwindling fast. I was

short of my fare back to England; another few quid would come in handy. Mr Angry had drunk enough.

'Come on. Let's go,' I said. We made our way into a carriage and it wasn't long before he was asleep with his coat on the seat beside him. I took out the cash he hadn't spent. I figured I was doing him a favour keeping him sober. He was drinking himself into an early grave.

I needed the cash so he was doing me a favour helping me get back to England. I threw his coat and mine out of the train window so when he awoke he would believe we were both robbed while we slept. I couldn't have left as when he awoke he would have come looking for me and I hadn't a clue how long a journey we had left. I decided to stay put and bluff it out. I fell asleep.

I was suddenly awoken by a very angry push.

'My coat. Where's my fucking coat?' His face was red with rage.

I shot up out of my seat and joined in the protest.

'Fuck. Mine's gone too.' He hadn't got a clue that I'd taken his money.

'Bastards,' he shouted at the top of his voice. I thought he would put it down to experience, have a moan and that would be the end of it. Not this guy. He started ranting on about killing whoever had taken it. He looked serious.

'Come on. Let's go,' he said. I followed behind him as he pulled every carriage door open, shouting abuse at whoever was in there.

'Where's my fucking coat, you thieving French bastards?'

I decided to sit down and disassociate myself from him. I knew nothing of this guy; I hadn't seen him in Aubagne. All I can imagine was that he joined the Legion and was binned the same day. The train pulled into a station. The piss-head had decided to sit down and every minute or so would scream out.

'French bastards.'

He was so pissed he hadn't noticed me sitting down. I slumped lower into my seat hoping he'd move further up the train. I noticed the train guard talking to two armed officers on the platform with serious looks on their faces. Just as the piss-head screamed his abuse at the French commuters they boarded. The guards approached the piss-head and barked out orders. The piss-head threw his hands in the air and told them to fuck off. He began shouting into the face of a female passenger his face exploding with rage. One officer shouted a French phrase and drew his weapon. Mr Angry froze. The other officer moved in and cuffed him.

'They've got my fucking coat,' he protested as they led him away. I stayed low in my seat until the train moved off. I was glad he was gone; having him around was like an irritating rash that continually itched and I had my own problems. Wherever he was going I figured he wouldn't need any cash. My conscience was clear.

I made my way across Paris and headed for Dieppe then boarded the ferry back to England. On the ferry back I gave myself a mental debrief. I tried to come to terms with why I had been binned from the Legion. The truth was I had nothing to offer. I expected them to take me in, feed me, train me and give me a new life. In return I would give them my life. I was nothing to them, nothing to myself. I had a shit existence. I blamed everybody but myself for my problems instead of standing my ground and dealing with them like a man. There were many legionnaires in there for reasons only they can tell you about. I realised I was trying to join the Legion for the wrong reasons and for me it was not to be. I pushed the memories to the back of my mind to be filed away.

I'd learnt one valuable lesson from my experience and that is you can run as far as you like but you can't run away from yourself. Far better to face your problems head on and cure them. I decided there and then that I would stop running and get my life in some kind of order. In the short time I was in the company of the Legion, they had inspired me to carry on with my life and try and make some sense of it! For that I thank them graciously. I went into the toilets of the ferry and took a long, hard stare in the mirror. For the first time in ages I felt proud of myself.

The ferry docked in England. I made way home via the train using the last of the money I had. I got off the train at Loughborough Station tired, hungry and paranoid, but glad to be home. I didn't know what I was going to do next. I'd have to sleep on it. I felt as low as a snake's arse. I still had my self-respect even though I was at the end of the snake. In my mind's eye I could see a ladder in the distance, a ladder I hoped I could reach and climb my way out of this miserable existence.

LONDON BOUND

I spent the night back in my old room. The family were excited by the story I told of my trip to the Legion.
'Their loss,' my mum said.
I had to smile to myself – mums are great and no matter how bad things were my mum always remained upbeat and positive. She would always pick me up and spur me on.

I couldn't stay in Loughborough for long because the police were looking for me and it wouldn't be long before they found out I was back in town. I had to lie low for a while to decide my future. A friend, Seamus McConnell, was a labourer doing some contract work in London. He couldn't offer me any work but he could offer me a place to stay for a while.

The digs were situated in the Queens Road – a rundown area of Peckham. The lady who ran the digs was an albino with a milky white complexion and the features of a Jamaican. She was a kind and warm person who made me feel very welcome. Because of my short hair she nicknamed me soldier boy. I felt relaxed In London even though I had no work or money. I was unknown around here so didn't have to keep looking over my shoulder for the Old Bill. I couldn't sign on the dole (the police would have been onto me immediately). I tried to find some casual work but I was too busy in my mind trying to suss out what to do next. As the days passed me by I got continually paranoid and expected a knock on the door. I began to feel like I was already back in prison. I might as well have been; I couldn't work. I had no money. In fact, I would be better off in prison. I felt like a coward.
I should have done the thing that my father bought me up to do: the manly thing. He always used to say, 'Son, if you've made a mistake and done something wrong be man enough to admit it and take the consequences like a man.' Easier said than done when you're facing years in prison but my train of thought was heading that way. I was no better than the dropouts and tramps living under the train bridges of this fair city: at least they had the bollocks to be something if only a tramp.

One weekend the Loughborough lads came to London to celebrate one of the lads' birthdays. I arranged to meet them in Covent Garden. I was looking forward to seeing the lads for the craic, in particular, my old training partner Ian 'Spider' Reeves. We had a great night out and I forgot about my predicament. Spider decided to miss the coach back and stay on in London for another night at the digs. We drank our way back via the Old Kent Road, dropping into pub after pub. We finished the night's piss up in a real old traditional pub complete with a Chas and Dave sound-alike duo playing all the classic, foot-tapping, cockney songs. It was hard to take them seriously. The night nearly erupted into a fight. Spider fell asleep at the bar and when he awoke he was like a bear with a sore head. He fell out of the pub and into a gang of London punk rockers. Spider erupted and they backed off. I gestured with my open palms, 'It's all right, lads. He's pissed,' as if they hadn't noticed! The punks understood a good night out and laughed it off. I walked Spider away and we made our way back to the digs.

We awoke the next morning hung over. Spider had to go back to Loughborough for work the next day. I'd slept on my thoughts of the day before. Seeing the lads free, listening to their talk of work and investing in this and that, I'd had enough of running. I'd been in London for too long. The six weeks felt like three months and the buildings felt like they were closing in on me. I decided to accompany Spider back to Loughborough so we caught the last tube out of London heading north. On my return there was only one thing left to do: hand myself in to the police. I spent a few weeks keeping a low profile. I didn't want to be inside for Christmas (I'd be doing a few of those anyway) so I bided my time. I decided to stay on the run and hand myself in on New Year's Day after spending Christmas with my family and friends.
On my last night of freedom the lads decided to go out in fancy dress. Four of them decided to dress as SAS troopers. I dressed the same and was able to walk the streets without the Old Bill knowing who I was. At one point a police officer bid me a Happy New Year.
I stayed sober knowing I was giving myself in. I wasn't a Ronnie Biggs. I was a violent thug and at times I felt as desperate as he must have. I got a glimpse into the uncomfortable world of the

criminal on the run and hated it. After spending New Year's Day with my family I prepared my clothes. Clothes that hopefully would look cool and still be in fashion on my release.

BACK TO THE BIG HOUSE

I contacted my solicitor and arranged to meet him. After a short chat he drove me to the police station. It was a crisp January morning and the low winter sun was shining; a welcome change to the dark clouds that had hovered over my head for the last few weeks. The frost on the cars remained even though they were in full sun. I took a deep breath and breathed out slow. The air smelt frosty fresh. I knew that would be changing very soon.
I looked behind me then turned and walked into the police station, knowing full well I would be locked up within the next ten minutes.
My solicitor approached the desk. 'I'm here with John Skillen. You have a warrant out for his arrest. He's here to hand himself in to your custody on his own free will. I'm here to represent him.'
The copper paused for a moment looking like he didn't quite know what to do.
'Right,' he said then he picked up the phone.
Within seconds two police officers arrived in the foyer. One took out his handcuffs and said, 'John Skillen, I'm arresting you for being in breach of a crown court warrant.' But before the copper could carry out his arrest my solicitor spoke to a CID officer who had joined us.
'I don't think there's any need for that, do you? Mr Skillen has handed himself in of his own free will. He's not likely to run away now is he? Shall we go through?'
My solicitor gestured to the door leading to the charge desk and cells. One of the coppers looked embarrassed. I loved the way solicitors could put the coppers in their place. He was a good solicitor and knew his job well. Even though I was facing certain incarceration I felt free: no more running and ducking in and out of doorways. The world I was carrying around next to the chip on my shoulder had suddenly been lifted off. A smile appeared on my face. It was the second time in my life that I had been responsible for my own destiny. I realised that I was in charge of my own life and I could change it, me and me alone.
At Welford Road Prison I went through the usual booking in procedure that was required at one of Her Majesty's finest hotels.

The officer accompanying me to my cell had a serious look upon his face. The cell smelt strongly of body odour. The walls and lights were dim. Inside was the usual double bunk and a single. The con lying on the top bunk gave the screw a death stare, then repeated the same look toward me.

I took the single bed and lay at the far end so I could keep my eye on my new cellmate who appeared to have a major social problem. The big Rasta was huddled up inside his blanket. I'd met guys like him before. His type did hard time. They don't interact with anyone else. They just try to sleep away their bird. This particular guy was a poet of sorts; he lay and mumbled repetitive phrases. It was as if he was if trying to put himself into a trance. He made no attempt to speak to me which was unusual, but then I wasn't in the mood for talk.

The pungent, musty smell of the Rasta's body odour and the stench of the piss pot thickened the air. It was going to be a warm, muggy night. One night alone in a cell with this poetic lunatic would be a sentence in itself. I'd tried to start a conversation but to no avail – the Rasta just blanked me. I couldn't sleep at all that night; I couldn't stand the Rasta's constant humming, and he hummed in more ways than one. I'd put in for a cell change first thing in the morning.

MOVING CELL

I eventually fell asleep and then awoke to the sound of repetitive riffs coming from the vocal chords of my new cell mate. It reminded me to arrange a move immediately after breakfast.

After slop-out I nipped off to breakfast. Prison is easy when you know the routines.
It's about knowing how to conduct yourself in front of the screws and more importantly the other cons. Take no shit from either!

Breakfast is the worst meal you'll get in prison. The others are just about bearable but breakfast is shit and you have to eat something. I joined the queue which resembled the one in the dole office. The only difference was we all wore the same washed-out, brown jeans, stripy blue shirts. The lack of fresh air, sunshine and the continual, slow release adrenalin caused by the fear of the unknown gave most cons a pale, sickly looking complexion.

I looked around taking in my surroundings. Nothing had changed since the last time I'd been here. I spotted a few familiar faces. I couldn't believe I was back in this Victorian shit-hole, shuffling along with coughing and spluttering, fag-smoking lines of social dropouts. But then again I suppose I was one of them!
I picked up a tray and approached the serving hatch. Inside, looking resplendent in their white uniforms were six of the meanest looking cons. Each hovered over a large cooking tray or pot. They had that sly 'come and get it' look on their faces. They toyed with the food, stirring and lifting it. The aromas drifted up into the air tempting me toward the first delicacy: scrambled egg.

The spoon clanged on my tray several times as the con serving me tried to release the solidified egg mix. Each time the spoon hit the tray I went to move on only to be held back by the hand of the con and the spoon hitting the tray repeatedly. The egg which was made from dried egg powder, was topped with several anaemic baked beans inside a watery, orange colour sauce the likes of which wouldn't make it through Heinz quality control. I moved on to the next con: a skinny looking chap with a blue spot tattooed on his cheekbone (the sign of an ex-borstal boy, the tattoo known as the borstal spot).

A tiny roll of streaky bacon with more streak than bacon was placed on my tray followed by a slice of fried bread which was about the third of a normal sized slice of bread and was deep fried retaining most of the grease it was cooked in. I stayed still and pushed my tray out further requesting another roll of bacon (the one on my tray measured one inch by one inch,) I liked my bacon. The kid looked left then right and plonked two more rolls on my tray. I winked at him: typical borstal boy – anything to fuck off the system. If he'd have been caught he would have been kicked out of the kitchen. So if I got caught I would say I'd nicked them. I picked up the fried bread and hid the bacon from view. I couldn't help thinking whether or not the cons rolled the bacon themselves or did they come pre-rolled? I was fixated by the delicious smell of the bacon, even Her Majesty's finest chefs couldn't fuck up its smell.

I moved on to the most talked about food in prison history – the infamous porridge. I moved toward the con making eye contact, a wry smile cut from his lips. He stirred the porridge in a figure of eight. I held my tray still staring into the eyes of the con. He stared back like a boxer about to start the first round and carefully placed the ladle of porridge on to my tray. When he lifted the ladle a second time, I caught his gaze and stared hard almost growling, daring him to put it on my tray. One ladle was more than enough for me.

'I'll have it,' a voice said from behind.

I moved on to the toast and picked up a couple of pieces. A spoon of marmalade was bashed onto my tray and I lay the toast across it. I walked off.

'You should always eat your porridge, mate,' the con behind me said. I turned around to face a short, dumpy con that had just had my ladle of porridge.

'You what?'

'You should always eat your porridge.'

'Oh yeah, why's that?'

'Well there's an old saying, you know.'

'Is there?' I said trying not to get too involved as you never know who you're mixing with on remand. He could be a nonce, a granny basher, or a child molester: people that nobody mixed with. I walked on. The con shuffled along beside me trying to keep up. He leaned against my shoulder almost whispering as if he was about to impart some great secret that if released could topple governments. I stopped outside my cell and listened to his wisdom.
'If you don't eat your porridge especially on your last day you will come back to finish it.' He gave me a sinister look then smiled and scurried off. I looked down at the gooey mess on my tray and smiled.

I remember the first time I'd tried prison porridge in Welford Road on the YP wing awaiting allocation to borstal. I picked up my plastic spoon and got stuck in expecting it to taste like Scots Porridge Oats, the brand I used to have as a kid sprinkled with milk and sugar. This version tasted like water with too much salt added. The sour gooey taste made me heave and I was almost sick on my tray. But when you're hungry enough you'll eat anything and I soon got used to it.

I got stuck into my tray of breakfast eating every oat of porridge, then started on the bacon. My humming cell mate (who hummed in more ways than one) looked at me in disgust.
'The pig is a dirty animal,' he said.
Fuck me. It talks, I thought. Then I squashed the bacon between the leathery toast and ate. After breakfast I requested a move to a different cell; if I stayed in the same one any longer me and the Rasta would be fighting. I needed to talk to someone to get my mind off the court case. The Rasta was well known to the screws, I wasn't the first to request a move. To my relief, I was allocated a different cell. This cell was cleaner, brighter, smelt of disinfectant and most importantly, smelly con free. A cell to myself. Luxury.

Just after tea, a pale frightened looking man walked in. He wouldn't look at me. As the door locked into place he glanced up at me. His sad expression reminded me of a lost dog.
'That's it, mate. That won't be open again until morning,' I said.

He fell back onto his bed, let out a sigh and pulled his top blanket over his head.

It was obvious he was a first timer. Guys who are weak minded can easily become suicidal. I'd felt heavy bouts of depression myself in the past few months and I can understand how they feel. Having a strong character led me away from suicidal tendencies. There was a clank of keys and the door unlocked; the man sat bolt upright in bed and looked at me as if to say, 'You said they weren't going to open that door again.' I smiled

'Late arrival,' I said. A tall skinny guy appeared in the doorway and immediately introduced himself.

'I've never been to prison before.'

'There's a first time for everything, mate,' I said. The first timer butted in.

'It's my first time inside too,' he said. Two first timers that's all I needed. The screws had given this one a bit of thought.

Well at least we'd have something to talk about. The cell door shut and the first con imparted the knowledge I'd given him earlier to his newest cell mate, word for word.

'That's it, mate. They won't open that again until morning.'

I lay back on my bunk and smiled. He'll be all right, I thought: quick learner.

I lay on my bunk listening to them talking about their families, their jobs and their lives, outside of the four walls that incarcerated us. I felt sad and helped them change the course of the conversation.

'What did you think of the one-inch bath, lads?' I asked.

That got them onto a less painful subject. I'd only been in for a couple of days and already I'd had enough. The eerie silence broken by prison keys clanking in the distance, cries, moans and abusive shouts echoed across the landings and filtered through the cell door.

To think I might have to spend the next five years or more listening to it made my skin creep and chilled my spine. I rolled over on to my side and snuggled up to my pillow as if it was a huge, cuddly toy.

'No shitting in the piss pots, lads,' I said. I pulled the itchy grey blanket over my head and drifted off to sleep.

The days passed by, the court date was now closing fast. I needed to get my head sorted out and organise my defence. I had to make sure what I was going to say was clear in my mind. I'd pleaded not guilty to the charge of wounding with intent as I hadn't used a glass on Regan. There was just a chance I might get a favourable result. Regan had a fiery temper. If I could just get him to lose it in court who knows! I felt my stomach spin over at the thought of standing in the dock. I felt queasy.

Whilst playing darts with one of my cell mates I overheard a guy being given advice.
'You want to go and see "The Barrister", mate. He'll tell you how to behave in court. Got my mate off easy he did.' It was the little guy who gave me advice about eating my porridge.
'The barrister! Who's the barrister?' I asked. Was this some new sort of prison perk I hadn't heard about, probably supplied by the prison service to help you get a result? The con told me all he knew about the man nicknamed The Barrister. He was a former accountant by trade, imprisoned on remand, accused of ripping off his clients and fucking off to Spain with all their well-earned dough.
He'd set himself and his family up in Spain with a new life never having to work again. Sounded good to me – I was impressed. They called him The Barrister because (according to him) he had studied law and his cell was full of law books. He was defending himself in court which was also impressive. He was tall and tanned with greying hair, very confident and articulate. He actually sounded like an army officer when he spoke.
'Now, John, tell me about your case. Did you actually do it?' he said. I paused. Do I tell him or not? He could be a prison spy planted to find out who was guilty. I let go of my paranoid thoughts and decided to tell him.
'Well yes and no.'
'Yes and no. Well you either did it or you didn't. Which one?'
I explained to him in detail about the fight with Jimmy Regan.
'You are pleading "not guilty" aren't you?'
'Yes.'
'Then stick with it. From what you've told me about his character he needs locking up, not you. The charge you're facing carries a

high maximum sentence. I will probably get three years for embezzling hundreds of thousands of pounds of my clients' money. I have a new life in Spain to go out to. I spent 15 years living it up. I've made fortunes using that stolen money. With good behaviour and the time I've spent on remand, I'll be out in less than a year then it's back to Spain and a life of luxury. You have a fight with a bouncer; a bully to boot, and you could get five years minimum.'

I grinned. I looked at him and thought, you wind-up cunt!

'What you have to do, John, is show the court that you're innocent. It doesn't matter what the judge thinks. It's the jury you have to convince and juries don't like bouncers. Most people growing up have had some sort of run in with them or heard some sort of horror story. You have to get the jury to believe that you are innocent.'

I listened very carefully to what the he was saying. It also gave me hope – something I was lacking. He continued.

'When you stand in the dock I want you to feel innocent. This will be easy for you as you didn't use a weapon. So you are halfway there, John. You have to become like an actor playing the role of the innocent man. When you speak, speak clearly and confidently. Don't mumble. Do not lose your temper. If you do, that will be it. When you're giving evidence make yourself appear small in the dock. Don't slouch. Be humble not cocky and remember, you are innocent until proven guilty.'

I felt excited and confident for the first time. The Barrister was a big help. I had thought of pleading guilty to grievous bodily harm to get a lower sentence, but not the wounding. Now I thought I might be able to win the verdict. The Barrister continued.

'You see, John, you have to learn to use the law to your own advantage. After all, it's our law, the law of the land written for us to protect us. You have to work within the confines of the law.' I turned to leave the cell.

'John.'

'Yes?'

'Would you be so kind as to close the door on your way out?'

I had to smile. This guy was so cool. He didn't give a damn about the system because he knew how to play it. His phrase 'work within the confines of the law' was one I would remember.

PROMISE TO GOD

"God helps those who help themselves"
Benjamin Franklin

It was a bright sunny morning on the outside. I could see the blue of the sky through the cell window highlighted by the gloom within. A spider had spun a web across the top corner of the ceiling. The spider was laying in wait for a fly to enter its trap. It seemed quite content to sit there and wait for its prey. Strange considering I wanted to leave this prison and couldn't, the spider had chosen to stay. His prey wouldn't have that choice. Like me, he'd soon be trapped.

I'd heard about astral travelling or out of body experiences from the hippies that frequented Devil's Kitchen. I put it down to psychedelic hippie bollocks but what the hell! I didn't have anything else to do. I closed my eyes and visualised myself walking out of my open cell door, down the staircase into the yard, past the prison guards and through the main gates. It actually felt real. I got excited. I was free. Nobody tried to stop me. I started to run getting faster and faster. I ran all of the way home, upstairs into my bed and drifted off to sleep.

Reality hit home like a slap in the face. I awoke once again to the dreariness of the cell. The spider had gone. All that was left was an empty web. Well so much for astral travelling, but hey I was desperate.

I dressed in my itchy black trousers, pastel cotton shirt, grey jumper and patent leather-look-alike paper shoes (standard prison issue), and made my way down to the prison chapel. Most cons will do anything to get out of their cells, even going to church (somewhere they probably never went on the outside). For me the chapel was a good place to think, a place to be alone that didn't resemble a prison. I began to feel depressed and in my depressed state all I could see was me doing a long stretch, anything from five to seven years depending on who the judge was. If I was found guilty I'd get a sentence for the wounding and a sentence for failing to surrender to a crown court warrant. I was shitting it. I buried my head in my hands and prayed like I did as a child.

Our Father who art in heaven
Hallowed be thy name
Thy kingdom come, Thy will be done on earth as it is in heaven
Give us this day our daily bread and
Forgive us our trespasses
As we forgive those who trespass against us
Lead us not into temptation but deliver us from evil…
Amen.

A strange feeling I'd not felt before eased its way into my stomach. I felt sick. I wanted to cry. I fought back against the pain in my throat. I felt my eyes well up. I couldn't take it anymore. It was like I'd finally given up on myself. I was fucked.
I felt a surge of anger. Within seconds of walking into the chapel I had become an emotional wreck. I was breaking down. I was squeezing my hands so tightly together they were white. My head pounded. I prayed harder covering my face so it couldn't be seen.

Hail Mary full of grace the Lord is with you
Blessed is the fruit of thy womb Jesus
Holy Mary mother of God pray for us sinners
Now and at the hour of our death
Amen.

I took comfort from the prayers and I spoke quietly to myself.
'Lord, I know I've not been the best of lads but I need a chance, Lord. If you give me one chance I'll try my best to lead a good life. I can't take any more of this life. Please, Lord, give me a chance.'
I left the chapel with my head bowed. I walked back to my cell thoughts racing through my mind. I tried to bring myself round, but the lump in my throat would not go away. It felt like a noose around my neck.
Being in the church in the peace and quiet without distraction made me realise how unhappy I really was with my life. I'd stopped running physically, but mentally I was still on the run. I had to stop running and accept the sentence whatever it was. After the Legion had binned me I had figured it out: you can't run away from yourself. The Lord helps the helpless, but he can only help

you if you begin to apply good morals and good work ethics into your life.

I also realised this was my life and I could change it. All I had to do was pay my dues, get a clean slate and start over. I decided to accept my fate. I thought of the worst case scenario and accepted it. If I get seven years I'll be out in four. I'll get out and I'll lead a good life and change my ways of violence. I accepted defeat like the Japanese samurai of old did before they went into battle. Now nothing could stand in my way. Sometimes life's a real bitch. You feel alone but the truth is you're never alone, even if you're not a religious person. You can always pray to the great creator, ask for help then take action toward what it is you want. It's true what they say, 'prayer is food for the soul'.

THE CASE

As I walked up the steps leading to the dock I wondered how many had walked these steps before me. I wondered how many were guilty and how many had got away with it: cold-blooded murderers, rapists, thieves, terrorists. I didn't consider myself a criminal in the true sense of the word. I had a scrap with a Neanderthal that wanted to rearrange my facial identity. I hadn't mugged some old lady or raped or robbed. It was just a fight. But in the eyes of the law I was guilty until proven innocent.

Those same angry feelings welled up inside me and began to rise again. I realised that was part of my downfall – the inability to control my anger. I had to control those feelings.

I couldn't let the anger show through. I had to sit and stay calm. I breathed deeply through my nose and let it out slowly calming the adrenal release. I walked into the courtroom and was ordered to sit down. I was grateful that my jelly legs could rest. The jury were to my left, the witness box to my right. The judge out in front had full view of the courtroom. I heard the familiar phrase.

'All stand.'

The judge entered the courtroom. He took his seat, shuffled some papers then peered at me taking a long, hard look over the rims of his half-moon spectacles. His name was Judge Jowett and he had a far bigger reputation amongst criminals than I did. He was known for his harsh sentencing. This guy had the power to send me away for a very long time. I could hear the voice of the con nicknamed The Barrister in my head.

'Try and feel innocent, John.' I did my best. It was made easier for me because although I had battered Regan I did it fair and square, me and him, and no weapons other than those attached to my body. I was summoned to the box, took the oath and was questioned by my solicitor. I felt comfortable and relaxed as I answered his questions looking at the jury each time I spoke. My solicitor sat down and the prosecution brief stood up. I felt the adrenalin playing with my insides. I stayed calm and breathed shallow. The cross examination came next.

I wasn't surprised by the tactics of the prosecuting barrister. It was usual in these cases for them to try and make you lose your temper, to show to the jury how aggressive you could become if buttons were pressed. He went through the 'make him lose his temper' routine by making false accusations at me and then trying to get me to argue with him. I stayed calm. In my mind it was spring flowers and sunny days. The adrenalin pumped up the beat of my heart. I felt flushed and hot faced. I avoided direct eye contact with the prosecutor, looking instead at the jury. I didn't want the tunnel vision I would get if I focused on the prosecution barrister – it would have triggered fight mode and I would become confrontational, which would be disastrous for me.

I took my time answering the questions. I didn't rush and relaxed my posture before I answered. Occasionally I feigned deafness giving me time to think about my answer. This had the effect of frustrating the barrister and making him appear flustered and amateurish.

When the barrister said 'no more questions' I felt a smile cut from the corners of my mouth. I dipped my head and hid it from the jury. For the first time in my life I had held that temper with success. I'd kept my cool where previously I would have lost it.

As soon as Regan was called to the stand he eyeballed me. It was the first time I'd seen him since we'd fought. I wanted to stare back at him. I wanted to let him know that I didn't give a toss about him. I wanted to shout 'Any fucking time you like, fat-boy'. Instead I showed no emotion. I was playing a game of bluff and the stakes were high. Instead of returning the gaze, I looked to the jury to see their reaction. I kept my hands in the prayer position to give the impression of a peaceful man.

Where the prosecution had failed, my barrister succeeded.

'I put it to you, Mr Regan, that you have lied in your accusations against Mr Skillen, and that you have lied in your statement to the police that Mr Skillen attacked you with a glass. Is that not true?'

'No it's not. He attacked me with a glass. He couldn't beat me otherwise.'

'Calm down, Mr Regan.'

'I am calm.'

My solicitor on hearing Regan's remark turned to the jury and raised his eyebrows.

'How heavy are you, Mr Regan, seventeen stone? Nineteen? Twenty?'

'I'm not sure.'
'You will admit that you are a big, heavy chap?'
'Yeah that's right.'
'And you have an impressive physique?'
'Yeah, I work hard for a living.'
'Besides your day job, Mr Regan, what other work have you undertaken?'
'What do you mean? I've done all sorts.'
'You are also a nightclub bouncer. Is that right, Mr Regan? As my brief said these words he looked toward the jury and made a facial expression as if to say, now you know who you are dealing with.
'Yeah, that's right.' Regan's attitude came over like that of a cocky teenager talking back to a teacher.
'How heavy is Mr Skillen, Mr Regan?'
'I dunno.' He looked across at me as if trying to gauge my weight. This time my gaze caught his. I felt the temperature rise but it quickly cooled off when I managed to look through him rather than at him.
'Well I can tell you he weighs eleven stone six pounds. That is considerably lighter than you. Correct, Mr Regan, is it not?'
The barrister paused and looked at the jury emphasising the fact to them.
'Mr Regan, I find it very hard to believe that an eleven stone man could defeat a 20 stone man with your obvious experience in dealing with violence.' Jimmy Regan took the bait and sealed his demise.
'That's right. He couldn't.'
'Couldn't what, Mr Regan? Couldn't beat you – is that what you're saying to the court? That an eleven stone man couldn't beat you in a fight?'
Regan looked confused like he'd just figured out he'd fucked up. He shouted out.
'He used a glass! He used a glass!' Rage turned his face red. His true personality was exposed. My barrister turned once again to the jury, taking his body to one side so that the jury got a full view of Regan losing it. This time he looked as if he was saying, 'See? The guy's a fucking animal.'
'I put it to you, Mr Regan, that you have lied to the police and have lied to this court.'

'I'm not lying.'

'Calm down, Mr Regan, and answer the questions I put to you.' The brief looked toward the judge. I shook my head from side to side and pulled my lips tight back to stop myself from smiling. 'I put it to you, Mr Regan, that you attacked Mr Skillen and that he acted in his own defence and that your injuries were caused by your own stupid, aggressive behaviour.'

Regan went ballistic. 'I'm not stupid. He couldn't beat me.' The judge ordered Regan to calm down or he would be held in contempt of court. Regan still hadn't realised that every time he said I couldn't beat him he was convincing the jury of just that.

On the second day I produced an unexpected witness in the form of Rob Brent. I'd known Rob for years. He was always in and out of prison. He had worked at Sammy's nightclub as a DJ. I'd talked him through what had happened and he agreed to be a witness.

Rob was dressed in civvies and stood proudly in the box looking like he did when he performed his set in the DJ booth. Rob told the court that he had seen Regan scuffling with me and falling backwards hitting his head and face against the door frame and on the floor.

He said that at no time had he seen me hit Regan. He told of how I struggled free from his grip and ran off looking too scared to do anything other. He also added that I was afraid to go to the police because of Regan's fearsome reputation. Even I believed Rob. He was that convincing.

When the prosecution took over they went straight for the jugular. 'Mr Brent, have you ever been in trouble with the police?'

'Yes I have.' Rob directed his answer confidently to the jury. The prosecution brief looked smug as he surveyed the courtroom.

'Could you tell the court where you have travelled from today?'

Rob was an old hand. He knew how to work the prosecution. 'I admit that I have been no angel throughout my life. I've come here today from Welford Road Prison to give evidence for Mr Skillen. I'm not on trial and I don't believe that my past criminal record will affect my memory of what happened that night. Mr Regan is known as a bully in Loughborough and it's high time he learnt his lesson.' The prosecution's smug look was replaced with a frown. The case was drawing to a close. The evidence had been heard. All that was left now was for the jury to make up their minds as to whether or not I was guilty. I squeezed my palms together and looked to the heavens.

THE VERDICT

I couldn't wait for the verdict. I remembered what the con we called The Barrister had said to me. 'You'll know if you've got a "not guilty" verdict, John. If the verdict is in your favour the foreman of the jury will look you in the eye. If it has gone against you he will not give eye contact.' I didn't know how true his statement was. After all he was dishonest. I was about to find out.

I sat poker-faced and waited. A whirlwind started spinning around inside my stomach. I felt sick. My mouth dried up which was unusual for me – it usually watered when I felt sick. My palms felt sweaty. The more I dried them on my trousers the more they sweated. I would either walk free from this court today or would be guilty and get five fucking years. I took a deep breath. My destiny was in the hands of the jury.

My eyes followed the foreman of the jury as they filed back into the courtroom. I looked directly at the foreman and waited. The jury sat down. The foreman remained standing.

The judge spoke, 'Have you reached a verdict that you all agree on?'

Before the foreman replied he made direct eye contact with me. I felt a tinge of excitement. If the dodgy accountant was right, I was home and dry.

'We have, your honour.'

'How do you find the defendant on the charge of wounding with intent, guilty or not guilty?' I held my breath. Come on say it. I closed my eyes and bowed my head, palms tight together. Come on say it.

'Not guilty, your honour.'

I wanted to scream out but kept cool.

'And is that the verdict of you all?'

'Yes it is, your honour.'

'Mr Skillen, the court finds you not guilty of wounding with intent.'

At this point the judge would usually say you are free to go. Instead he said:

'Please remain where you are.' His voice was stern. I felt despair. 'The jury is dismissed. You may leave. I now have another matter on which I have to deal with concerning Mr Skillen.' The foreman of the jury looked confused at the judge's remark and turned and filed out with the rest of the jury giving me one last look and a comforting smile as he left.

'Mr Skillen, on the matter of failing to surrender to a crown court warrant, I'm sure you're aware it is a very serious offence and I'm going to treat it as such. For failing to surrender to a crown court warrant I sentence you to five months in prison.'
I'd forgotten about the failing to surrender to the crown court charge. Surely he should have dismissed the charge considering I was found not guilty? I stood perfectly still. I showed no emotion. I was grateful I'd been found not guilty of the wounding. The judge obviously thought differently. I was wrong about the jury deciding my destiny. The judge was the one with the true power.
Five months? I'm found not guilty and I still get five months? I was paying the price for a reputation that had preceded me. But five months is better than five years. I took it as a good result. I was once again a convicted criminal.
I'd meant what I had said when I prayed to the Lord, and I had got what I had asked for, the not guilty verdict. I had fought Regan and was guilty of that, even though I considered it a pre-emptive attack. I'd gone too far and in the eyes of the law was guilty, but not as charged. Sticking a glass in someone's face is a horrific act and could so easily cause serious disfigurement or even death.
I would keep to my promise and on my release build my new life and try and live it as a good person. I accepted my punishment like a man and decided to get on with my time.

CRAZY STIRRER

Back in Welford Road, a lad from Loughborough known as Terry, transferred into my cell. Terry was an all right lad. The last thing I wanted was another dodgy cell mate. At least with Terry I could have a laugh. He wasn't the type of lad I would have hung round with but we'd grown up on the same estate so we stuck together. Outside of prison life he was always involved in all sorts of criminal activities, but inside he was a sound lad and as honest as you could be in the prison environment. We two-ed up for a while and cell life had a certain sanity to it, until I was called to the landing office by the duty screw.
'Skillen, we're bringing a prisoner up onto the landing after tea. I don't know if you've heard of him or not but he's known as "Mad Harry". He's in solitary confinement at the moment. We've decided to put him in with you as we realise you're not easily intimidated. He won't be with you for very long. We expect him to be back in solitary very soon. He's that type.'

Later that evening as we lay talking about fuck all, the cell door burst open.
'Get your fucking hands off me, screw,' the voice said. Mad Harry entered the cell. He was five feet seven inches tall with bulldog features and a deep red complexion. He had the same attitude as Ben Kingsley's character in the gangster film, *Sexy Beast*. He rubbed his hands over his shaven skull as if trying to stop his head from hurting. He scanned the cell like he was looking for a way out.
'I'm fucking Harry. I fucking hate screws.' He grabbed a metal chair which had plywood backing and rested the chair back on one hand. He then smashed his fist through the wood backing. 'Fucking screws!' he said.
I'm sure his actions would have intimidated a lot of cons. All it did was reinforce what the screws had already told me – he was a fucking knob.
'What's your name?' he demanded. The guy was a psycho all right and had to be toned down a bit before he got out of hand. I'd met his type many times before.

'I'm John and that's Terry. We're both from Loughborough.'
'I know Loughborough; I did a job there once. Nice to meet you, lads. Do you know who I am? I'm going to write a book, you know. I've done just over 30 years and all I did was rob a post office. I got five years that turned into 30. I should have been out years ago. They can't beat me, you know. They can't fucking beat me.' His complexion turned a fiery red as he ranted on.
'Come on. Let's have a riot. We'll smash up the cell, barricade ourselves in.'
He walked towards the door and banged both fists like hammers against it as if trying to smash it open. 'Fucking screws.' His sentiments were echoed throughout the landing. I interrupted the loony cycle.
'Listen, Harry.' Harry ignored me. I raised my tone and the risk of a scrap. 'Harry, sit fucking down and listen.' I got his attention. 'You ain't going to smash this cell up while I'm in it. Do you understand me? If you want to cause a riot do it in association time not in here. Me and Terry are doing easy time. If you want it hard that's up to you.'
I was expecting Harry to have a go. I was surprised how quickly he settled down. I'd already informed Terry that if Harry got out of hand then I would fill him in, and that's what I was prepared to do. Harry was a psycho; just tolerable but not to be trusted. I would be watching my back during his stay with us. According to Harry he spent most of his time in solitary confinement. He bragged that his goal was to be the con to have spent the most time in solitary. Great goal I thought. With his attitude it shouldn't be difficult to attain. He was just a big lump trying to be a hard man. Harry chilled out after our little chat. He loved singing 'Danny Boy' and various Irish rebel songs, telling and listening to jokes. The man was fit though. He could set up the best cell gym I'd ever seen. The three of us worked out every day: benching, pull-ups, dips, curls, press-ups, sit-ups. He had a workout for each muscle group. Well what else do you think about when you're in solitary confinement? Harry loved his press-ups. He was 54 years old and as fit as a fiddle.
I noticed the training seemed to tame him, exorcising his aggression. The trouble with Harry was he was literally like a

caged animal. He hated the system. He was what I feared becoming.

One morning he woke with a notion. I could tell by his expression he was deep in thought. I stood in the cell doorway at slop-out. Harry came and stood behind me.

I felt vulnerable and could sense something was wrong. I adjusted my position so if Harry turned bad and I had to I could get the first whack in. He looked pissed off. He gestured with a nod of his head. 'See that cunt over there.' I looked across still keeping one eye on Harry. I checked out a lean, medium built man in his early 20's.

'He was fucking staring at me yesterday. Come on, John. You, me and Terry will go and fill him in, and when the screws come we'll fill them in as well.'

'Harry, he ain't done anything to us. Leave the kid alone.'

'Fuck him. He's a cunt. I'm going to take him. Are you in?' This guy was like a live grenade on self-destruct and he was just about to pull the fucking pin. I had to distance myself or I would be drawn into his explosion of violence and a world I didn't want part of.

'Harry, if you want to kick off, then kick off but you do it on your own.'

'All right, John. I understand.' He offered me his hand. I kept my eyes on him and slapped his hand in a friendly gesture.

'You and Terry are going to be in my book. John and Terry from Loughborough – great lads.'

He skipped off creeping in and out of cell doorways. He got to the doorway which the kid would have to pass on his return from slop-out. I stood with Terry watching the game unfold. If it wasn't so sinister it would have been funny. Harry looked comical creeping in and out of doorways. Warning the lad wasn't an option. I didn't have a clue who he was. He might well have a problem with Harry. It was between the two of them. I noticed more screws on duty than usual as if they were ready for Harry's antics. Harry waited, jostling from side to side as if busting for a piss. As soon as the kid was in range Harry surprised him with an almighty inside of the forearm strike. It landed like a baseball bat striking a ball but with far less impact. The kid jolted backward as Harry pressed forward with the attack.

Harry's continuation attack fell short of its target and the kid let rip with a barrage of punches too fast for Harry to cope with. Punch after punch landed on Harry's face. It was plain to see the kid was trained in the art of pugilism. The hard shots ripped his skin open, the claret flowed. Within seconds the screws ran toward the fight like worker ants moving in to feed. The panic alarm blared out a high-pitched intermittent sound that cut through my ears and set my heart racing. The screws descended on Harry ignoring the kid. Harry started scrapping with the screws. They overwhelmed him in an instant like schoolboys doing a pile on. Harry managed to get back to his feet. The screws got control pinning him first to the wall then to the floor. That was the last I saw before I was manhandled into my cell.
'Bang up!' echoed throughout the landing. Me and Terry giggled as we listened through the door. Harry was getting a beating I was sure of that, but by the sound of it he was giving as good as he was getting – if only verbally.

We saw Harry a few days later walking across the landing escorted by two big screws.
'I'm being shipped out, lads,' Harry shouted with a big smile on his face.
'See you, lads. Don't take any shit from these bastards.'
The burly screws ushered him on his way. Harry had a claim to fame if you can call it that. He attacked John McVicar, another notorious con, with a pot mug and bragged he'd knocked him out. Truth was he hit McVicar then locked himself in his cell when McVicar challenged him. Harry was certainly a character and one we were glad to see the back of. I think the screws were too. Harry had trouble written all over him.

The next day I was informed that I had been de-categorized from a 'B' category prisoner to a 'C' and was being transferred to an open prison, H.M.P. Ranby near Nottingham. I'd heard that Ranby was an easy nick. The food was better and there was plenty to do. No cells, just open dorms and a cracking gym. I was looking forward to getting my time done as quickly and as quietly as possible.

A couple of days before the transfer I noticed a commotion on the landings. A category 'A' prisoner, usually a lifer or a con deemed extremely dangerous, had arrived from a maximum security prison. I hadn't seen Terry this excited. I thought he was being released.
'It's Frankie Fraser. Mad Frankie Fraser. He's finishing off a life sentence for murder,' Terry said obviously in awe of him.
I paused on the landing to check out Mr Fraser. He looked very ordinary except he was flanked by four screws and walking like he was a king and the screws his bodyguards.
Terry gave me a short history lesson. 'He's one of the old gangsters from the Kray era. He used to work for the Richardsons. He was an enforcer for them. A real nasty bastard.'
I'd heard of the Krays but mad Frankie Fraser was a new one on me. I looked at him and wondered how he could do all that bird and stay sane. He looked cool and surprisingly fit after spending 30 odd years inside. He had raven black hair and a tough looking weathered exterior. He walked tall and proud like royalty. Even the screws seemed to curtsy as he passed them by. The landings were buzzing with stories about Fraser, the Richardsons and the Krays. I found out that he was actually finishing off a ten-year sentence for torture. In this world this man was a real celebrity.

The following morning Terry and I were chatting as we walked the yard with the rest of the cons. The yard was flanked by a huge wall on one side and the prison on the other.
It was a sharp chilly day. The sun was shining but not on us; we were still in the shadows. The pace of the walk was brisk. The cool air tasted of freedom. Out came two screws followed by Frankie Fraser with two more screws behind him. Frankie walked toward the circle of cons.
Terry tugged at my sleeve. 'It's Fraser.' I looked at Terry. His face was on fire with excitement. 'Fucking 'ell he's joining us.' Frankie got in line and tagged along with me and Terry. He didn't speak immediately. He just quietly paced along. The circle of cons went silent as if waiting for him to make a speech.
'How you doing, lads? I'm Frankie Fraser.'
I introduced Terry and myself and we walked on.
'I'll soon be out, lads. Do you know something?'

I looked at him and for a moment was transfixed by his eyes. They were set deep in his skull and the iris appeared black. He had a presence, an aura about him like a movie star.

'In all the time I've been inside they still don't know how I got rid of the bodies,' he laughed.

'It's pigs you know. Pigs will eat anything and everything, clothes and all.' He laughed again like he had done some mischief and got away with it. He talked about getting out and writing a book about his life. We were guided back into the prison doors whilst Frankie continued his walk. I wished him good luck in his new life and walked on. I found Frankie Fraser to be far from mad. He came across as a very friendly and articulate man, but dangerous? Oh yes, you could see that in his eyes, the mirrors of the soul. I couldn't help thinking what a waste of 30 years.

RANBY OPEN PRISON

Ranby was very, very boring and the time passed slowly. It was a bit like a small town. Most cons knew somebody in there and if they didn't it wasn't long before they were incorporated into somebody else's clique. I met Andy, a lad I'd grown up with on my estate in Loughborough, a lovely lad, who had fallen in with the wrong crowd and was now paying the price. Another lad from just outside Loughborough was also in residence, a lad known as 'Cockney'.

Cockney loved the romance of the big time villains as he called them: the Krays, Richardsons, Ronnie Biggs. He loved the big jobs that went down. Cockney knew more scams than most. He was a sharp individual, a man who loved the finer things in life, but he didn't look so sharp dressed in prison issue clothes. I couldn't understand his mentality. He loved the good life but to get it by depriving others of their hard earned goods was a big mistake. We all make mistakes. That's why there are rubbers on the end of pencils, tippex in the office and a delete key on the keyboard. Cockney introduced me to a few characters and at one point I felt myself being drawn into their circle. I kept my distance. I didn't want to make any more mistakes in my life.

Most of my association time was taken up in the gym. It was a beautiful gym with more than enough equipment to get a full body workout. I teamed up with Andy. I spotted for him on the weights and he repaid the compliment. I worked hard in the gym exorcising my aggression. There was a skipping rope available for use, a rare piece of kit in a prison gym due to its possible misuse as a noose. I skipped round after round punishing my body with sit-ups and press-ups. If I had gleaned one lesson from my short association with Mad Harry then working out on a daily basis was it! I got so involved in my training it became all I lived for. When I was in the gym the world seemed like a different place, I felt free and happy.

Inbetween the gym visits I would get to hear the sob stories of the cons. Most were guilty by their own admission but portrayed a hard done to exterior. Prison can be a miserable place if you hang around with the wrong people – the people who haven't accepted the fact they have committed a crime and deserve their lot. Far better to accept the time and get on with it. You become negative if you hang around with negative people. One lad in particular was hard done to. He was an ordinary looking lad, an unfortunate caught up in a street fight and arrested. I sympathised with him. He was finishing off a hefty sentence for a crime circumstance dictated.

He was involved in a street fight with a gang of opposing football fans who had invaded his town. He got punched to the ground and was being booted to bits by several lads. A carving knife fell to the floor where he lay taking boot after boot. He reached out for the blade and with a mighty roar scrambled half to his feet and started thrusting the knife into his attackers. The blade penetrated a man's stomach and he fell to the floor dead from the thrust of the blade. Fear had caused him to commit the ultimate crime. He was given ten years for manslaughter. He was 17 at the time. In an instant not just two lives were destroyed but many: the families of both men living with the consequences of a weekend scrap. The kid was remorseful. He didn't think about picking up the blade. He didn't think about anything other than getting to his feet and saving himself. The real sentence he got for life was the fact that he killed another human being. Somebody's little boy gone forever. And he had to live with it. The futility of violence.

Whilst I was in Ranby I took part in the Football Association amateur referee's course which would, if I passed the course qualify me as a football referee. The course was boring at times but very enjoyable on the whole. Anything to keep my mind off my time. A few weeks had passed and I was due to take the referee's exam the very next day. Whilst we practised on the field I was called to the prison office and informed that my appeal against my conviction had come through. I'd appealed as per instructions from my barrister. I'd forgotten about the appeal having resigned myself to getting on with my time. I didn't want to go. I'd spent about eight weeks in Ranby. I had another two months to go. What really bothered me was the referee qualification. It would have been the first course I'd ever passed and I would have got a certificate validating that I was good at something.

'Do you want to go on this appeal or not?' the screw asked.

I was about to decline the appeal when another screw commented, 'No one has ever got out of here on appeal. You're wasting your time, Skillen and ours.'

That did it for me. Fuck you, I thought, and decided to go for it!

WEEKEND OUT

I boarded the minibus for the long journey to two of Britain's most notorious prisons. First stop was Brixton where I would spend the night before being whisked over to Wormwood Scrubs which was closer to the Court of Appeal. Brixton prison was playing host to several notorious characters who were involved in the Brinks Mat bullion robbery and were considered heroes by the majority of the Brixton inmates. They stole 6,800 gold bars weighing three tons. The haul also included platinum, diamonds and travellers' cheques valued in total at approximately 26 million pounds.
As the police hunted the gang the gold was melted down and sold on. I once heard a tale that any gold jewellery bought after the Brinks Mat robbery probably contained some of that bullion. Fascinating to think that anyone of us could be in receipt of stolen goods without even knowing it.
These guys were the talk of the prison. I heard a commotion on the landing and went out to see what was going on. Three cons being taken through the prison.
'Who are they?'
'You don't know? It's the Brinks Mat boys.' They were dressed in smart suits, open necked shirts and I swear they were wearing gold chains around their necks. Cheeky bastards, I thought.

Brixton was no different to Welford Road. It smelt the same, felt the same and when the door slammed shut it had the same effect. I couldn't wait to get out of this shithole.

I arrived through the gates of the Court of Appeal and was taken upstairs into the dock.
I thought I'd be waiting around for hours. The screw said:
'Don't worry, Skillen, it won't be long before we're heading back to Ranby. We're on first.' He smirked. I smiled a sarcastic smile.
I'd be glad when this charade was over and I was back at Ranby so I could get on with my time. I looked out into the courtroom to see where the judge was seated. The courtroom looked huge: all dark wood with that same polished smell. There was an eerie silence to the place and the lighting was dim giving the room a Victorian feel

to it. A door creaked breaking the silence and adding a sinister tone to the proceedings. My barrister briefed me and then awaited the arrival of the judge. He looked far more nervous than I was. I was just enjoying a day out. It was interesting to be sitting where many infamous people probably sat awaiting judgement. The court entrance had appeared on the news many times before.

The judge looked older than anyone I'd seen before, almost skeletal, as he shuffled some papers. I always wondered why they did that. They never seemed to read them. The barrister stood tall and looked like he was reading to himself from the papers he was holding.

'Come on then, man. Get on with it,' said the judge. I was surprised at the outburst especially as he looked like he should have been buried a long time ago. The barrister looked embarrassed. He stammered his words then started his legal rhetoric. He outlined the case then explained his reasons why he thought that I had been wrongly imprisoned. Put simply I had been found not guilty of any crime so therefore had no bail to answer to. I was innocent and could not be in breach of a crown court warrant.

'Yes, yes, yes, man. Quite right. Is that all?' the judge said.

'Yes, your honour.'

That was it – five minutes – my case heard. What a waste of government money.

The judge looked at me and said:

'Mr Skillen, you should not have been convicted for being in breach of a crown court warrant. You should not have been sent to prison. You're free to go.'

The judge got up and left. One phrase and I was set free; now that's true power. I sat, still feeling a bit numb.

I felt nauseous and not at all excited. I turned to the screw. He splayed his arms and shrugged his shoulders.

'That's a first for me,' he said. I collected up my property and a rail warrant plus a few quid travelling expenses and was told to leave the court house. I walked down the steps of the appeal court and onto the streets of London. Around me the traffic buzzed, black cabs, red buses, irate drivers filing through the streets going about their daily business. I was free.

I giggled to myself. Fucking hell. I'm out. It's over. I felt like crying with happiness.
I jumped into the air then realised where I was. I legged it across the road and into the tube station. I made my way back to Loughborough, a free man.

Even though I had been released I didn't feel free. After the initial euphoria I felt incredibly depressed. I really didn't want to be out. I was fucked up in the head. Fear ate away at my senses. As I drifted off to sleep, the motion of the train soothing me, I remembered the promise I'd made to God. He'd delivered the verdict I'd asked for then given me a bit of time to consider my life. I had to change. It was now my turn to deliver. I was fit, strong and able. It was time to get a job and make a life worth living for myself.

BACKWARD STEP

The promise I made was soon forgotten as the first beer took effect. The Blackbird public house on the Sharpley Road council estate was the regular of Regan, my old adversary and the meeting place of the lads. I walked into the sound of the pool balls clacking together on the blue baize table and the babble and friendly banter of the lads at play. The scene brought back memories of the Saracen's Head – a big, old, dirty boozer that saw more fights than Madison Square Garden. I'd been barred from that pub more times than any other. The pubs in town like the Blackbird were being closed down or refurbished into disco pubs which resembled nightclubs. A tradition was being lost.
I was on my third pint of lager and it was making me feel aggressive. Not openly toward anyone in particular, I just felt aggressive. One of the lads came over to me and whispered in my ear.
'John, I thought I'd better warn you. Regan's next door. He knows you're here.'
It was a tip off I didn't need. I decided to play it cool and ignore the fact he was here.
I knew Regan wouldn't let it go. It was inevitable that our paths would cross. A few more beers and who knows how I'd react if we bumped into each other. I felt like going home. There was no reason why I shouldn't other than me not wanting to appear like I'd bottled it in front of the lads. Peer pressure was again dictating my lifestyle. I decided to stay.
I was fitter and stronger than the last time we met and wiser. A rematch didn't bother me. Getting arrested did. He grassed me last time and I knew he'd do it again. I was sure of that. The beer was now well and truly in the veins relieving me of my conscience. I made my way to the toilet for a piss. The smell of the urinal reminded me of slop-out in Welford Road and for a split second in my mind's eye I was whisked back there. I finished zipping up my flies. The toilet door opened and in walked Regan. He stared at me for a second as if trying to figure out what to say. We were only about four feet from each other. I seemed to be making a habit of

meeting Regan in toilets. At least this time it was the gents and not the ladies.

I remained calm ring his gaze. I could feel tension rising.

'Yeah?' I said staring back at him. I'd forgotten how big he really was. Last time I'd fought him I was angry and had a reason. This time he had reason on his side. I felt a jolt of adrenalin kick in. I pushed any thoughts of prison and the police to the back of my mind. I couldn't have those thoughts clouding my decisions. Regan was a formidable character. If he saw the slightest chink in my mental armour he would go for it. His type preyed on fear and weakness. If it kicked off now I could face prison again or if I bottled it I could get filled in. I countered the negative thoughts in my mind. Fuck it. If he wants it he can have it. If I hesitate I would become his punch bag. I struck first with the verbals.

'You got a fucking problem with me?'

Silly question really considering I'd put him in hospital last time we met.

'Yeah, you glassed me,' he said. Before I could reply the toilet door opened and in walked one of the lads. Kev assessed the situation immediately and didn't waste any time in getting involved. He knew both me and Regan well and knew the history between us.

'Now, now, lads,' Kev said, standing between us like a referee in a cage fight. Regan was a family friend of Kev's parents but Kev was also like the proverbial big brother to the lads. He liked things all fair and square. With Kev as ref I decided to tell Regan a few home truths. Get things out in the open.

'You fucking know I didn't glass you. So does everybody else. You're a fucking bully and I beat you fair and square.'

'Leave it, lads,' Kev butted in. Kev was very streetwise; he knew when it was about to go. We were in the negotiation stage; one wrong sentence or move and we'd be scrapping like dogs.

'No stay out of it, Kev. He started it.' Kev kept quiet.

'Listen, Regan, if you want a fucking go we'll go outside now into the car park and sort this out. One on one just like last time.' Regan got braver. He had an audience and didn't want to appear weak in front of Kev.

'You glassed me. You couldn't have beat me if you hadn't used a glass.'

I stayed cool.

'I didn't use a glass. I can prove it.' I gestured toward the door. Regan stared at me. I repeated the offer. Final chance. I stepped forward toward the door. He stayed perfectly still.

'Fuck this. Outside. Let's go.' I waited inside the doorway. It was Regan's move.

'You what?' he said, repositioning himself so that he faced me square on.

'You heard me. Would you like me to spell it out for ya?'

Kev moved in toward me and put his hands in front of me as if to hold me back. He never touched me. Kev was old school, he'd worked the doors and fought all his life. He knew that if he touched me it would click on my adrenalin and could erupt me into action. Kev just wanted peace. 'Leave it, John,' he said.

'No. Fuck him, Kev. He's a cunt. He's the one who won't leave it. If he wants another go we'll do it now.' I stared at him over Kev's shoulder.

'Outside.' I gestured for him to lead the way. He broke off the stare that was threatening me and turned his back. He undid his zip, pulled out his cock and faced the toilet wall.

This was a clear sign. I didn't need to hear what he said next. But I wanted to hear it.

'We'll leave it at that. I don't want to fight you again!' he said.

'Okay fair enough. You make sure that you squash the rumours that I used a glass on ya.'

I laid down an open offer.

'If you ever want a go you know where I live.' I left the toilet. I felt better for having the confrontation. It cleared the air. I felt buzzed up.

I returned to the bar. The room fell silent when I entered. Everybody looked in my direction. The juke box started up and Paul Weller and the Jam soothed the atmosphere with the distant echoes of far away voices. I noticed Regan leaving the bar almost immediately.

A couple more beers, a few pats on the back and I was off. It was a big deal for me being accused of using a glass. Glassing somebody is a coward's game. I also believed Regan was a hypocrite. He'd dished out enough violence himself. One beating and he runs to the law.

If he'd have put me in hospital the night we fought I wouldn't have gone to the Old Bill.

I would have accepted the beating then I would have trained, bided my time and fought him again. I had no respect for him and as far as I was concerned it was over. But I would always watch my back with that one.

I realised that I had managed once again to hold my temper when usually I would have steamed into Regan without talk. I put this down to confidence in my ability and whilst I stayed cool and negotiated with him, I was fully prepared to go all the way even if it meant prison. I also found out that alcohol, particularly lager, made it harder for me to control my aggression.

REPELLING BOREDOM

When I was 14 years old, I'd had a telling off and disappeared to my room. The wallpaper was so damp it had fallen off in parts and was in dire need of redecoration. But times were hard and money was in short supply. What we did have went on food or booze. I decided to do a bit of my own decorating. Day-dreaming was common for me. I had a strong imagination. I was enthralled by Bruce Lee in *Enter The Dragon* and Chwi Chang Cain from the TV series, *Kung Fu*. I'd leap up and down practising the moves. I never missed an episode. I loved the philosophy of Cain: 'I do not wish to fight' – a fantastic deceptive phrase, which meant if you don't fuck off out of my face, I'm gonna kick the shit out of you in a way you've never seen done before! Priceless. I wrote a message on the bare wall; 'I've run away to China for five years to practise the martial arts.' Running away seemed the logical thing to do at the time. Bruce Lee was the man. I used his posters to cover most of the bare walls in my bedroom, along with the front covers of the boxing news and a few pictures of scantily clad and topless models. I didn't have the money to buy real glue so I stuck them up with glue made from flour and water. I promised myself that one day I would become a black belt in kung fu.

My brother Sam had recently had a car accident. He was the passenger. The lad driving was out of his head on amphetamine sulphate (speed) and he drove his car into a tree. Sam was badly injured and was told he'd always walk with a limp, as one leg would now be shorter than the other due to the bones in his pelvic girdle breaking on impact. He had his liver stitched, his stomach sewn up. He lost about three stone in weight. During his rehabilitation he decided to start up an exercise regime to help himself back to fitness. He chose kung fu under the tutelage of Steve Faulkner. Within a year of starting kung fu you couldn't tell he'd ever been in an accident other than a scar that ran down his torso. Kung fu training made a major difference to his stature, physical fitness and ability. It also helped him control his aggression – something I needed help with. Sam encouraged me to go along with him to a session to try it out. I was a bit sceptical at first but you can't argue with the facts. It had done wonders for Sam. I went along and lined up with the kung fu students. They wore black suits and around their waists were coloured belts made of a silky material. I was impressed with how smart they looked. Some were barefoot, others wore thin black slippers. The style of kung fu was known as Lau gar; a Chinese system of self-defence based on the five animal style of the Shaolin temple: tiger, crane, leopard, monkey and snake. The instructor was known as the 'Brockton Blockbuster' for his ability to smash his palm heel through a stack of concrete edging slabs (in which he held the world record). He wore the only black sash in the hall. Steve was from Birmingham and had a soft Brummie accent which was difficult to understand.

The lad next to me wore a white sash. The sashes went up in ascending order, white being the first grade, then blue, green, yellow, purple, brown and black. The black belt seemed a long way off. Every three or four months depending on your attendance and your ability you would take an exam. If you passed you received the next coloured belt, eventually reaching the black belt. Kung fu was very different to boxing. In boxing you used four punches thrown in a variety of angles, hooks, uppercuts, straight, and jabs. In kung fu they would use a multitude of strikes including all the punches from boxing, kicks, sweeps and takedowns arranged in to a series of movements known as sets which appeared to be a very complex form of shadow boxing.

It wasn't long before I had the ability to take my first grade. I was nervous standing in front of the Brummie. The techniques were shouted out in Chinese. Chinese was hard enough to understand but when it was said with a Brummie accent it was like someone had invented a new language. I demonstrated the techniques to the best of my ability. It was hard to shake off the style of the boxer and I felt awkward holding my hands out in front of me like my old idol Chwi Chang Cain. I kept looking along the line to check if what I was doing was correct.

One week later the Brummie read the names of the people that had passed and the people that had failed. I was more nervous than I was when I stood in the dock waiting for the verdict. The Brummie paused before he read out each name which made the feelings worse.

'Promoted to first kup white sash,' he looked along the faces of the line then said, 'John Skillen.'

I felt so proud of myself. That first grade meant everything to me. It soon hit home. I was now on the first rung of the ladder and climbing. Seven more belts and I would attain the coveted black belt.

Through the kung fu teachings I realised that achieving the grade represented a goal in my life and now I had another one. My next goal was the blue belt. I couldn't wait to get stuck into learning the new techniques. The first three belts were short term goals, the next three midterm goals and the brown sash and the black, long term goals. Goals were something that was missing in my life until now. Yes I'd done stuff but never really knew where I was going with it. I now had a reason to train to keep myself occupied. I felt great. Boredom passed me by. I still didn't have a job but, for the first time in ages, I felt like my life was worthwhile.

GIZZA JOB

If your ship doesn't come in,
Swim out to it.
Jonathan Winters

It was the mid '80s. Unemployment was still rife in Loughborough unless you had a trade. Most of the lads I knew had their lives in check. And although they had problems similar to mine they had dealt with them. They learnt a trade, endured the low wage of an apprentice and reaped the benefit of a secure and stable employment. That's what I should have done instead of fucking around feeling sorry for myself, all because I didn't get it handed to me on a silver plate.
I had to get off the dole and get a job I could stick with and earn some good money. I loved looking and feeling smart and to do that I needed cash. I hunted everywhere for a job to no avail. I felt intimidated by the fact that I'd been in prison. Who would employ an ex-con? I also had issues about my education; my spelling and writing skills were atrocious. I'd tried to improve them in borstal some years ago. The advice I was given by one of the English tutors was that your handwriting mirrors your character. She pointed out to me that doctors were educated men but you couldn't read their writing.
She decided to help me by getting me to write in German. She said that the forming of the letters in a language I didn't know would help me concentrate and correct the shape of the letter. It worked and my writing became more legible. But I still had a complex about it and about filling in application forms. When the time was right I would go to college and study for the new GCSE English exam. For the moment I was caught in the benefit trap that sucked so many men into bad ways.

Dave, an old friend of mine, worked at the Brush engineering firm on the far side of town. People joked if you got a job there it was a life sentence. The Brush was one of the biggest employers in the town. I'd tried on numerous occasions to get a job there but failed. It was one of those places where if you knew somebody that already worked there you were more likely to get a job if they put a good word in for you.

I met Dave and had a chat with him about work and how I was struggling to find a proper job. I'd done lots of short term jobs on the side getting a back-hander here and there but it wasn't regular good money. Dave had a cushy little number as he put it, driving an electric delivery truck around the brush shop floor taking components and stores to different parts of the factory. He was a shrewd character and to supplement his earnings he'd wheel and deal his way around the factory selling all sorts of typical market stall goods from sweatshirts to trainers. If it was near Christmas it was cheap toys, Easter it was chocolate eggs. His dealings weren't restricted to the factory. I'd often see him with his boot open selling something or other out of it.

Dave put in a good word for me and got me an interview. I asked him how he'd sorted it. He said, 'the guy owed me a favour.' I couldn't believe he'd got me an interview so easily.

I later found out that Dave supplied the lad with videos and they weren't the type you'd let your mother watch. I couldn't even get to speak to anyone to get a job at the Brush. I was always told come back in six weeks. It's true what they say; it's not what you know it's who you know that matters.

I had the interview and was told there and then that the job was mine. I was now a trainee laminator making fibreglass soundproof boxes, panelling and fibreglass components. I had to clock in at 7.30 a.m. and clock out at 4.00 p.m. unless there was overtime to be had. I was very grateful to Dave for getting me a job. True friends are the ones that help you when you're down on your luck or going through a tough time.

Dave fancied himself more than the average guy – five feet nine with blond hair fashionably parted down the centre and a moustache (also fashionable at the time). He loved soccer and played of course, up front. His short, powerful legs propelled his 13 stone frame toward the goal every Sunday. Dave was a tough player giving out more than he got. There was another side to this multifaceted character. At night he became a nightclub bouncer, always a smile on his face until it kicked off. Dave worked six nights a week at Sammy's nightclub. During a shift at work Dave

offered me a job on the door. He joked 'you can have Regan's old job.' Dave was there the night it kicked off with Regan.
He despised Regan because he was a bully and said he deserved all he got. 'I will have a word with the other lads and see if I can get you in, John.'

Dave's brother-in-law, Big Dave McKnight, was the manager at Sammy's. The only way to get a job on the door was if the bouncers agreed to have you in their team. There were two requirements: firstly you had to be able to scrap and secondly be able to stand a pull from the coppers and keep your mouth firmly shut. Being cool was another requirement (which you couldn't have if you didn't have the former two). I fitted the bill nicely but had my reservations about working the door. Dave tipped the balance for me.
'John, you will be earning instead of spending and you're still on the town. And the women love bouncers.' He rubbed his hands together and smiled. I needed the money. I also needed to keep myself occupied. Boredom is a killer and leads to most problems in life. I'd done one or two jobs on the door, nothing permanent just a quick earner here and there. I'd once spent a long weekend in Manchester with an old friend Lincoln. The job was for the Rebecca's nightclub chain. The club sacked their head doorman – a brave decision as he was the hard man of the area and the rest of the doormen refused to work the door. They had been threatened with violence if they did. Rebecca's management also owned a Rebecca's in Loughborough before it was sold and became Sammy's. Lincoln worked for Rebecca's and was asked to sort out the door problem. He asked me to accompany him as the job entailed taking over the door. Door work was always territorial and if you weren't from a certain area you didn't work that door. It was seen as an invasion of someone's turf.
The rest of the door team refused to front the door. That became our job. We would stay there for five nights going up on the Wednesday and working from Thursday to Saturday, returning Sunday. The door team was well tooled up for what was threatened to be a bloodbath. Everyone that came to the club on the first night was vetted and searched. Most name-dropped the old head doorman saying that they didn't have to pay because they were

friends of his. Lincoln took no shit. He was a good bouncer and, everyone for the first time since the club started trading, paid. If they said they knew the manager then they were told to pay and see him for the refund later. This stopped a lot of the shit from arguing the toss.

There was one guy who refused to pay and demanded entry. He had a few lads with him. I could see the regular door lads were nervous. The lad was well over six feet and built like an old-fashioned shit-house. Solid.
'You're a fucking marked man,' the lad said to Lincoln in his Manchester spiel. Lincoln moved forward and faced the lad square on. I pushed through and stood side by side and scanned his mates. If it was going to kick off they were in for a shoeing. I gripped the bat tight in my hand. I held it at the back of my thigh just out of sight. It was a short stumpy heavy bat ideal for swinging in small spaces. One word from Lincoln and I would be swinging.
The guy moved in on Lincoln but before he could raise a punch Lincoln's huge fist landed a thumping blow in the middle of the man's chest. The blow had all of Lincoln's 15 stone behind it sending the man reeling backwards and dropping him to one knee. It was a great shot. The kid was helped up by his pals who had a look of disbelief on their faces. The kid was carried off head bowed. The word soon spread that we weren't going to take any crap. We kept the shit out and the weekend went smooth with no trouble in the club.
The only piece of real action was when a car screeched through the shopping precinct which at that time was deserted. It reversed into a TV shop smashing the plate glass window open. Two lads jumped out wearing balaclavas, threw a load of electrical items in the boot and drove out of the precinct. It was known then as a ram raid and one of the first of many to plague the country. The copper that attended the scene said afterward that it was a new craze and a gang was operating in Manchester. The copper told us that the gang was being trained by a former rally driver. The way the kid drove was more like a stock car driver. Shortly after that incident shops were regularly raided. Precincts all over the country built entrances and started to lock them up at night. And shops started using shutters. I went home that weekend with 75 quid in my

pocket plus my expenses. It was easy money. With that thought in mind I told Dave I would think about it his offer.

The next day Dave told me he'd spoken to the door lads and if I wanted the job I was in. I decided there and then to take on the job of nightclub bouncer.

BOUNCER

I looked in the mirror. The jacket felt tight against my shoulders. I threw a couple of straight punches toward my own reflection, then a couple of hooks. 'Bang bang,' I said out loud. I straightened the collar on my shirt which appeared almost luminous beneath the black jacket. My punches flowed and although the jacket felt tight I was surprised how easy it was to punch in it. This jacket was made for the job. I looked myself up and down: shining black Airwair shoes, black trousers, gleaming white shirt, black jacket with shiny posh collar and to finish off the look – a neat black James Bond-style dickey-bow. All that was missing was the Walther PPK!

I straightened my tie and reached for the Old Spice aftershave. I poured it into my hand and splashed it all over. I took one last look in the mirror just to treat myself. One word personified my image – cool!

The smell of the aftershave and the thought of the new job excited my senses. This was my first night as a fully-fledged bouncer. Could I cut it? With the risk of being arrested, forever a very real prospect, could I cut it?

I felt my heart turn over at the thought of being arrested again. I had to be careful. One fuck up was all it would take to send me back to jail. Working in a violent environment and trying to stay out of trouble with my record was hard enough. When the police despised you like they did me, they don't forget easily when you've hit one of their own. I was about to tread on hot coals; only trouble was I didn't want to get burnt.

Dave was due to pick me up at eight thirty. I walked down the stairs.

'Whoa! You look smart. Where you going?'

'I'm on the door tonight at Sammy's, Ma. It's my first night.'

She straightened my dickey-bow.

'You be careful,' she said. I could tell she was worried for me, not because of the fighting, she knew I could handle that, it was the police involvement.

I walked outside to wait for the arrival of the babe magnet Dave. It was still light. A warm summer breeze and clear skies made it appear earlier than it was. A small child aged about eight called Duncan stood at the gate. Duncan was a very old eight and very inquisitive, sometimes to the point of irritation. He was a scruffy angel with a dirty face usually covered in chocolate.

'Where you going, John?' he asked.

'Work,' I replied not wanting to get drawn into a conversation with an eight-year-old.

'Work, dressed like that? My dad don't get dressed like that when he goes to work.'

Duncan had a Sheffield accent and his little voice took on a manly quality.

'Well this is what I have to wear.'

'Why?' He looked at me. His freckles matched the colour of his hair. His eyes were wide open waiting for my reply.

'I don't know. It's my first night. Anyway shouldn't you be in bed by now?' I said.

I wanted to say, 'Piss off home.' The nerves were getting to me. I remembered that Duncan was just a baby. He wanted to know about the world and everything in it. I settled for, 'Go on. Run home now, Duncan. It's getting late.'

Duncan stared at me for a second then split, sprinting off across the road to his house shouting, 'Got to go now, John. I've got jobs on.' He disappeared into his garden. I heard him shout in the distance, 'Have a good night, John.' I had to laugh.

Dave pulled up with music blaring out of his car windows.

'Come on, Skillybob. Get in.' Dave sat with his jacket off, his shirt collar open. The car stank like the perfume counter at Boots.

'Fucking hell, Dave. That's strong. What is it?'

'It's Kouros aftershave. The birds love it. Come on shut the door. We'll be late.'

We drove off in the direction of Sammy's.

SAMMY'S

Sammy's nightclub was situated in the old cattle market area of Loughborough, housed inside part of the Curzon cinema. The entrance was through a set of double doors which were raised up and set back from the pavement. Two double doors formed the entrance, one of which opened outward toward the wall. The foyer was about the size of a small living room. To the left was the pay-desk, to your right a seated area and in front was the cloakroom. Above the cloakroom was a small CCTV monitor. To get into the club you had to climb two flights of steep stairs 20 feet up which led to the dance floor and the bars.
I'd been in there a couple of times since the fight with Regan. What stood out most was the state of the club. It was well worn compared to what it had been in its heyday as Rebecca's. With the lights off it looked fine. Put them on and the local health and safety would be asking a few questions.
The smell of stale beer and tobacco mingled in the air with the smell of bleach and disinfectant: someone's attempt to make the place smell nice. The cleaning lights were still on. Dave sprinted ahead of me as if running to a fight.
'Come on, John. We'll have a half before we start.'
I stopped and looked down again. How was I supposed to get somebody down the stairs without falling myself? I followed. Dave passed the ladies' toilet where I'd had the fight with Regan and went through the double doors into the club. I remembered Regan standing there arrogant and bullish surveying the club. I'd been on the other side of the fence then. I knew what it was like to be singled out – to be picked on. I took a deep breath and smiled. Then I made a promise to myself to do the job right. I would be firm but fair.

Sammy's was a disco townie club. The room was so full of smoke I lost sight of Dave.
The lights passed through the smoke creating multicoloured beams that hit the mirror ball and scattered in all directions. I noticed the pool table in the top corner next to the main bar: a new addition. At the side of the main bar was a fire door which when open sent a

signal downstairs to alert the door staff that it had been opened. The doorway led into the cinema and was a fire escape for the club in case of evacuation. But it had another use. It was used to take out unsavoury customers. To the right of the bar was the lads' toilet. I'd had many a scrap in there over the years. The DJ booth was in the middle of the club on the far wall overlooking the dance floor. From there, all of the club could be seen as long as it wasn't too smoky.

I joined Dave for a half. 'Here you go, mate.' Dave handed me a flat half of lager.
'Right, John. If it kicks off next to the pool table the quickest way to get them out is through the cinema exits. They lead down the stairs and out the front doors to the pavement. You have to be careful taking them out as there is usually a cop van parked up outside.'
As Dave was talking he walked me through the cinema and out through the exit then back in to Sammy's through the front door.
'Here's the buzzer system. They are all named. If the buzzer goes off, well you know what to do. Just make sure you see who has pressed it before you sprint off. If it kicks off on the dance floor we take them out through the front doors. When you come through the double doors, John, start scanning the club. You will soon spot the aggro. Look to the DJ booth, the bars. If they have seen it they will be pointing to it. The idea is to get there as fast as you can. If they're fighting, they're out, no discussion. It doesn't matter who they are or how big they are. They go, unless of course it's one of the lads.'
I felt a tinge of excitement at the thought of a kick off. I felt the old stomach whirl around. We went downstairs and I was introduced to Big Dave McKnight, a huge Scot with 18 stone plus of relaxed muscle. He had a head and face full of hair. He looked a right handful. The first thing I realised about big Dave was his manner. He was a real gentleman with a big smile and a great sense of humour. My old friend Bullet appeared through the doors. He'd been working with Dave for some time now. They were a good pairing. Their moustaches matched almost perfectly except for the colour.

Bullet was as fast as a card sharp with his hands. When he balled his fist he had a cracking right hand and a steel grip that when curled around your throat signalled the end. The staff filed in and within no time at all a queue formed outside the club. It was Saturday night and Sammy's was the place to be. The music exploded from the huge speaker next to the staircase. Dave leant into the pay-box and turned it down. It was just loud enough to hear the spoken word. The sound spilled into the night air.

Sammy's filled up quickly on a Saturday night. People queued early for the early doors discount and to make sure they got in. It was now 11.30 p.m. and the club was packed. I made my way upstairs behind Dave and Bullet. The air had now become warm and thick with the smell of perfume, cigarette smoke and basket meals.

I was greeted with the sounds of disco and the choking mixture of the artificial smoke the DJ had filled the room with. Lights flashed and rolled and bounced off every wall. The dance floor was so packed the crowd appeared to move as one. I noticed a small bloke wearing a huge dickie bow. His nose was spread across his face and his ears protruded out to the sides half covered by his long loose perm. In the dark his silhouette made him appear like a caricature of the FA cup. His dickie bow was twice the size of a normal fashionable one. It looked comical. I imagined it to have flashing lights on. He had a handful of pint glasses in his hand as he stopped in front of me.

'You're John Skillen aren't you?'

'Yeah that's right, mate.'

With that said he walked off reaching down every so often to pick up another glass. He had the pace of a Spanish waiter in a quiet bar. He didn't seem to be a full ticket.

Dave asked me to position myself on the speakeasy steps and observe the dance floor. The speakeasy was a small bar area enclosed by a partition. It was an old eating area now darkened by the lack of lights and used for the eating of tongues. The speakeasy steps were a good vantage point. I could see right over the top of the dance floor toward the pool table area: one of the major flash points. In fact, thinking about it, the whole of Sammy's was a major flash point.

As I scanned the area I noticed two lads on the dance floor squaring up to each other.

One said something to the other then turned away. I could see the lad wasn't going to leave it at that. He tapped the lad on the shoulder. He was about to go for it. I moved in, making my first mistake. I should have alerted Dave and Bullet about the situation unfolding but I didn't have time or any way of communicating to them. It was all eyes and ears. I ran over and grabbed both lads a little too enthusiastically. I spun them round to face me by levering both shoulders apart.

'What's going on?' Before they could answer I told them both to calm down or they would be out.

'Sorry, mate. We weren't arguing. He's my brother, we're only talking.' I realised they were raising their voices to be heard above the music which was far too fucking loud. Raising the voice made them look more aggressive than they actually were.

'Sorry lads,' I said and walked back to my vantage point. Bullet was standing watching over me like a guardian angel.

'Take it easy, John. It will kick off soon enough, mate. It always does.'

He was right. I was as tense as a Korean border guard. I wanted to do a good job. The 20 minute stint was soon over and we exchanged places with the lads downstairs on the front door. I was glad to get out of the loud music. It was harder to tolerate when sober.

Punters were still coming into the club. I vetted them as they came through the door with Dave as my guide. I weighed up some of the lads wondering how I would handle them if they kicked off when Dave suddenly slammed the door shut to the ear piercing sound of the panic alarm. Bullet was already on the stairs with Dave in hot pursuit, I followed. Dave screamed out 'Top bar,' as he ran.

I charged up the staircase and was breathing heavy as I reached the top step. The smoke filled my lungs and burnt. I blasted through the double doors and swerved past one of the lads who was dragging a lad by the hair, punching and kicking him as he resisted.

'Pool table,' the doorman shouted. I sprinted through the crowd knocking them apart as I went. Another doorman passed me, his arm wrapped around the neck of a youth who looked unconscious.

He was followed by a lad swearing and cursing, his shoulders firmly held by Bullet who frogmarched him toward the entrance. The DJ was pointing to the pool table area which was surrounded by on-lookers.

'Get back,' I shouted. There was a pile of bodies scrapping in and around the pool table. One kid was smashing a pool ball into another kid's head. The knuckles and boots were flailing. I dived in, whacking the first person within range. He went down too. Lads were locked in each other's arms. I fed a hand through and wrapped it round his neck. I held him back. The lad he was fighting with surged forward but his attack came too late. Bullet, who had returned to the brawl, caught him square on the jaw with a peach of a punch and down he went. Dave was pummelling a couple of guys in the corner switching from one to the other. I dragged the youth I had round the neck off toward the entrance. He stopped struggling.

'All right, mate. I'm going. I'll walk out.' He felt the need to repeat what he just said. I kept a firm hold of him until we reached the top of the stairs.

'You have two choices; walk or be thrown down.'

'I'll walk, mate.' I let him go and he ran down the stairs and tripped falling head first down the second flight. I followed. He shot back up uninjured from the fall and ran out into the street, his face bloodied from the fight and his shirt partially ripped off. He stumbled across two unconscious bodies. I slammed the door and sprinted back up the staircase. 'It's clear, it's clear,' Bullet said laughing. We walked back down to the foyer.

The lads that had been kicked out were now scrapping with each other outside the club.

I watched through the small window in the door as the police pounced, dragging bodies into their van for a night in the cooler. Bullet and Dave were joking with each other about who was the fastest to the fight. I held my chest and coughed, the smoke having irritated my lungs.

The rest of the night went by without incident except for a few pukers and piss-heads being escorted from the premises. I thought I was fit but my legs had turned to jelly and my throat burned from inhaling too much smoke. It was a sprint from cold that caused the feelings. I needed to do more running.

At the end of the night we gathered upstairs for a drink. The dickie bows were off, the tension eased. The lads laughed and joked about the evening's activities.

'Do you think you'll stick the job, John?' Dave asked. I looked at the blood splattered on the front and cuffs of my shirt and caught a glance of myself in the mirror at the back of the bar. I looked around at the lads that had watched my back throughout the night. I looked at the cash in my hand and shoved it into my pocket.

'Yeah Dave, loved it.'

'Well if you want it the job's yours.'

At home I lay on the bed and felt comfortable. I couldn't wait until the next shift. I also wondered how long it would take for the ringing in my ears to stop.

LONE WORKING

After the realisation of jelly legs and the burning chest I decided to get back into my old running routine. The course I set for myself was a three mile circuit between Loughborough and nearby Quorn across open countryside. I wore steel toe cap boots for added resistance. At the end of the run I jogged to the old railway bridge and started a sprint routine. Ten press-ups, sprint to the top of the hill about 40 metres, ten sit-ups then walk down the hill backwards for recovery. Ten times was sufficient to recreate the feelings I had during kick-offs at the club. Three times a week gave me a high standard of fitness. I always finished with bag work.

Working the door alone is not a good idea. It only takes two people to start a fight.
The benefit is that working alone you will learn a lot about tactics and deception really quickly. You have to. So when Dave asked me to take on his Monday night session on my own I was slightly reluctant to take the job on. On Monday nights the club could get anywhere from 50 to 200 punters in.
'What's the routine if it kicks off, Dave?' I asked.
'It never does, John. It's just a few scoobies and art students having a laugh. It's like their weekend,' he said. 'You'll enjoy it, John. It's a right laugh and it's easy money.'
I detected a hint of deception in Dave's voice. 'The money's a bit less than the weekend but it's money for nothing,' he said.
'All right. I'll do it.'

Bill was the duty manager and an ex-doorman himself. He knew all the scams that went on and would always watch your back for you, especially if it kicked off. His motto was: 'You're the fucking doorman. Sort it out.' Bill would watch the door if the buzzer went off. He'd work the pay-box until the till went upstairs at 1.00 a.m.
My job was to keep the townies out unless they were into that particular scene or had student union identity. Two scenes don't mix and if you do mix them up the atmosphere of the main scene would die and trouble would ensue. The Indie alternative scene was one of those risky nights: full of all kinds of weird and

wonderful people. It was a very young scene, mainly art college kids with a smattering of like-minded individuals of varying ages. It was occasionally invaded by one or two of their college tutors trying to keep hold of their youthful arrogance and fit in with their students. I was the filter system to ensure that only people into the scene were allowed in. If any townie or squaddie slipped the filter there could be trouble. Usually if they did slip by they didn't stay long. You either loved the music or hated it.

Most people dressed completely outrageously or in second-hand clothes picked off the rails at one of the many charity shops or jumble sales that were springing up all over the town. The night had its characters; most looked like a cross between Russell Brand and Pete Burns.

It was one big Rocky Horror Show. There was always the musty smell of patchouli oil and the sweet sickly smell of dope. Those punters that didn't suit the scene were easy to spot. Most of the confrontation was on the door. I could go through the night without a hint of trouble upstairs.

The buzzer pierced the silence and shocked me out of my daydream into action. I climbed the two flights of stairs. My breathing changed as I hit the top step. My heart raced. I turned right. I didn't have time to think about what I was about to face. I crashed through the double fire doors and scanned the area as I ran forward. All eyes were on me. I sped past the speakeasy. The first bar was clear. I ran up onto the raised area looking over at the DJ for an indication of where the trouble was located. No response from the DJ. I pushed by a man in long red dress who resembled Shirley Bassey with dodgy make-up and ran to the pool table in the main bar area.

'Who's pressed the buzzer?' I shouted to the barman. He shrugged his shoulders. I looked again to the DJ whose head was still bowed thumbing through his record collection. I could see the light on above his head indicating that he'd hit the buzzer.

'You've just pressed the fucking buzzer, you fucking dick.'

'Sorry, mate. I'm real sorry. I didn't know I pressed it.'

'Don't press it unless you see a kick-off, all right?'

My chest was heaving. I sucked in a deep breath trying to get some good quality air to my lungs to feed the working muscles and get them ready for action. Trouble was there was no action to be had.

Fucking false alarm: the worst thing that can happen in a nightclub. I must have barged about ten people on the way through. That in itself can cause trouble when some twat turns on you for spilling their drink. I made my way down the staircase. I recovered my breath quickly. My new training regime of hill sprinting was paying me dividends.

Bill sat on his stool in the pay-box sipping an ice cold lager with a smile on his face and froth from the lager on his moustache.
'Fucking false alarm, Bill.'
'Well not to worry, Skillybob. It will keep you fit.'
Bill's laughter brought a smile to my face. Two girls appeared behind me. I was still hyped up from the panic alarm and didn't notice them until one of them spoke.
'Excuse me but when you ran past us you knocked my friend's drink out of her hand.'
'Did I? I'm sorry, mate. I'll see if I can sort it for you.' I approached Bill.
'Bill, these two girls' drinks got knocked out of their hands when I ran past them. Can you sort it out for them?'
'Here, give 'em a couple of drinks vouchers and get them to tell Rob the bar manager to bring me a pint down.'
'There you go, girls. Hand this voucher into the bar and they will give you a half pint each.'
'We were on pints!'
Bill was in earshot of the girls and interjected. 'Fuck her. Half's good enough. They'd probably drunk half already anyway. She said it was her mate's drink. So get her to buy her mate a pint using both vouchers and she can go without. If she don't like it tell her to fuck off out of the club.' Bill's customer service style left a lot of room for improvement.
I didn't have to repeat what Bill had said. The girls were also in earshot.
'You heard, him girls,' the girls walked off slightly put out at Bill's abrupt nature. But to Bill who was off the same council estate as me, the alternative lot were just a bunch of posh kids, acting weird.
There was a knock at the door. I peered through the glass peephole. Two lads dressed in weekend townie gear stood on the top step. I opened the door and was immediately hit by the smell of burgers

and fried onions emanating from the breath and clothing of the lads.

'Yes, mate?' I said.

'What time do you close?'

'2.00 a.m., mate.'

'How much is it to get in?'

'A quid, mate.'

'And how much a pint?'

'A quid.'

The lad who had questioned me turned in the direction of his friend.

'Shall we go in?'

'How much is it, mate?' the lad asked again as if trying to be sure he heard right.

'It's still a quid.'

'That's cheap. It's usually more than that at the weekend.'

'Yeah I know, but it's not the weekend is it!'

I watched the quiet one, whose eyes were glazed over from too much beer. It was a warm evening yet the kid looked cold. Both his hands were firmly in his pockets. They went to walk into the club. I blocked their path and broke the bad news to them.

'Sorry, lads, you won't get in tonight. Try again at the weekend.'

'Oh come on, mate. We've just got a taxi from Leicester. It cost us a fortune.'

'I'm sorry, mate. You can't come in.' I shut the door under the instructions of Bill. I felt sorry for the lads; they just wanted a piss up. I knew that if I let them in, there would be trouble or I would have to babysit them till they left.

The door rattled. 'Open the fucking door!' I heard someone shout. I ignored the rattle. The lad with the glazed eyes had his face pressed against the small glass window peering in at me making him look like Quasimodo, the bell ringer. He looked like he was trying to climb in through the glass like some crazed zombie. He pulled back slightly then pressed his finger against the glass pointing it at me. He had become an abomination of himself. The alter ego Mr Hyde had appeared. The way he had changed from an ordinary lad to a nasty one reminded me of the way the CID used to play good cop, bad cop routines. I opened the door to explain the situation to him and he surged forward in kill mode. He was too late. I let rip with a low front kick into his groin. The boot hit him solid. He doubled up dropping his hands to cover his bollocks. I gave him a second warning – the first being the kick in the knackers.

'Don't kick the fucking door.' He surged forward again. I held on to each side of the door frame for balance and booted him again. I leant back slightly to give me more power, raising the knee to the required height. This time the kick was a lot cruder and full on. The guy winced and doubled up for a second time. I raised my tone. 'I meant what I said.' This time he got the message and backed off down the steps.

I pulled the door shut. 'Fucking twat,' I exclaimed. Bill sniggered over the top of his pint glass.

'Knock him out, Skillybob.'

It was all just a laugh to Bill. The door rattled again. I'd now had enough. I snatched the door open ready to lay into the kid. Pete, the owner of the club, reared backward.

'Whoa! It's me, Pete.'

Pete was over six feet but hunched over due to the excessive amount of alcohol he had drunk. Pete was a party animal. When he was pissed everyone and no one were his friends. Pete had a habit of bringing in people that he had only just met, ordinary people whom he latched onto. Most of the time it would be some celebrity. They wouldn't pay, they'd just walk in. It was good for business, Pete would say. It would have been if we had got some, some kind of advertising or profile after the visit or a recommendation, Pete couldn't see that he was being used. I didn't like the way people took the piss out of him. He was a fair bloke.

Pete walked through the door. I put my arm out to stop the next two who were about to follow Pete in.

'It's all right, John. They're with me.'

I forced the two townies back out of the door and off the steps. I followed and stood on the top step.

'Fuck off. You've been told twice, now fuck off.' I'd already given them a chance to leave.

I felt like knocking the pair of them out. Instead I gave them the instructions that I hoped they would adhere to.

'Fuck off.' I underlined what I'd said with a cold stare and a sideways upward movement of the head like I was trying to flick water off my hair. They got the message and walked off toward fat Pete's burger stand pushing at each other. I kept my eyes on them until they got into a taxi and drove off. Pete the owner put his hand on my shoulder.

'Sorry about that, John.' Pete slurred his words and spat out the offer of a drink.

I liked Pete even though he was a pain in the arse when he was drunk, but aren't most people? Pete wandered off upstairs.

Just as I was dropping into deep thought I was panicked upstairs by the buzzer. I could hear Bill shouting in the background. I sprinted through the double doors and headed for the dance floor. The room was over the top with disco smoke. It was hard to see what was happening. I spotted a group of lads pushing and shoving each other. At first I thought they were slam dancing – which consisted of the crowd pushing shoving and jumping into each other. I would have stopped there and then if it wasn't for the DJ pointing frantically at the group.

I had no time to decide who was guilty and steamed into the centre like a rugby player going in for the ball. The group collapsed into a heap as I rammed them. One remained standing. I gave him a short right, enough to stun him then grabbed him and twisted him into a neck-hold. I dragged him to the top of the staircase. He struggled and refused to move. I grounded him, grabbed his trouser bottoms and dragged him down the staircase. His arse hit every step on the way down. Bill was waiting.

'I have him, John. Go.' I left him in Bill's capable hands and sprinted back upstairs. Two girls were pointing to a lad standing at the side of the dance floor who was trying to look innocent.

'Come on. Let's go,' I said. As I grabbed him he put his hands up as if I had a gun.

'All right. I'm going, mate.' I stepped in behind him and walked him to the top of the stairs. The guy kept his cool and did as I said. I got him to the top and passed him onto Bill who was waiting at the bottom. 'Down you go, mate.'

'Don't hurt me, mate,' came his pathetic plea.

'Fuck off outside.' I waited till Bill had him then went back inside.

The lads were followed by about 15 other punters. Trouble didn't go down well with the alternative crowd. It freaked them out, especially if they had been indulging in psychedelic chemicals or some type of whacky baccy. As people left I apologised for the trouble. The alternative nights were a good early week earner for the club and for me, while I got the chance to work them. A week later one of the lads came back to the club to thank me for my timely intervention. He'd been standing with his friend when I'd stepped in stopping his mate from getting a pasting. When the crowd had gone over from the force of my entry into the *mêlée*, he'd broken his leg and due to the chemicals in his body he didn't realise until the next day that it was broken.

Bill was a good laugh and knew how to have the craic; I was never bored in his company. He was a good doorman and manager having saved Sammy's from what could have been a serious fire. Whilst on routine patrol around the club, he spotted an improvised incendiary device. Someone, for whatever reason, had been compelled to plant the device under one of the seats inside the club, on the busiest night of the week. Had it gone off, the place would have been devastated and lives lost. The culprit was finally caught and got a big sentence for his crime. Bill Barras was truly one of the lads and a good friend.
I knew every part of Sammy's that the public were allowed to go into. It was a big club that regularly held several hundred people. Sammy's was the classic, townie, disco venue. I'd fought in every corner of the place and knew the flash points because I'd been in them. I could spot trouble before it kicked off. I'd got used to that after ten years of scrapping round the town. I'd proved my worth in many a gang brawl and I knew how to deal with violence because I knew how violent people thought. I'd done my apprenticeship on the streets, in DC, borstal, prison, in the pubs and clubs and now I was a professional. I was getting paid for taking out the trash. Where before I was classed as a troublemaker by the police and hounded by them, I was now doing the same job. Only I didn't lock people up. I dealt with the problem there and then: judge, jury and executioner.

This was my trade. Like all good tradesman I needed the best tools to do the job. My tools were my hands, feet and brain and any other part of me that I could use to defeat the violent when our paths crossed. I'd always been able to punch. I found it easy to land a punch on the button. I was a knockout specialist. One punch was usually enough. A quick question and bang, straight out. It's not difficult to throw your fist into someone's head. I kept up my boxing training, but since working at Sammy's I found that something was missing from the toolbox. I needed another edge. A lot of the time I would find myself in a grapple, pulling or pushing people out. It wasn't always advisable to punch someone and besides not everyone required the tough treatment of knuckle and boot.

I decided to take up judo. I chose judo after becoming aware of the sport via Brian Jacks of *Superstars'* fame. Brian Jacks was 'the man', the hero from TV's *Superstars*. His throwing, sweeping and grappling skills were legendary. He was the most widely known judoka in the public eye. With 1970 and 1973 European Championship wins and his 1968 World bronze medal most people knew of him. His Olympic bronze in 1972 set him apart from other athletes of that time. It was Brian Jacks' judo that inspired me to take up the best grappling martial art available to me.
I started my judo at the Trinity Judo Club in Loughborough, with a local lad by the name of Ian Stores. Ian was a very good judo player. He encouraged us to train and fight hard and travel to different clubs in and around Loughborough, Leicester and Nottingham. One of the toughest was Leicester Judokwia on Sunday mornings.

The club was above an old church and was full of brown belts and Dan grades. Most good competition fighters went there for a workout. I used to get hammered in the beginning, then eventually I started to get the upper hand. I was hungry for the club fighting and never really considered competition. All I wanted the judo for was to give me the edge on the door or in the street. Many lessons were learnt mixing with the tough guys and serious competition fighters who would thrash us and then like all good judoka, tell you where you were going wrong or congratulate you if you did well. Judo is a tough art.

I started to incorporate judo into my door work. During kick-offs certain things started to shine through over the months and years that followed. The techniques were being pressure tested for real. I found a major improvement in my gripping strength. The grips worked immediately. After all, door work is about getting control of situations by fair or by foul. The leg trips and the feel for controlling and feeling the bad intent in body movement gave me an advantage in that I could pre-empt their attack. The head- and neck-holds I was using became chokes and strangles. Chokes which I was using before the judo training became far better due to the increase in grip strength. My reactions improved. The close-in, crowded stuff never seemed to bother me. I didn't care when someone pushed their face into mine. I dealt with it by using rising elbow chokes, throat grabs, pulling and pushing. I could feel and pre-empt body movement. Judo gave me great tactile awareness.

The first time I used a rising choke was during a family feud which had kicked off one Saturday night. They were a close-knit bunch of friends but mix beer, women and men, add in a little bit of controversy and you have a very potent cocktail with a very dramatic kick to it. I knew all of them which made it worse.

In-fighting is common at family do's especially if there is no common enemy. Dave and me knew them best and had to sort out the problem and try and calm things down without the argument breaking into a fight and spreading. We couldn't just go steaming in; these were our friends and associates.

The group separated the two fighters and were pulling and pushing and holding each other back. Each one of the group had either somebody holding them back or they were holding someone else back. It was a very fluid situation. Twenty or so bodies cluttered the double fire doors in front of the ladies' toilet. No one dared leave through the scuffling for fear of being drawn into the situation. It was tense as we moved in to calm things down. Our presence rekindled the fight. Both fighters were now fully engaged. Dave grabbed one, I grabbed the other and we broke them apart.

The guy I grabbed hold of was a fiery tempered individual with a strong reputation as a brawler. We'd had our run-ins in the past. He had the temperament of an enraged pit-bull on a leash.

I placed my hand on his right shoulder and asked him to stay cool. I could feel his intent. He went to push forward. I raised my elbow and pushed it across and into his throat, pinning him against the wall. I found that if I eased it off he was still pinned with my body weight. If he tried to surge forward I could apply the choke and push him onto his heels, making it difficult if not impossible to surge forward from this position.

I had one problem: my back was exposed to the rest of the group.

My old friend Spider had appeared on the scene and was watching my back. That's what real friends are for, which gave me peace of mind. If nobody was watching my back I would have had to spin my man around into a headlock or knock him out with the choke to get him out. That was an option but not one the crowd would take too kindly to. I knew he could go a bit and that he favoured the head so I rendered this useless. I pressed my forearm against his throat, using the shoulder as a hinge point. I had my body weight pressing into his chest. I dropped my weight lowering my hips as in judo so I could force the pressure up. I could see his eyes getting wider as I held the choke on.

I eased off the pressure to let him breathe, then told him again to calm down.

'You're choking me,' he said.

'Calm down and I will let you go.' His anger had subsided, he had become compliant.

The rising choke worked well under pressure in the dojo, usually whilst on the ground. I had adapted it there and then and pressure tested it for real with no rules but my own morals.

Judo became a necessary part of my training. I noticed that the rising choke was very similar to the upper block in kung fu or karate. I could restrain safely without putting myself in too much risk. The judo fitted in nicely with the roughhouse boxing I always practised. Punching was my main artillery. It was the distance I found myself at most of the time.

I felt safe and confident knowing I could drop a man with either hand. My left fist was as hard as my right, because I had damaged my right hand knuckle after I threw an uppercut into someone's jaw. Due to lack of targeting I hit the teeth instead of the underside of the jawbone. The teeth are full of germs and the knuckle became infected. The red lines – the sign of blood poisoning – were climbing up my veins. I was in bandages for ages but carried on training isolating the injury and concentrating on training my left hand punch. My left hand became as strong as my right.

I had the tools for the job and like a good tradesman kept them in good condition. I trained every night during the week usually before work and Saturday mornings. This gave me an edge. Having confidence in my ability enabled me to hold back in situations when normally I would kick off immediately. I was starting to learn how to weigh up the pros and cons of a situation. Being pre-emptive is the way, but I didn't want to be fighting if I could negotiate a way out.

BLINDSIDED

"Constant awareness is the cornerstone of good personal security."
The modern bodyguard by Peter Consterdine

Working the door is dangerous without a doubt. People who are driven by alcohol or some other drug don't act in a rational way. I remember one lad being so angry he crushed a pint glass in his hand as he contemplated sticking it into someone's face. I watched another repeatedly smash his face against a small pane of wired glass until it cracked: a mash of blood made him un-recognisable in seconds. Whilst working the door you need 360 degree awareness and someone to watch your back. And still you can be caught out. 'After the battle tighten your helmet straps', is an old Japanese samurai warrior saying that definitely rings true within the realm of the bouncer.

Being caught on the back foot was common in the early days of my door work. Unlike fighting in the street with where I could hot foot it into the night whilst discussing the intricacies of booting someone's head off their shoulders. On the door it was different. On the door you had to stand your ground. Oh yeah, there was the occasional time when one or two of the lads had to disappear for fear of being hauled in for questioning by the Old Bill, but generally staying put was the only option. Running, after all, could be construed as guilt or worse, cowardice. I was being paid to do a job. It was our door which we protected even if it meant a kicking. It was an honour to stand and fight. And if you're getting paid to do a job then that's what you should do. Whilst on the door I was constantly reminded of the fact. I couldn't even go to the toilet for fear of being accused of hiding from trouble.

If your bottle was suspect you were out. The lads just wouldn't work with you. Sticking together as a team was what it was all about. Together we were strong. Dave and I were a two-man team most of the time and I had a good reputation as a bouncer in the circles that mattered.

A new fun pub was opening in Loughborough. Fun pubs were the new craze sweeping the country. It was good business to attract the new breed of young drinkers that were going abroad in the summer, then coming back to the UK expecting the party to continue. People wanted more from the English pub. They wanted a party and the fun pub was delivering.

Pub crawls were the 'in thing'. If the pub was good then it would be packed for longer. The concept bar had arrived just in time for the youth explosion that was gripping the cities and towns. I was approached by the manager of the new fun pub, prior to it being opened. He wanted a couple of bouncers to protect the new venture. He'd heard of my reputation for doing the job right. He explained that the pub was to be more like a nightclub atmosphere at the weekends.

Pubs were just starting to take on doormen but they were generally rare. In Loughborough nobody worked the pub doors – this was to be one of the first. Me, Dave, Bullet and Sean made up a team of four on the door. The pub was a big success and we sorted out a deal with Jon, the new manager of Sammy's, enabling us to work the pub first then Sammy's after. We would boost the reputation of Sammy's whilst we stood on the busiest pub in town, giving out tickets and promoting the place.

People felt safe with bouncers on the door. Soon pub doors sprung up all over the town.

They were a major part of the scene. If you had bouncers on the door you could almost guarantee a good crowd. It was a much-needed boom time for pubs and clubs and everywhere seemed to be busy. More bouncers were needed to sort out the confrontations that were ever present when the blood was saturated with alcohol.

The bouncers in the town stuck together and became one big team; you fucked with one you fucked with them all. We had our own system to keep out the shit and were a law unto ourselves. We created our own Asbo so to speak. If you were barred from one venue you were barred from them all. We formed an unwritten door code: if one door was in trouble the other lads would join forces and sort the problems out. The doors in Loughborough were run by Loughborough doormen. Anyone else were considered outsiders and not welcome. It was the same in other towns and cities – you didn't work on someone else's patch and they didn't work on yours, unless you were invited in.

We'd just got back from Sophie's Bar, which was very busy at the weekends, and saw a kick-off with a gang of out of town lads. The door lads were outnumbered and we jumped in to help out. Due to this we were late opening Sammy's doors. A queue had formed and they were getting restless.
'What time are you opening?' asked a girl who was not far off from being a dwarf. I looked down at her and smiled.
'Now,' I said.
Before I could give the instruction to come in, I heard the manager say, 'Dickey-bow, John.' He adjusted his own dickey-bow to underline what he had said.
I delved into my pocket pulled out my neat little dickey-bow.
'I thought you'd forgot it for a minute there, John. I thought you would be wearing the bat,' said Dave.
The bat was an old fashioned dickey-bow of gigantic proportions. I remembered the glass collector on my first night had been wearing it and he looked a complete clown. The manager, backed up by the bouncers, insisted you wear it if you forgot your own. It was a bit of a laugh at the expense of somebody else's ridicule. It made you remember your dickey-bow. Being smart was the key to a successful door. We had to set the example to the punters. The queue pressed forward up the steps of the club and filed their way to the point where my outstretched arm prevented any further forward movement. From this position I could control the flow of the eager human traffic.
Dave was positioned on the door opposite me staring out of the inspection window with a face as serious as an immigration officer at passport control. He was checking for undesirables, underage drinkers, known troublemakers, and gangs of lads likely to kick off once inside.
My eyes scanned the queue checking like Dave for possible knock backs. Four eyes are better than two. It was our job to make the club as safe as possible by preventing the shit from getting to the fan.

All seemed well – just the time when things go wrong – when you least expect it to.
Dave gave me the nod that a group of lads had pushed to the front of the queue and were walking up the steps to gain entry. Their attitude was one of 'We're too good to queue up'. They now stood facing me, daring me to refuse them entry. I scanned their faces, not catching anyone's gaze so I didn't get drawn into a staring match and lose sight of the others in the gang.
'Yes, mate. Can I help you?' I asked. I was always polite.
'Yeah. We want to come in.' I didn't recognise any of the lads and between both Dave and myself we knew everybody in the town that was worth knowing. I decided to use a time-honoured tactic: get the crowd on my side. I gestured toward the queue
'And so do all of these people who were in front of you.' A group of girls at the front gave the lads some stick.
'Who do you think you are? Haven't you heard of ladies first?'
'Yeah get to the back,' said the short girl.
'Wait your turn,' somebody else said.
'You heard them, mate,' I said trying to make light of the situation that was evolving.
'I ain't fucking queuing up.' The lad's arrogance intensified. His aggressive nature shone through like the low winter sun shines through your car windscreen, irritating as fuck.
He obviously took my light-hearted reply as a sign of weakness. The guy was acting like a fucking jerk. I stood tall trying to give him a subliminal message not to fuck me about. The crowd went silent sensing a kick-off. They waited for my reply. I stayed cool. I was aware of Dave's manoeuvring closer to my side: another indication it was about to kick. I held onto both sides of the door in a relaxed manner ready to launch a front kick to his unsuspecting groin area – a big target, difficult to miss. One good boot would distract him from my follow-up attack. Or get him to capitulate.

I could tell from the way he was standing he was about to be sucked in to my trap. Otherwise, he would have stepped back or stood side on.
I gave my reply,

'If you ain't prepared to queue up like everybody else then you ain't coming in. I suggest that you and your friends go and join the queue.'

I changed from a friendly tone to a serious one. The lad stared at me. He was the man. If he accepted my suggestion so would the others. He was key to peace. If he went for it, they all would go for it. I stared back, waiting for the first sign of his attack. I wasn't going to succumb to his aggressive stance. I knew too well his type. I had to show my strength of character. If he sensed weakness he would go for it.

I didn't give a fuck about him or his mates. I was ready. He needed to know that.

The silence was broken when he blinked nervously. Like a boxer accepting defeat before the fight starts he broke off the stare that was about to draw me in to physical confrontation. He turned away and said to his friends:

'Come on. It's a fucking shit hole anyway.'

The group of girls that had ridiculed the gang erupted into laughter when one of them parroted in a high-pitched voice what he had said. The lads stormed off. The crowd shuffled forward.

'That told them,' another of the girls said. I smiled politely breaking the aggressive feelings I was battling with. A deep breath helped the smile break through. Dave had moved behind me during the confrontation so the lads could see we were a team. I had noticed one of the lads having a good look inside the door as I was negotiating their withdrawal.

Ignoring what had just taken place and making light of the situation, Dave leaned over to my ear.

'Do you know what, John? I think it's going to be a busy one tonight.' 'The best disco in town' by the Ritchie Family piped through the speaker in the foyer. The atmosphere was building. The punters made their way upstairs. Brian, the cloakroom attendant, a tough 16-year-old, was chatting up a group of girls whilst he hung up their coats. I kept the banter going with the crowd, making them feel welcome as they waited to party the night away. It also helped to ease the feelings of fear that were racing through my veins due the confrontation I'd just had.

I'd just started to relax when bang! The queue at the front door was forced apart as the gang stormed into the foyer. I was overwhelmed by the speed and aggression of their unexpected attack. The first punches missed but forced me onto the back foot and onto autopilot. I returned fire and hammered home hook after hook not worrying where the punches were landing. I just fired them into the bodies that were in front of me. I forced one back into the wall just inside the foyer and continued my barrage. As he dropped to the floor I turned and was met with another ferocious attack. I ducked and surged forward banging in punch after punch. I was now alongside Dave who was pummelling one of the attackers against the wall. Brian the cloakroom guy had leapt over the counter and was scrapping with another. One of the attackers made a run for the door panicking his mates into flight mode. They followed him taking hits as they went. The mouthy one who had started the ball rolling was a bloody mess after Dave's barrage of punches. I let go a perfect right hand punch and sent one of his crew to the deck just as he fled the scene. I stamped on his shoulder then rolled him with my boot down the steps. The crowd cheered. Dave stood alongside me as the lads grabbed their wounded and made off. The queue which until now had been a bit unruly stood in perfect order not wanting to get involved. The scene calmed down and the queue once again filed in.

We had to get ourselves back to normal as quickly as possible. Smiling and a bit of humour cleared the tension. 'Disco Inferno' by the Trammps got the crowd buzzing as they shuffled in through the door. Me, I kept one eye on the steps just in case.

Later, after the crowd had gone in, I nipped upstairs to watch a re-run of the video tape and make sure that a new tape was put into the video. The old one disappeared in case the police became involved or wanted to view it later. I watched the footage on the CCTV. It took one minute from when they rushed into the foyer to when they left but it felt like ten. I'd learnt another valuable lesson: always be prepared for a comeback especially straight after a confrontation. Tighten your helmet straps and remember: it's not over, until it's over.

THE KNOCK BACK

Getting rejected or ejected from a club can be embarrassing. People don't like rejection. We all want to feel like we belong, that we can take part in what our peers take part in. But as a fact of life we don't fit into every scenario no matter who we are.

'No trainers tonight, lads,' said Jon the manager as he passed us by on the staircase. Jon was ex-navy, a smart 30-something and new manager of Sammy's. He meant what he said. And no trainers to us meant just that. Even if the Queen turned up wearing trainers she'd have to get changed or get refused entry. I have lost count of the arguments I've had trying to explain to one of my own friends that they couldn't come in due to wearing the wrong attire. It's a tough call to turn away a friend because they don't fit the bill. But then again, a friend wouldn't put you in that position if they were a true friend. It makes it equally difficult when you're turning your own friend away from the door and sod's law delivers the owner on the doorstep with one of his friends wearing trainers! When a manager gave us instructions we carried them out to the letter – not really the right thing to do. What you should do is be flexible. But in the early days of my door work I was far from flexible. No trainers meant no trainers. Sorry, Your Majesty.

It was a Tuesday night, student night at Sammy's. The club was heaving by 10.00 p.m. It was their big night out and the town was overrun with students on the piss. Most of the students were taking advantage of the cheap drinks that were on offer to entice them into the club. Drinks with names like 'snake bite' (cider and lager mixed) or 'purple nasty' (lager, cider, and blackcurrant); these drinks were very potent and at the end of the night the staff and punters would be wading through a variety of differently coloured pukes.

When the beer was in the students got stupid. A small incident could become a major fight especially if it involved one of the rugby team. Loughborough played host to some of the top university rugby players. Most would go on to play international standard rugby. I enjoyed the hectic atmosphere of Tuesday nights.

I also felt very small at times weighing in at around 80 kilos facing lads of 100 plus but I had heart, bottle, and plenty of street savvy which more than compensated.

Dave and I worked the door with hundreds of students dancing the night away. It really was the only place to be if you were a student. The nights became legendary. Some of the most famous of athletes attended Sammy's, most before they were famous. Some had already reached those dizzy heights.
'Sorry, mate, no trainers,' I heard Dave say.
'Come on, guys, it's student night.'
I countered his observation.
'Listen, mate, I wouldn't even let my own brother in tonight if he was wearing trainers.'
'I'm sure you wouldn't,' came his sarcastic reply.
The guy was otherwise very smart. Jet black hair. A lean physique. His clothes didn't quite fit the student look. It was like he had dressed the way he did just to fit in with the Sammy's crowd. I noticed the quality of his trainers. They must have cost a fortune and were probably the most expensive thing the guy was wearing.
'I'm sorry, mate you can't come in those trainers. You'll have to go home and get them changed and then come back,' I said taking the onus off Dave.
'Look guys, do you know who I am?'
We did but we didn't let on.
'I'm Sebastian Coe, the 1500m world record holder.'
I couldn't stop myself from saying what was coming next, it just seemed appropriate.
'Well mate, it won't take you long to run home and get some shoes now will it.' Dave turned away and started to laugh. I realised what I had said. Sebastian Coe took it well. He even smiled himself and saw the funny side. He went off home and came back a short while later wearing shoes. We let him in for free. After all, he was a celebrity.

I met a few celebrities who turned up at the venue over the years. Thursday night, 1.45 a.m., I was standing on the door waiting for the punters to leave. A tall, well-made guy stumbled out of a taxi and almost fell flat on his face. Doing well to regain his balance stumbled up the steps and stood in the open doorway looking at me with glassy eyes.

'Sorry, mate. We're closed,' I said.

'I'm here to see Pete the owner. I'm a friend of his.'

'Well Pete's not here. He's gone home and I suggest you do the same before you fall over.'

'He said he'd be here.'

'Well I'm not lying to you, mate. He's gone.'

'Well can I nip in for a quick drink?'

'No, mate. Last orders went ages ago.'

'You know who I am. I've been here before with Pete.'

I recognised the man and knew that if I let him in I would have to spend the next hour trying to get him to leave. Sleep was calling me so that I could rest before my 6.30 alarm went off.

'I'm sorry, mate. We're closed.' Then he hit me with it!

'I'm Peter Shilton, the England goalkeeper.'

'I know who you are and you're playing at the weekend so an early night will do you good, Peter.'

The quick quip stunned him. He stayed silent then said with a smile on his face, 'You're right.' He turned and got back into his taxi.

Peter Shilton played a brilliant game that following weekend. It amazed me considering how drunk he'd been. He became a short term regular at the club. He probably won't remember as he was always drunk. That aside he was the best goalkeeper England has ever had and a lovely man.

THE THREE AMIGOS

Working through the week at the club and holding down my day job at the Brush became too much for me. I hated the boredom of the factory. And I was constantly having arguments with the foreman. There was just something about him I didn't like. I decided to hand in my notice. Just before I did a good friend of mine, Pete Rake, who was one of the area's top lads in the '60's Mod era and a good scrapper, gave me some top advice. This led me to stay on a couple of more painful weeks. I got offered voluntary redundancy. Six weeks' wages and accrued holiday pay meant I got a big payout. Something I wouldn't have got if I'd have given in my notice. Never jump the gun! I thanked Pete for his advice and told him anytime he needed a favour I'd be there for him. For me, my only income now was from my job as a bouncer.

We named Thursday night 'Fight Night.' Every Thursday the local Royal Army Signals base would release their civilian clothed ranks onto the streets. The squaddies seemed to have only three things on their minds: women and lager. The women usually caused the third thing: scrapping. Meet them in the cool light of day, alcohol free, and they were a great crew of lads, but get them drunk and they were a real pain in the arse. The squaddies were major binge drinkers and scraps would break out all over town. The local lads gave out more than they got. There were no rules in street warfare; once it's kicked off, anything goes.

We closed the doors at 1.00 a.m. to prevent the undesirables from gaining entry. The undesirables were punters who had tried getting into another club usually out of town and had been unlucky or had got in but were ejected for fighting or drunkenness. A bloodstained youth stood in the doorway with a couple of his mates. 'All right, John,' he said.
'Sorry, lads. The club's shut now and you know the rules: no entry after 1.00 a.m.'
'It's not 1.00 yet, John.' The kid's attitude immediately pissed me off. He was right but the fact he was covered in blood was a clear

indication that he had been fighting and for all I knew the lad he fought could be inside. If they met it could all kick off again.

There was one other thing that pissed me off; he was talking to me as if he knew me. I'd seen him around before but he didn't *know* me. He knew *of* me. I liked to keep a distance from the lads using the club. I might have to chuck one of them out at some point and it's a lot easier if you don't know them. I decided to ask them about the trouble they'd been in. If it was a good story, who knows. I might let them in.

'What happened, lads? Where's the blood from?'

'Oh I've had a right good scrap,' he said. He sounded very proud of himself.

'I battered this squaddie to fuck.'

'Yeah he fucking killed him. I was there. The squaddie didn't have a chance.' The second kid looked at his mate like someone looking at a famous star.

'Where's the lad now?'

'Oh he ran off.'

'Didn't you chase him?'

'No he'd had enough, John. He was a fucking wanker.'

I looked the lad up and down. He was covered in dirt and congealed blood. 'Listen, mate. You really can't come in looking like that.'

'Ah come on, John, I only want a quick drink.' Dave appeared and gave me the nod.

'He's all right, John. Let him in.'

I got the message and remembered Dave's wheeling and dealing. He probably had a hidden agenda. I changed my tone and said, 'Well seeing as you know Dave and you won, well I will let you in.'

That meant that the kid now owed Dave a favour and as my brother Sam says, 'a favour's better than a fiver', and Dave would definitely call it in at some point.

The kid went to walk in. 'Hang on a minute,' I said. I noticed blood seeping from the side of the kid's head. I turned him around to face me.

'What?' the kid asked.

'You did win didn't you?' The kid put his hand to the side of his face.
'Yeah why?'
'Well, where's your fucking ear?'
The kid put his hand to where his ear used to be. 'The squaddie bit it off.'
'Well don't you think you should take the ear and get it sewn back on?'
'I can't.'
'Why not?'
'The squaddie swallowed it.' I looked at Dave and made a face of distaste. Dave started to laugh.
'Go on. You better go and get a drink.' The kid wandered off with his mates holding on to the root of his ear.

The violence in town on Thursdays was a sickening sight. It was common to have a gang of lads stamping on a single guy. The drunken squaddies would then high tail it back to base to hide behind the uniform of the armed forces. You can't blame the squaddies for sticking together in a strange town. They weren't always the instigators of the violence and they did bring much needed revenue into the town. The pubs employed more door staff because of the squaddies' willingness to do battle so we weren't complaining. Not all squaddies were violent lager louts; most were just lager louts.

Thursdays were usually empty until the pubs kicked out then the queue would form outside the club. Sometimes we'd keep them waiting to make the venue appear busier and to build up the excitement factor. Then we would start the selection process. 'Sorry mate, not tonight,' were the words nobody wanted to hear. I stood firm with Dave; he was a good partner to work with: loads of bottle and a great laugh. He had one other major quality: he was brilliant with a cosh and fast on his feet. If he was chasing you were caught.
I remember one night there was a kick-off on the door. A group of lads tried to storm in and just before they ran in, we ran out and surprised them. After seeing one of their lads getting sparked by my right hand they fled. We gave chase and whilst still in a full

sprint Dave laced one of them over the head with his cosh. I was about a foot away when the cosh landed. The sound echoed round the empty streets and the kid's head opened up like a zipper on a raincoat. The kid tumbled forward but regained his balance. Dave didn't give chase and stood back to watch the kid leave a trail of blood behind him. It looked like a bad oil leak on a car.

Before the rush on the door, one of us would nip down to Fat Pete's burger van. Fat Pete was one of the good guys of the night. What Pete saw he kept to himself.
Hot dog men go through some shit being parked up in town. When I was running with the lads we would regularly rock the van – a dangerous thing to do and once or twice it went over.
As burger vans are very violent places we had a kind of a deal going. Pete needed looking after; he would supply us with food during the night and we would keep an eye on him.
If anyone gave him any shit we were up there like a shot. If there was ever any trouble Pete would see nothing and say nothing. Not just me but many other lads avoided prosecution due to Pete's stance on not getting involved.
Pete's appearance never altered. He wore a jumper beneath his apron even though the van was hot inside. His tired, unshaven looks gave him a dirty appearance, but his burgers and food were as clean as haute cuisine. He was always nervous and jittery; not surprising the amount of shit he took night after night. I do think that Pete hammed up the nervous streak a bit so we would feel a bit more compassionate towards him but he didn't need to. He was a likeable character.
It was my turn to do the burger run whilst Dave got the halves of beer in to wash them down with. I noticed a group of lads standing at the van. As I got closer I noticed that one of the lads was Fez. Fez was short for Ferret but his real name was Jason Beeby. Jason was my adopted brother. When he fell out with his dad, he left home and came to live with our family at Manor Drive. Fez was a lovely lad. The wimp that moved in with us had become a fiery tempered lad who would fight for a slice of bread if he was hungry enough. He'd learnt how to fight whilst living with us. I'd given him training, teaching him how to fight by punch bag work and

sparring. Fez got further fighting experience from the many bars, chip shops and kebab shops he used to frequent.

Fez stood with my dad watching over him. My dad could drink like a true Irishman and he loved the craic. He would often approach the lads in town and have a laugh with them. He could fight but that was the furthest thing from his mind. I didn't like my dad in the town on fight night.

Three other lads were standing to the side of the van scoffing burgers and fucking about like lads do. They were poking fun at my dad. Fez looked nervous.

'All right, Fez?' I said as I got within verbal range, letting the lads in earshot know I knew him.

'Yeah I'm all right, John,' he said looking slightly relieved I'd turned up.

'Aye up, Dad.'

When my dad noticed me his face lit up. He was very proud of me and wasn't afraid to show it in public.

'Hiya, Johnny boy.' He went into his usual rhetoric. 'Lend us a couple of quid for a drink, son.'

'You look like you've had enough, Dad. Come on. Let's get you home. Fez, get him a taxi. He's going home.'

'We're waiting for one, John,' Fez said.

'Usual, John?' Pete asked.

'Yes, Pete, two of your finest burgers, mate.'

The three lads at the side of the van were making piss-taking gestures to my dad.

'Hey Irish,' one of them said, then he jokingly teased my dad with his burger bun. At first I thought they were just having a giggle with my dad. He liked a laugh when he was out and about.

'What's their problem, Fez?' I asked.

'They're squaddies they've been taking the piss out of your dad because he's Irish.'

Fez was drunk and becoming emotional and was close to kicking off.

'I'll deal with this, Fez,' I said. I didn't want Fez steaming in whilst my dad was there. My dad couldn't fight sleep the state he was in. I had to deal with this situation swiftly. The army boys appeared cocky. I knew from the run-ins I'd had with them before that they were up for it.

'Are you ready, Fez? I'm going to give these fuckers one chance. If they don't take it I'm gonna take them out.'

I turned in the direction of the squaddies walking between them and my dad, making my presence felt.

'Hiya, Dad,' I exclaimed, letting the lads know that the guy they were taking the piss out of was my father. I was giving them the opportunity to walk away and stop bothering him. Anyone with any sense wouldn't pick on somebody's dad, especially if that someone was dressed as a bouncer. Fez was raring to get stuck into a fight. Fez knew the score; that I wouldn't want my dad involved. He stayed back a step or two which gave me the room I needed to manoeuvre. I faced the lads head on. I noticed Fat Pete move the ketchup and mustard from the front of the counter to the back shelf. He always did this just before a kick-off. Pete had learnt through experience.

The lads remained where they were. They were now silent. It became obvious to me that they were ready for trouble and wanted it. The uniform I was wearing hadn't fazed them. If they didn't want aggro they would have moved away from the van.

They hadn't realised that we were in the same trade; only I was the unarmed expert. They might be handy with a rifle or pistol in the hand but when the gloves were off this was my living. They were over-spilling with confidence, so much so that they didn't realise they were being set up.

The problem with the squaddies was they didn't respect the fact that they were in someone else's town. They had no fear of the local law. They knew the army would deal with them. They were in effect immune. They would probably be confined to barracks or get a slapped wrist at most. To the army they saw it as the lads letting off a bit of steam. To me and my friends they were invading our territory and for that they had to pay the price. I didn't consider the consequences of what was about to happen. I couldn't face three lads of unknown ability and think about getting arrested or worse beaten. I knew that hesitation would be my downfall. Hit first and let the coppers ask the questions later. It was as they saw it a three on three situation. I considered it a one on three situation and that's how I was going to deal with it.

I tested their bottle. 'What's your fucking problem?' The biggest squaddie in the middle of the group spoke.

'I ain't got a fucking problem.'
'You fucking have now.' The lad eyeballed me but never made a move.
'I think you owe this man an apology,' I said gesturing towards my dad.
The kid looked in the direction of my dad. I moved in closer as I spoke. I'd asked the question that would either end the confrontation or cause all out conflict. One of the youths positioned himself to the right of the talker. This enabled me to get a better angle on the talker. His other mate discarded his burger. This was an indication to me that he at least was up for it. Why else discard the burger? He also gave me the indication that it was going to happen immediately. I had to act. I repeated the question to the talker shuffling in to punching distance. I wanted the talker well and truly in the line of fire. The kid that had discarded his burger stepped a little closer. I raised my open palms just above waist level and turned my right shoulder through to my left, disguising the loading up of the left hook.
I pointed to the advancing squaddie, 'Keep out of it you. It's between me and him.'
As the talker turned his head toward his mate, I let go the left hook catching the talker flush on the jaw. I stepped out with my left foot toward the guy on my left, landing the right cross with my full bodyweight on the front of his jaw. The first lad, the talker was now silent and spaced out on the floor. The second one followed. And the third joined them as a left hook landed high on his cheekbone. All three were now horizontal to the pavement and unconscious. I lurched forward and momentarily lost my balance as a fourth punch which was already on the way hit mid air. It was not needed. I looked around me taking a mental note of all who witnessed my attack, fearing the watching eyes of the Old Bill. It was quiet at the van and the action was over in a couple of seconds.
'Fucking 'ell,' Fez said.
'Never mind that, Fez. Get in the taxi and take my dad home.'
'Fucking 'ell.' Fez felt the need to repeat himself. He bundled my dad into the cab and off they went. My dad hung his arm out of the cab window and punched the air.
'That's my boy,' he said and flopped into the cab.

If I'd learnt one thing about fighting over the years it was don't hang around for the glory, just fuck off and deny anything happened. Fat Pete replaced the ketchup and mustard and made up two quality steak burgers.

'Here's your usual, John. See you later. I won't say anything. You know me, John.' It was obvious Pete wanted me gone. Pete's nervous twitch flickered across his face which he usually got after a ruckus. I took the burgers and wandered off. I knew Pete would keep his mouth shut. He'd tell everybody else but not the police.

One of the lads was starting to come round and was sat upright. He looked completely confused and stared around his surroundings. He looked at his two mates on the floor beside him then looked up at me. I smiled and took a bite from one of the burgers.

'All right, mate?' I said as I walked off in the direction of Sammy's.

The quick continual movement of my feet enabled me to complete the multiple knockout, something I found easy to do. Dave had left the club door and was on his way to me after some girl had told him I was about to have a scrap. Dave slowed down his pace when he spotted the three lads on the floor and me walking back from the van. We strolled back to the door and enjoyed our burgers.

The smell from the burger lingered in the foyer much to the manager's distaste.

The club was busy. The crowd were enjoying themselves. I could see the dance floor on the small CCTV screen. The crowd's feet were moving to the sound of the Gap Band's 'Oops Upside Your Head'. Some were sitting in long rows holding each other's waists swaying and singing along. An aggressive shout at the top of the stairs got my feet moving toward the top landing. The aggressive shout had come from a friend of ours: a bouncer from one of the pubs in town who was in for a drink and had over indulged. By the time I'd got to the top the bouncer had changed his grip from the lad's attire to his throat. He squeezed tight around the lad's neck using a wide grip pinning the lad to the wall with a straight arm. From there he was telling the kid that he was out of order. I intervened.

'Sorry, John, but this cunt's out of order.'

'Let him go. I'll take him out.' At this the bouncer rammed his forehead into the lad's forehead. Then he issued him a warning.

'Don't ever fuck with me again. Do you understand?'

The kid looked surprised as the bouncer then turned toward me and started to walk down the staircase. I put my hand on his chest.

'It's all right, John. I'm going.' I was pissed off at the bouncer for his disrespect toward me. I'd already offered to take the lad out. My anger eased and I started to giggle. I couldn't help myself. The bouncer stared at me in disbelief.

'What's so funny?'

'I think you'd better get your head sorted out. It's pissing with blood.'

The blood from a cut, which was about two inches long and wide open, streamed down his face. The lad standing behind the bouncer was still shocked and stationary.

'Go inside, mate. I'll sort this out. Forget what happened.'

I was covering for the bouncer so the lad didn't go to the police. Letting him stay in was usually enough. When Dave saw the bouncer he too erupted into laughter. We patched him up and sent him on his way.

The lad came down a short while after saying that he'd walked into the bouncer and spilt his drink. He'd said sorry but it wasn't enough. My brother, Peter, who was working at the time confirmed the story. The lad didn't have a mark on him.

A valuable lesson learned: when head hits head the softest one will rip first. What the bouncer should have done if he felt the need to butt someone was hit anywhere below the eye-line of the antagonist. Personally I only use the head-butt as a last resort, for the reasons above.

I always giggle to myself when I think of that head-butt moment when a bit of poetic justice took place.

As the lad left for a taxi, my three amigos from earlier in the night appeared at the front door looking dishevelled. I said the words that nobody likes to hear: 'Sorry lads – not tonight!'

THE DEMISE OF SAMMY'S

When I began working at Sammy's it was a cool place to be. People wanted to be there. The club was always packed. We could choose the best from the queue and keep the shit out. Now it was on the decline: carpets worn down; lights not working; the furniture stunk of a mixture of puke, piss, beer and disinfectant; the cleaner's attempt to disguise the former. Sammy's nightclub was being run down. The owners, who also owned the cinema, wanted the space back so it could be incorporated back into the cinema complex.

It was a sad demise. The once exciting atmosphere became stale and boring and boredom leads to trouble. It was also the fact that the door policy changed; Pete, the owner, wanted us to let in as many people as we could. The dress code was practically nonexistent – it was all about getting them in and getting as much money out of them as possible before the club closed its doors for ever.

Fights that were the norm increased. We would stand in the front foyer scanning the dodgy CCTV monitor for signs of trouble. We got so good at spotting trouble we could see it building before it happened and in some cases got there before the fight started. I felt more comfortable being up inside the club in the thick of it, rather than standing down on the door just waiting for the buzzer to go off. Sammy's was always kicking off due to the variety and mix of local and out of town punters crossing paths when drunk. But now the mix was far worse; fights were happening every night.

The quietest night of the week was Wednesday. It was so quiet boredom forced us to play pitch and toss – an old gambling game where coins are thrown against the wall. On this particular night we were playing a round of pitch and toss. I had a handful of coins which hit the ceiling and scattered around the foyer when the buzzer went off. The sound of the buzzer chased me up the stairs heart pounding.

'Where Dave, where?' I shouted. Dave was hot on my heels.

'Bar,' he shouted back. We ran through the club and into the fight. Dave wrapped a neck-hold on one of the guys as I wrapped mine into a strangle. We dragged them to the top of the staircase and walked them out. It was crazy. They were the only two punters in the place!

Most people started taking the piss. Some even gave it! One Friday night I walked through the doors on my routine stint. I was confronted by a scene that infuriated me. One thing that really got my back up was punters being disrespectful to the club. The club was a shit hole I know but you can still have a bit of respect. It was now common knowledge that Sammy's was shutting down for good, so being barred from the place was no longer a deterrent.

Two local lads stood in front of the once busy bar that was now shuttered and in darkness. The two lads were play-fighting: something else that irritated me. I watched making sure it was just that. I had thrown out lots of lads for so called play fighting: an innocent game that can cause a bad atmosphere, at worst a real kick-off. Never play fight in a club, do it for real or don't do it at all. They hadn't clocked me standing in the shadows watching them. One of the lads pushed his mate to one side, sank his pint in one swallow and dropped his glass on the floor. He removed his cock from his pants and pissed, attempting to spell his name out on the carpet. He took great delight in spraying it from side to side focusing on his aim. I sprinted forward and focused on my aim – a well-timed right cross.

I bounced him off the wall and into the neat puddles of piss which had settled on the carpet. I didn't throw them out; they were regulars. I told his mate to tell him when he woke up to have more respect.

Sammy's was very much an old school type venue; when there was a kick-off it got sorted out the hard way by knuckle, boot and cosh. If somebody hit a doorman they got what they deserved: a fucking good kicking. We took it to the point of leaving the door and chasing them or getting ahead of perpetrators and ambushing them. It was a risky thing to do but with the likes of the sqauddies or football hooligans they had to be given the right message: 'Don't fuck with the bouncers'. We were our own law, judge, jury and executioners.

We meted out violence to those that deserved it and protected those that didn't. A little like Robin Hood robbing from the rich to give to the poor, only we were beating the bad guys to protect the innocent and it worked. There is no doubt in my mind that the old school style of door work protected more people than it harmed. I'm not condoning violence for violence sake but necessary violence for the protection of the weak or innocent. Sammy's had been good to me over the years. Despite the hundreds of confrontations, fights and brawls, I had a direction in my life and a trade I enjoyed. I can't remember once not wanting to go to work. I loved every minute of it. That's the thing about door work; once it's in your blood you can't get it out. If I had a night off I didn't really enjoy it. I felt I should be back on the door. Going out on the town wasn't the same for me. It was boring. I loved the buzz of working the door, not knowing what was coming next.

The last night at Sammy's came and passed. It was the busiest we had been for ages and funnily enough I can't remember one single incident. At 2.30 a.m. the owner let the staff and a few of the bouncers from around town drink what was left of the stock, washed down with a load of chips from the nearby chippy. Parts of the club were neatly dissected and taken home as mementos. The beer and chips got a hammering. I left the club for the last time not knowing how I was going to supplement my earnings. The early morning sunlight threatened to blind me as I opened the door at Sammy's for the last time. I squinted and took one last look at the door I'd fought so hard for. I walked away feeling the same way I felt when I had been binned from the Legion. Gutted. Whilst at Sammy's I worked with some good doormen. They know who they are and they too have many memories of Sammy's door!

REPUTATIONS

When you're off the door and out of uniform you're just like everyone else; unless you have a reputation. Some people's spread far, others remain within the boundaries of their own towns or cities. Having a good reputation as a bouncer is like any other business.

Like a good joiner, electrician or mechanic, if you have the tools to do the job you do the job better. In our game you need to be sharp, quick thinking, fast on your feet, deceitful and have lots of bottle. With a strong character you won't buckle under the pressure when some alcohol-crazed bruiser offers you out for a one-on-one or threatens to shoot or stab you into an early grave.

Like all good craftsmen my reputation was very important to me. If you want the best jobs you have to protect your reputation. That meant a lot of fighting. I would not back down to anyone. But I did choose when and where I fought – even if I had to wait months for the right moment to strike. Now I was off the door I'd be watching my own back.

MR CHRISTOPHER'S

I'd already been tipped off about another club opening up in the town. It was a bit hush, hush. Mark Walsh had left the doors a couple of years previously and was working with his friend and business partner, Eric Schofield. Eric and Mark were a canny business partnership prepared to risk all they owned for a business venture they believed would be successful. They had built up a sound business in the UPVC market selling windows, doors, etc. and were about to cash in their family homes so they could fund the buying of a club by the name of Mr Christopher's on Loughborough High Street. Dave had tipped them off that it was up for sale. Mark and Eric offered Dave the position of manager and me the position of assisting Dave and running the door once the venue was opened.

Mr Christopher's was a very cheesy cabaret club on the top floor of an old Co-op store. Cabaret clubs were a left over from the '70's era. Even the big cabaret chains like Bailey's and the Commodore Rooms were in decline. Punters wanted more from a night out than a dodgy singer or some comedy group taking the piss out of the crowd. Besides that was something your mum and dad did at the works' Christmas do! (If they were lucky enough to be in work.)

Disco was big business and was on the rise. New clubs were being opened or refurbished and people were becoming choosy. If they couldn't get what they wanted in town they would travel to one of the bigger cites which were only a taxi or bus ride away. The town needed another good venue. See a need, fill a need.

Whilst I waited for the job to call me I concentrated on trying to build up a business that my brother Sam and I had been earning from during the week: ice cream sales. I would often be standing on the door when someone would make a comment about me being an ice cream man. I used to feel slightly embarrassed then in my defence I would quip that I only sold hard ice cream.

The ice cream business hit problem after problem. 'Fucking hell. What's that?' Sam said.

'Fuck me. It's a wheel,' I said. The wheel rolled on chasing the car in front. 'I wonder whose wheel that is,' I asked, almost laughing.

Sam stayed quiet, then my stomach rolled over and I got that sinking feeling as if something was terribly wrong. The van surged forward and dropped on to the tarmac then slid along completely out of control, eventually stopping after an almighty scraping sound and the crash of the front nearside wheel arch becoming wedged on to the kerb stones. The van filled with the smell of burning steel and smoke. I panicked and got an incredible depressed feeling realising the wheel was off the front of our van.

The ice cream business was a good little earner. We also ran a light haulage firm – very light. We had one truck, but after repairs and maintenance, insurance, tax, MOTs, cleaning products and uniforms, all we were getting was a very low wage based on the hours we had to do – no real profit. Both me and Sam decided to ditch the businesses and never go near transport again. We got our accountant (yes we had one) to wind up both businesses properly so we had paid our dues.

I learnt a lot about business from those early dealings, the main one being you need capital to set up a business and good organisation; oh yeah, and a bit of knowledge of what you're getting into!

I had a steady girlfriend whom I'd met whilst working the door at Sammy's. She was a real stunner. Her eyes captured me and lured me in. She was a friend, a lover and so much fun to be with. Both me and Tina decided to invest in a home. It felt good to have my own house. I felt as proud as a father holding his newly born child. My life was a million miles away from where it had been. It felt good to be in full-time work. Working as a bouncer meant I had the money to enjoy the good things in life. We wined and dined, travelled to hotspots and cities. One of the cities we regularly visited was Paris. It was on one of our visits to Paris that I decided to surprise Tina with a special gift. I realised that I loved this woman and in the hotel room just before we left to go on the town I produced a diamond engagement ring from my pocket, thrust it toward her hand and asked her to marry me. It was the most frightening thing I have ever done. She refused to take it unless I got down on one knee and asked her properly. I felt like some knight in shining amour. We kissed after she accepted, then it was into Paris for a memorable romantic night. A year later we were married. My life was transforming.

I needed to secure the job at Mr Christopher's. The call for the job at the new club came through just in time. I was back on the door.

Once the previous owner had finally left, Mark and Eric started to make changes. They had big plans for the venue. First we had to shake off the old image of a cabaret club.

There was a good buzz in the town and much talk of the new venue opening. Dave who was now the manager wanted to attract the old Sammy's crowd so we put a sign on the old door giving directions to the new venue which was to be called Crystals nightclub.

Dave's idea worked and the club became busy from the off. Especially the student night. We also used some of the Sammy's bouncers who were used to the crowd we would attract.

The glass collector shouted to me from the bottom of the staircase. 'You're needed in the kitchen, John. There's trouble.' I sprinted the steep flight of stairs followed by my door partner for the night, Sooty, an experienced bouncer.

My mother and father were doing a part-time stint washing the cutlery and crockery from the night's meals for a bit of cash in hand and a few beers. They'd just finished and were having their fag break near the exit when they had heard a commotion in the kitchen. My dad looked in and caught a six foot five rugby player standing on the work surface pissing on the clean crockery and cutlery. 'Get down, you dirty bastard,' my dad shouted. The student turned nasty. My dad shut the door and locked him in. I now faced the prospect of going into the kitchen to ask a pissed up, pissed off, pissing student, to leave for taking the piss.

I opened the kitchen door and peered in. The piss-taker was trying to find a way out. He reminded me of the headless chicken I met all those years ago. He knew we'd be coming for him. And I knew his adrenalin would cause him to panic and that made him dangerous. 'Oi. Let's go,' I shouted. I moved towards him. Sooty appeared and stepped in front of me. Sooty was a few inches bigger than me and solidly built: a good doorman, one you knew would back you up when it kicked off. We encroached on the rugby player type trying to get an angle on him. I expected him to charge forward in true rugby player style; instead he turned and ran for the fire exit door. The exit door led into the room which was being refurbished. He was trapped with nowhere to go but toward us. He turned and faced us without thinking. We both lurched forward and moved in noticing at the last minute that he was carrying a butcher's steak knife in his right hand. The blade was at least 12 inches long and three inches wide to the point and razor sharp on both edges.

It was too late to think. I had to act before he presented the blade. I grabbed his arm with the blade in it by the wrist with both of my hands and pinned the arm back against the stack of old furniture. I had him off balance. At the same time Sooty charged into his chest pinning him to the pile of debris behind him. He was bent backward and unable to lunge forward. I held onto his wrist until Sooty prized the knife from his grip and grabbed it by the handle. Once the knife was out of the way we punched and booted him until he was subdued, then dragged him out of the fire exit and dumped him in a pool of stinking stagnant water.

I took a deep breath and laughed. It was a close call. Butchers' knives, which are designed to cut meat from bone, are deadly weapons in anyone's hands, never mind a drunken, pissed off, rugby player with intent. If we hadn't rushed him when we did it could have been a tragic end to a new beginning. We didn't report the incident to the police. They had their way of doing things that didn't fit with ours.

The rest of the night went without incident until the rush to the cloakroom. Seven hundred students all seemed to want their coats at the same time. The cloakroom attendants in their haste to please leant a little too heavily on the already straining makeshift coat rail. It collapsed sending the coats off their hangers into disorganised un-numbered heaps. The only way the coats could be verified to the owner was by a paper ticket with a number on it which was attached to the coat hanger. A nightmare unfolded. Angry students jeered and shouted at the attendants so much that one girl was in tears. It took over an hour to sort out the problem. Every coat had to be identified by size, colour and anything they could say was in the pockets. Talking to students at the end of a piss up is like trying to catch fish on a fishing rod without a hook; impossible.

After the knife incident it was deemed that the kitchen would be closed and converted into a new cellar, with smaller basket meals prepared in a kitchenette to comply with the nightclub licensing law. The rest of the club would be converted into a two room venue: the best type of club. Two rooms give you versatility. The new club would target the townie and student crowds from in and around Leicestershire. I was given the position of Club Manager and Head of Security and made it known that everyone in the town including known troublemakers and people barred from Sammy's were given amnesty. The club would start from scratch giving everyone the chance to enjoy the new venue. The trouble was not everyone was worthy of a second chance. But a job's a job and if you take the money then you do the job right. We agreed to the amnesty; we knew the bad would fuck up again and when they did we could take pleasure in taking out the trash.

I decided to put together my own code of conduct of necessary violence. Every possible way out would be given to the aggressor and violence would be a last resort. I would work within the confines of the law. After all, it was our law written for us, to protect us. I knew that dropping some kid on his arse for being out of order was morally right if that kid was about to do it to me. But to then stomp him into the ground was going too far. I had a right to protect myself and that's exactly what I would do. I would only fight when I deemed it absolutely necessary. Only then could I live with the consequences of my own actions. If I ended up in prison again it would be because what I had done was absolutely vital to my or someone else's safety.

I wanted to pass on this code of conduct to any of the bouncers that would be employed at Crystals. In that code was a rule, a very strict rule: nobody was bigger than the club. If they had to leave they would leave. If they were refused entry then they stayed out. The door staff would be firm but fair and would stick together as a team. If you threatened one you threatened us all. A nightclub can only be successful if the right door team are chosen for that venue and a good door team needs to have a mix of special qualities. Too many talkers and you get walked over. Not enough and you're always fighting. Then of course there is the visual deterrent – commonly known as a big fucker.

BIG UNS AND LITTLE UNS

*It's not the size of the dog in the fight.
It's the size of the fight in the dog that matters.*
Old saying.

The club progressed and became extremely successful, so in order to protect the venue which had a capacity of a thousand, we employed a team of 15 door staff. I drew my doormen from either the boxing gyms, judo halls or purely for their street or previous door experience. If I didn't know them or they were deemed dodgy (drug dealer types, nasty fuckers, steroid freaks or worse, cowards in the face of adversity) they didn't get the job. Sometimes I went on gut feeling. Some guys just look right. One such doorman was Nigel Parker. Nigel, by his own admission, had never had a fight in his life. I could see why. He was wider than Arnie and at six foot eight, a Goliath of a man. His pastime was tug o' war and his hands were built for pulling ropes.
Once he donned the uniform of the bouncer he became the ultimate visual deterrent.
One thing struck me about Nigel when I first met him and that was his demeanour. He was a real gentleman. If ever there was a gentle giant Nigel was it. After a short discussion about money Nigel accepted my offer.
I nicknamed him 'Tiny'. I would train the man mountain in the art of the door.

Tiny's first brush with violence came one Thursday night. I had given him the task of watching the main room door on his own whilst the other doormen patrolled inside.
The club was quiet and would remain so for most of the night as the local fairground, which took over the town centre each November, was in full swing. There was one order given that night: no fairground workers were allowed in. Thursdays were still known as 'fight night' and if any of the fairground staff got hurt we could be fighting the rest of them (which had happened on a few occasions over the years). One of the lads, a good friend of mine, Lee Williams, was riding the big wheel and during one of his

antics of spinning the seats over he fell to the ground and smashed his skull. Lee, a tough fucker, survived the fall ending up in hospital smashed up. This was to trigger a conflict which became known as the battle of the speedway. A major kick-off with the fairground folk ensued. The speedway became a battleground with the Loughborough lads winning the first half. I can't recount the full story as I wasn't there. I also missed the second half of the battle which finished with some of the Loughborough lads trapped in a bedroom in a terraced house whilst the fairground crew tried to axe the doors down. Every year that the fair came to Loughborough conflict was in the air. The truth was: Loughborough was our town. The fairground was just another invasion. Unfortunately, the fair lads thought the same way. It was their pitch they had been coming here for years. We decided the best way to avoid further conflict and keep the peace was to keep them out.

I was on the front door having a laugh with the pay-box girl and a couple of the doormen when the buzzer stopped the conversation dead. In a second or so, I was at the top of the stairs through the double doors and witnessing Tiny surrounded by 20 or so fairground workers. A third of them were women. Tiny was throwing bodies off him. When one flew off another jumped on him. It was like a scene from a King Kong movie. By the time we got to the fight Tiny had forced them into the corridor next to the rear entrance door. We joined him and after a tirade of abuse from the fairground workers, they left. I turned in the direction of Tiny and said, 'Welcome to the world of the nightclub bouncer.' Through deep breaths he laughed. Tiny had single-handedly ejected 20 or so rough customers. He'd made up for his lack of fighting experience in one night. He became a solid member of the Crystal's team.

If Tiny was the biggest doorman, then Paddy was the smallest. At around nine stone Paddy was an amateur boxer and as fit as any man could be. Paddy wasn't a talker. He was quiet and always had a smile on his face which lit up the room. Paddy was a cool customer. When the smile disappeared it was time to duck! Paddy had a dynamite punch. I can honestly say I witnessed Paddy knock out cold, lads twice his size and bigger with a single punch. He was a one hit wonder. When you woke up you wondered what had hit you. Although I witnessed Paddy's knockout technique I never once saw the punch land; it was far too quick for it to register. Paddy was dangerous. When he stepped up to the mark he would be the only one stepping back from it. What appeared to give Paddy his strength of punch was his aggressive intent coupled with good technique. He transformed from a nine stone smiling gentleman into an aggressive explosion of forward driving power in an instant. Paddy always stuck to the moral code. If one lesson was to be learned it was never underestimate any man regardless of size. Violence was always a last resort action for Paddy, a valuable asset in a doorman.

Another doorman of repute was Marios Tinentis. To look at him you would consider him to be overweight and unfit. I first met Marios one afternoon after he'd rang the club asking for work as a bouncer. He told me he had previous experience working at the Rock City venue in Nottingham city centre. Marios was sporting a rock-a-billy style haircut which was similar to the Elvis Presley GI cut. He was around six feet tall, 250lb, with a barrel chest and was dressed in denim jacket and trousers. He looked very rock 'n' roll.
One thing I noticed about Marios was his presence. I followed him upstairs and introduced him to Dave who was standing on the dance floor. I winked at Dave.
'Right, mate. If you really want this job you have to do a little test. All the door staff has to do it. I mean that's if you really want the job?'
'I'll do it, John. I really need this job. I'm skint, mate.'
'Okay. I want you to go down to the front door. Once you're there wait for the panic alarm to go off. As soon as it goes off, sprint up the staircase as fast as you can. I'll time ya. If you can get up the staircase and over to these fire doors in ten seconds, bang out 20 push-ups you can have the job.'
I'd already decided to give Marios the job but boys will be boys and a laugh is a laugh. The real test was for his sense of humour.
Dave smiled. 'You cunt, John.'
'He'll never make the stairs. Look at the size of him.'

Dave went to the bar and hit the panic alarm. We heard a crash then the pounding feet on the staircase. The doors to the club burst open and Marios sprinted toward the fire doors like a rhinoceros on heat. He was extremely fast for a big lad. He dropped down banged out 20 push-ups then stood tall.
'Do I get the job?' he said between deep breaths.
I looked at Dave then back to Marios.
'Sorry, mate. You weren't quick enough.' Marios's face dropped.
'I'll have another go,' he insisted and started making his way back down the stairs.
I couldn't hold back the laughter.
'I'm only kidding, mate. I had already decided to give you the job before you did the run.'
Marios looked pissed off then the look of anger gave way to a bellow of laughter. That's what a doorman needs: a good sense of humour. Marios held his stomach as he laughed which reminded me of the big bear in *The Jungle Book* film. We nicknamed him Balloo, the name of the bear in the movie.

Training for new doormen was mostly on the job. I advised any that weren't doing the physical training to get involved with some, either judo, kickboxing or boxing. One or two didn't need to. One such man was a South African by the name of James. James had applied for a job at Crystal's before. But I'd turned him down at the time. He was well overweight and just didn't look the part. Six months down the line he came back and re-applied. He looked like a different bloke. He'd shed a couple of stone and looked fit. That takes commitment. I gave him the job then invited him to the gym. After taking James on the focus mitts, I quickly realised that he had a terrific right hand which he threw in a very unorthodox manner. When it landed it landed sharp and solid. James was a crafty bastard. Deception was his tool. It was like he didn't fear the consequences of his actions. His main plus point, which I believed to show a high level of intelligence, was his absolute conduct and mannerisms.
He gave off an aura of sheer confidence in his ability in a ruck. In male company he gave no quarter and his gentlemanly demeanour gave him an edge to women. He was a true gentleman. To me he was a model doorman and although he was very much his own

man he was one that stood by you. You knew your back was safe. James was worth his weight in gold. Another doorman of repute was Ian Moffat, a tall, lean, muscular framed man, a man I could trust to watch my back whenever the going got tough! With the door team we inherited from Sammy's we had a good mix of old school and new school. The door team at Crystal's remained pretty much intact over the years. We had one or two additions. Some stayed, some moved on. They all have their own stories to tell of life on the door.

FAMILY NIGHT OUT

Saturday night and the club was buzzing;
'Excuse me,' said a busty blonde in a low cut dress.
'What's the problem, girls?' I said as they surrounded me.
'It's those idiots over there. They keep coming over and pestering us.'
The girls were barely 18 and not long off the playground. It showed in their lack of maturity. This was playground courtship in the disco. I glanced over to see three, very happy, young lads, arms wrapped around each other dancing to Jeff Beck's 'High Ho Silver Lining' – a real arms in the air track that transcended age.
Not one to spoil a party I said to the girl, 'They probably just fancy you.'
'Do you reckon?' she said looking interested.
'Come on, Julie, the lads are only having a laugh,' said one of the other girls who hadn't stopped dancing during the whole conversation. Just to make sure that the lads were on the level and to make the girls feel more comfortable I decided to have a word to sound them out. I approached the group and pulled them to one side.
'Listen, lads, the group of girls over there, go steady on them. They are feeling a bit intimidated. I know you're only having a laugh but cool it a bit. The truth is, lads, I think they fancy you lot.'
'I told you,' one of the lads said.
I left them to it and carried on around the dance floor checking out the atmosphere and keeping an eye out for potential problems.
I popped over to chat with the DJ, 'Soul Mick,' as he was known. Mick was an old school style DJ who knew how to work a crowd. His set was real dance around yer handbags stuff with lots of cool soul tracks thrown in to the mix. The small room in Crystal's was packed every time he played. I stood next to the DJ booth and looked across the dance floor. Both bars were now two deep with punters and the dance floor heaved as one. I walked away to the sound of James Brown's 'Feel Good' and the hissing sound of disco smoke filling the room. I noticed the group of girls had now mingled with the lads. Many a relationship blossomed at the local nightclub; families were created out of drunken passion.

But families can be a real problem when the booze is in and when they kick off it's really difficult to sift out the shit especially when you know them.

I checked out the main room. It too was buzzing, courtesy of Rob Brooks. Rob was a star, a very confident man with a smile which was far brighter than any of the lighting effects he worked with. He was very good at spotting situations and never panicked. If he spotted trouble his finger would be on the button. A good DJ is worth a dozen mediocre doormen. If they are doing the job right they will be scanning the crowd looking for a reaction to what they are playing.

Rob brought my attention to a group just inside the main room doors: a local family known for their sporadic outbursts of violence. I thanked Rob and made my way over. They all looked worse for the drink as I stood back and watched. One of the lads was staring at a group of three young men on the edge of the dance floor who were scanning the crowd obviously on the pull. The lad's expression gave away his intent. His eyes were focusing on the lads with a piercing stare like that of a tiger about to attack its prey. Experience told me he was about to make his move and confront the group. Before he did, I made my move. I placed my hand on his shoulder. I needed to get his attention and break his stare before he decided to scrap it out. 'They're not worth it, mate. They're not in your league,' I said leaning close into his ear.

I was bigging him up, making him feel like he didn't need to fight. He turned; surprised I'd got so close to him without him noticing me. The fact he had tunnel vision due to the adrenalin made it easy for me to approach him unseen. He knew me and my reputation for not fucking about when it came to aggro. I needed to know what they'd done to him or his family to warrant so much attention. I suspected it was very little. But when the booze has taken hold of the brain functions (which wasn't hard with this group) then the smallest of problems became reasons to go to war.

'That cunt over there keeps eyeing up my missus.'

'Well at least she's worth looking at,' I said trying to make light of the situation. He looked at me and lightened up.

'Yeah they'd never get one as good as her.'

'Stay out of trouble, mate. I'll see you later.'

The rest of the group gathered round him. I knew full well that something was going to give. I hoped it wouldn't.

I made my way through to the foyer and spoke to the door lads letting them know about the possible kick-off. I felt like a concerned parent informing the babysitters of the bad traits of my children. Whilst I explained the situation the door to the main room opened and the three lads who had been on the edge of the dance floor walked through.

'Can we get out this way, mate?' one asked.

'Why, what's the problem?'

'Well we don't want to leave by the other door. There's a bunch of potato heads in there screwing us out. We don't want any trouble.'

'Listen, lads. Stay in and enjoy yourselves. If there's any trouble we'll sort it out. That's what we're here for.' The lads declined the offer and left. I decided to go back inside the club and keep an eye on the potato heads. As I entered the main room I caught sight of them going through the middle doors between the two rooms. The space between the double fire doors and the small room formed a fire break and customers were kept out of the area. It was meant for passing through only.

The void was the size of a small kitchen. I slipped through the door to find out what they were up to and stood un-noticed in the shadows listening to them arguing and jostling each other about. It was like I was watching a live version of the *Jeremy Kyle Show*. The lad that I'd spoken to earlier wanted to give chase to the lads that had just left the club. His girlfriend was trying to talk sense into him but he was having none of it.

I stayed back hoping the situation would fizzle out. If I intervened right now I might become their common enemy and actually make matters worse. They were all related in some way or other. I remained an observer like a mini United Nations' peacekeeping force. The boyfriend became more aggressive the more the girlfriend tried to convince him to stay put. He accused her of flirting with the lads and sticking up for them. I watched his anger grow until it boiled over into blind rage. He aimed a punch at her, then fired his balled fist into the wall.

'I'll fucking kill 'im!'

I remembered watching my dad do the same thing to my mother many years ago during an argument. I was eight years old. He'd lost his temper like this guy had, but didn't want to hurt his woman. The situation was turning nasty. I intervened.

'Oi, there's no need for that.' Before he could answer a fat bird who looked like she was chewing a lemon retorted.

'Fuck off. It's nowt to do with you.'

This bird was so ugly that if the offer was on the table you wouldn't know whether to fight it or fuck it! You couldn't drink enough booze in one session to warrant taking it home. I gave her some back in the language she'd understand.

'Shut your fucking mouth and keep out of it, I'm talking to him not you.'

I hated dealing with women like this but if they were going to act like men then that's how they should be treated. I've seen some nasty bitches over the years who would stick a glass in your face without hesitation and I wasn't going to let her get that confident. Her boyfriend who knew me quite well pulled her back.

'Fucking leave it. John's only trying to help.'

I had an ally. I turned back to talk to the girlfriend but it was too late. I had become embroiled in the middle of a family feud with no backup. The girlfriend pushed her boyfriend back and slapped him across the face. He returned the compliment and then rammed her into the wall by her throat. The corridor exploded into a free for all. The fat girl whacked the lad from behind. She was joined by her boyfriend who was then attacked by the lad's brother. I lost track of who was hitting who and grabbed the nearest person to me. It was every man for himself. I had a human shield which I used to get through the doorway. I signalled to Mick who had already heard the commotion and had pressed his buzzer.

The fat girl had hold of one lad swinging him round by the hair as the doormen burst through the doors. 'Get them all out!' I shouted and threw the shield into the doorman's grip. I wrapped the first one I saw around the neck: the lad that had kicked it all off. I turned him. It was difficult as his own were kicking, punching and tearing at him as if he was their worst enemy. I dragged him into the small room. He struggled violently, the alcohol adding to his strength. Within seconds of the strangle being applied I had complete control of the potato head. The crowd had parted. I paused at the side of the dance floor and shouted into his ear, 'Fucking walk or I break it.' He became compliant as I applied the pressure to his neck, by clamping either side of his neck muscle with my bicep and forearm. This temporarily cut off the blood supply to his brain and gave me control. He was seconds from unconsciousness.

One of the door lads appeared and I passed him into their arms. 'He's barred for good. Get him out.' I spun round and sprinted back into the void. Others had joined in from the main room, some trying to calm it, others getting stuck in. I ran toward the pack that resembled wild animals fighting except that the snarling was louder. A glass smashed against the wall close to my head as I waded in. I felt punches hitting me from behind. I spun my antagonist into the door using his body to open it and punched my fist into the small of his back to enable me to get control of his bodyweight. 'Fucking calm down,' I said.

'Let me go. You're choking me.'

'Fucking calm down then and I will let you go.'

I stopped at the top of the staircase and released my grip. 'All right I'm going.' He shrugged me off. It was the wrong move. I was pissed off with this goon. He was going out the hard way. I grabbed his legs and pulled them from beneath him and dragged him down the staircase by his ankles. He tried to stop himself by putting his hands down, adding to his downfall as his arse hit every step on the way down. I dumped him at the bottom and ran back upstairs. I was left with the last one: the lemon eater.

I encircled her body with my arms trying to pin hers to her sides. Her body was squidgy and hard to grip. She struggled, cursing me and fighting. I switched grips and spun her into a right side headlock and pulled her toward the doors. She leaned back hard bracing her arms against the doorway. I didn't want to harm her so I applied the neck-hold without much pressure but I could feel her head slipping out of my grip. She started flailing, trying to get at my face with her nails. Suddenly and without warning she felt the full force of a GP 300 radio on the forehead. She yelped and struggled more violently. The bouncer raised his radio for another crack.

'No,' I shouted. 'It's a woman.' I let her go expecting her to fall but the mixture of alcohol and adrenalin had anaesthetised her to the feelings of pain. She shrugged me off. She was a tough bitch. The bouncer's expression of anger turned to one of horror. Fear engulfed him when he realised he'd whacked a woman. Her forehead had split wide open. The gash was deep but no blood flowed from the wound which was unusual for a cut forehead.

She ran down the staircase not yet aware of her injury. I followed her expecting her to keel over at any moment. She ran out into the street where the fight was continuing. Police vans and dogs had arrived and arrests were taking place. I watched the lemon-eater run toward the potato-head who had started the fight. He looked in her direction.

'You fucking bitch!' he shouted as he ran toward her and she to him. When in range and in full view of a police officer he head-butted her smack bang on the forehead where the bouncer had hit her. She dropped to the pavement and for the first time since the fight started was silent. Potato Head was cuffed and bungled into the waiting police van, the lemon-eater carted off in an ambulance.

The bouncer had a lucky escape. In the heat of the moment he reacted wrongly but it was an easy mistake considering how aggressive she was. All he saw when he came through the doors was me in a ruck with what he thought was a very violent man. I eased his mental trauma when I told him what had happened outside.

'Families: they're nothing but trouble,' he said.

Although he looked relieved that he hadn't been arrested for assault, he never really got over that incident. He could have killed the woman. The bouncer left the doors shortly after the incident due to, believe it or not, family problems!

I've had to deal with many different family situations over the years. It nearly always ends up in a messy kick-off either in or out of the club. A week later they're all friends and you end up being the villain of the piece for getting involved. But hey, that's the job.

After a comical debrief with the door lads, I noticed that the girls and lads I'd met earlier had paired off and were embracing each other, smooching to one of 'Soul Mick's' erection section classics: 'Easy' by the Commodores.

BRAWLERS

'Out of chaos comes order'
Nietzsche

Dealing with gangs of lads, whether they're football hooligans, stag parties, or some other cultured group, needs a special kind of touch. If it's not handled right it can turn into a nightmare. When it kicks, it kicks. There's no time for line ups or verbal deception. It's time to think on your feet, time to duck, dive, roll and keep swinging until they drop.

It was 10.00 p.m. at Crystal's. We'd been open for about 50 minutes and the club was slowly filling up.
'It's going to be a busy one tonight, Dave, the town's heaving. The pub across the road is rammed.'
'Yeah, there's a coach load of lads in from the brewery on the piss, some kind of celebration,' Dave said.
Occasionally we'd be given a tour by the brewery company and Dave would organise a piss-up, a kind of let your hair down, ease the stress and pull us together as a team. After the tour we'd be treated to as much free ale as we could drink and when lads get together they are peer pressure driven. I wouldn't have said we drank the brewery dry but we had a fucking good go on a few occasions. Dave could definitely organise a piss-up in a brewery!

Now it was the turn of the 40 strong brewery lads to dip their toe into our world.
'I'd better give Rob a call and see how he's coping. They were a bit lively earlier on. It might kick off.'
Dave was good at foreseeing trouble; he'd been in more kick-offs than Alan Shearer.
'I'll send a couple of extra door lads over, Dave. If they see we're a team – they might think twice about kicking off.'
It would be easier go over there and get rid of them instead of babysitting them waiting for them to kick off. But interrupting a lads' piss-up when they aren't doing anything other than having a good time is asking for trouble.

I sent the rest of the door team over to the pub with orders to make their presence felt.

I got a call from one of the door team on the radio. 'John, you had better get over here, mate. The brewery lads are well pissed. We've already had words and it looks like it's about to…' The radio went dead.

I made my way over to the pub at a steady pace; I didn't want to go running in there and nothing be happening – I'd look a right prat. Besides, it wasn't my style. I'd found out the hard way that it's better to be calculating and weigh up the situation as you approach it.

I could hear shouting above the pulsating beat of the music emanating from the pub.

I quickened my pace and expected the worst. Before I could get through the main entrance, the exit doors sprung open and a couple of lads stumbled out into the street. The inside of the doors were a bottleneck with a mix of bouncers and brewery lads engaged in a free-for-all brawl.

I sprinted inside to join the lads and was met with a cheer as the DJ announced my entrance. The DJ was treating the brawl like a game show and he was the host. He kept the music going whilst he gave a running commentary over the microphone and continued to make light of the trauma: a sign of real experience.

The lads were struggling to clear the doorway due to the amount of bodies in there. It was like a mass rugby scrum or the opening day of the old January sales. We were seriously outnumbered. A lad ran towards me and stopped on the dance floor. He was jumping about, splaying his arms out to his sides.

'Come on then,' he screamed at me. I sat him on his arse with a well-timed right hand.

'And down he goes!' announced the DJ.

I was immediately confronted by another who was impersonating a drunken version of world welterweight boxing champ, Sugar Ray Leonard. He danced around, his guard held mid height flicking out jabs and frowning. When I was in range I left front kicked him in the groin and launched a right cross to his now exposed jaw line. He did a strange kind of jig then crumpled and sprawled out face down in front of the DJ

'And down goes another one!' the DJ cried.

I felt embarrassed by the DJ's comments; this was serious. I ignored his jibes. He was making a good job of a bad situation keeping the crowd entertained. I turned to the fracas in front of the fire exit. Doorways are great; you can easily hold a gang of 30 or so lads back if you stand your ground. A doorway is designed to fit one maybe two people through at a time. So there could be 100 in the gang but still only two can come through at once. If you slug it out and use loads of verbal you can do all right. I ran toward a lad on the staircase who was about to dive into the *mêlée*. I grabbed him and slung him into the line of fire of a muscular six footer who was grappling his way back in.

As the six footer bent and surged forward I hit him with an uppercut just as the door team came pressing down on to him. The combined weight of the door team and the six footer crashed into my accelerating fist. I felt a searing pain in my wrist He dropped to the floor and was dragged out and thrown into the street. The doormen then slammed the door on the now protesting brewery workers.

Now order had been restored the doormen began to let in a couple of people at a time. One of the brewery men approached me after a heated discussion with a few of the gang. He raised his arms and showed his palms, a sign that maybe he was speaking the truth.

'No trouble mate,' he said. I could tell by his body language that he really didn't want any trouble but it could have been a deception so I took no chances.

'Look I'm sorry about what happened,' he said.

'That's fine, mate, just get rid of your boys and we'll put it down to experience.'

He reached his hand out to shake mine. He was sincere but I made no gesture toward his hand. Instead I nodded. He turned away head bowed and walked back in the direction of his gang. They made their way off down the High Street arguing, pushing and shoving at each other. Me and a couple of the bouncers went back across the road to the club to make sure none of the brewery workers got in. They were now all barred from most premises in town.

By the time I had walked the 100 yards or so across the road my right hand had swollen to twice its size and had took on a rubbery like condition. The pain was almost unbearable. I got a damp cloth, filled it with ice and applied it to the wrist. I put a bandage around the wrist to keep it in place and compress the ice. The swelling went down and it felt OK.

I finished my shift and went home to bed. I didn't make a big issue out of the swollen wrist. I slid into bed and went to sleep too tired to care. By morning my wrist had swollen to twice its size. I made my way to hospital returning a few hours later with my arm in plaster. I'd fractured a couple of the scaphoid bones in the middle of my wrist. I'd figured they had broken when I threw the uppercut in the midst of the ruck in the doorway.

If I learnt anything from that situation it was do not throw an uppercut unless you have a clear shot at the underside of the jawbone. Saying that though, sometimes in the heat of the battle you don't get the choice; you just do what it takes and hit what you see.

FOREIGN EXCHANGE

Being a doorman was seen by some as a cool profession. You got good money, your pick of the women and all you had to do was stand on the door. After a while you get fed up with the 'I want a job, mate' night callers who haven't got a clue what they are letting themselves in for in the very real world of violence.

I got a call on the radio. 'John, there's a big foreign bloke looking for you, sounds Scandinavian or German. He wants to know if there is any work going. He says he has done security before in his own country.'
'Give him my number and tell him to ring me on Monday. I'm very busy at the moment if you know what I mean.'
It was best practice to know how many people were in the club at any one time in case of a visit by the fire brigade or police. It was done using plastic tally counters known as clickers. I popped down to the door to check the clicker and to enquire further about the big Scandinavian bouncer. 'How many on the clicker?' I asked.
'Eight hundred, John.'
I then asked him about the big Scandinavian who was after a job.
'I don't think he understood what I'd said, John, he was looking a bit drunk.'
One of the other lads walked away giggling.
'What's so funny, lads?'
'Well he was pissing us off so we sent him across the other side of the club to see the lads on the other door.'
The lads were taking the piss out of him, sending him from one doorman to another each time he asked for a job. He must be getting frustrated. I sensed something afoot.
I got another call on the radio.
'The foreign lad is still looking for you, John. He says he can't wait until Monday and wants to see you now.'
'Is he pissed up or sober?'
'He's had a few?'
'Did he pay to come in?' I asked just in case it was a scam for free entry.
'Of course he has.'

'Okay, just ignore him. Don't wind him up. It's probably the booze talking. If he keeps giving you hassle he'll have to go.'

Between the double doors of the club a guy was lying unconscious. Puke emanating from his mouth formed the shape of the map of Britain. I immediately called for backup. I hated pukers. The stuff smells and sticks like shit to a blanket. I would sooner sort out a dispute in a crazy hen party than look after a puker.

I remember one guy whose mouth opened and ejected everything out of his stomach that he'd eaten and drunk in the last four hours. A projectile tube of vomit headed for me about three feet long. It looked like a white plastic guttering downright pipe attached to his lips.

It appeared that his jaw had unhinged to get more puke out. I ran onto the landing just in time. The projectile vomit hit the carpet, then the doorway and splattered up the wall. The guy's stomach rolled, he bucked and another projectile was released. I was glad that I had been sprint training regularly or I might not have got away in time.

The one I was walking away from right now wasn't that bad but still a puker. I made my way to the office and passed Ram, an off duty bouncer from one of the pubs in town.

He was talking to a huge foreign man I took to be the big Scando. He was looking a little pissed off. Lads are lads and taking the piss is normal, especially if you're a six foot three Scandinavian giant who doesn't comprehend that 'come back Monday' means 'come back Monday.' I walked toward the office noticing Ram pointing at me through the back bar mirror. I was about half way down the steps when the giant Scando caught my attention. His body language gave me the impression he meant business.

What I didn't know at this time was that Ram had said to him 'If you want a job you have to be able to chuck that man out. He's the boss.' I never got a chance to talk to the Scando. He leapt on me from the top of the staircase shouting, 'You have to go. You have to go.'

The o in the word 'go' stretched out from his voice and triggered my response. I grabbed him by the throat in mid-air, spun him around and through the office door which was ajar.

I drove him backwards forcing my thumb and fingers deep into the sides of his larynx and directed his huge frame onto the chairs

which were neatly lined up against the wall and pinned his head to the seat. His facial colour drained pale then he started to turn blue. First his lips then his cheeks. Veins were growing in his neck and forehead. I screamed into his face.
'What's your fucking problem?'
The cashier who was sat behind me shrieked.
'John, stop! You're killing him.'
I released my grip slightly to allow him oxygen.
'You fucking move and I'll kill you. Do you understand me?' The 'kill you' was a figure of speech meant to frighten the Scando into staying still. I unclipped my radio from my belt. 'Office now, office now,' I shouted. The door lads appeared in seconds.
'Get this piece of shit out of here,' I said. The lads stiff armed him and started to walk him out of the office with just a hint of a smile on their faces. Just before he left the room the Scando turned round and said in a croaky foreign accent, 'So, I don't get the job then?' I had to laugh.
I felt for the big Scando. The lads had wound him up, then set him up, a joke that backfired. Well you know what they say, 'All's well that ends well'. The situation also reaffirmed that wherever the head went the body would follow. Spinning throat grabs became an integral part of my training.

A RARE NIGHT OFF

The annual judo club meal had just finished. I'd been presented with the student of the year award mainly for winning a national championship and was in an excitable mood.
'Come on, Tina. Let's nip into the club for one,' I said as we passed the front of the alleyway leading to the entrance. It was a rare night off for me. Saturday was usually too busy to have a regular night off. We went to turn the corner when I spotted a gang of lads at the front door. I paused sensing trouble. The club policy was no gangs of lads unless they were booked in. The party was less likely to kick-off if we had a contact name. It also gives off an air of professionalism. If we had a problem we could approach a party of lads knowing at least one person in the group. The club was busy on Saturday night. There would be around eight doormen on duty, spread over the entire club but as I ran security at the club's feeder bar Busters, four of the bouncers were on duty over there, which left only four on duty. They would be stretched over two rooms, two upstairs on the move and two on the front door. The two doormen were heavily out-numbered which was par for the course. The lads in the gang were displaying aggressive body language and citing racial reasons for not being allowed in. The doormen were standing their ground. 'They're going to kick off,' I said to Tina.
'Are you sure?' Spider who was lagging behind caught us up.
'Wait there, Tina. Come on, Spider,' I said.
'Be careful, John,' she said.
Spider followed me I felt a tinge of excitement. The alcohol was masking my true feelings. Normally I would be feeling a bit anxious due to adrenalin. I made my way through the crowd followed by Spider. The plan was to team up with the lads hopefully preventing any trouble and give them our moral support.
'Excuse me, lads,' I said as I walked through the middle of them. They parted arrogantly but parted nonetheless. One blocked my path.
'Excuse me,' I said as I passed giving him full eye contact. He would be the one that would start the situation off. I could sense his arrogance, his demeanour. He was the main man.

'Everything all right, lads?' I said to the doormen, making sure I was heard by all in the vicinity of the door. But before one of the doormen could answer. The lad at the head of the gang, a stocky Jamaican, butted in.

'Cha man is everyting all right. Who da fuck are you, mon?' he said.

I took off my suit jacket and passed it to the cashier, took a breath and said.

'I'm the fuck who's going to be stopping you from coming in here.'

I stared at him. But he was having none of the psyche out shit. He was street. He knew the game.

The crew shuffled closer.

'You reckon, mon?'

'Yeah I reckon.' I stared hard at his face. If he thought he could take me he would go for it any second. If he wasn't game he'd spout off some abuse then leave. Either way I was ready. I had already dropped my chin and was shifting bodyweight from foot to foot.

'What's the problem, mate. Are you racist? Is it because we're black?' The standoff was broken for a second as my old friend Ram a big Asian bouncer and a good friend of mine, who had just finished his shift at a nearby pub, waded through the gang in his black and whites and trumped the racist card that was being played.

'It's nothing to do with the colour of your skin. The reason you're not coming in is your attitude and the fact you're not booked in.'

The lad looked behind himself, probably checking his crew were still there. Then he said with absolute confidence, 'Who's going to stop us from coming in?' He'd given a direct challenge to the door. He'd done the numbers thing and felt confident having his crew behind him.

He dropped his shoulder and rushed forward triggering off my right hand punch. It missed his jaw and skimmed his forehead. A free for all brawl ensued. The foyer was tight with bodies. This was about forward momentum and grappling now not punching. It's hard to connect with a clean shot in a *mêlée*. The judo skills came in handy. Spider had his head down charging forward throwing low hooks. Within seconds we had the doorway clear and had pushed the gang into the alleyway.

An old friend Lefty turned the corner as the gang fled and was met with a right hand that sent him sprawling to the ground. He was already halfway there before they hit him; you could have blown him over he was that pissed. That was all the reason we needed. The chase was on.

It must have looked comical. The gang stopped every few yards and blows were exchanged then they were off again. The man with the mouth turned and faced me off. I launched a jumping front kick to his head. I don't know what made me throw the kick, it just came out. The mouth leaned out of range which wasn't necessary. I was already on the floor.

I'd slipped on a chip wrapper. The mouth moved in and threw an almighty kick of his own. I felt the wind of it skim my skull. I had already covered my head with my arms. Spider ran in from the side screaming. The mouth turned and ran. It was like a mini Olympics. We'd won the fighting but we had no chance in the running events. When we realised what we were doing we stopped, shouted a few insults and started the long walk back to the club.

We arrived back to find Ram guarding the door for us looking as cool as fuck. One of the Jamaican lads had dropped his Ray-Bans and Ram was wearing them. He had a big 'fuck off' smile on his face.

'Not tonight lads. You've been fighting,' he said.

'Everything all right now, John?' Tina said with a wry smile on her face.

PRESSURE POT

It was a quiet night on the door. The local students that gave us all of our trade on a Tuesday night were going through their exam period. Some were under immense pressure from their parents to get good results. There were horror stories of students jumping out of the local tower block and ending it all because the pressure had got to them. We noticed the rise in stupid incidents inside the club: silly arguments and irritability that led to outbreaks of violence or vandalism. The students were tired and nervous. The pressure pot could boil over at any time.
I usually stopped with the lads for a quick beer before driving home. We'd have a couple of halves to unwind after the night's frolics. It was a kind of relaxed de-brief of the night's events. Then after the beer we'd all leave together or in pairs just in case of a comeback. They are rare but they do happen. The night had been uneventful so there didn't seem much point in me hanging around. I decided to skip the beer.
I bade the lads good night and made my way to my car.
It feels kind of lonely driving home after contact with so many people. The streets are deserted, litter is strewn everywhere and the odd taxi is hunting down the last fares of the night. The hot dog man was dismantling his pitch. I spotted a lad in a gleaming white shirt leaning against a plate glass window. As I drove past him his eyes opened. He raised his arm as if to hail a taxi then dropped his arm and closed his eyes again. He was pissed and falling asleep. I laughed to myself; I'd been in that state myself once or twice. He'd had a good night all right.

I made my way home via the Ashby road, the main road which led to the M1 bypassing the university. The Ashby Road area is the main student area known to the local estate agents, as 'the golden triangle'. It was the most lucrative lettings area. Students are big business in Loughborough. They contribute to the local economy, though most people don't see that. All they see is the negative side: a rowdy bunch of piss-heads who vandalise for the fun of it and fill the streets with puke.

I was doing around 20 miles an hour and increasing my speed. I manoeuvred the car off the roundabout and onto the straight approaching the crossing. I saw a dark figure of a man standing in the middle of the road directly in front of me. I ignored the fact that as I got closer the figure never moved. It stood perfectly still facing in my direction. I was travelling at just under 30 miles an hour.

Suddenly the figure started to sprint toward my car like a hurdler sprinting toward the first hurdle. I carried on driving knowing the humour of the students. One of their tricks when pissed up was to sprint toward your car then at the last minute run out to the side, or leap off the kerb at you as you passed. They were dangerous games. One I'd played a few times myself, showing off in front of the lads. But the sinister thing about this guy was there was no gang of lads to show off to – he was fucking serious.

The sprinter got faster and then closer. I hit the brakes. The car screeched as I pressed the brakes full on. Then like a scene from a 3D movie the student's face scrunched up as it hit my windscreen. I instinctively covered my face by crossing my arms like an X factor goon. His legs flipped backward then his body somersaulted and he was gone over the top of the car. Fearing the worst I leapt out of the car. 'Fucking hell, mate. Are you all right?' I was still trying to come to terms with what had just happened when the sprinter jumped up and tried to run off. I grabbed him by both shoulders and pinned him to the car.

'What the fuck are you doing? Where you going?'

'Fucking leave me. I just want to die.' His eyes were tearful red rimmed and full of anger. He tried to pull away from me.

'You ain't going anywhere. Stay where you are.'

Again he tried to bust loose so I swept his legs, taking his balance and his legs from under him. He sat on his backside with my knee pressing him against the car.

'Don't fucking move. You ain't going anywhere You could have fucking killed yourself and me. I have a wife and two kids.' I got angry as the realisation of what had just happened hit me as hard as the car had hit him. As I screamed niceties at him, I noticed that both of his wrists were slashed. Some looked just like scratch marks rather than a real attempt to kill himself. I felt concerned and disgusted at the same time.

'What have you done that for?' He started to cry.
'I've had enough.' I felt sorry for him. A big lump the size of an apple formed in my throat.
'Listen to me. You need an ambulance.' I pulled him to his feet and stood him against the side of the car.
'Just let me go. I want to die.' My anger took away the lump from my throat.
'Listen to me, you fucking wanker, you ain't going anywhere. You need help.' I vented my anger trying to talk some sense into my new friend.
I began to realise that the cuts on his wrists were a cry for help. His last attempt was deadly serious. I wanted to shake him real hard and wake him up to the real world. They're only fucking exams, I thought.
I was so concerned about the student I hadn't heard the car pull up behind us until the bright lights emanating from its rooftop made me squint. I put one hand up to my eyes and the headlights dimmed for a second then went back on. Through the lights I could make out the silhouettes of two traffic cops. I held on tight to my friend who was now a blubbering mess. The copper approached me.
'What's going on? Let him go.'
'No, not unless you cuff him.'
'Let him go.'
'No fucking way. Look what he's done to my car.'
'I'll take care of him, you go and sit in the vehicle,' he gestured toward the police Jeep.
'Okay. But don't let him go. He's just tried to kill himself by running at my car.'
The copper raised an eyebrow! I got into the vehicle and started to explain the reason why I had a student pinned to the car at 3.00 a.m. The copper I sat next to made no reply; he looked me up and down. The uniform of a bouncer was all he needed to see. The officer returned and questioned me on what happened. When I'd finished he asked me if I had been drinking. I hadn't.
'I want to take a specimen of your breath. Have you been drinking?'
'No.'

'Okay. Take a breath and blow into this bag.' I was cool about the breathalyser. I'd been pulled a few times and knew the routine. One particular night I was pulled and asked to take a breath test twice, half a mile between stops. The second breath test didn't take place after they realised I'd just been tested. Not bad considering I only lived two miles from the club.

The policeman's face was stern. His breathing changed as he waited for the result to appear.

'Why don't you look at the guy's wrists? He needs help.' On saying that an ambulance pulled up. The copper looked up at me. Suspicion spread across his face. They owed me no favours. Our relationship was one of mutual disgust for one another.

'I know you don't believe me, but get the paramedics to check his wrists. That will verify my story.'

I could understand the way the copper must have been feeling. My story was a little hard to believe. I hardly believed it myself and at one point I was worried I would be charged with an offence. I continued trying to convince the copper of what had happened.

'Go on. Ask him why he cut his wrists.' The copper's curiosity got the better of him and he approached the paramedics, who thankfully confirmed what had really happened. If the kid had died I could have been charged with manslaughter. The copper took the rest of my details and said I could go. 'What about the damage to my car?'

'It's a civil matter. I can't get involved.'

'Well give me his name and address.'

'I can't do that.' But as he said those words he turned his note book over so I could read the kid's details for myself. He gave me a reassuring wink.

I made a mental note of the kid's name and address.

'You get off, mate. We need to have a word with your friend.'

I wanted to thank the copper but just nodded a nod of satisfaction in case his partner didn't agree with his ethics. As I drove off the shock of the event began to take hold. I started to run different scenarios through my mind. I felt sick. When I got home I woke Tina. 'I've just run a student over.' As I said it I realised as tragic as it was, it was actually quite funny. I started to laugh and couldn't stop.

I remember being like it on holiday once when me and a couple of friends of mine went out onto a balcony. I had just got back from being refused entry for an early morning swim to ease my hangover when we were told that a man had been found dead in the pool. We became hysterical. Shock can have a weird effect on you.

Tina was confused when I related the sprinter story to her. At first she doubted it then realised I was serious.
'He could have killed you. If his head had come through the windscreen it could have smashed into yours. You could be dead now or seriously injured.' I felt very lucky to be alive. I fell asleep thanking God for keeping me safe.

The next morning I got a rough quote for the repairs. Twelve hundred quids worth of damage. It was time to pay my friend the sprinter a visit – if he was still alive. I drove round to his address and parked. I was still angry. I knocked on the front door. If he didn't answer I'd have to kick it in. It wouldn't be the first time I'd kicked somebody's door in. I was once awakened in the small hours by a friend who'd had a problem with a couple of lads. He wanted me to accompany him to show him where the lads lived and to watch his back whilst he had words. I owed the guy a favour and it was time to pay it back. I took him round to the lads' house on the council estate where I lived. When we got there he went to knock on the door.
'Listen they ain't going to answer the door. We have to take them by surprise,' I told him. The lads were proper crooks, steal anything, burgle you while you were still in the house and brutalise your granny if she got in the way.

The only way to enter their domain was shock and surprise. I shoulder barged the door to loosen it then leant back and booted the door where the lock was located. The door flung open and in we went. The crooks scattered around the house fearing a police raid. Then the lad my mate wanted a word with burst into the kitchen, claw hammer in one hand and if that wasn't weapon enough he launched toward a carving knife sitting on the side of the sink. He paused when he saw who we were. He knew us well. I ragged him into the corner and left my mate to it. Meanwhile I checked the living room and warned the rest to stay out of the way. My mate sorted the problem out and we were gone. Now I was faced with another door and kicking this one in could easily get me arrested.

I gave the door a good bang. I knew there would be more than just him in the house and I knew what I was doing was wrong. If he called the police I could be in deep shit, but it had to be done. The door opened.
'Does Steve live here?'
'Yeah, mate. What do you want him for?'
'It's private.'
'All right, mate. I'll get him for you.'
'Never mind that. Fuck off out of the way.' I didn't have time to fuck around. The student was surprised at my attitude. He obviously had no idea who I was and why I was there.
I barged past him and he didn't try to stop me. He slammed back against the wall.
The buzz of adrenalin made my eyes feel wide open. I didn't know who was in the house and I didn't care. 'Where is he?' I shouted at a big rugby type student lad.
'What's the problem, mate?' I kept up the crazed appearance.
'Fuck off back in your room and stay out of this.' The kid did what I demanded. Another student who was on his way down stairs looking pasty and hung over saw me and ran back upstairs.
I heard a pathetic sounding voice from the kitchen doorway, 'I'm in here.' He sounded very humble and scared. I stood outside the door for a second. His voice reminded me of how nervous this kid was. I calmed myself.
'Come in. I'm sorry. Please don't hit me,' he said.
'Don't hit you? You've changed your tune. Last night you wanted to kill yourself now all of a sudden you've gone completely off the idea of pain.'
'Please shut the door. Don't let them hear what's going on. They don't know about last night. If they find out I will be a laughing stock.'
'All right, calm down.' I shut the door.

'Look I won't tell anybody else about what happened. As far as I am concerned it's between you and me.' He looked weak. I felt sorry for him.
'Look I don't want anything from you and I don't want to hurt you, but you will have to pay for the damage to my car.'
'Please, I'll pay for the damage but don't tell my father what I did please.' His eyes filled with tears. I almost walked away at that point.
'We'll tell your dad that you were drunk and you ran across the bonnet and roof of the car when it was stationary, (another old student trick I have seen done a couple of times and one an old friend of mine used to do to police cars including kicking the lights off the top). I got him to sign a piece of paper saying he owed me £1200, gave him my address and left him to get in touch with his dad.

That next day his dad made a two hour journey and paid me a visit. I proved the damage via a quote and he wrote me a cheque there and then for £1200. I agreed I wouldn't take any further action against his son. The matter was ended there and then, well almost.
The son's father was very concerned and couldn't understand why his son would do something stupid like run over a car. It was a head scratcher for him and it seemed the itch wouldn't go away. I'd given my word to the kid not to tell his dad the real story of what happened but I had two kids of my own and felt for the father.

I knew if I didn't break my word and tell the truth and the kid did himself in I would never forgive myself. It would be like I was killing him. He needed help and his parents needed to know. It was break my word which was living a lie or tell the truth and hopefully save a desperate soul.
I decided to keep my promise to the student. After all, I'd given him my word. But just like the police officer tipped his notepad over to show me the kid's details without breaking his own police rules, I decided to give the father a big clue and help him help his son get out of his predicament. The father turned toward his car, thanked me one last time and bade me well.
I called after him.

'Do you know this is the time of the year that students are under immense pressure, some even attempt suicide.'
'What do you mean by that?'
'I think you need to have a serious word with your son.'
His eyes lit up with urgency. 'What are you saying?'
'Listen, mate I made a promise earlier today and I won't break it.'
'You need to talk to your son. He needs your support right now.'
The realisation of what I was saying left him silent for a second. I watched the wheels of his mind turn working out just what it was I was telling him.
'Oh my God,' he said. 'Thank you, I'm sorry for all the trouble.'
He turned and walked away rubbing his head.

I never knew what became of the student. I saw him a few weeks later at the club and he appeared more confident than the last time I'd seen him. I briefly spoke to him on the door and ever so quietly he said, 'Sorry.'

The unexpected chance meeting on a road at 3.00 a.m. could have ended in tragedy for two families. Every time I drive past the spot where I hit the kid, I see him standing waiting to sprint toward me. Then I see his face on the screen before it flips over. Some images cannot be erased from the memory.

DEFENDING THE HIGH GROUND

The main room in Crystal's was usually closed on Thursday nights due to a shortage of punters, so private functions were encouraged. A crew of lads from a nearby city had approached us and wanted to put on a night. Urban jungle music was the theme.
I don't mind private functions. What does bother me though is urban music. Confrontation oodles out of it: in-fighting between different gangs, intimidation, anger, drugs, it comes with the package. I don't want to sound political but there is usually a lot of resentment to authority. And if you get drawn into their internal conflict you become the enemy and it can all go wrong. There are many stories of shootings and stabbings connected to this and other cultural scenes of the same ilk. We were fully aware of the situation when we took the booking, but were under pressure from the owners to get the money rolling in. So the gig was booked and about to start.

The attitude of the *clientèle* was enough to put the most hardened of doormen on edge. Thursday night fight night was also in full swing in the small room and the very last thing we wanted was for the two scenes to mix. It would be like having a fireworks party on a petrol station forecourt.
Jungle music at the time had a mixed race following, gangs of lads and girls with big attitudes and the odd big butt. I stood on the door with Tiny and Johnsy, a doorman of good repute and loads of real experience. They were tasked with searching the punters as they came in.
We kept it tight, keeping them on the staircase and ourselves on the flat landing, letting in a couple at a time and giving us an advantage if anyone decided to get shifty and kick-off. Because of the attitude that goes with these nights, everyone was tapped down for weapons. The majority would have been turned away from a mainstream night.
I'd been getting uptight all week waiting for this night to happen. The rumours of shooters increased my feelings. I knew what damage those babies could do. I regularly visited a shooting range in Nottingham with a friend: Andy. I couldn't get a licence of my

own but he used to sign me in and gave me the opportunity to try out some of the weapons on the range. I fired most of the big pistols. It's frightening what they can do at close range. My awareness of these weapons put me on edge. But at least I had some knowledge as to where a weapon would be concealed and how to make one safe. I also knew that the weapon wasn't the danger, but the person with the intent to use it!

As we couldn't lock the middle doors (they were fire exit doors) I took the precaution of putting a bouncer on the middle doors separating the two rooms. His job was to make sure nobody went through them, no matter what. Steve was a relatively new bouncer but he'd been tested and was fine.

We'd been open for about three hours and everything was going really well. The room was heavy with smoke; a mixture of cigarettes, disco smoke and weed. The dim lighting highlighted the smoke into beams which cut through the darkness. The organisers had brought in two big strobe lights. When the strobes flickered they flashed intermittent silver blue, silhouetting the shapes of furniture and turning everyone into gyrating robotic forms. Inbetween the strobes of light it was pitch black.

The atmosphere was becoming more sinister as the night progressed. I got an eerie sensation in my stomach, a foreboding of things to come. Watching this spectacle unfold before me was both totally disorientating and disturbing. Gangs of lads huddled together. The dark recesses were crowded and formed into circles of lads and girls. There wasn't a smile amongst them.

I could feel the bass booming inside my chest like a second heartbeat. The hairs stood tall on my arms. I was on edge. I had to leave the dance floor area and get a breather. I went out into the foyer to ease down a bit. I made a few wise cracks, but they fell on deaf ears.

I waited in silence, watching the CCTV monitor which covered the far door.

I saw the light on the wall above the door flash before I heard the piercing sound cut through the silence and register in my eardrums forcing me to sprint into the club. My heart was pounding harder and faster than the bass rhythm. I blasted through the doors scanning the area as I went. Visibility was low. It was like being in heavy fog at night with no street lamps. I looked toward the bar which stood out like an oasis in the darkness. The barman was pointing to the middle doors. Through the smoke I could see a struggle taking place. Before I could make any headway through the crowd I was hit with a flash of strobe lighting which temporarily blinded me. When my vision came back I could see punches and kicks being exchanged between doormen and a gang of about ten lads.

A free for all had erupted on the middle doors and threatened to spread throughout the club. Steve was in the middle of the exchange. I had a choice to make. Do I go in or do I put on the lights? I chose the latter. Steve was doing all right and had been joined by two more of the doormen from the small room. I had to get the lights on so we could see the situation clearly. They were situated behind the DJ booth which meant I would have to run the gauntlet through the crowded dance floor and put the lights on. I would at that point become a target for a very pissed off crowd. But it had to be done and quick. Steve was in the shit!

I got to the booth and flicked the switch. The room lit up cancelling out the crazy, disorientating effects of the strobes. Now I could see. I ran into the *mêlée* and knocked out the first person I came into contact with. I grabbed hold of the nearest person and tried to apply a strangle. I got grabbed from behind and pulled backward. I spun and faced a group of black lads.

'Stay out of it, man,' one said.

'Fuck you,' I said and grabbed the kid. I ran him to the foyer doors looking around me as I went. I was closely followed by Johnsy. He passed me by and dispensed with another, using the lad's head to get through the doors. I followed suit throwing mine into the waiting arms of Tiny.

I ran back in and went to the aid of Steve who was fighting like fuck against two lads in the doorway. Johnsy was rolling on the floor with another.

I pulled one off Steve. Steve now free, turned and threw a punch just missing my head.

'Steve. It's me,' I shouted. I pinned Steve to the door. The brawl had temporarily stopped. The lads involved had run out into the foyer after their crew. They would be regrouping and I feared for Tiny. I ordered Steve to go into the small room and press the buzzer for the rest of the doormen to come through. Me and Johnsy ran to the door but were stopped by another gang of lads trying to get out. The foyer door was being held shut. We were stuck inside the main room. We could hear a brawl going off inside the foyer. We had to get in there. For all we knew Tiny was taking a kicking. I directed Johnsy through the food hatch.

'I won't fit through there,' he said.

'Yes you will.' I picked him up and forced him through, then dived through myself. The food hatch led into the kitchen and the kitchen door led to the foyer. I ran for the door. Johnsy picked up a tool.

The last thing we needed was to give them a reason to tool up.

I didn't want to douse the flames in petrol.

'You don't need that, Johnsy, come on.' I ran through the door expecting to run into a barrage of trouble. Instead Tiny was holding the foyer door shut and shouting instructions which were being obeyed.

'Leave now,' he said. I just caught the backs of the gang as they left cursing saying they would be back.

They had left divided, but once outside they would regroup and try again.

I was sure of that. They were too arrogant not to.

'Fuck me, Tiny, I thought you were getting a kicking,' I said. Tiny smiled as two other doormen arrived from the small room to boost the door. We moved to the top of the staircase.

'Where's the promoter?' I asked.

'He left ages ago, just after that gang arrived.'

The promoter had taken the money and left us to deal with the trash.

'Okay. Let's hold the door.' We waited for the possible return of the gang.

As I made my way down the staircase I heard voices and then saw the gang at the bottom.

I stepped back up sharpish and stood on the top step. If they were armed I would be the target and the staircase would become the shooting range. They'd already made threats to shoot us as they left. I didn't think of the consequences of the situation. The adrenalin was flowing and time was moving fast. If they were armed I was fucked anyway. I stood my ground. They were halfway up the staircase before I'd got onto the top step.

'Nobody stops us from going anywhere, man. We go where we want to,' said the heavily built lad.

I counted seven lads ascending the staircase. I'd been here before in this same position and I knew what to expect. I knew how to defend the high ground. They continued, obviously blinded by their arrogance. I almost laughed when the big lad came within range, his head at my boot height. I let him have the full force of my neatly timed left roundhouse kick. There was a sickening cracking sound that echoed around the stairwell. The foot duster did its job. My leather covered steel toe cap caught him on the side of the jaw. Steel on bone switched him off instantly. He paused statue like for a moment, then fell back into the arms of his gang causing several of them to reel backwards. I broke the silence.

'Now come on, you fuckers.' My aggression was tearing at my insides. I wanted to run down and finish the job. Instead I stood my ground.

'Take your man and fuck off.' My aggression was high. My temper under control.

'We're going man. Leave it. We're going.' They backed off. I could feel the weight of the support of the lads beside me. They left the club and order was restored.

We'd given them a way out, probably not the one they would have liked. Without their leader they were in turmoil. They left almost immediately in two cars racing off at high speed. The night continued without any more trouble. I switched doors and kept a low profile in case we got a visit from the Old Bill.

It was the last jungle night to be held at Crystal's. We'd kept control of the venue. As they say it was a good night: no one got shot!

BATTLE OF THE HIGH STREET

Football violence was rife through our towns and cities. The hooligan crews dodged the coppers as they sought turf to fight on.

The notorious 'baby squad', followers of Leicester City football club, were on their way into town hell bent on firing up trouble. They had a reputation for kicking off when the odds were in their favour and thought they would surprise us, but one of their own who shall remain anonymous, tipped me off through a third party and during what was to follow kept well out of the way.

When they arrived in town, word spread fast and we were kept informed of their whereabouts and were ready for them. We were used to fighting with the odds stacked against us and fought harder knowing that every one of us counted.

I'd fought in many gang fights over the years with different hooligans and they're all basically the same: a few tough lads who might be able to stand a toe to toe one on one, with the rest, a bunch of marauders using hit and run tactics; the hits not being very hard and the running extremely fast! They carry or use anything they can get their hands on. The usual weapons were: Stanley knives – a very sharp workman's tool, very easy to obtain, gas of the CS type, knuckle-dusters and sharpened coins. The most common weapons were bottles, furniture and glasses. Their methods were to blind-side and attack the weak and vulnerable, or who they thought were vulnerable.

I walked across to Busters followed by five other bouncers leaving another three on the club door tooled and ready to go. I'd beefed up the door via a phone call to Big Ken Schofield who was running a club in a nearby town. The doormen Ken brought over were veterans. One in particular, was Carl, a real tough fucker with loads of bottle. Fifteen in total – we stood the door and waited for the kick-off.

I organised the team like a general preparing for a last defensive stand. Our real plan was one of attack.

'If they come, shut two of the front doors and congregate on the single front door. Remember there might be a 50 out there but they can still only fit in a couple at a time. Keep an eye out for the CS gas and the blades.'

Most of the lads had experienced this type of fighting. The nerves were evident in the not so experienced. The others hid their feelings of fear. Oh they weren't afraid. If they were they wouldn't be standing on the door. Fear is a natural feeling. Controlling it is a skill developed through experience.

I knew how the squad would behave as I knew how they thought. They didn't care about the law. They didn't care about whom they hurt and didn't need a reason to cause harm or damage. The cause they chose to follow was meaningless.

They came to the door two at a time doing a walk-by checking out the door to see how many doormen were on duty. They acted as if we didn't know who or what they were. Most of the lads stayed inside while they did their dry run. They would see only two doormen and probably estimate four at tops. The walk-bys were an indication of a possible attack. If we knew, then the police should know, but there wasn't one copper in sight. We soon found out why.

We gathered in the foyer and waited. Waiting was the worst part. That's really what being a doorman is about – waiting for a kick-off or the possibility of one. Yeah it's nice to able to nip it in the bud, but a lot of the time it doesn't work like that. People are unpredictable when intoxicated by alcohol or drugs, so waiting was the norm.

The pub was double checked to make sure nobody had slipped the net earlier. It wasn't unusual for the squad to put a couple of lads inside to open an exit door and let them in.

I knew the tricks. We used the fire exit routine ourselves a few times when raiding a club or letting in barred friends.

After about five minutes we got a definite message that they were on their way; it's nice to have someone on the inside running with them and reporting back. I stood behind the lads. As they got closer I noticed within their ranks were several police officers, powerless to stop them. It was an awesome sight to behold: around 60 hardcore hooligans all dressed similar. There didn't appear to be any organisation, but I knew there would be. We crowded the door. As they got closer I instructed the lads.

'Stand your ground. They want to be able to say they took us. No fucker comes through that door.'

'It's all right for you. You're at the back.'

I injected some humour.

'The general always sits on the hill.' All that stood between the door and the hooligans were four feet of tarmac and two feet of slabs. I sent one of the lads inside to clear the customers away from the glass windows at the front of the pub just in case they got smashed in. The bouncers ducked and covered their heads as bottles whizzed past smashing against the foyer walls and thudding against bodies. From the back the bouncers looked like they were doing some kind of weird twisting dance as they avoided the incoming bottles. Cans flipping and spinning, spurting their contents over the crowded doorway added to the mayhem.

The police looked on and waited. It was early. They were undermanned and waiting for backup. If we let them get away with coming into the town and causing trouble with no consequence we were making a rod for our own backs. I'd learnt the way was to go for it regardless of the odds. If we were aggressive enough we would win through. The fans surged forward in a bid to overrun the door. Knuckles and boots were exchanged. Then like the tide they backed off, only to surge forward again. The movement was constant. And the noise deafening.

'Don't fucking go yet. Hold the door,' I shouted. 'They can only come in two at a time.'

The windows were shattering as the bottles hit. I shouted to Rob the manager to bring a bottle bin to the door. It was time to equalise. I picked up a 1.5 litre Martini bottle. This was to be the signal to go.

'Keep down, lads. When this bottle lands we're gonna run the bastards.'

'You're joking, there's too many of them,' came the reply.

'Fuck 'em. We're going out.'

I could see several youths running in looking for a way forward, not daring to overstep the mark. Their faces were ugly with aggression and hate. Kids barely off the playground. But very dangerous in a pack.

'Stay low,' I shouted. On those words I hurled the bottle into the crowd, narrowly missing a policewoman. She turned to the side as the bottle smashed into the forehead of one of the hooligans. He went down and we went out. With a mighty roar we charged into them. Their lines broke right and they scattered. We had a window of opportunity.

'Go. Fucking go, destroy 'em!' I pushed the doormen forward and ran through.

'Come on then,' I shouted as I ran forward. They hadn't expected us to run them. Within seconds bodies littered the streets. We were joined by other doormen from other pubs. Over 100 lads were now fighting along the 200 metre stretch of the High Street. Weapons were being swung like it was rounders or baseball practice. To my left I had Carl and to my right, Tiny.

I shouted to Tiny to hold the door. I could tell by the look on his face he wanted to carry on scrapping, but if they got into the pub they would claim a victory. He stayed. We now had the momentum. I found myself in front of four of the mob who stopped running and faced me off. I drilled the first one and we were fighting. Knuckles and boots fell short of their targets – it's hard to connect in a running battle. It's harder still to keep your footing.

Carl was now whirling a set of nunchaka above his head like he was doing an impersonation of a helicopter. Behind Carl a police officer was trying to swoop on him but was unable to because of the whirling nunchaka. The copper managed to grab Carl's arm. I turned grabbed the nunchaka and thrust them into the copper's hands.

'Take them. He just took them off those lads.' The copper looked dumbfounded but bought the explanation. Carl laughed and shouted as he ran: 'Fucking 'ell. They're my best set. Cheers, John.'

I heard a helicopter above us, its searchlight flickering from doorway to doorway, lighting up the whole street. Beyond the fans I saw several police vans screech to a halt. A youth splayed his arms out to his sides as if inviting me in, his oppos each side of him doing the same. 'Come on then,' he shouted.

I silenced him with a left hand power slap which took him off his feet. His oppos sprinted clear and disappeared into the crowd which had now gathered at the end of the High Street. Their mate lay unconscious at my feet. Everywhere I looked scraps were happening. It was chaos. I hunted for my next victim. The police had now arrived in full force, one or two officers were beginning to run in and grab certain people. They were trying to herd the squad into one group; it was a cool manoeuvre. A suited guy shouted my name. I took him to be a high-ranking copper.

'John. Call your lads off. We'll take it from here. You've done a good job. Let us do ours.'

'No problem,' I said. I dodged from man to man.

'Cool it. Let's go. Leave it. Get back to the doors.'

We walked back through the High Street un-challenged by the police as they closed the trap on the hooligans. Order was quickly restored to the High Street. The helicopter overhead added to the seriousness of the event; this would cost a fortune. The squad were herded away like animals inside a police cordon, not as wild now they had been tamed. People eager to see the action were now roaming free along the High Street as the pub filled and the music blared out as if nothing had happened.

We were in an 'us or them' situation and exercised our right to pre-emption. It was the only way to deal with the situation: go forward and do the business. Protection was what we were being paid for. If we hadn't been ready for the visit, the pub and everyone in it would have been trashed without a doubt. The total damage to the pub was a few pounds worth of glass. The police bill would be far more significant. The lads on the door fought courageously and none were arrested or injured: a miracle considering how many bottles were thrown. Tiny took some stick for staying on the door. I made sure the lads knew I had told him to stay and the reasons why: the protection of the building and everyone in it.

The lads all had a tale to tell and everyone starred in their own show. It was a major kick-off and we still had another four hours of door work to go.

The following week the local papers were full of 'the battle of the High Street' and several of the hooligans were arrested and charged.

TEEING OFF

Whilst working the doors is a venue job, it regularly becomes a policing job of the street. I've often had to leave the door to help out some unfortunate lad who's on the wrong end of a few size nines.

One particular night I saw a gang of young men chasing a lad past the end of the alleyway which led to the club. I ran out to see what was going on and the gang of 15 to 20 had surrounded the lad and were kicking fuck out of him. He was curled up on the floor in the foetal position. 'That's somebody's son,' I thought. The boots were landing so hard they moved the lad's body. The gang were relentless. They were going to cause him some serious harm or worse kill him if they carried on. I felt the rush of anger and charged toward the gang screaming a kia like a karate exponent.

I jumped high into the air with a leaping side-kick like something out of a Jackie Chan movie. My timing was perfect. I landed smack in the middle of the gang and in true Jackie Chan comic style fucked up and ended up curled in the same foetal position as the lad. But the blows I was expecting to land on my head and body didn't materialise. The lads had scattered at the sound of the kia. I picked up the kid and dusted him down.

He was dazed but okay. He said one of the lads had accused him of staring at him. He'd denied the accusation and legged it when they threatened him; he slipped and became surrounded.

Another time a woman came screaming through the Crystal's entrance way.

'Help me, you've got to help my boyfriend.' With no hesitation I followed the woman.

She was hysterical. We headed into the High Street. Two cars were parked up opposite the club. All of the car doors were open. Two youths were fronting up another group of lads. One in particular (I took this to be the boyfriend) was about to take a golf club across the skull. The youth with the club looked like he was about to tee off on the golf course but couldn't quite get the swing right. I approached the youths with my arms splayed followed by two doormen.

'Hey mate what's going on?' He turned his attention away from the lad and directed his swing at me.

'You what?' he asked.

'Put the club down,' I said in a firm voice. As the lad backed off I got closer trying to keep the distance from his swing angle. Suddenly I was in danger. All he had to do was swing the club. He raised his arms. If I stayed put he would have copped me. If I went back he probably would still have copped me. The only way was to go in close beyond the swing. All of the power would be in the end of the club. I jumped forward sweeping the lad's legs from beneath him. He took off. He floated parallel to the floor for a second then landed with a thump. If we'd been in a karate tournament I would have scored Ippon, but this was no tournament. He immediately bounced back up and ran to his car. I picked up the club then in a firm voice shouted:

'Get in your car and fuck off.'

'You fuck off,' was the abuse I got as the lad's wheel spun away. The girl thanked me and the other bouncers and got in the car with her boyfriend. The argument was about the boyfriend cutting the other lad up at the lights. Door work will always be a policing job; after all doormen are the first emergency service. They are there on the scene way before the police or the ambulance service and are a necessary force.

MACHETE MADNESS

Cutting through the air thrashing from side to side the blade caught the light and sparkled. The crazed youth charged forward into the attack without a thought for his own or anyone else's mortality.

Violence always appears dirtier midweek. It's a different kind of violence compared to the classy kick-offs at the weekends. There seems to be more hatred involved and the perpetrators always appear more desperate.

Balloo, the big cuddly doorman of Cypriot origin, was on his soapbox trying to solve the Middle East crisis single-handedly and thought that I should listen to his ideals. The one way conversation was interrupted by the crackle of the radio. It crackled out muffled broken sentences. 'Hello this is John. Can you repeat the last message? Over.'
'Yeah, John, sorry about that. The aerial's fucked. I've swapped radios now. I just got a call from the pub. There's been some aggro over there with a group of out-of-towners. They have been refused entry into the pub, they had a run in with one of the Loughborough lads, Nigel, a few weeks ago and Nigel was out for revenge.'
'Don't let them in the club. They're real trouble. If they bump into Nigel he'll kick it off! He's on his way to the club,' Dave said.
'Okay, Dave. No problem,' I replied.
'A description would be handy though,' I added. Dave laughed.
'I'll come down to the door.'
'Notorious Nigel' was a friend of mine and one of those rare breed of lads that really lost it in a fight. This was something that by his own admission he wasn't great at, but when he flipped he really flipped. He was a true psychopath. He'd been to see a psychiatrist on more than one occasion and he'd spent time in the cuckoo's nest. I remember saying to him one night, not knowing he was serious about having psychopathic tendencies, that anyone who goes to see a psychiatrist wants their head examining! He didn't find it funny. He just gave me a weird look as if he didn't get the joke. Nigel was a lunatic when it came to fighting and would use

any weapon that was within his reach. He'd had a fall out with a local gang of lads he'd known for years and instead of talking it through with them like most lads do he got frustrated about the whole situation and decided to track them down.

He cornered them in a local town centre pub with a shooter. He burst in while they were having a quiet drink, pointed the gun in the direction of the group and laid down his terms for peace. He didn't realise straight away that he was on camera. When he did he scarpered and left the country until the heat died down. Funny thing was, the camera wasn't recording that night and he spent months in Greece for no reason. Things didn't ever seem to work out for Nigel. Relationships were a nightmare; his life was violent but in a comical sort of way like a cartoon violence where nobody really gets hurt. He never seemed to see the danger in what he did.

Dave joined Big Ken, me, and Balloo on the door. I'd told Ken about Nigel's run in with the out-of-towners. He shook his head from side to side. Ken was a ruthless doorman to those that deserved it. He pulled no punches when it came to meting out the necessary. He was a keen rugby player and powerfully strong. He'd boxed as a heavyweight and knew the ropes. He also knew the streets. Big Ken was a real gentleman. I had a lot of respect for him, a true friend.

I stood in the doorway waiting for the out-of-towners to appear at the end of the alleyway which led to the club doors. The alleyway was well lit and covered by CCTV. It was a warm summer's night and the streets were quiet. The smell of takeaways drifted in the air. A couple were staggering in the doorway to the hotel opposite the alleyway trying to gain entry. They appeared comical stumbling around, fondling each other almost to the point of tearing each other's clothes off, as if they couldn't wait to get to their room.

The door lads were now silent, a stark contrast to the chattering that went on before we got the call. These lads we would be turning away were strangers to us. We didn't know who they were or what they were capable of doing. Whether it would get physical or not we'd have to wait and see.

They appeared in the alleyway. A scruffy bunch who looked pissed off. I decided I would be the one to break the bad news. Balloo manned the middle doors with Dave. Ken stood behind me. I straightened up, making myself appear bigger like animals do in the wild when they feel threatened. I always felt confident when working the door. I trained as hard as any athlete and knew the game well.

I gestured to Balloo and Dave as if to say 'are you ready to go?' There were five of them in total, all big lads and they looked arrogant and intimidating. It was fight night and the entry ID to the club was either a dole card or army pass. I observed their mannerisms as they strode cockily toward the doors. They looked like they were going to walk straight through us. I positioned myself in the doorway blocking their entrance. They stopped in front of me. I spoke to whom I considered to be the main man: a big pissed off looking lad who appeared to be suffering from male PMT.

'Yes, mate. Can I help you?' I said politely hiding my fear of confrontation behind a smile.

The big pissed off youth who had taken a central position in front of me, tried to brush me aside as if I wasn't there. His breath stunk of kebab meat. The rest of his gang stood either side of him forming an arrowhead formation.

He never answered me and stared inside the foyer checking out who was in there.

He continually moved around fidgeting He was very agitated and looked like his temper was about to boil over. He looked at me as if to say 'are you a fucking idiot?'

'We want to come in.' I kept eye contact to let him know I was talking to him and him alone. His lads were now irrelevant. They were still a threat but I had entered negotiations with him. His reply would decide whether this would become personal or not.

As soon as he had finished taking mental notes of the situation his brain in the form of one of his mates worked out a reply. 'We want to come in,' he said.

Fucking 'ell, I thought, that took some figuring out. At that point I knew he and his crew were of low intelligence.

'Well I'm sorry, lads. You won't get in.' I scanned the group including them back in to the conversation so I didn't get drawn in to tunnel vision with pissed off. Pissed Off challenged my decision.

'Why not?' I felt a surge of adrenalin at his aggressive reply. If he was going to strike first he missed his chance. There was no use trying to be civil to this twat. He'd only see it as a weakness. He was up for it so I gave it to him straight. I countered his open ended question with a brain teaser.

'Because I fucking said so.' I kept eye contact and waited for his reply.

I was already positioned to whack him if necessary. He was, at that point, in control of my right hand. I waited. First he broke eye contact and looked over my shoulder.

'Fuck you,' he said and turned and walked away. I countered. I probably should have kept quiet at that point but I couldn't help myself.

'Fuck you too,' I said. His lads followed his lead. Then without further warning Pissed Off turned and sprinted toward me as fast as a sprinter coming out of the blocks. Only he resembled a rhinoceros instead of a finely tuned athlete.

One thought ran through my mind, Come on, you fucker. I thwarted his attack with a well-timed, front kick aimed into his pelvic girdle halting his sprint and bending him forward at the waist. Both of his hands dropped to protect his vitals. He turned and walked away cursing to himself.

'Fucking good shot,' I heard Ken say. Laughter filled the foyer. Dave winced when the kick landed and was now giggling. Balloo joined in.

I smiled, which was my way of switching off the adrenal tap. I'd found out over the years that humour helped me to return back to normal after a kick-off. Before I learnt this I found myself taking out my feelings of anger and frustration on the next person that stepped out of line. They'd be dealt a severe attack whether verbal or physical, when they probably didn't deserve it!

As the laughter died down Ken gave us the benefit of his experience.

'They'll be back' he said. Pissed Off was now probably really pissed off. Had already checked out how many we were. He'd fancied his chances and failed in his first attempt. I'd made him look foolish in front of his mates and they would be winding him up. Once over his embarrassment of being stopped by a solitary front kick he might try again. We waited.

Shouting emanated from the street. The couple who were still trying to gain entry to the hotel were looking nervously toward the left of the alleyway: the direction in which the lads had gone. I figured the lads were perhaps fighting amongst themselves and best left to it. A scuffle broke out in front of the alleyway, then a scattering of bodies running in all directions. The man still trying to get into the hotel was now frantically banging on the door in a state of panic. The woman clung to him as if her life depended on it.

'What's happening?' said Dave. Before I could answer, Pissed Off appeared looking really pissed off. His face was a contortion of evil caused by his extreme anger and the mass of adrenalin he must have been experiencing. I didn't want to believe what my eyes were telling me. Ken believed his.

'He's got a fucking machete,' he shouted. Pissed Off charged forward, eyes wide open now looking like Linford Christie when he neared the finish line. The intent in his eyes fed my adrenalin. I needed every millilitre of it. I grabbed hold of the door handle and positioned myself in the middle of the frame. I held my other hand on the opposite frame. I figured I could take him with another front kick. It was a gamble but I felt I could do it. If I missed I was fucked.

'Shut the fucking door,' Ken shouted. Dave and Balloo joined in the cry.

'Fuck him,' I said. I was calling his bluff. I stood firm. He raised the blade high in the air ready to strike me. My mind was very calm and clear. He was almost within striking distance when I realised he wasn't bluffing. He was out of control. I read somewhere that a stabber never shows and a shower never stabs. Good phrase, but I wasn't taking any chances. He cried out as if in pain and swung the blade to the sound of the door slamming shut like a huge shield. He sliced at the doors like a maniac. Blow after blow hacked away at the oak.

Ken laughed nervously, 'Fucking strewth that was close. Keep that fucking door shut, John.'

I wasn't going to let go. The attempted destruction of the doors stopped and Pissed Off pressed his face against the small porthole of glass and screamed. Then he turned and walked away holding the fearsome tool in his hand. He looked invincible. His crew were at the end of the alleyway waiting to welcome their hero.

I couldn't bear to see him walk away and try and claim a victory. I took a glance at Ken before I opened the door. Dave moved into position with Balloo at the fire exit doors adjacent to my door. We'd crashed out of them many times before. This time we'd be facing a maniac with a blade. The tension was high.

'Oi cunt,' I shouted. Pissed Off turned round, his aggression subsided and he had a look of disbelief on his face.

'Is that the best you've fucking got?' I said. I stood tall and defiant. I was supercharged with adrenalin. I felt taller. The phrase had the desired effect. He exploded with rage once more and hurled the machete at me. It turned over in the air as if it was travelling in slow motion. I watched it coming toward me like a boomerang in flight. Then it got faster. I snatched the door onto my body, once again using it like a shield. I felt a sense of relief when I heard the blade bounce off the door and hit the floor. The relief tripled when we crashed the doors and Dave took control of the machete which had broken in half.

We gave chase not knowing whether or not the rest of the lads were armed. Pissed Off and his crew were out of the blocks once again and sprinting up the High Street. Dave armed with half of a machete was in hot pursuit, with me, Balloo and Ken following on. The quiet of the High Street was broken by the screams of 'Get the bastards.' We couldn't have pissed off with his crew claiming victory over us. It would open the floodgates for more idiots to try their mettle. As we ran past the pub where the aggro had started Notorious Nigel joined us. His pace was fast. He overtook us all and gave chase to the mob. As Notorious Nigel neared the gang they turned left and dived into a waiting taxi. Nigel carried on running, took a leap of faith and landed on top of the taxi roof. He held on like a stunt man in a spy film. I didn't know what he was trying to achieve. Whatever it was he failed as the taxi shook him off and he rolled onto the tarmac. The taxi sped away into the night. I could just see the faces of the lads in the cab flicking the Vs at Notorious Nigel.

We fell about laughing as the mix of Notorious Nigel's antics and the euphoria of what had just happened hit home. The laughter got worse when later we found out that the half machete that Dave was carrying up the High Street belonged to Nigel. The scuffle at the end of the alleyway was Nigel attacking Pissed Off and his mates for jumping him the week before with a machete. Notorious Nigel had tripped, fallen and let go of the blade. When Pissed Off picked it up Nigel was already gone leaving us to deal with the machete loony!

The incident brought back memories of other attacks reminding me of how deadly a machete is in the wrong hands. The machete is cheap, easy to get and a tool that can become an extremely dangerous weapon in the hands of those with bad intentions.

EXTRA CHILLI SAUCE

The doner kebab goes perfectly well with at least 15 pints of good quality lager. The extra hot chilli sauce is a must.
'Large doner please, mate. Sling in plenty of meat, not too much salad, leave the cabbage out – it gives me heartburn,' says the unsuspecting youth as he stands there swaying gently from side to side.
'No problem, my friend, plenty meat for you. You wanna the chilli sauce?' The reply sounds sinister and you can see why: one bite and you're liberally splashed with eau de cologne de kebab. Yes; the kebab is a classic part of the British nightlife. I've often wondered whether it was the devilish hot chilli sauce, mixed with the lager that leads to the metamorphosis that turns well-mannered men into brutal fighting machines, that make them want to rip off somebody's head and play football with it down the street. Maybe it's the fact they haven't pulled and it's merely sexual frustration that drives them to a session of head dancing.
The kebab house, it's a real dangerous place, but where else can a man drown his sorrows when the pubs and clubs have shut?

The car pulled up outside the kebab house. It was the first night I'd had off in ages. When you're working the doors full time it does you good to have a break. Me, Tina and a few friends had all been out for a quiet drink. It was closing time so in our wisdom we decided to get a kebab. Dave hopped out and vanished through the kebab house door rushing to get served before any type of queue formed.

'Do you want a kebab, Tina?' I asked as I got out of the car.
'No thank you!' came her disgusted reply as if she knew something I didn't. I ventured toward the kebab house which was a few yards away from where the car had pulled up. I noticed two lads standing next to the passenger side door window of an old jag which was parked just outside the kebab house opposite the glass fronted window and door. One of the two lads was leaning his head towards the jag window talking to the driver.

As I approached the doorway the two lads made their way into the kebab house but made no attempt to queue up, staying just inside the doorway. My path was immediately blocked by one of the lads. I thought back to the times I'd been in here before. It always started like this, some twat blocking your path, pushing in front of you or nicking a piece of your closely guarded kebab. I remembered why I stopped coming in here.

'Excuse me,' I said, attempting to move around the youth which due to the size of the doorway was virtually impossible without him giving way. He didn't seem interested in buying anything; he was facing out of the doorway and made no attempt to place an order. His mate, standing to the left of him, never moved. I was unnerved by his cold stare. He was far too close for comfort. I walked through him pushing him back against the wall so I could get by. He came back at me blocking my path again. I immediately grabbed him by the throat rammed his head against the wall, pinning him with my elbow against his chest. I tightened my grip so he couldn't move. My nose was almost touching his.

'What's your fucking problem?' I asked glaring deeply into his eyes trying to see what was going on inside his head. My hand squeezed tighter as my temper level rose. I could feel his windpipe collapsing, his eyes bulged wide almost popping out as my thumb and fingers dug deep into his flesh.

Silence fell as I waited for his reaction, my gaze switching momentarily from his only to see what his mate was doing. The silence was broken by the voice of the unshaven, tired-looking Turk behind the counter.

'No trouble in here please. You go outside if you want to fight.' He raised his kebab knife like an ancient Turkish warrior raising his yatagan.

I spun the youth off the wall and towards the open doorway, my hand still gripping his throat.

'Fuck off out of my face, you cunt,' I said, launching him backwards into the street. His mate shuffled out after him. My gaze met theirs. They stared back at me in defiance making no attempt to come forward.

'Come on, get your kebab,' said Dave.

I felt angry that I had lost control over two dickheads. I smiled and turned toward the counter. Before I could place my order an aggressive voice shouted in my direction.
'Oi cunt!' I stole a quick look at Dave expecting him to answer the call! Here we go I thought.
I turned in the direction of the call. Standing on the pavement in front of the two lads was a bearded hulk of a man who wouldn't look out of place as a villain in a Bond movie.
'Pick on someone your own size,' the hulk said. His face was on fire with rage and aggression. He was way over six foot four and a commanding sight. I was already feeling the effects of the adrenalin from the previous confrontation and the sight of this hulk in front of me pushed it through the roof.
'You what?' I replied.
'You heard. Pick on someone your own size.'
I quickly weighed up the situation. He stood in front of me like a huge bear. His arms hung by his sides almost touching the floor. This guy was built like a WWF wrestler, he even looked as mad as one. I couldn't help thinking I'd been set up. Were those boys deliberately sent to wind me up so he could have a go? I didn't need this shit. All I wanted was a bite to eat.
I felt myself being caged in by my own fear. I looked around me. I felt nervous, trapped. I'd fought outside here many times before and paid with my liberty. I got my first stretch on this very road where I was now being threatened. I didn't want to get arrested but here in front of me was one big fucking guy that wanted to rip me a new face and I didn't know why.
The two lads stood there smirking. They made no comment or move and seemed to be staying out of it for the time being. I recognised the hulk. But the two lads were an enigma. I couldn't think of a reason why he would want to fight me. I must have upset someone along the way. Being a nightclub bouncer that was inevitable.

The hulk moved into position on the pavement. He obviously thought he could beat me. It was time to make a move. I left the safety of the doorway and walked toward the car and away from the hulk. On seeing this the hulk dipped his bread. 'That's it. Fucking run, you coward.' His aggression deepened his voice. He was now ridiculing me in front of the lads that had caused this confrontation. I could sense his confidence growing with every step I took. He continued his abuse of me as I made my way to the car door.

'Go on, that's it. Run just like the coward you are.' I got to the safety of the car, opened the door and took a deep breath to ease the feelings of adrenalin flooding through my body. I threw my jacket into the back of the car. As I slammed the car door shut I heard Tina shout.

'Somebody stop him. That man will kill him.' I cast all thought from my mind and turned and caught the hulk's stare.

'I'm not going anywhere, you fat fuck,' I said. His face painted the picture I wanted to see almost instantly. The look of confidence disappeared from his face and the colour drained from his skin.

I'd led him to believe that I was a beaten man. The battle he thought he'd won wasn't over yet. He tried to adjust his stance and fire in his attack but was blinded by his own panic and wasn't prepared for the low swinging left hander that whipped in from the hidden stance I'd adopted. It caught him high on the forehead. There was a smacking sound as it landed. Ready to follow up with the right I paused as he froze in mid-air unable to respond. Everything around me became still.

For a split second nothing seemed to move, like someone had taken a snapshot in time. The image became firmly imprinted in my mind's eye.

I could see everything around me. It was like I was above the action watching it unfold. I didn't notice the large gash on his forehead until he crashed to the floor landing on his knees as if asking for mercy.

He remained there in the silence, finally falling forward onto his palms braced by only his hands and knees. The silence was broken by the sound of the blood hitting the pavement as it flowed like a beer tap on a busy Saturday night. It made a puddle between his hands: the only thing keeping him from falling onto his face.

I lined him up for a boot to the face to finish him off but he'd had enough. He looked a beaten man remaining there on all fours as the bloody mess on the floor started to congeal into a crimson sticky mess. I lurched forward over his body and screamed into his face.

'Don't fucking mess with me again, you fucking wanker,' I said as the fear gave way to the euphoria that always follows the realisation of victory.

He turned his head towards me and stared for a second then stared back at the floor peering into his own bloody mess. Motionless. The blood slowed to a single repeated drip. I felt sorry for him, even though I knew he wouldn't have shown me the mercy I'd shown him. I didn't think he'd heard what I said. But the message wasn't for him as much as for the two lads and the small bloodthirsty crowd that had gathered. He started to crawl along the pavement towards his car, unable to get to his feet. The two lads stayed well back and didn't attempt to help the defeated hulk. I looked in their direction. They both looked to the floor.

I was about to leave when two well oiled youths came out of the kebab house door. Seeing the sticky mess on the floor one of the lads bent down as if to scoop the up the blood with his kebab.

'Look', he said to his mate.

'Extra chilli sauce.'

I learnt a valuable lesson which you should heed next time you fancy a kebab: send somebody else to get it for you! I certainly will. Better still, give your arteries a break and cut them out altogether. They can be killers.

ON THE RANK

'The enemy of my enemy is my friend.'
Ancient proverb

'I'm just nipping across the road for some change. If anybody wants me you can get me on the radio,' I said.
'Do you want an escort, John?' said Balloo trying to be helpful.
'No it's all right, I've got a Sierra,' I said as I made my way out of the club.
'Your jokes get worse,' said Balloo.
'It's working with you lot. You're cramping my style.'
I heard Balloo's infectious laugh as I turned out of the alleyway and into the High Street.
The High Street was always quiet at this time. The well oiled masses were either in the clubs or had long since gone home, although there were always a few stragglers roaming about too drunk to realise where they were or even who they were. I noticed one youth sitting in a shop doorway. He was leaning against the window half asleep. Suddenly he awoke, erupted all over his lap then drifted off again. He was like a semi active volcano.
I looked down the long line of taxis, the faces of the cabbies temporarily lit up until they realised I wasn't a potential fare. Taxiing in the summer is a cut throat business.
'Many in, John?' asked Brains leaning towards the passenger window of his cab. I called him Brains because every time I saw him he had his head inside a book.
'Absolutely chock-a, mate. All you want now, Brains, is for it to piss it down at kicking out time,' I said. Brains laughed then dropped his head back inside his book.
I continued down the line of cars gesturing to each one in turn. Some drivers were sitting having a chat inside the taxi parked behind or stood chatting through the driver side window as they waited patiently for a fare. I always got on with taxi drivers; there were some real characters on the rank. It's a hard job and they have to take some real shit. Many a cabby has been attacked over the years. I'd helped a few out and they in turn helped me and a few others out. A good taxi driver sees all and says fuck all. As I

walked across the road I noticed a small crowd of Thais coming out of Loughborough's only Thai restaurant. I listened to the babble of the Thai language and wondered how difficult it was to learn. I noticed in front of the Thai House two men standing talking. One in particular got my attention. He looked across at me and stared. Then without taking his eyes of me he mouthed something to his mate. The way his mate reacted I figured what he'd said wasn't good.

I felt my heart race. I knew this kid well, a lovely lad. But now I barely recognised him. He was indulging in steroids and pumping big weights. The steroids were so strong they had changed his facial features and his body had grown to a size you could not get to in such a short time. I knew him and his family when he was a nice lad growing up on the estate. Now he was an arrogant bastard with a bad steroid-induced attitude.

My heart pounded and the negative voice inside my head warned me, you might not be able to take him. My anger grew and cancelled out the negativity. This abomination of a human being had been present when my good friend Spider had been jumped at work by a gang of three lads.

Spider was tired after a day's graft and he and the rest of the workforce were filing out of the various vans and trucks and heading for home. Spider, a good doorman with many years of experience, hadn't a clue what was about to happen. The last person he expected to see was a man known as Jack Glover.

Glover was a local drug dealer who had indulged in his own products and had become a pumped-up steroid freak. The once nine stone boxer had transformed himself into a monster of a man. He was massively built but short and bald. He was so out of proportion he resembled the Dunlop Michelin tyre man without the friendly smile. This became his nickname. The Michelin man was a nasty piece of work; his regular steroid rages made him appear a fearsome character. He suffered from delusions of grandeur and thought himself a hard man. He was dealing in various hard and soft drugs including the death drug heroin. Death drug not because people die from it but because it steals people's souls and destroys countless families' lives. The users become prisoners of the parameters of both mental and physical pain and live a life of degradation whilst the dealers get rich.

The money they made from their dealings enabled them to buy their own gym in a small town a few miles from Loughborough. Whilst working at the club one night I was approached by a group of young lads. They'd upset the Michelin Man over drugs dealings. They were scared and wanted advice from me on what to do. They told me that the Michelin Man had kidnapped them and had put them through some kind of ordeal. They wouldn't tell me what kind of ordeal and appeared ashamed of themselves. I didn't agree with the drug thing. I'd seen what drugs did to people, how it tore lives apart. I told the lads they would become who they hung around with. And I gave them a piece of advice: stay off the gear and stay out of the Michelin Man's way.

The Michelin Man had an insatiable appetite for steroids, sharing his stash with his associates so they too became like him. His reputation was built on fear and he surrounded himself with people who were weak minded so that he could control them, people that would feed his ego. It was also rumoured that he was in possession of firearms. With this knowledge in mind I banned the Michelin Man and several of his close friends from the two clubs that I was responsible for. The fact that I had barred him from the club and pub infuriated him but he didn't have the bottle to face me. He preferred a continuing feud of words. I recommended that other doorman friends do the same at their place of work. Some took the advice; others ignored it stating that the Michelin Man was all right! There were two friends in particular who were very close to Glover. They were the Korman brothers. Spider was the first doorman to implement the banning on my instructions. The Michelin Man was livid and threatened a comeback against Spider, singling him out.

As Spider got out of the van at his place of work, he came face to face with the Michelin Man and a match fight ensued. Spider could have taken Glover but the consequences were stacked against him. As a family man with a wife and two children to support, he couldn't afford to lose his job, having to fight it out in the very yard where the offices of the directors where based. Plus he was out numbered.

Spider still fought the Michelin Man and held his own even though he'd been engulfed by a major adrenal dump which was enough to stop the best of men. Spider's experience and skill enabled him to cope. The Michelin Man was waiting for Spider to fall so he could stamp his way to a reputation. When Spider told me about the incident I got angry and offered to help. He refused. Spider wanted to sort out the Michelin Man in his own time and his way. I agreed with Spider. It was a matter of honour for him.
'Okay you deal with Glover.' What I didn't tell him was that I'd deal with the others.

The lad that had circled Spider whilst he fought the Michelin Man now stood twelve feet from me looking at me like I was a piece of shit. I wanted to ignore him and walk away: after all it wasn't my problem, it was Spider's. Why should I get involved? I knew why: Spider was my friend, my ally. We had stuck together over the years and fought back to back when times got tough. Your friends are the ones that stick by you and watch your back when the shit is spread wide and far by the fan.

I know what it is like to be alone and right here right now I was going to change the stakes. I was going to show these cunts that as friends me and Spider would stick together, no matter what the odds.

I calmed my anger and approached the abomination. My adrenalin was already racing round my system. I couldn't contain myself any longer. I used the fact he was staring at me as an excuse to confront him.
'What's your fucking problem?' I stared into his eyes and made my way to where he stood.
'I ain't got a fucking problem.' His tone was arrogant and harsh.
I weighed him up; he was at least three stones heavier than me and very aggressive. If he rushed me I'd have a problem. I figured he didn't have the bottle but guys on steroids are unpredictable. I had to take him out quickly, pre-empt him. I gave him an ultimatum.
'Stay out of it,' I said positioning myself ready to whack him.
'Stay out of what?' He knew what I meant but was playing dumb.

'You know what I'm on about,' I said. I didn't want to tell everybody in earshot that it was because he had jumped Spider. But I needed him to know that was what it was for. I had to protect Spider's reputation. I didn't want people thinking I was fighting his battles.

He clicked on and said, 'He fucking deserved it.' I countered what he said matching his aggressive state.

'I barred Glover and the rest of you from the club. If you have a problem with that sort it out with me!' I could see his face contorting with rage. Had he the bottle to go for it? I wasn't going to wait to find out. He dropped his head slightly and grimaced. This was a precursor to attack and I sensed he was about to explode into action. I'd had him within striking distance since I'd faced him off. My hands hung down at my sides relaxed. The initial idea was to warn him off, let them know Spider had an ally. I was carrying five grand in my left hand and was surrounded by witnesses. I didn't want to get into a fight here in the street. The police could pass by at anytime.

The abomination stepped forward aggressively and spouted a couple of words that didn't register. Before he could finish his manoeuvre or get out a full sentence I threw a right hand slap from the hip. The slap caught him flush on the side of the jaw just below the ear. He went down quicker than a pint at last orders.

'Fucking stay out of it,' I shouted. The phrase would have meant nothing to those watching but at this point I had no control over what came out of my mouth. I turned and walked coolly away. I felt pretty smug. I was used to switching off my aggression as quick as I had switched it on. I didn't have to follow through and stomp him in to the ground. The real message was for the Michelin Man. I wanted him to know not to fuck with me or my mate.

I'd taken him out with one slap. It was that easy. The slap had cut through the steroid rage.

Rob, the manager of the pub, stood at the doorway. He'd witnessed the slap along with the line of cabbies and the small crowd outside the restaurant. The message would soon get through to Glover. Then if he fancied his chances he'd know where to find me.

'Everything all right, John?' Rob said.

'Sort of, mate.' No sooner had those words left my lips when I heard the abomination shout out to me.

'Is that all you've got, Skillen?' I turned to see him standing there like a B-movie gunslinger waiting to shoot it out with me

The group of Thais and the cabbies were now staring at me waiting for my response. I should have finished the prick when he went down and now I had my hands full. I had awakened the rage within him. I handed the five grand to Rob and turned toward the abomination. He continued his abuse as I approached him.

'You're fuck all, Skillen, fuck all.'

They were the last words that left his mouth. As soon as I was in range and before he could take action I drove a low front kick hard into his groin using the toe end of my foot. The surprise impact caused him to lurch forward. He dropped his hands to protect his vitals then leaned back and pulled to his right where his jaw met with my leather clad toecap shoe as I followed through with a solid roundhouse kick. The sound of the toecap impacting on his jaw seemed to echo in the night air. It was a sickening crunch and like somebody had flicked a switch his body shut down instantly.

I smelt a burning sensation in my nasal passages brought on by the adrenal rush. He fell backward and crashed into the boot of a taxi, then rolled to the floor. The boot broke his fall stopping his head from getting a secondary hit from the pavement. I stared at his body for second. A feeling of panic sped through my body. I looked around then bent down and put him in the recovery position. I stood back up and like a scene from a movie the crowd of Thai waiters and chefs cheered loudly, waving their hands in the air cheering and chanting Thai boxing! Thai boxing! They chattered away in their mother tongue. Shocked faces stared at me from the line of taxis. I scanned their faces. I noticed not one caught my eye and no one came to help the abomination. He wasn't liked since he'd become an arrogant bully boy.

I eventually got my change from the pub and when I came back out again some 20 minutes later, he was still unconscious. I checked his breathing then passed him by. He was alone. I took the change into the club and went back outside to check he was okay. I felt sorry for him. But better him lying there than me. He eventually came round.

I walked back into the club passing the semi-active volcano on the way. He was now leaning against the plate glass window only his shoulders were off the floor. The puke had run down the front of his jacket and shirt and onto his lap creating a neat little pile of spew; he looked in a sorry, self-induced state. I didn't say a word to any of the other lads on the door until Rob came over later and spread the word. I wasn't proud of what I'd done even though he deserved what he got.

I saw him a few days later. His jaw was broken and had to be wired up to hold it in place. He stopped hanging around with the Michelin Man after that incident, which he later found to his benefit. I'd done him a favour in a roundabout way. Me? I lived the next week or so worrying whether or not he would go to the police. He didn't and a few months later the reason why would become clear.

NEAR MISS

Keep your friends close, and your enemies closer.
Tsun Szu, Chinese sage.

Sunday, day of rest. No such luck for a man with a family and a home to keep in good shape. All of the big DIY stores were packed at the weekends. I hated doing DIY jobs. It just wasn't me and I always end up getting injured due to being overtired. I'd sooner stand on a door and face a crowd of football hooligans than do DIY.

I ushered Tina around to the bathroom aisle.
'Take the lads with you. I'll catch you up in a moment,' I said.
'Where are you going?' she asked.
'It's all right, Tina. You go round there. I'll be around in a minute.'
She'd spotted the scrotes like I had on the way in and was fully aware of who they were and what could happen if they approached me with the kids present.
'Come on, lads,' she said to my two sons, hurrying them along with a worried look on her face. My two young boys giggled and ran off chasing each other with Tina reluctantly on their heels.

When we'd pulled into the car park I'd noticed two men, one of whom I'd had a run in with outside Crystal's nightclub a few weeks before.

That man was Rakesh Korman, one of Glover's sidekicks and heavily involved in his dealings. He'd spotted me going into the store and followed me in. I couldn't help thinking that going shopping was stressful enough without having to watch my back. But running a nightclub door isn't confined to the club; it can follow you around haunting you wherever you go. The last time I'd met Rakesh Korman was on the door, when I refused him and several others entry into the club. They started to mouth off, laying down threats to kill. They were buzzed up on alcohol and drugs and acting very brave. During the confrontation which had moved from the door to the street one of the brothers got too close for comfort so I chinned him and put him on his arse. What happened next was like a scene from a Laurel and Hardy movie. The guy I chinned, fuelled by the drugs, quickly jumped back up and sprinted off in the opposite direction. He was confused; the adrenalin was too much for his system to cope with and he'd gone into flight mode. Everyone there except his associates erupted into laughter as he ran smack into a lamp post resulting in a second knockout. His brother backed off shouting threats then turned and ran into the same lamp post and smashed his nose which poured with blood. It was difficult to take them seriously after that performance.

I saw them re-enter the store. They headed straight towards me. I thought about ignoring them instead of courting confrontation but I knew from experience that if I tried to ignore these pricks they would grow in confidence by feeding on my unwillingness to face their threat. I knew both of the lads were out of my league when it came to a brawl and not a problem to me. But the fact that they still approached me in a disrespectful manner told me they were confident. And if they were confident there would be a reason. They would be high on the gear that was for sure, but were they armed? I watched their body language closely. They were both irritable and looked nervous. Knowing their involvement in hard drugs and rumours they had firearms meant they could be very dangerous.

I took this threat in front of me as serious. Something was making this guy very brave and that un-nerved me. Maybe they thought it safe to approach me in the store, assuming that I wouldn't fight in front of the kids. They were wrong. A lot of people find it hard to deal with confrontation whilst they have children with them which is only natural. Me? I will fight anywhere if the need to protect my family arises.

I noticed Korman had put on a lot of weight, mainly bloated muscle. He was broader and more thickset. I came to the conclusion he been stacking up on the gear but wasn't training hard enough for it to turn into muscle. He looked fat. The drugs obviously gave him more bottle; steroids bring out an aggressive nature more prominently. I've seen normally mild mannered lads turn into crazed loonies.

'I want a word with you,' Korman said in an aggressive tone.
'Have you got an appointment?' I said mocking him. He looked like a monkey looks when he's trying to take an apple from a small jar, where the neck is too small for the hand covered apple to come out, or like an Irishman put in a round room and told to sit in the corner. I changed my expression and tone to one of a serious nature.
'The best thing you can do is fuck off.' I coupled the phrase with a serious tone.
'Jack's not happy with you barring us from the club.' Shuffling a step or two closer like he was trying to get an angle on me.
'Tough shit. Tell Glover to go and fuck himself.' I looked around, people were starting to take notice of the evolving situation. I watched the pair of them, closely, switching my gaze from one to the other. I didn't want to lose sight of Korman's mate which can happen when the tunnel vision effect of adrenalin kicks in.
His mate looked away when I got eye contact. His heart wasn't in this confrontation. When they break eye contact it usually means their bottle is waning and they are feeling the fear. The other cunt, Korman, was too ballsy for his own good.
'When are we allowed back into the club?' He made a small step to his right as he primed me with the question, moving his hand toward his back pocket. He never took his eyes off me. I quickly posed him a question countering the question he had asked me and lining him up with my lead hand. Does he have a knife? I thought. He was close enough to stab me if he did have a blade. But did he have the bottle? He was fidgety. I subtly countered each move he made, controlling the distance between us. What a coup for him if he could bury a blade in me. If he was going to attack it would be now.
I made the safe assumption he was armed. Better to assume he's armed than not. I asked the question and waited for brain engagement. I wasn't interested in his reply. I just wanted to occupy his mind. I took a quick glance around me, took a deep breath and exploded an almighty left hand slap to the side of his head. A thwacking sound echoed in the open space of the store. Korman hit the deck with a thud! I shouted at his accomplice.
'Do you fucking want some?'

The sight of his mate on the deck and the shout caused the kid to jump well back and say, 'No trouble, John, I'm not getting involved.'

Korman tried to get up; it was like he was glued to the floor. He wasn't unconscious but the only part of his body he could lift was his head. Korman was completely disorientated then he scrambled back to his feet and raced off to the far end of the store with me in hot pursuit. 'You've done it now, Skillen. Glover's going to fucking shoot you.' He sprinted off toward the back of the store in such a blind panic he didn't notice that he was running past all types of weapons: axes, hammers, planks of wood and Stanley knives.

He ran through a warehouse door followed by his mate and locked himself in. I could see him through the shelving racks and wire mesh. I was smiling at him now, teasing him, showing the bloated fucker I didn't care about him, his brother or the Michelin Man.

He continued shouting his abuse repeating that Glover was going to kill me. In the background I heard one of the witnesses say that the police had arrived. I made myself scarce, telling Korman to give a message to Glover. 'Tell him he had better not miss.'

I went to find Tina and the boys on the other side of the shop. Tina suggested we leave immediately. I told her the police had arrived and I wasn't in a position to leave.

I became pro-active and walked toward the police officer. 'Can I have a word with you?'

Another officer appeared and said to the copper about to question me, 'Don't let him go anywhere. A man is making a complaint of assault against him.' Korman had grassed me up as soon as the coppers had arrived. In the old days it was a sin of the street to grass but the rules had changed a long time ago. Now they would fight you and if they lost they would still go to the police. Usually the one that gets to the police first is on to a winner. I had to get myself out of this situation. If I got arrested Tina and the lads would be vulnerable.

'I'm glad you're here I want to make a complaint,' I said to the copper. I knew the officer that had approached me would listen to my side if I was civil about it.

'You're John Skillen, aren't you?'

'Yes mate,' I said.

'What happened?'

'I was here with my wife and two kids shopping when two men approached me in a threatening manner. I told my wife and children to go out of the way as I feared for their safety. The lads were being abusive toward me. I had previously banned them from the club I worked at on suspicion of dealing in drugs and they wanted to know why I wouldn't let them back in the club. One of the lads I know as Rakesh Korman gestured to his back pocket. I'd heard a rumour that they carried knives and at that point I thought he had a knife. He was very aggressive and started to move toward me. It was at that point that I thought he was going to stab me and feared for my life. I thought I was going to die. If I hadn't taken this action my wife and children were in danger too.'

The copper stared at my spiel with his mouth slightly ajar. I continued telling him about the situation, hamming it up.

'I struck him once with the open palm of my left hand to prevent him from attacking me further, then told him and his mate to stay back. They backed off and I shouted for someone to call the police then I waited for you to arrive. I'm so glad you came or I would have been in serious trouble.'

'That's self-defence. Come with me,' the copper said.

'Well can I make sure the wife and kids are safe?'

'They'll be all right now, John. Come on.' I smiled as Korman passed me. This had the effect of sending his temper into overdrive.

'You bastard,' he shouted.

'Hey there's no need for that,' the copper said warning Korman to be quiet. The copper asked me if I wanted to press charges.

'Of course I do. People like that shouldn't be allowed on the streets.'

The copper looked at me shaking his head in agreement. I had a friend.

When the police searched Korman they informed me there was no knife. I kept quiet.

I had given my story, no point in confusing matters. I knew Korman was dangerous in his state of mind. I could have told the copper the truth: that I didn't give a fuck about him or his mate but that would have got me arrested. I didn't mind appearing the weaker party if it meant my freedom. I knew I was sitting pretty. Korman was still aggressive and was shouting at the police to arrest me. He was warned to calm down but every time he looked at me the smile sent him crazy. Another copper approached us.

'Are you sure you want to press charges?' he asked.

'Listen I don't want to cause you any paperwork. If you tell him to stay away from me and my family I am quite happy to walk away and forget the whole incident.'

'Wait there,' the copper said. Another heated conversation took place and Korman was allowed to walk off. My friend, the policeman informed me that no charges on either side would be pursued. The matter was closed. I didn't know whether Korman had a knife or not, but I did notice the copper's reluctance to arrest him. They had more than enough evidence, but they chose not to. I was suspicious. Something didn't quite add up.

HAPPY ANNIVERSARY

It was a beautiful August morning. I could hear the birds chattering away in the trees. I rolled over and pulled the covers over my head to block out the sunlight that was threatening to blind me. I felt groggy after working the night before. Unfortunately the pigeons cooing loudly outside the bedroom window didn't appreciate that fact. I could still smell the cigarette smoke that always clung to my skin. I crawled out of bed and into the bathroom and took a long hard stare at myself in the mirror. It was my wedding anniversary and I was looking forward to a nice relaxing day with my wife and children. We planned to have a barbecue and enjoy the heat of summer.

On my way to the supermarket I held on to my sons' hands, being careful not to hold too tightly for fear of hurting their delicate bones. I love my boys and I felt proud to walk with them hand in hand. It was fun watching them grow up. That was one of the plus points of being in the nightclub game. I got to see more of my children in the daylight hours. I felt lucky. I went to work, they went to sleep.
We made our way round to the toilet block at the front of the store. I could smell doughnuts in the air.
'Smell that, boys,' I said teasing their taste buds. Their faces lit up.
'What, Daddy?' said Luke with a smile on his face which could melt the hardest heart.
'Fresh doughnuts. Now if you're good lads while we're shopping you can have some doughnuts to take home to the barbecue.'

As I walked along I subconsciously checked the area I was walking into. It was normal after years of door work behind me. I was fully aware that I could bump into a multitude of old enemies made whilst doing my job, anywhere at any time. Awareness is the key. They say you should never take your work home with you. Unfortunately for me, and hundreds of other doormen all over the world, working the doors is a job that you take with you wherever you go. It eats into the very fabric of your daily life and many a relationship has been destroyed due to the nature of the job. Late nights and violent encounters, not to mention the opposite sex. Frustration, fear, anger, temptation are emotions that need to be exorcised out of your system before they build up and lead to a breakdown of self-control. Some relationships have been through the forge and survived, others have failed miserably.

Tina walked behind me. Tina is a beautiful woman, bubbly, fun loving and a strong-minded woman who won't take any messing. For any woman who is having a relationship with a bouncer or venue manager it's all about trust. Some women are attracted to the men that do these jobs like metal to a magnet. I have a lot of respect for the woman that has enough self-confidence to trust her man to stay faithful.

We were discussing what to buy for the barbecue when I spotted one of the Korman brothers heading in our direction. Pradip Korman was Glover's closest friend and as some said 'his bum chum'. He was dressed like a typical bodybuilder: shorts and vest and looked like he had just finished a training session. Heavyweight training workouts fuelled by anabolic steroids had pumped up the veins in the muscles of his neck, arms and legs. He looked incredibly fit and strong, a formidable character. I was surprised. I'd seen him only a few months before. He was about eleven stone then, now he weighed in at least 15. He'd become over-inflated just like his ego. He continued towards me.
'Well if it isn't hard man, Skillen,' he said, his voice firm and strong. I felt a massive surge of adrenalin known as 'the adrenal dump'. My mouth dried up. I felt sick to my stomach.
I felt my knees turning to jelly. My heart pounded in my chest. It was so strong I could feel it in the throat. I'd relaxed for a moment and became unaware just enough for the dump to take me by surprise. I remained silent taking a deep breath to slow down the feelings that were overpowering me.
I carried on walking gathering my composure. I trained for times like these when the adrenalin was so strong it weakens you. But no matter how much I trained it always felt the same. You have to control it or it will destroy you. I wasn't afraid. I knew about my body, how it reacted to fear. I stared into the eyes of the fucker that had dared to insult me. He was speeding toward me now. The cunt

was going to attack me whilst I was holding the hands of my children. Anger cleared the feelings of the dump.
I now had control of the adrenal rush. I felt a calmness descend over me. I kept hold of my boys' hands until Korman closed the distance. I had to get the timing right. I couldn't afford to miss. I waited, then releasing the grip from my son's hand I exploded a right hand punch in a straight line to his jaw. It landed with a crack. I heard a popping sound and he was unconsciousness. He thudded to the floor.
'Fucking wanker,' I exclaimed, leaning over him. I could have destroyed him right there on the floor, kick ten different kinds of shit out of him but I couldn't let my sons see their dad behaving like an animal.
I looked around me. Several people witnessed the punch. I stared at them as I passed, not one caught my eye.
'Come on, lads, toilet time.' In my rush to get the boys to safety, I forgot about Tina.
I left the lads in the toilet. 'Stay in here, boys. Mummy will call you in a minute,' I said rushing outside in time to see the steroid freak rising up from the pavement.
The punch was more than enough to take out an un-drugged opponent, but the drugs had given him incredible powers of recovery. I was now considering the consequences of what I'd just done. He immediately got on his mobile phone to none other than the Michelin Man.
I noticed a few yards behind on the road was a parked car. Five men were cramped inside paying particular attention to the scene. When I scrutinised the vehicle the passengers and driver appeared to get erratic and sped off sharpish. The car and its inhabitants made me think: coppers.

Korman was on the phone and getting frantic.
'You're fucking dead, Skillen. Oh you're a fucking dead man,' he said with a passion in his voice.
'That's funny 'cause I feel very alive.'
'You fucking won't be. Jack's going to fucking kill you. We warned you before. You fucking done my brother. You're dead. Dead!'
On that phrase Tina and the kids came out of the toilet.

'Come on, Tina. Let's go.' The freak got through on his mobile.
'Skillen's just fucking dropped me.' I couldn't believe how much the drugs effected his emotions. He was raging like a mad bull and running around in circles.
'He's coming down now, Skillen. He's on his way. You're going to get it!'
'Fucking bring him down. Tell him I'm here and I'm waiting for him.'
People started to pass by taking a wide berth. He shouted to them trying to gather witnesses.
'He hit me. You saw him. Get the police.' In the next breath his personality changed again.
'Jack's going to fucking shoot you. You're dead. He's coming down.'
'Tell him to hurry up then. I ain't got all day.' Tina was now waiting in the store with the boys who were looking a little worried. Korman shouted at the store supervisor who had come outside to see what was going on.
'You saw him hit me didn't you?' he said. I interjected before she could side with him.
'Did you see me hit him?' I said to the supervisor who knew me.
'No. All I heard was him shouting and threatening to shoot you,' she replied.
Korman's demeanour was frightening. She cowered away from him. I left and made my way to the manager.
'Have you got somewhere safe for my family to go until the police move on that nutter outside?'
'Yes, over there is the door to the canteen. You can wait in there. The police are on the way.' I led Tina and the boys to the canteen and questioned one of the staff as I passed him by.
'Excuse me, mate. Are there any cameras covering the front of the building?'
'No mate, I'm sorry there isn't,' he said.
I wasn't sorry. I was glad. I would deny ever hitting him. It would be easier than trying to explain my actions to the police. Korman was still busy outside trying to build a case against me.
Tina sat in the canteen looking very pissed off. She knew the game was to stay cool.
I spoke to the manager again.

'Listen, mate. I need your help. Some drug-crazed man has just threatened to shoot me in front of my wife and kids. Can we stay out of the way here until the police arrive? I don't want to go outside again in case he's still there. I'm not bothered about myself, it's the family.' At that point the manager became my ally.
'No problem. Stay here as long as you like. I'll bring the police to you when they get here.' I thanked him.
When the police arrived I spoke to an officer who knew me from the doors.
'What's the problem John? He causing you some hassle, mate?'
I explained the situation to him leaving out the fact I'd dropped him.
'Say no more, John. He's giving the lads some real stick out there so he's being moved on. If he doesn't calm down he'll be arrested. You stay in here until we get rid of him.'
When the police officer returned he asked me if I wanted to make a complaint against Korman for threats to kill.
I told the officer it was my wedding anniversary and I just wanted to finish shopping and go home and have a nice day.
Korman was warned but not arrested. I had started to put the puzzle together in my head. Why were the police so reluctant to arrest Korman? The shit he was giving them outside would easily have warranted a breach of the peace. It was the same with his brother Rakesh. Were they being protected in some way?
On the way back home my son Luke asked me a question.
'Daddy, why did you hit that man?' I was struck dumb by his question. It surprised me coming from someone so young. Tina spoke up in my defence.
'Daddy hit that man, boys, because he is a naughty man.' I looked at Luke's facial expression in the rear view mirror and fell into deep thought. Had I done the right thing?
I was still angry when I got home but pleased I hadn't been arrested. The key was to play on the things that set me apart from the likes of Korman; I was a family man with children. He was just drug dealing scum. No contest in the eyes of the law.

We struck up the barbie. And for the first time that day I started to feel relaxed in the heat of the sun. The smell of the barbie mingling with the sweet summer air tantalised my taste buds. I was almost dozing off when I heard Tina shout me into the kitchen.

'John, I just saw a car go really slow over the top of the road.' As we spoke I spotted the car go past again. I could make out Korman in the passenger seat of the car checking out the house. The cheeky bastard dared to come near my home. I ran toward the car; it was time to do a number on this cunt. As I got closer to the car it burnt rubber and skidded back out of the street. I could just see Korman giving me the gun hand.

The situation was beginning to get out of control and I couldn't let it carry on. I would have to take the fight to the Michelin Man and put a stop to this irritation once and for all. It was clear to me the visit was just a token gesture to make Korman feel he had done something. He could now say he'd been to my house when all he'd done was drive into the street. Once we were sure the uninvited guest had retired for the day, we got on with the barbie and celebrated our anniversary late into the night.

Although the day had started out rough it hadn't fazed us. Tina and the boys would soon forget the incident. It wasn't the first time they had seen their dad fight. They had been sitting next to me in the gym since they were born watching me workout and spar. I reported Korman to the police letting them know that he had passed by my house in a threatening manner. The police appeared to ignore the report. As for Korman I found out a few days later I had broken his jaw.

THREATS TO KILL

The following day I went to work around midday. I unlocked the club, took off the alarm and made my way to the office. Inside the office was another room which housed the safe and the telephone answering machine. There were three messages on the phone; two were erased from my memory by the third. I recognised the voice instantly. It was Pradip Korman.
'Skillen, I told you Glover's going to shoot you and he means it. You're dead, Skillen. That's not all. We're going to kidnap your kids and some sick bastard is going to...' I stopped the tape before I'd listened to all of the message. A tremendous amount of anger rushed through my veins.
I replayed the tape several times. There was a sinister tone to Korman's voice. All I could hear was 'Some sick bastard is going to interfere with your kids.' This was a serious threat.

This confirmed the rumours that I'd heard, that Glover was interfering with young boys. I grabbed the phone knocking it off the desk. I fumbled for the keypad. My hands were shaking with anger. I tapped in the number and waited. The dialling tone rang. Nobody answered. I slammed the phone down and went back into the safe room and replayed the message again. I took the tape carefully from its housing and put it in an envelope as the front door buzzer sounded. I walked downstairs and let in my brother Pete. He instantly saw something was wrong and accompanied me to the office.
'Pete I want you to come and listen to this message.'
Pete was furious at the message. He too was now clear in his mind that Glover was now very dangerous. 'I'm going to kill that fucking wanker,' I said.

I tapped the number into the phone. I was getting anxious for someone to answer, someone I could vent my building aggression on. I waited, then I heard the voice I didn't want to hear. It was Pradip Korman. 'You fucking cunt, you dare to threaten my kids. You're the fucking dead one, you fucking scumbag,' I continued not letting Korman get a word in.

'You put that big fucking gay wanker onto the phone now, you fucking shit. Next time I knock you out I'm gonna stamp all over your face, do you fucking hear me? Now put that overblown steroid freak on the phone.'

'He doesn't want to talk to you. He's training.'

'You fucking put him on. Tell him I said he's a bottle-less, gay paedophile and when I get him I'm going to wipe the floor with him. He's going to wish he never heard of me. Tell him, tell him now, you cunt.'

The words just flowed from my mouth as the arrogant shit on the other end of the phone threatened me again. But I could tell by the sound in his voice it was a feeble attempt to cover up his own feelings of dread. He knew I would hunt him down.

'He's going to shoot you. He means it.'

'Tell him he'd better not fucking miss.' The phone went dead. I instantly rang it back. He answered. 'Put him on the phone, you cunt, and if you hang up I'm coming over to your gym and I will fucking batter him in front of every fucker. Nobody threatens my kids, you sick fucker.' The anger I was feeling wouldn't subside. The phone went dead again. I redialled.

'Put him on.'

'He doesn't want to talk to you. He's training.'

'Put him on now.' I could hear the Michelin Man's voice bellow out in the background shouting abuse.

'Put him on the line now or you're going to get it first.'

A gruff, aggressive sounding voice screamed down the phone at me.

'Yeah! You're a fucking wanker, Skillen. You're fuck all. I knocked you out before and I'll knock you out again.' The delusions of grandeur that he suffered just got grander.

'You fucking fat freak. You never knocked me out before. You've never even fought me before. But I tell you what, I'm coming over there now and I'm going to knock you out and stamp your fucking head into the ground in front of your fucking little minions. And when I've finished you, they're next.' The phone slammed down again. I redialled. Korman answered again. 'You tell him that I'm on my way over there right now.'

'He won't be here; he's going in a minute.'

'Put him back on the phone.' The aggressive voice was calmer now, I could hear the fear as he spoke.
'I fucking told you, Skillen. You're fuck all.' I used phrases that I thought would infuriate him so that he would be engulfed by adrenalin.
'Listen, fat boy. You meet me now and we'll sort this out once and for all.' But he was using the same tactic.
'You watch your kids, Skillen.' I nearly ate the phone in my temper.
'You fucking meet me, you prick.' He was gone and Korman was now back on the phone.
'He doesn't want to talk anymore.'
'Listen to me, you bum boy. You tell him to meet me on Derby Road playing fields at 3 o'clock or I'm coming for him. And make sure that all three of you are there, 'cause when I've battered him I'm going batter you and your brother as well.' The phone went silent, then Glover's voice blurted out of the ear piece.
'I'll fucking be there, Skillen.' The phone went dead.
Pete sat stunned by what he'd heard on the speaker phone. 'I'm coming with you.'
'No. I go alone. That tosser is going to learn some fucking respect.'
I was concerned about being shot. I knew he had the means to do it. I was sure he wouldn't be alone when he came for the one on one but if that was the case then I would fight whoever came with him. This was about honour.
I had considered going to his gym, but knew from another source that he'd left just after the phone call. There was no doubt he could scrap but he wasn't in the premier league, he was first division having been relegated long ago. But he knew how to use the fear factor against people to make them think he was better than he was. When we met I would make sure he wouldn't be walking off that field.

WAR OF WORDS

I went home and changed into my training gear. The conditions were dry. The Derby Road playing fields were well out of the way from prying eyes.
I made my way onto the field and stood on the edge where I could be seen. He would approach from the front and would be in full view of me. I'd heard he had a pistol and a shotgun. The shotgun would be easy to spot and I was confident if he pulled a shooter I could be out of range before he could fire it.
I checked my watch. He was late by five minutes. Come on, you wanker!
I spotted a car pull into the car park in the distance. I walked out into the middle of the field and waited his arrival. The car turned and drove off again. I turned to walk back and noticed to my left a police riot van pull into the car park just behind a mud bank. The van looked to be full of police. The bastards must have had the gym phone tapped. How else would they know we were meeting here or had they someone on the inside at his gym?
I retreated back out of sight and waited. I couldn't go until at least an hour after the deadline for him or he could claim a victory if he turned up.

I waited for just over an hour. I was disappointed he hadn't turned up. It confirmed my thoughts on him: he was bottle-less. I slipped away back into my car and drove home. I would make sure I let everyone know he bottled it! Wars of words are psychological battles that when waged can mentally destroy or weaken an enemy without the need for actual combat.

I stared at the children who were fast asleep in their beds. They looked like angels, sweet and innocent. If anyone ever harmed my children I would kill! I had to make sure they were safe. This war of words with Glover and his cronies had gone on for long enough and now my children were at risk. I had to play both games and make sure the coppers understood the seriousness of the Michelin Man. I stood by the rule of the street – never grass. But this cunt was beyond the street; he was a sexual deviant, a beast and a dangerous drug dealer stealing lives and destroying them and had no right to walk free. I would take the tape to the police and let them know what the Michelin Man was about.

At the police station I approached the desk and asked to speak to an officer about making a complaint. I briefly explained the situation to him. The police kept me waiting for 45 minutes. Then when a copper arrived he said, 'There is no one available to take your complaint yet, Mr Skillen. Can you come back later?' I was gobsmacked. This was fucking serious and the coppers were treating it as if I was reporting a lost dog or something.
'No I won't come back. I want to see somebody now and I want this cunt arrested.'
I was warned about my language and told if I didn't calm down I would be arrested. I kept quiet and waited. A higher-ranking officer took me into a side room for an interview. I told him what happened except about the arranged meeting and waited for his reaction.
'Can you prove any of this, Mr Skillen? It's all just hearsay. Have you any evidence?'
'I have the tape of the threats to kill me and interfere with my children.'
His attitude changed immediately.
'Let me listen to the tape,' he said. When he returned it was another officer who spoke.
'John, you're going to have to trust us on this one. We're fully aware of Glover and his antics. Stay well away from him.'
'What about the threats to harm my children?'
'You go home and look after them. That's all I can tell you at the moment.' I stormed out of the office.
'If anything happens to my kids I will hold you responsible,' I said.

The following morning I got a phone call. 'Is that Mr Skillen? I'm just ringing to let you know that an officer will be calling to see you later today to discuss the complaint you wanted to make yesterday.'
I took note. A couple of hours later I got another call. It was my brother Pete.

He was very animated. 'Glover has been arrested. The lot of them have been pulled in,' he said. Their houses were raided last night. I felt a smile blossom on my face. Finally they'd caught the cunt. Now I knew why they wouldn't arrest them before. They were waiting for the right moment and probably had been watching them for months building up a case. And there was me nearly wrecking it for them! They must have been so frustrated.

The Michelin Man and several of his gang including the Korman brothers were arrested and charged with serious drug offences, kidnap and sexual offences including rape of a minor and assault. It was now out that the Michelin Man was a nonce! He and his gang were eventually sentenced to over 50 years between them.

A lot of lads that had associated themselves with the gang now shied away from the very mention of his name. Like Judas they denied his existence and that they were ever friendly with him. Me? I just smiled knowing that I had judged his character right and for the next 20 or so years he would become what I always thought he was before he got banged up: just a wanker. And his life inside would become his own living nightmare.

SEVEN YEAR ITCH

Crystal's was becoming tired and worn down and the rumours were it was up for sale. The rumours stopped when the club was given a mini refit and became known as Pulse nightclub. The club started to attract more people and was on the up once again. It was a successful business but once again rumours spread that it was up for sale. The rumours filtered down to the punters. I noticed the respect for the club begin to dwindle. Not knowing whether or not you will have a job from one day to the next makes working an uncomfortable experience. I approached the owners and asked them outright if the venue was up for sale. I was told, in Eric's own words: 'Everything is for sale at the right price, John. If you run a successful business and someone offers you a million quid for it, what would you do!' He was right, it was his business, and he was in it for profit.

A couple of months down the line I was called into the office and told that the club had indeed been sold to a big nightclub chain. I met with the area manager of the new company. He began to tell me about a club he was responsible for in the city of Hull. His eyes sparkled with a mischievous sparkle when he spoke of the Tower and he looked like he was holding back a smile. He didn't tell me much about the place, only that it was a very busy club, but in need of a refurbishment, which he told me was going to happen soon. I was worried that if I didn't take the job at the Tower I would become another unemployment statistic. I'd been at the club for over seven years and now it was the time to move on. I was still carrying the mental burden of being an ex-con. Not only an ex-con but I had on my record a police assault. I had been told if I couldn't get a liquor licence in Hull, my career with the company was over. I had three months in which to prove my worth to the company. I remained apprehensive but positive. A friend of mine, Mick 'Aga' Steans, one of the bouncers at Pulse summed it up for me.

'John, no matter where you go in the world you are the same person. You will do fine wherever you go,' he said. Those words were a strength I would pull on many times over the years and gave me the realisation of who I was. I wasn't running away from my past anymore.

Moving to Hull was a big move. I hadn't worked this far off my patch before. Could I cut it with the locals? What level of aggro would I be walking into? Who was the man? I didn't know anyone. If got myself into shit I would be the only one to dig myself out. I accepted the offer, I was now the new acting manager at Hull's Tower nightclub. Little did I know that acting was to be a big part of it!

Whilst Tina stayed at home and looked after our two boys, I went to Hull to visit my new place of employment. Tina really didn't want to move, but I needed this job. I had something to prove to myself.

HULL

Hull: England's forgotten city, sitting on the Humber estuary was a cold, damp, smelly place. The once great fleets of fishing vessels docked here, one of Britain's main sea ports. Now just a dark shadow of its former self.

The Tower nightclub, a grade two listed building, was a scab on the back of a city looking for an identity. It was situated on the outskirts of the city centre nestling in the red light district of Analaby Road. Inside the Tower were very ornate moulded cartouches, swags, sways and pillars. It looked more like a derelict cinema than a nightclub. The 1983 conversion consisted of taking out the screen and chairs and putting in a couple of bars. A staircase led to the ornate balcony which for some reason reminded me of a scene from Romeo and Juliet only with a fat bird playing Juliet and a tattooed fuckwit playing Romeo. There were a few lighting effects that would struggle to fill the room with light. I dreaded to think what the sound system was like.

The plaster was falling away from the walls and the original carpet, in order to make it look better and stop it from wearing any thinner, had been painted black. Yes you read it right, painted black. The incredible thing was it actually worked! The Tower smelt of antiquarian book shops, musty old ladies, stale beer and piss.

The Tower pulled its crowd from Bransholme, according to the locals the biggest council estate in Europe with one of the worst reputations for unemployment, drug abuse and crime. But the Tower was successful. It was filled in excess of its capacity of 900 every weekend.

On the desk in my new office was a fax message from my old friend Mat Halford at Loughborough. It was a photocopy of a newspaper article about a visit made to the Tower by the famous boxing promoter Frank Maloney who wrote:

'Boy what a night out we had in Hull last Monday after my young fighter Paul Ingle retained his British featherweight title. The ring

card girls were just as exciting but afterwards the entertainment had to be seen to be believed. Myself, Steve Lillis and another couple of journalists went into the Tower nightclub where the slogan is 'Have an hour in the tower, for a snog with a dog'. I'm actually gonna write to Tony Blair and tell him to close the club down or at least put a sign outside with a warning telling any male who enters, that he takes his life into his own hands.

When I was introduced to the local women if I'd met one under fifty five I would have been amazed. To compare these women to dogs was an insult to the canine race and their loyal owners. I came across one woman bigger than Billy Britain dressed up like a spice girl with layers of fat asking Lillis if she could show him her tits. Even he said no and if you knew what he'd kipped with over the last few months it would tell you how ugly she was.

Just when I thought it couldn't get any worse a sixty year old grabbed hold of me and told me she was a woman of the street who could handle any man in the club. The next minute she whipped out these big saggy tits 'Screaming have a look at these boys.' My lager went instantly flat. Please Mr Blair before you do anything close this club down for humanities sake. I love Hull but the next time I come I'll do my drinking in Lexington Avenue nightclub or the ringside pub.'

When I first read the article I thought it was a joke. I was to soon find out it was definitely no laughing matter.

After my visit to the Tower I decided to look around the area for somewhere to live. I'd asked the company if I could commute daily. They said if I wanted the job I could live in a hotel from Thursday to Sunday then commute home after, returning each Thursday until I found somewhere to live. They would pay for the accommodation for six weeks. I felt the emotion of being away from Tina and the boys. Bouts of depression threatened but a phone call home each night allayed the feelings. I missed them intensely. A major part of the depressed feelings were because of the slow release adrenalin I was experiencing. The slow release is the worse feeling you can have. If you let it take over your mind it leads to panic attacks. Usually when I suffered slow release I would go to the gym and have a roll around on the mat, punch bag or have a really hard weights session. This used up the chemicals that caused slow release. I promised myself that as soon as I was settled I would get myself into a routine at the hotel gym. Then I would find a boxing club and a judo club. Finding somewhere to live in Hull was like trying to find the Holy Grail or maybe even Atlantis. The city housing estates were so different. There was literally something for everyone. That's if you like city life. I'd been all around the city. I even followed Hull's famous fish walk which led me to within a stone's throw from the old red light district. I must say for all its mismatched buildings and quirkiness Hull city had a nice feeling about it, neglected yet loved at the same time. I felt sorry for her.

I popped into a couple of estate agents grabbed some info and made my way in the direction of Beverley, a town seven miles from the Tower. If Hull was the cheese then Beverley was the chalk. It was a lovely, old market town with a Ye Old Worlde atmosphere, a walk around the famous Beverley Minster, fish and chips at Sullivan's and a pint of real ale at Nellies, the oldest pub in the area, still sporting gas lamps and brewing their own award-winning ale which sold at a fraction of the cost of some of the other brewers' ales. The seaside town of Hornsea was 20 minutes' drive away.

I drove around trying to suss this lovely area out. I drove past the Minster and turned into Long Lane. It was quite long as well, two and a half miles exactly. At the end of the lane I came to a T-junction. My heart fluttered when I saw a house called Toll Bar Cottage. It was a Victorian toll house with a 'for sale' sign reaching out to me. With only £40,000 to spend on a house I turned left and drove on thinking the house far too expensive. Every house I looked at didn't compare to Toll Bar Cottage. I headed back to Loughborough having left my details with a few estate agents to send us any info on houses that came up in the Beverley area. I left the house-hunting to Tina. She would check out any housing advertisements that were sent to us. The following Thursday I moved up to Hull to start work at the infamous Tower nightclub.

TOWER FOR AN HOUR

The dome's mosaic glistened in the morning sunshine, standing proud. The Edwardian features looked out of place on the road that prostitutes walked and dealers dealt their evil. 'Ladies' night every Thursday, free entry b4 11pm, the posters proudly proclaim.
The Tower nightclub, where the prostitutes drop their prices to compete with the locals. If the prostitutes had posters displayed they would probably have read: free shag before eleven, £5 after plus a free drink.
The dealers have no problem selling their wares; white powder, brown, ganja, skunk.
Like a mobile chemist they dispense their misery, a temporary high the equivalent of a free shag and lasting about as long.
The Tower's glass doors reflect the characters of Analaby Road. A devious rag tail bunch of misfits. Yet the building stands tall, still proud of its past where once came the famous, all be it on rolls of film. Much joy, love, peace, war, horror.
Darkness will soon shroud the Tower in the misery of the night enlivened by the people who come to dance, drink, socialise and fight.
The bouncers those guardians of the night looking like movie stars at a premiere add to the image of this once famous picture house. Emotion once again dominates.
The atmosphere creates, fun and frolics, the boy shouts, 'Come on, lads, Tower for an hour, snog a dog and shag a bag.'

I was given a guided tour by Brian, a big man with a big smile. Brian was joint partner of a door agency who supplied door staff to the Tower. I could tell by the way Brian looked at me that he was unsure of my ability to run the place and who could blame him? I was just a southerner to them. I could feel his eyes penetrate my skull trying to see what was going on inside my head. It was natural for him to be suspicious: whenever there is new management, change is inevitable. Jobs will be at risk. I put myself in the hands of Brian and let him show me the ropes. I needed as many allies as I could muster. I remembered the phrase: 'One enemy is too many and a thousand friends too few.' At that moment I had no friends and would probably find many enemies. I was the new kid on the block, but I was unknown and untested. People fear the unknown and test the untested.

It was 11.30 and the club was heaving. I followed Brian into the foyer where two bouncers were ejecting a lad. One bouncer pulling him by an arm, the other had his arm wrapped around the lad's neck. The man was protesting his innocence and refusing to go. He was about 40. I noticed on his cheek an infamous tattoo: a single blue spot known as the borstal spot, the tattoo of the borstal trainee. I moved aside and watched the man fly through the door and land in a heap on the floor. He jumped up, gave the bouncers some abuse and then wandered off cursing. In the background 'Another One Bites the Dust' by Queen boomed out of the speakers.

Brian acted as if nothing was happening, his big grin hiding his annoyance at his bouncers. Brian was trying to make a good impression. After all it was my first night. Brian and his partner Terry were the only members of staff who knew that I was the new manager at that point.

We walked from the foyer which still housed the original ticket booths and made our way up the central staircase. If it wasn't for the smell of piss and perfume, cigarette smoke and the beat of the music, I would have sworn it was still a cinema.

I got to the top of the first flight of stairs. There were two toilets either end of the landing. I realised I was standing in a puddle of water. The only roll of decent carpet was soaked in water and piss from an overflowing urinal in the gents' toilet. A pile of sick was becoming diluted and trodden in to the carpet. I imagined that's how the original carpet met its fate. As I turned the corner to take the next flight of stairs I heard moaning and groaning. In front of me gyrating to Dexy's Midnight Runners 'Come on Eileen' was a fat bird on top of a lad who looked like he was being raped and crushed.

And in no particular order.

'Oi that's enough of that,' said Brian. I was sent mute by the sight of this huge girl.

'All right. Keep yer hair on,' she said lifting herself off her victim.

'I was just on the vinegar stroke,' she said. The lad pulled his jeans up and scarpered up the staircase. He was more afraid of the fat girl than Brian. I laughed and followed Brian.

The small bar at the top of the second staircase was full of cheesy pictures of Hollywood stars. Brian informed me it was called the Hollywood Bar. Nice touch I thought. We took yet another flight of stairs past my office and through a set of double doors onto the balcony area. The sickly smell of cannabis and skunk weed hung heavy in the air mingling with tobacco and disco smoke. The balcony was dark, the occasional lighting effect, if you can describe it as that, flickered by catching the silhouettes of the people giving a sinister seedy and intimidating effect. I felt cold. The shell-suited *clientèle* eyed me up as I followed Brian across the balcony area to the balcony end which looked out across a large dance floor.

A row of lads leaning on the balcony looked like a police ID parade. Brian walked on, it was obvious he didn't want me to linger for very long. It was as if it was a no-go area. I noticed a big doorman leaning against a fire exit door, his arm up the skirt of woman twice his age. He looked about 30-something with boxer's features. A few yards away from him an unshaven, tattooed bunch of men in their 40's were skinning up joints. One held a lighter below a chunk of cannabis, its smoke drifting into the air. I walked on as he crumbled the softened cannabis onto the cigarette paper.

We made our way down a staircase which looked like it was made from thin scaffold poles. The staircase split into two halfway down so you could walk right to the bar or left on to the dance floor and the rear fire exits. Brian pushed me back as a scrap broke out on the staircase. Brian stopped still blocking the upper staircase off. Within seconds the bouncers arrived from both directions trapping the aggressors in the middle of the small central landing. The bouncers grabbed the first people they came into contact with, put them into headlocks and dragged them toward the door. Whoever was in the way regardless of whether they were involved or not was un-ceremoniously dragged to the fire exit at the rear of the club. I was reminded of my first days as a bouncer at Sammy's. I felt like joining in but I was the acting General Manager and couldn't put a foot wrong or my job would be gone. The DJ who had been shouting down the microphone 'fight on the staircase' played on, a big smile on his face.

The bouncers were quick and ruthless but it wasn't all one way traffic. Paul, a tall, ex-kick boxer was battling with a lad trying to restrain him. He managed to grab the kid in a headlock then let go as he reeled back in pain. One hand going to his back, his white shirt immediately turned red. He pulled out a broken bottle which had lodged in his kidney area. Brian jumped in and he and Paul dragged the perpetrator through the rear fire exit door. I followed and witnessed several of the bouncers doing the river dance on the kid's head and body. Order was quickly restored. The bouncers looked nervous as they went back to their positions. I never commented on the incident. Brian, again acting as if nothing had happened, led me through the crowd toward the main bar.

The main bar area was set back from the dance floor and so low down when you stood at the front of the bar the servers were lower than you were. I saw a man at the far end of the bar helping himself to a drink from the beer tap. The bar was four deep; it was full of hardened drinkers, people with shit lives drowning their sorrows in cheap ale. The staff behind the bar were of the same ilk and took no shit. I noticed they made sure they took the money before they gave out the drink.

'Who the fuck is this, Brian?' I heard a woman say. I looked across at the woman aged about 60-ish with bleach blonde hair and a very low cut top with two huge breasts and tattoos on her biceps any sailor would have been proud of.

'Now then there's no need for language like that. This is the new manager,' Brian said. The secret was out.

She leant forward, pulling down her top.

'What do you think of these then?' she said revealing her youthful looking breasts complete with two erect nipples that looked like chapel hat pegs (not that I was taking too much notice). I smiled. She cupped them in her hands and shook them at me.

'Come over here and give 'em a suck,' she said. I looked at Brian and laughed a nervous laugh. A cheer went up from a nearby group of lads.

'Put 'em away, Angie, or you'll be out,' Brian quipped.

'It's all right, Brian. It's only a bit of fun,' she said.

Brian shoved me in the side and we moved off and onto the dance floor which was heaving except for a circle of space around where two women were playing tug o' war with each other's hair. One of the woman's dresses was ripped open, a saggy tit dangled beneath her head which was bowed by the grip of her opponent's hands on her hair. As the Chairman of the Board sang 'Give me just a little more time and our love will grow', two bouncers appeared and grabbed one woman each underneath the arm and around the waist and carried them to the fire exit whilst the women kicked and frantically flailed their arms.
'Is it always like this?' I asked Brian.
'Oh no,' he said. 'This is a quiet night.'
A lump in my throat temporarily stopped me breathing.

It was getting late, not far off kicking out time. A stocky Jamaican guy about 50 was standing in the foyer sporting short brown and greying dreadlocks with tattoos covering his face. I recognised him as being one of the men skinning up on the balcony. He was giving anyone who would listen a rendition of Al Jolson's 'Sonny Boy' and definitely wasn't a full ticket. A warble at the end of each word made him sound like he was gargling with mouthwash and his mumbling along with the tune told me he knew very little of the words. He was on a cannabis and beer high and a candidate for the next X Factor. Mind you he probably wouldn't get through the first round.

Last orders hadn't come quick enough for me. As the punters piled into Anlaby Road, a mini riot had erupted between two rival council estate gangs. Sagging bodies littered the roads as the boots rained in on them. The ones left standing scattered at the sight and sound of the police riot vans as they screeched onto the scene like the cavalry, a little too late.
I knew now what I had gotten myself into. There was a knock on the door. A copper stood on the top step. Brian opened the door.
'I don't suppose you have the video of the premises and the street, do you?'
'There isn't a camera in the place, mate,' Brian laughed.
I couldn't believe that in a place so obviously violent there weren't any cameras. The club was stuck in a time warp. Once the police

had left I made my way across to my hotel (ironically it was called 'The Friendly Hotel').

On my way over I noticed that I was wrong about Al Jolson. He'd made it through to the next round all right. He stood under a street lamp, one hand pointing to the heavens and the other on his chest serenading an imaginary passer-by. Beside him in the dark recesses of Anlaby Road a heroin ravaged prostitute, trying her best to earn her next fix, shook uncontrollably. I felt like jacking it in and going home.

SETTLING IN!

It wasn't long before we had sold the house in Loughborough and bought the one just outside Beverley at the top of Long Lane. After some intense wheeling and dealing the house known as Toll Bar Cottage was ours.
It was an ideal location, a small village with a school and more importantly superb five, seven and nine mile runs through the East Yorkshire countryside.

We settled in quickly. The East Yorkshire people were friendly and upbeat. The boys attended the village school and were both very happy and I was enjoying the challenge of the Tower. My brief was to keep the club busy. Just give it a tweak they said. What they hadn't told me was that the Tower had had three management changes in less than a year. No one wanted the job, the reason being it was an unsafe licence and the club was a major hassle to run. I had a meeting with licensing officer PC Craddock. He warned me of Brian's partner, Terry.
'He's a bad one,' he said. 'I don't want him on the door at the Tower.'

Terry was one of the lads, an ex-pro boxer and I did what I always did in these circumstances and drew my own conclusions. I found him to be a gentleman. What he did in his private life was nothing to do with me. When he worked the door he was professional and a great addition to the team. I liked Terry. Finding out the licence was unsafe made me feel like I had been set up. The truth was I should have been brave enough to tell the company to stick it and stayed in Loughborough, even if it meant getting another job somewhere else. I'd made my decision and rightly or wrongly I moved my family there. If the licence was unsafe I would do my damnedest to make it safe. I would do the best job I could at the Tower.

My aim was get control of the drug abuse and prostitution. It is an offence to allow a prostitute to ply their trade in any licensed premises. I had to take a gamble and show everyone the new kid on the block wasn't going to be pushed around. It was time to make a stand.

On Friday night I called Brian into the office and told him I intended to search every single person that came into the club that very night. Brian strongly advised me not to.
'If you do that you'll have a riot on your hands. This is Tower,' he said.
'And it's my club,' I said. Brian stared at me in silence. I could see in his eyes he was probably thinking I was another interfering dickhead.
'Fuck it, Brian. Everyone will get searched even if I have to do it myself.'
'All right. Have it your way but don't say I didn't warn you.'
I organised for a bucket to be filled with lime cleaning fluid as a dump for any drugs we found on the searches. I didn't want PC Craddock or the punters accusing me or any of the bouncers of keeping any of the drugs haul I knew we'd get!
Hull was trying to clean up its act and the authorities appeared to be very anti-drug, yet there was no Club Watch scheme in operation. They had tried but it failed miserably when not all clubs supported the scheme. I put up a sign saying 'Amnesty'. I doubted any of the Tower lot would understand what amnesty meant. What it did mean was if they put any drugs in the bucket voluntarily I would allow them to still come into the venue and nothing else would said about the matter. If they argued they were out on their arse and banned. No personal details would be given to the police.
I stood next to the bucket not knowing whether or not the bouncers would back me up. From what I had already witnessed in the last couple of weeks there was no reason to suspect they wouldn't. I told Brian if anybody refused to be searched they were out. Brian looked nervous. There were some tough fuckers using the Tower and Brian didn't want to piss anyone off. I can't say I blame him. After all he lived here and I was just some guy brought in to do a job nobody else wanted. I told them to warn people that there was a drugs' search going on inside the doorway before they entered so they had a chance to walk away. There are certain people in Hull you just don't want to piss off!

I took charge of the search myself. I knew how to talk to these people – we had a lot in common. I had few complaints and it wasn't long before the bucket was half-full of a mixture of drugs that included speed, coke, ecstasy, heroin and cannabis resin. There were other potions I didn't recognise, plus pills and syringes. The only real tense moment came when a guy entered the club and came directly to me

'Have you got any gear on you, mate?' I asked.

'Why?' he asked.

'Well tonight we're running an amnesty, that means if you have got anything on you, you can put into this bucket of lime cleaning fluid and you can still come in the club.'

Letting them in the club after being caught with something was a risk but I figured out they couldn't get into any of the other clubs and this being the only one might swing it. I didn't want to hand anyone over to the police. I wanted to re-educate them to not bring the gear into the club. If I survived the night, the message would be out there loud and clear. The lad stared at me for a moment and put his hand in his inside his coat pocket and pulled out a block of resin the size of a giant Yorkie chocolate bar, except it wasn't in chunks just a smooth plain bar known as a seven because it weighed seven ounces – a valuable bit of gear.

'How do I know that you're not going to keep it?' he said. I explained to the lad that he was putting it into lime cleaning fluid which was a powerful type of bleach.

'No police involvement?' he asked

'No police,' I said.

He dropped the seven in the bucket and walked off into the club mumbling to himself. He was a big lad. Who knows what might have happened, so just in case I'd had him lined up the whole time. One wrong move and he would have been unconscious.

Surprisingly enough the night went by without a hitch except for the usual scrapping that took place nightly at the Tower. I'd learnt one valuable thing about the Tower crowd: they loved the place and the desire to be a part of the crowd was strong, far stronger than the power of the drugs I'd collected.

Whilst I lay in bed later that night I thought about what I'd done. I didn't realise the implications it would have on my reputation. Some of the Tower crowd were drug-free, but a large proportion weren't. I earned a little bit of respect from both sides. I now had to protect myself and the club's licence. The next morning I went into the Tower earlier than usual and telephoned the drug squad to report the situation. They would already know by now what had gone on the night before. If I didn't call they would most definitely call me. I spoke to a duty sergeant. 'This is John Skillen, the new manager at the Tower nightclub. I put a search on everyone that came into the club last night and collected a considerable amount of drugs. The drugs are still on the premises and I would like to hand them in for destruction.' The phone went quiet for a moment. 'Hello?' I said.
'Just a minute. Tower, you say, on Analaby Road?'
'Yes that's right.' The phone went quiet again then an officer came on the line.
'Hello, Mr Skillen, there will be an officer down to see you right away.'

Half an hour later two plainclothes officers from the drug squad dressed in jeans and baggy jumpers inspected the bucket of drugs and questioned me. I told them the new policy of the Tower. They warned me to be careful and offered me their backup if I needed it.
I went back to the hotel gym for a workout, then later returned for the nightshift. When I arrived there was a police officer waiting for me. We went inside.
'I have come to commend you for your actions in drug prevention at the Tower last night. What you did sent shock waves through the police station. You have earned the respect of the station. Well done. If you need any support or help just contact us.'
I was gobsmacked. My relationship with the police was built on mistrust.
I knew they had spoken to the Leicestershire constabulary before I arrived at the Tower and who knows what they had told them. But now they could see for themselves what type of person I was. I wouldn't be licking arse, or grassing, that's not what I'm about, but I would work within the confines of the law.

I received a letter signed by Chief Inspector Bell stating that he now considered the Tower a drug-free zone and thanked the staff and management for their co-operation. This letter sealed my position as General Manager and shortly afterwards I applied for and got the liquor licence.

I remember attending in court for my licence – the first time I'd been in a court and not on a charge! The thing was I couldn't help feeling guilty as if I was about to be banged away again: a very distinct possibility especially working at the Tower. The licence was, from that moment on, safer than it had ever been. The company, now taking the Tower seriously, invested money in CCTV, radios and smart staff uniforms. The Tower had become a safer place for me and the staff to work. Well as safe as it could be.

PROFIT

"Profit is not a dirty word, John"
Michael Holland – Showman

After having a meeting with the Area Manager he wanted me to maintain the profits at the Tower which were incredible for the size of the place. I didn't mention to him that something was amiss with the figures as his and my wages were based on the club's profitability. But I had noticed a few things that were affecting the figures and disguising the true profit the club was achieving.
Whilst I was cashing up the tills one particular night I noticed a large tub of money in mixed coinage sitting next to the till. 'What's this money doing here? How come it hasn't been cashed up?' I asked.
'It's our tips,' the girl informed me.
'You're not allowed tips. This is a nightclub not a bar or restaurant,' I said. 'You're on a wage and a good one too. Does everybody get a share of these tips?'
'No, just the bar staff,' she said. I left the conversation there.
There was something else going on which I found to be strange. We had a Greek cellar man. He couldn't speak very good English and my Greek was shit, but we communicated. I picked up a couple of empties that were half full of ale. These were drinks people were too pissed to finish and were left on the side. In fact the whole club was littered with half-full glasses and bottles. I noticed the Greek was tipping the lager into one bucket and the bitter into another. I thought it was just coincidence that it appeared he was keeping the beers separate from one another until I poured both glasses of slops into his lager bucket and he went ballistic. I backed off and went up onto the balcony area and watched him from a distance. Eventually my curiosity got the better of me; I'd caught many a glass collector mine sweeping over the years and pissed on the job, but this particular glass collector seemed to be taking the mine sweeping to a new level. Was he collecting it to take home and drink! I followed him into the cellar which was absolutely filthy and in very poor condition.

Neatly in the centre of the cellar floor were two barrels side by side and a gas bottle. Both barrels had their tops removed: something that was only done by the brewery. The Greek was tipping the buckets of beer into the appropriate barrel. Now I knew why he didn't want the slops mixing. I was completely taken aback. I'd heard of landlords putting the drip trays slops back into barrels which was relatively clean beer (illegal all the same and very bad practice) but to put the slops back into the barrels that people hadn't drunk was beyond my comprehension. I watched in silence as he screwed the lids back onto the barrels and re-gassed them and connected them back up. I slipped out of the cellar before he noticed me.

Instead of confronting the Greek outright I decided to play a game with him. I would take away the one tool he needed to do what he was doing and that was to take away his degasser, (to open a gassed up barrel of beer you first have to take out the gas to relieve the pressure in the barrel. The lines that bring the beer to the pumps are long tubes. When the barrel is connected to the system, gas is pumped into the barrel. This gas forces the beer into the tube. When the tap at the bar is pulled open the beer flows into the glass. No gas, no beer). What the Greek had done was get an old head insert with a length of beer line on which wasn't connected to the system, fitted it to the gassed barrel and released the gas pressure from the barrel. It was very simple and took about five minutes from start to finish.

What the Greek was doing was affecting the stock report, the profit report and covering up possible theft. It had to stop. I took away the Greek's barrel head and tube. When he came into work that day I asked him why he was putting the beer back in the barrel. I had a real hard time convincing him what he was doing was wrong but made it clear he must stop. He left, giving up his job a couple of days later. My regime of doing the right thing was not suited to his methods and he moved to another club.

I had a meeting with the glass collectors that night and informed them that what he'd been doing was wrong and appointed another glass collector as cellar man and head glass collector. I issued the glass collectors with new uniforms so it was easy to spot where they were at night when on shift. That same night I had a meeting with the bar staff telling them from that night on, tips were not allowed. I had noticed that on the main bar where the old staff worked was a large tubful of tips and on the bars where the new staff worked they had none. I came to the conclusion that the tips were not coming from the customers as tips but drinks that were not rung in. The Tower customers were not the type to tip! It ended there and then. Stopping the tips made me a very unpopular type of guy, but I wasn't there to be liked, I was there to do a job. Stopping the tips meant the tills would be easier to figure out and the true figures would start to emerge.

On the Saturday night I got a message that one of the bar staff, a real troublemaker, wanted to see me in the foyer. I could see the bar staff were gathered at the bottom of the staircase waiting for my arrival. The troublemaker looked confident, her eyes sparkled like a mischievous school kid. 'What's going on, why are you off the bar? The club's packed. Get back on the bars.'
'No, we're not going back on the bars until you re-instate the tips. That's our money, not the club's and we deserve it,' she said. Here I was on a busy Saturday night and all of my staff were going on strike until I re-instated their tips. I had to think fast. I decided to make a stand.
'Right, you either get back on the bars or you're suspended from work as of now.'
'And who's going to run your bars?' the troublemaker asked. Looking around at her colleagues I asked them again individually, 'Are you going to get back on the bars?'
They all said 'No' except one lad who answered, 'I need the money, John. What bar do you want me on?' The others stood firm with stubborn looks on their faces.
'Brian, these bar staff are refusing to work, I want them off the premises,' I said.
Brian and two of the door staff escorted them off the premises under protest and I was left standing in front of several glass collectors. The troublemaker called to them to leave the building. I butted in before they could react. 'Listen lads, did the bar staff ever give you any of their tips? This is not about you, it's about them. Why should you lose your job over them?' What the bar staff didn't realise was that I had trained up several of the glass

collectors as bar staff. I'd shown them how to work the tills. 'You and you on to the main bar. You're on triple time tonight.' I then sent the rest to the other bars. Brian came over to me and took off his dickie bow.

'I'm sorry, John,' he said. Fuck! I thought. The last thing I needed now was the doormen to go on strike. I looked at Brian and he said, 'I'm off the door. Me and two of the lads will help on the bars.' I let out a sigh of relief. Then Terry came over with two girls from one of the bars in town. Terry had arranged for them to work for an hour through the busy period. We were back in business!

The bar staff that were suspended staged a protest outside the venue as they waited for the press to arrive. I stayed well out of the way when the press photographers came outside the club. The following Monday the local paper headlines read: 'Manager sacks bar staff after they go on strike.' The case went before a tribunal when I refused to give them their jobs back. I knew they were fiddling the tips but couldn't prove it. I also knew they were giving beer away and not charging for it. After a long drawn out affair the tribunal ruled in my favour and the bar staff withdrew their complaint.

The stock report showed evidence of gross stock deficit for the first time since the company had taken over. The deficit in itself was proof that major theft was taking place at the Tower. Whether it was the bar staff or not, without concrete proof who knows? It would have been easier for me to leave things as they were and not rock the boat. After all the figures would have made me look like I was doing my job but I couldn't do that. Somebody was paying me a wage to do a job and if you're taking the money then you should do the right thing no matter what the consequences are. With the old staff gone I could now train the new staff to do their jobs right.

STRIPPERS

The Tower strip nights were legendary; the usual line up was one male stripper to keep the girls happy and one female for the men. They were full nude strip shows with the usual and some unusual accessories: baby oil, whips, chains, talcum powder, various vibrators and a collection of dressing up costumes for adults. Every stripper booked had their own show and they were all different.
The Tower also ran an amateur strip night. The amateur show was like pop idol for exotic dancers. Volunteers were pulled from the willing Monday night crowd. The DJ would entice a punter male or female up onto the stage to strip. Sometimes they would get a couple of lessons with the pros first and then on to the stage to convince the crowd they were the sexiest up there and professional enough to last the pace. Most of the time it was jump on the stage and get your kit off and win a bottle of bubbly and a bit of cash. There were also a lot of impromptu strippers in the audience peeling of their attire just for the hell of it. The Monday night crowd were the roughest of the week: a mix of half-decent weekend punters and a social security waiting room. And for the most part they looked like a human tattoo exhibition with a few sadomasochists thrown in to the mix.

On Mondays I stayed well out of the way. When the Tower women got horny it was dangerous to be anywhere near them.

At 10 o'clock I got a call on the radio. It was Brian requesting my presence at the main bar. He sounded serious.
I ran down the staircase from the balcony almost going arse over tit on the way. 'What's the problem, Brian?' I asked through heavy breaths.
Brian pointed in the direction of the stage.
'Look at the tits on her,' Brian said. The beaming smile on his face broke into laughter.
I looked up to the stage area. The fattest bird I'd ever seen had completely stripped off and was gyrating her hips and holding her long tits in each hand, raising them up to her mouth. She kissed then sucked each nipple alternatively to the cheers of the crowd.

'I bet you'd like to take that home wouldn't you, Johnny lad?' said Geordie George, a local licensee who ran a pub called the Earl Grey. The Tower crowd frequented his pub for the stag night specials; two girls raised up in a cage enticing the stag of the party to get in the cage. There they would strip the stag naked and he would be sexually abused then ridiculed whilst everyone else looked on. George was a streetwise character who enjoyed a good laugh.

All eyes were on the fat bird; she was far more entertaining than the act and she was cheaper. As the fat bird was celebrating her win Geordie said, 'You might want to check out the toilets, John.' I made my way into the toilet, followed closely by Brian. I could hear voices in one of the cubicles: one male and one female.

Brian banged on the door of the cubicle, 'Right out you come,' he commanded. Whoever was in there didn't answer. Brian reached up and peered over the top of the toilet door.

'Fuck off, you dirty bastards,' came the shout from within. Brian looked at me and gave the universal signal for a blow-job. I sniggered like a naughty school boy. The cubicle door opened and outpaced an unshaven man in his 30's.

'Sorry about that, lads,' he said with a satisfied smile on his face. 'But you know how it is.' The woman was tucking a tenner down her top.

'How much did he pay you?' Brian asked.

'Not enough,' came her reply.

'You know you're not supposed to turn tricks in here. Out you go.' Brian ejected the prostitute. She didn't seem too bothered. She'd score some gear outside which would keep her on the streets late into the night.

There were always a couple of prostitutes knocking about in the Tower especially when the cold north wind blew in from the Humber Estuary. I went back to the foyer thinking about the lives of these reprobates. They didn't have a lot going for them.

WHY?

'Main bar!' I shouted to the bouncers who were already heading through the doors into the club. I looked up at the camera. I could see them bringing out a lad. The lad walked out holding his arm. Blood dripped from his sleeve. At first I thought it was beer that was soaking it. The blood gushed out.
'Fucking 'ell,' I said. 'What have you done?'
The back of the man's hand was sliced and ripped open. I could see the tendon, ligaments and bone and the skip flapped to one side. Most of his fingers were severed and hanging limp. I ripped open a thick bandage, clamped the wound and told the lad to hold it in place. The bandage turned red as soon as I applied it. I put another one in place. It too went red. There was nothing else I could do. I shouted to the till girl to call an ambulance immediately.
'There's another one, John, in the cloakroom,' Terry said. 'He's worse than this one.'
Brian and Frank were nursing the other guy. I spoke to the girlfriend who was waiting just outside of the cloakroom door. I asked her what had happened.
'This lad ran at Mick and stuck him with a pint glass. He never spoke to us, he just attacked Mick for nothing. He rammed his pint glass in his face. Is Mick going to be all right? It looked bad,' she said.
'Is that your boyfriend's name, Mick? Well look you're safe now. Wait here. I'll tell him you're waiting for him.'
I went into the cloakroom and was shocked at what I saw. This was the worst glassing I'd ever seen. Mick's face was being held in place with a tea towel. I ripped open another bandage and gave it to him.
'Listen, mate. You're going to be all right. The ambulance is on its way. Your face is in a real mess.'

I should have just kept him calm in case he went into shock, but his face was so bad I couldn't help describing it to him. When I removed the tea towel revealing the bloody insides, his nose was almost severed, the eye was cut top and bottom and the ball inside

the socket gaped like a fish's eye. He also had a long deep cut down his other cheek.
'What the fuck happened?' I asked.
'Some guy stuck me with a glass.'
'What for?' I asked.
"I don't know. I didn't even speak to him and I hadn't seen him before. He walked up to me and I thought he'd punched me.'
I left the lad and went to the guy in the foyer. I needed to know why he'd done what he had done.
'Why, mate, why did you glass him?'
The kid looked at me then the floor.
'Because he was staring at me.'
'You stuck a glass in a man's face scarring him for life because he stared at you?' I asked.
'He's a cunt. He deserved it.'
'But he says he doesn't know you.'
'I don't know him, but no one laughs at me and gets away with it,' he said.
I asked him to lift up his arm and his fingers flopped down. He was lucky he hadn't severed a main artery. He'd severed almost everything else.
'Look at your fucking hand. You've destroyed it, all because you thought someone was staring at you.' He dropped his head to the floor again in shame.
'Come with me,' I demanded. I led him to the cloakroom with Terry covering him from behind in case he did a runner.
'Look at the lad's face. Look what you've done to him. You've scarred him for life,' I said. Mick stared at the lad and uttered in low painful voice.
'Why mate, why?'
The glass merchant hung his head low and said, 'Sorry.'
'Sorry, you fucking bastard, sorry? Look what you've done,' his girlfriend said.
I wanted the lad to see what he'd done, to see the pain he'd caused. He'd have to live with the sight of the lad's face hanging in bits forever.

Due to the severity of the injuries we detained both lads and the girl until the police arrived. The police were always quick to respond in these situations, especially at the Tower. If either party's friends or family turned up mayhem would ensue. As soon as the police arrived the lad who did the glassing admitted what he'd done. He was arrested and taken to hospital. The other couple left in an ambulance. I never saw any of them again.

As I filled in the First Aid book, I flicked back through its pages. Three books were filled. The majority of injuries were from glassings with pint glasses, which were supposed to be safety glasses which crumble on impact. Maybe they do I thought, but not before they caused serious wounds. I was already aware of the damage a glass could do. I had my own way of dealing with them, but how do you deal with an unprovoked surprise attack!

I viewed the glassing on the CCTV. There appeared to be no dialogue at all. All I could see was a quick glance from one guy to the other. I watched on screen as the glass merchant took the last swig of his pint before he walked toward his victim and without warning buried the glass into his face. One blow was all that landed before the bouncers arrived to stop a further attack which could have ended Mick's life. I was angry at the glass merchant; two lives ruined in a moment of madness. I went into the main bar area and found the glass on the floor near where it had shattered just leaving the jagged base intact.

The glassing left me feeling on edge, I realised this when the loud crack of the stripper's whip startled me. I looked across to the stage to see a small tattooed arse being whipped by a stripper.

The kid screamed out in pain every time the whip hit the target. The pain was nothing to what the glass merchant and his victim would be feeling.

MINIMUM FORCE

Under British law: You can use as much force that is necessary to stop yourself or others from being attacked as long as you have the true and honest belief that yours or their lives are in danger. You don't have to wait for them to strike you first before you take action to defend yourself, you have the right to pre-emptively strike first.
Case law, Regina v Beckford

The job of a nightclub manager is a diverse career and it is a stressful one. The Tower was never far from my thoughts. I had to work every day except Sundays. If I wasn't working nights I'd be on days promoting the business or away at a meeting somewhere across the country.
When I wasn't working I was training, lifting dumb-bell weights and punching focus pads in the garden. I attended the Fisher ABC boxing club and the local BJA Judo club in George Street. I would run on average 20 miles a week. This type of training kept the stress levels well under control and my confidence high. I knew the law regarding self-defence having studied it from both sides. I knew how far I could go to defend myself and my family and I would do whatever it took. I had been a member of Geoff Thompson and Peter Consterdine's British Combat Association for a few years and had trained with some of the best instructors in the world, picking up information and techniques and adding them into my repertoire.

Working for a major company was like treading on egg shells and trying not to break them. There were so many ways to fuck up and lose your job.
The Tower's licence was safe for now and I knew the company appreciated my services. I'd had a strong relationship with the police, the crux to keeping the club open.
I re-ignited the local Club Watch Scheme by bringing the managers of the other venues together by way of pressure from what I'd achieved at the Tower.

Every club wanted to show that they were doing their bit. Some paid lip service, others did it like me for real. I was asked to join the local drugs administration team meetings to exchange information on the misuse of drugs. There I was, John Skillen, the lad off the council estate, an ex-con sitting in the company of high ranking police officers, drug squad, solicitors, prison bosses and a host of government officials and agencies, all employed to help stop the growth of drug abuse in Humberside. I had become a respected member of the community and I felt proud of myself.

Hull's nightlife was expanding. At one point there were over a dozen nightclub licence applications presented every week. Some got through the courts, others were rejected. I was in court more times objecting to licences on behalf of my company than I had been when I was a bad lad! I had more to lose now than I ever had. The consequences of my getting into trouble through violence had well and truly stacked up. And at the Tower I was never far away from trouble.

The queue outside the Tower was 100 deep and growing by the minute. Big Dave and Thunders stood proudly on the door waiting for the nod from me to open. The thump, thump, thump of the bass reverberated around the foyer awakening the senses like tribal drums. Big Dave was an ex-rugby player. His giant frame sat well inside the uniform of the bouncer. He knew his job: firm and fair. He had a marvellous sense of humour – a great trait for a team player. I lost count of the times he brought me to laughter.
Thunders, his partner on the door, wasn't in control of his personality like Big Dave was. He switched between being a gentleman and a ruthless bastard. By day he worked behind the counter of the DHSS dealing with the lowest of the low, people who had no respect for authority or themselves. The only thing they seemed to respond to or respect was violence. Thunders fulfilled his role as a bouncer working and looking after the same people that pissed him off every day at work. He came from one high stress job into another then wondered why he lost his temper so easily. When he wasn't pissed off he was as funny as fuck although at times his temper would take him off the rails and it was like working with two men not one.

'How yer fucking doing, Skillen?' I ignored the shout from the front of the queue.

The huge girl repeated the phrase.

'How yer fucking doing, Skillen? Show us yer willy.'

'Mind your language, you or you won't be coming in!' said Thunders in a tone that was intimidating. It was like he had realised he was being nasty and was having an internal battle against his subconscious to remain nice to these 'low lifes' as he called them. He laughed to ease the seriousness of what he'd said and the way he'd said it.

'Come on, Skillen yer bastard. Let us in.'

'Yeah come on. We ain't got all night. We need a shag,' said her equally large companion.

'Yeah Skillen, Tower for an hour snog a dog and shag a bag,' shrieked the huge girl.

She was known simply as Miss Hollywood after the Hollywood Bar where she did most of her stalking, trying to find a victim: usually a 'shag anything' drunken lad out for a laugh with his mates or a shy or lonely man.

No man was safe when she was around and no willing man need worry about sex ever again. When Miss Hollywood was teamed up with her mate they were known as Essex and Wessex as they were the two biggest counties in England.

Big Dave moved into position and opened the other side of the double-sided fire exit doors.

'Hey what's your fucking game?' said Wessex as she realised what Big Dave was doing. Dave and Thunders stood aside and everyone in earshot started laughing as they opened both doors wide enough for the two big girlies to walk in. I was struggling to keep my laughter bottled up.

'I'll fucking have you, Skillen,' Miss Hollywood shouted as she disappeared inside the club.

As the laughter and friendly banter died down I noticed in the queue a real horrible bastard who had been ejected from the club a few weeks previously for beating up his wife.

I'd asked Big Dave why he had beaten his wife up. Big Dave had laughed and said, 'Have you fucking seen her? If she was my wife I'd have beat her up.'

I was surprised to still see her with him. Don't they ever learn? Once a wife-beater, always a wife-beater. The trouble with some women is that they make excuses for their men saying that one day they will change. If a man beats up a woman just because he's on a power trip then in my eyes it makes him a coward. I was brought up to respect women. I have no time for guys of that ilk.

The wife-beater got twitchy as he got closer to the door. His wife clung onto his arm. I felt sorry for her. It was obvious he meant the world to her. When he got to the front Big Dave had words with him then lifted his ban and allowed him back in to the venue. This was due to the wife-beater's wife telling Dave all was now well between them. The wife-beater apologised for causing trouble in the club. The soft, trusting side of Dave gave him the benefit of the doubt and a second chance.

The wife-beater was an arrogant shit. I could tell by his expression and body language that he'd taken Dave's decision as a sign of weakness. If this had been any other club I would have over-ruled Big Dave's decision. But this was the Tower and one more aggressive person wouldn't make any difference.

The infamous Tower crowd was becoming charged like Frankenstein's monster, the atmosphere was electrified with a sinister glow. I was sure it wouldn't be long before the beer monsters of the Tower awakened. It would be quiet on the door until we got the late rush of rejects who hadn't made the doors of the more upmarket venues. The lads that had failed to pull would rush to the Tower in an attempt to score the birds nobody sober would want. And if they still failed they could fall out of the doors and into the waiting arms of the Analaby Road lamp post accessories. For a price of course.

There was a very strange time in the Tower between midnight and 12.30 when an eerie silence seemed to creep into the vibrant atmosphere and the expressions of the *clientèle* would become zombie-like. I could feel the tension in the air. I didn't know whether or not the Tower was haunted but at this strange time in the early hours it felt like it was. I would often feel a cold chill just before pandemonium struck. Skirmishes between boyfriend and girlfriend would start, then a fight would break out, then the whole club would become embroiled in hatred for its fellow man. It was like all the shit of the week was being exorcised from the minds of the people at the same time.

At 12.15 the lads on the door were unusually quiet. 'Brian it's happening,' I said.
'What?'
'The twilight zone.' I opened my eyes really wide, Brian looked at me. I mouthed the theme tune to the popular TV series *The Twilight Zone.*
'Look there's a fucking monster over there,' Brian said pointing out some big, ugly woman who looked like she'd been chasing parked cars all her life. The foyer filled with laughter which was immediately silenced by the panic alarm.
'Main bar,' shouted Brian as the bouncers ran in different directions. I remained in the foyer and instructed Thunders not to let anyone else in the club until the problem was sorted.
I made my way across the foyer past the zombies who were now lounging on the staircase. As I reached for the fire exit internal door catch to shut off the doors, I felt a cold chill like someone was watching me from behind. I looked behind me rubbing the back of my neck to take away the sensation of goose bumps. I looked across to the staircase. The wife-beater stared down at me. His face contorted with hatred. I paused and caught his gaze but he didn't hold it.
I turned and started to close both doors next to the exit to stop the zombies on the staircase joining in the scrap if the lads brought someone out. Before I could shut the doors they became wedged open by falling bodies. Bottles were airborne and beer sprayed. A full-blown scrap was taking place between bouncers and punters, hell bent on staying inside or keeping their friends in the club. The two doormen were reinforced by the arrival of Thunders and Brian (the ex-para) and Brian who was making his presence felt by barking out orders.
I felt a hand on my shoulder and turned to be confronted by the wife-beater. He pressed his face into mine.
'Your fucking doormen are out of order,' he said. His tone clicked on my animal instincts.
I countered his aggression with stronger aggression.

'Keep your fucking nose out of it. It's fuck all to do with you.' I turned away and watched as a youth's head was thundered into the cigarette machine knocking him unconscious. One of the bouncer's boots followed him to the floor catching him high on the forehead.
'Back off him. He's had enough. Get them outside,' shouted Brian as he pulled the bouncer off the kid.
I spotted the wife-beater moving toward me.
'Oi I'm talking to you – your fucking doormen are out of order. They're going over the top.' I felt his nose press against mine for the second time. His breath smelt like he had a decaying tooth. I hit him hard in the chest with both hands driving him backward into the watching crowd. This gave him an intense hit of adrenalin and his aggression took over. He charged forward and felt the full force of my right open palm. The power slap took him completely by surprise. His legs gave way as the violent shaking of the brain and the disturbing of the balance in his inner ear caused his central nervous system to shut down.
One of the doormen dropped to the floor and encircled the neck of the now unconscious wife-beater. The doorman threw him out of the fire exit doors and into the gutter where he belonged. Order was restored. It always amazes me how quickly order can be restored when clean knockouts are witnessed. The doors slammed shut blocking out the abuse coming from the gang that had been ejected. Big Dave called me over to the doors.
'John, your mate's at the door. He wants a word with you.'
I walked to the front of the queue. 'What happened? Who hit me?' he asked. I wasn't in the mood for niceties I replied with strong verbal.
'I fucking did!'
'Look, I'm sorry for what I did. I can't remember what it was but I am sorry,' he said almost in tears. It was comical. To think a man of his size and aggression could be reduced to jelly in an instant.
'Can I come back in?' he said, his voice child-like.
'Listen, mate. You'll never get in here as long as you've got a hole in your arse,' I said.
Big Dave and Thunders looked at each other and like the double act they were laughed simultaneously at the wisecrack. The laughter broke the tension.

Shortly after, the wife-beater's wife appeared in the foyer.
'Has he gone?' she said.
'Yeah he's gone. Are you going after him?' I asked.
'Well, is he allowed back in?'
'Never again.'
'Then I'm staying.'
'Good for you.'
As she wandered off smiling Brian (the ex-para) approached with an excited look on his face.
'How did you knock him out with a slap? I've never seen that before.'
This was the normal reaction when witnessing the power slap for the first time. It was hard to believe but you can generate awesome power behind the slap and it's safe to use for both parties: no lasting injuries minimising the risk of you getting arrested. There's also a bonus to it: memory loss.
After the knockout the doorman's attitude toward me changed. I was no longer un-tested.
In their eyes I now had history. I thought back to an example given to me by the self-protection expert Geoff Thompson.
'Slaughter the chicken to train the monkey.'
The wife-beater never came back to the Tower and his wife finally left him. She had witnessed his downfall from the staircase and at that moment realised she didn't really love him. If she did she would have tried to help him. She visited the club regularly after that with her new man who, as she said, knew how to treat a lady.

TROUSERS PLEASE

Whilst working at the Tower I witnessed some unbelievable things, some evil, some stupid, some weird and others just as funny as fuck. It amazed me the lengths some people would go to get in.

A gang of Geordies on a stag night grouped together, instead of splitting up like they normally would to gain entry. The Tower was the only club that would let the stag nights in together. The club had more than enough women on the pull to go around and whether it was a stag night or not, trouble was never far away. So it didn't really matter who came in as long as they were dressed appropriately. We let the lads file in checking their attire as they passed us. Brian stopped one lad for wearing trainers and negotiations began between the two lads, Brian and myself.
'Why can't we come in? My mate's no trouble. Look at him. He couldn't fight his way out of a wet chip wrapper.' I looked at the kid thinking, why would he want to be in one? and also realised he was probably right. They were both pissed – far too pissed to get in a club, but this was Tower.
'Look, mate, if you go away and get some shoes on you can come in,' I said.
'Where are we going to get some shoes at this time of night?'
'I don't know,' I replied.
'But you can't come in trainers.' Instead of continuing the argument the lads left, arms across shoulders, and vanished.

A short while later the Geordies returned. Both were standing side on to me and Brian. They looked like they were in a position to attack the door, but showed no sign of aggression or doing an attack. I realised that they were standing side on to us to hide the fact that the cheeky bastards had changed footwear. Each of the lads was wearing one shoe on the foot facing me and Brian and one trainer on the foot furthest away from us. I looked at Brian and we both started to laugh. 'Come on. In you go, just for your cheek,' Brian said.
'And make sure that you don't change your footwear back again. As long as you stay like that you can stay in,' I added. They

danced by us in high spirits and were greeted by their mates waiting just inside the foyer.

It was around that strange time of 12.30. Most people were already in a club, on their way home or munching at a take-away. Some were sleeping it off in the cells or getting medical attention at casualty. The rejects from other clubs were trying to make the doors. The dress code was the best weapon against the undesirables. The road outside the club was dimly lit and the lamp posts and doorways had their usual attachments, either waiting to be picked up or waiting to pull a client. There were a few stragglers walking the streets and the odd kerb crawling car passing by. One would pull up and a girl would jump in and the car speed off. Prostitution was a dangerous game. It wasn't long ago that a prostitute was found chopped into pieces and dumped in Hull's drainage system. For all its horrors it was the only way some of the girls could get their fix or feed their families. Sad but true.

The lights of the Tower were a warming sight to anyone walking Analaby Road at night. The Tower stood out as the last bastion of entertainment on the edge of the city.

Like a good manager I stood on the door with Terry the bouncer vetting some of the rejects from various venues. Most were okay but some were not even acceptable to the Tower. We were having a giggle about something or other when a man appeared at the bottom of the steps. He was scruffy, unshaven and his eyes fierce and untrusting.
'Am I all right to get in, in these jeans?' he said to Terry. The very fact he asked highlighted that he probably already knew they weren't all right.
'No. We don't allow jeans in on a Saturday. You know that,' Terry said.
The kid was known to Terry: a real troublemaker who lived on the notorious Bransholme estate and according to Terry, a real soft twat. I took it to mean soft in the head. Nothing between the ears. Come to think of it he did look like a potato head. His jeans weren't the only problem; his shirt looked like it hadn't seen an

iron in weeks. All in all, he looked like he'd just spent a couple of nights in the local police cell. I kept quiet and let Terry do his job. The kid started to get aggressive. His attitude now matched his attire. It stank!
'I want to see the manager,' he said. I stood back out of the way.
'The manager's busy at the minute,' replied Terry.
'Well I ain't going anywhere unless I see the manager. I'll stand here all night and I'll make sure no one else gets in in jeans.'
The kid was becoming a pain in the neck. I butted in to the conversation.
'I'm the manager. What's up?'
'I want to come in.' I repeated what Terry had already told him and waited for his reply. The cogs were slowly turning in his head trying to find a loophole which would allow him entry to the venue.
'So you're saying I can't come in because I'm wearing jeans?'
'Yes mate. That's right. No other reason.' The coin had finally dropped through the mechanism. The kid was starting to get edgy. I didn't want to give him a reason to get knocked out, so I let him down easy.
'If you go home and get changed and come back in a nice pair of trousers I will let you in.' I doubted very much he'd have a nice pair of trousers, let alone a home. The kid shot off. Terry giggled.
'Soft twat,' he said in a lovely Hull accent.
I walked into the foyer to stretch my legs, had a quick chat with the cloakroom attendant then made my way back to the door. As I passed the old cinema front doors, I noticed a commotion going on across the street, the sight of which was enough to make you walk into a lamp post. You know that feeling you get when you see something happening but you don't quite believe it, the feeling that makes you want to rub your eyes and open them wider to make sure what you are seeing is actually true?

I stood with my jaw agape watching a man lying on the floor fighting to retain ownership of his trousers. Holding on to his waistband with both hands was the very lad we'd just turned away from the door. I could hear the man screaming.

'Fucking let go of my trousers.' He was literally caught in the red light district with his pants down. Not good. The tug of war champ was getting emotionally involved.

'Give me your fucking trousers,' he demanded. The guy shouted back at him.

'You can have my money, take it, all of it.'

'Fuck off,' the kid replied.

'I don't want your fucking money, I want your trousers.'

I ran to the front door to inform the doormen. A small crowd had gathered outside to watch the antics of the trouser mugger. Everyone was speechless, then once they realised what was going on broke down into laughter. The laughter was infectious. I carried on watching the action unfold. Another man walking toward the mugging quickened his pace.

'Oi fucking get off him,' he shouted as he got close. The mugger ignored the protest and continued to drag the man's trousers from his legs. The mugger then let go of the man's trousers and turned on the guy who'd tried to rescue the victim.

'Give me your fucking trousers,' he said committing himself to a new mugging. He punched the guy on the jaw, dropping him to the pavement. He leant over him and started to remove his own trousers whilst he was disrobing himself. The first victim fled doing up his trousers as he ran. The mugger was now standing over his new victim in his Y-fronts. He tugged at the guy's trousers as he was about to lose his pants to the mugger. One of the bouncers asked if they could stop the mugging.

'Yeah you'd better,' I laughed. The bouncers sprinted over shouting as they neared the mugger. The bouncers were finding it hard to be serious as the mugger ran for it. He looked a right sight running down Anlaby Road in his underpants with his jeans in his hands, being chased by three hysterical doormen in dinner suits. I was in tears with laughter.

That was one mugging that wouldn't be reported to the Old Bill. I mean how do you explain that one?

HOLLYWOOD DOMESTIC

As I shut the office door I heard a commotion coming from the Hollywood Bar. I made my way down the staircase and heard a woman shouting.
I turned the corner and saw a woman in the doorway of the Hollywood Bar laying the boot in on a shaven headed man who was lying on the floor. She was cursing and abusing him. He laughed at her like a madman. The more he laughed the crazier she got.
Dealing with domestics is a minefield and I was just about to walk into one.
I didn't bother getting involved I just observed. The situation got worse when the stamps the woman was inflicting started to draw blood. I stepped around the big guy and instructed the bar staff to press the panic alarm. The buzzer sent its signal to the bouncers that there was trouble in the Hollywood Bar. Stepping around the big guy and pressing the buzzer was enough to make me the common enemy.

As the door staff arrived I was about to exchange words. The couple were now both vertical and I was the centre of their attention. As soon as the door staff appeared it was showtime in the Hollywood Bar. They cursed at me. The door staff were being over nice to them. I suspected they all knew each other. The big guy was wearing the black and whites of the bouncer without the dickie bow and jacket. The doormen stood around as the big man verbally abused me. I felt my adrenalin rise and shouted at Brian:
'Get them out Brian, now!' I was beginning to lose it.
'Get them out? You fucking get me out,' the shaven headed man said. This guy looked like one of the heavyweights from the Ultimate Fighting Championships or K1. He also reminded me of the '70's detective, Kojak, without the hat or lollipop. I'd been on edge most of the night. The challenge from this guy sent a veil of red mist across my eyes. I lost control.
'Come on then, you fucker,' I said as I surged forward. He responded mirroring my verbals. We hit thin air as we were both

held back from behind. He was pulled into the Hollywood Bar. I was pulled back against the outside wall.

'Come on, come on,' I screamed. 'Fucking let me go.' Terry F another of the bouncers had me from behind holding both arms: a bad position to be in. If I'd have got free I would have ripped into him there and then. I pushed back against the door in an attempt to free myself.

'Leave it, John. We'll deal with it. He's a cunt. He'll kill ya!' Terry F said.

'He'll fucking what? I'll fucking kill him.' I was raging.

'Get your fucking hands off me, Terry.' Brian came over to me to calm me down.

'John, let's go to the office while we get him out of here.' I looked across to where four bouncers were restraining Kojak in a respectful manner. They were all mates, I could tell that much, but not enough to let him scrap in their venue. The sign of good bouncers. I walked up the staircase with Brian. My aggression subsided quickly. I'd learnt how to control it over the years, laughter or humour, even just a smile tricked my body into believing all was well. Then as the aggression petered out, in came wave after wave of consequence.

'You could lose your job. He'll beat you.' Negative after negative invading my mind.

Brian didn't help matters. 'He's a bad one, John. You shouldn't have messed with him.'

'This is my club and I make the rules. If I say he goes, he goes. No one man is bigger than the club. Brian do me a favour go down there and get that cunt out or I will.' Brian had other ideas; he wanted to avert a situation he might become embroiled in and he was right to avoid it at all costs.

'You stay here, John. Leave it to us. We'll get him out.' I cooled off and left it to the lads. I shook with anger. I watched the CCTV footage to see what was going on. Brian told me that the man and woman were married and always behaved like they did wherever they went. The man was a bouncer who worked the doors of various venues in Hull. I didn't know how hard he was and I didn't care: he'd challenged me and I was up for it.

Brian, he was just looking out for me. He didn't know me very well and was judging me on what he knew of me. A big mistake. I knew my capabilities. Besides I didn't care about winning or losing. I get stuck in and what happens, happens. Brian came back to the office. 'He wants to speak to you at the front door.' Before I could answer Brian continued, 'I wouldn't go down there if I was you, John. He's got his son with him. He's a handful too.'
As we spoke his wife appeared on camera storming out of the building, a glass in her hand as she got close to the door. A tall, suave-looking man in a nice suit (a rarity for the Tower) appeared in the doorway. He immediately felt the full force of the glass in his face and she ran out of the door. The guy was still stood in the doorway when me and Brian got downstairs. He was in shock. I gave him a bandage. I couldn't help feeling that the woman mistook him for me. It was a classic case of being in the wrong place at the wrong time with a complete lack of awareness. Kojak's wife and son had vanished just before we arrived. Good timing I thought as he may have got what he wanted there and then.
'Brian, he's barred and so is his missus. They never get in here again,' I said. I went up to the office to secure the video tape in case of police involvement. The guy who got glassed didn't want any. Truth was he probably didn't want anyone to know he had been in the Tower or even on Analaby Road: the haunt of prostitutes.
Kojak returned whilst I was on my tour of the club asking to see me again.
I knew the game; this was one of intimidation, deception and patience.
He wanted to see what he would be fighting and get a glimpse into my psyche. He also wanted to fight on his terms. Well, he'd challenged me so the ball was in my court. It was a simple equation. I either had the bottle to fight him or I didn't. This wasn't about money; it was about honour, *my* honour. Do I let this cunt walk all over me or do I make a stand even if it means losing everything? I'd already made my mind up years ago. Nobody walks over me. I knew what I had to do.

I had a lot to lose and I wasn't going to throw it all away on a prick like Kojak. He'd get his scrap but on my terms not his. I'd choose the time and the place then the ball would be back in his court.

'Brian, go downstairs and tell him if he wants to fight me I'll meet him outside the back at 2.30 a.m. once I've finished shift and locked up. Tell him just me and him and no one else. If his son wants a go, tell him I will fight him after I've fought his dad. Brian, tell him he'd better be there.'
'Listen, John. You don't know this man. He's a fucking animal. He's been sacked off a few doors, well asked to leave really, but he refuses to go and no one can get him off the door. They had to pay him a grand to get him off the door last time. Nobody fucks with him.'
'Just fucking tell him, Brian, or I will go down there and tell him myself.'
Brian informed him and the fight was on at 2.30. There would be only one left standing: either me or him. The guy had really pissed me off.
It shouldn't have, but pride was beginning to slip into the game. The guy had threatened me in front of everyone. I couldn't let this one go. He might be tough but as an ancient Chinese warrior sage Sun-tzu said, 'Know your enemy, know yourself. A thousand battles, a thousand victories.'
I knew my capabilities and I knew of his ilk. I would find out just how tough he was at 2.30. The adrenalin started to flow again. I took a deep breath and let the feelings run around my body. Having a set-to round the back was stupidity. I shouldn't have arranged it. I should have just let things take their course. I used to think that a one-on-one match fight was the right way, the honourable thing to do, but it was dangerous. The guy could have a blade, a shooter or a few friends waiting to jump me, but it was my only option. I didn't want this confrontation spiralling into a feud lasting weeks, months or even years. I had to live and work here. For me there was no multiple choice, this was the only option. If he beat me I'd be back on that door the very next night, no matter what injuries I sustained and then, if I had to fight him again I would and I would keep fighting until it was no longer required.

Since I had moved to Hull I had kept up my training. Seven miles was an easy run for me. I did that several times a week. I lifted weights, punched the bag. I visited the boxing club and judo clubs twice a week. I'd had hundreds of fights and so many knockouts I'd lost count. As far as I was concerned, I would be the only one walking away from that alleyway.

I cleared the customers and the staff out as quickly as I could. The building was empty. I was having an internal battle as I walked around the club turning off lights. I kept checking my watch to see what time it was. Ten minutes to go. I took solace in the fact I'd been in this position before. If he was going to beat me he'd know he'd been in a fight. So like the samurai of old I accepted defeat then pushed it to the back of my mind using positive thoughts to counter the waves of negatives that wouldn't go away. I switched all of the lights out and made my way through the main bar for one last check before I left the building. I imagined him out there waiting for me. I knew he'd be feeling the adrenalin as well. I knew he'd be feeling the negativity. I was the unknown. Would he be prepared to risk his reputation? He'd be out there now building himself up into a frenzy. That thought too was pushed to the back of my mind. I wanted to get out there and get it over with.
I was alone. Well, at least I thought I was, until I came across Brian, Terry, and Big Frank another of the doorman. 'We're coming with you,' said Brian.
'No, it's all right, lads, I can look after myself.'
'Listen, John, he's a fucking wild one. He won't think twice about using a tool on you or he'll have someone with him. We'll just make sure things are even. Make sure no one else joins in,' Brian said.
I was taken aback by the offer of help. I hadn't known these lads anywhere near as long as they'd known Kojak. But they were prepared to watch out for me. Either that or they just wanted a ringside seat. Frank was built like a tank. He was a quiet man but he took no messing. He looked like a real hard bastard. His shaven head and cold stare could make hell freeze over. I could tell they meant what they said. I went with my instincts even though it made me feel uncomfortable.

'Okay,' I said. 'Wait outside. I'll leave on my own. I don't want Kojak thinking I'm a dick that needs protection. If you want to watch my back then you will have to follow me round. I'm going round there on my own.' They left and waited down the road. If it was me waiting for Kojak I'd jump him before he got round the back. So once I put on the club burglar alarm I shut the front door checked around outside then locked it as fast as I could. I secured my watch and keys and was ready to do battle. The adrenalin increased in my system. I felt wide-eyed and fresh. I slowed my breathing, taking a couple of big gulps of air to fill my lungs with oxygen to feed the big muscles.

It was a warm night. A prostitute stood under a lamp post looking restless. Her head was twitching from left to right as if she was waiting for someone. The rest of the street was dark and lifeless, not a soul to be seen. It was an eerie sensation. The lights of the Indian takeaway gave off a warm glow and stood out like an oasis in a drought. I made my way to the car park. I passed Brian and the lads. They almost had their heads bowed. I felt like I was going to a funeral. I hoped it wasn't mine.
I had to control my adrenalin, let it run around my system. I didn't fight the feelings; that was the worst thing I could do. Just go with it. Ride the wave as the surfers say. In a strange way I was enjoying the buzz of it. I breathed in deep through my nose letting out the breath slowly from my mouth, slowly and deliberately easing the feelings. I wanted to explode all over this fucking wanker. This was it. I would be met with a tirade of abuse then we'd clash. It was me or him. I'd go for the knockout. If I fucked up, I'd gouge his eyes out, then strangle or choke the life out of him. Then stamp all over him. My aggression began to build as I neared the car park. I turned the corner. The adrenalin had narrowed my vision. I was in hunter mode.
I scanned the area then splayed my arms. 'Come on where are you?' I shouted. I looked around. He was playing the waiting game. I stood alone. The lights of the hotel beaming down on me like I was a Las Vegas boxer waiting for my opponent to enter the ring. I looked over to Brian who stood back at the entrance to the courtyard. 'Where is he then? Where's the so called animal?' Brian looked confused and surprised.

I kept scanning expecting him to rush out at me any minute. The lads looked at each other, shades of embarrassment showing on their faces.

'I'm here, one-on-one and he hasn't showed.' I felt cheated and relieved at the same time.

'Fucking hell. He's bottled it. I didn't think he'd bottle it,' said Brian chuckling.

I walked toward them. 'When you see him, Brian, tell him I said he is a bottle-less cunt and if he ever wants a go he knows where I am.' If he wanted me I was the easiest guy in the city to find. The ball was now well and truly in his court. I added his face to my long list of faces to notice in a crowd. He'd be back and when he came I'd be ready.

Although I hadn't had a physical go with Kojak. I considered it a mental victory and if I could beat him mentally, I could beat him physically. I drove home that night feeling good but tense. I made sure I wasn't followed. I needed a good night's sleep. If he returned the next night, I wanted to be fresh. I was again prepared for the comeback. That's the beauty of always keeping yourself in good shape no matter what your age.

I later found out there wouldn't be any comeback, well not immediately anyway. Brian had seen Kojak that day and told him what I'd said. He also added that I'd said if he ever comes near the club I would give the video footage of his wife glassing the well-dressed man to the police. I wasn't happy about that, but considered Brian's over-protective nature was for the best. Our paths never crossed again.

THE FULL MONTY AND A HALF

Boredom, the fruit of negativity;
negativity the killer of the soul!
John Skillen

I found out through experience that when the Tower crowd got bored they started scrapping. Violence was part of their lives: a necessary evil. They were desensitised to violence like veteran soldiers are desensitised to killing. They saw it all too often. The Bransholme estate was split into areas with gangs from different parts of the estate opposed to each other's existence. They would gather at the Tower. On some nights all four corners of the Tower would become their territories. A stare, a bump, chatting up the wrong girl: all could trigger the sleeping volcano of violence.

I had to get the entertainment right. They loved getting involved in the action. They were real people who just wanted to forget their shit lives. The Tower was like all good clubs should be: a place of escapism, somewhere to go to forget the stresses of mundane modern living.

The Monday night strip night catered for the lower end of the market who mingled freely with foreign merchant seamen. They brought the prostitutes in from the cold and competition was rife from the local girls who obviously didn't charge a penny (well maybe a few beers and if you were unlucky a lifetime of child support agency payments). They all got their fair share of seamen, if you know what I mean.

The other venues in town, LA's, a big brassy First Leisure nightclub, and the Waterfront club also targeted the sailors. They usually played host to the higher ranks. Tower got the lower ranks or 'ratings' as they were known. The ships' crew brought in much needed revenue because if there was a good spend on the bar it meant a bonus for me at the end of the month.

As soon as a ship was about to dock I would arrange a deal for the sailors and put up banners with the name of the ship on and make them feel welcome. There was little fighting when the ships were in. The ejections on these nights were usually for shagging in the toilets or in some dark recess of the club. The girls would be all over the sailors like the girls in the film *Officer and a Gentleman*, only these girls would be happy with a beer and a shag rather than marriage.

One night I booked in a trio of strippers billed as an all-girl revue show. I had a word with their manager at the start of the night and told his girls to keep it clean. The local environmental health officer was coming to the venue that night to investigate a complaint. The complaint had come from one of the local clubs jealous of the competition at the Tower.
'Everything will be fine, John. Trust me. Instead of the usual *ménage-à-trois,* they will simulate, you know, John, not actually touch each other,' he said. The show was set.
I watched the girls peel off their clothes, purely from a professional point of view you understand! It's a manager's job to check out the acts and make sure they are up to the required standard. Well somebody's got to do it!
The crowd was responding well. The girls kept the show entertaining and lively, teasing the crowd. I nipped off to check out the door clicker to see how many we had in. I didn't want the environmental health officer coming into the club if we had exceeded the capacity. When I returned to the balcony I noticed that the music had taken on a more sultry atmosphere. The DJ was peering over the balcony as if mesmerised – not usual for somebody like Mick who was always up for a laugh and never shut up even when the act was on. I looked out over who were normally a lively bunch. The crowd too were almost stationary on the dance floor in a state of hypnotism. Everyone was staring up at the stage in disbelief. I looked at the girls on the stage. They were locked in a circle. Their long tanned legs entwined. All three were completely naked and involved in simulated oral sex; only it was far from simulated. The girls somehow interlinked their legs and were still able to perform oral sex on each other, the classic *mange-à-trois*. I panicked and skipped down the fire escape onto the stage and up to the DJ booth which was housed above the stage.
'Fucking 'ell, Mick. Stop the show. Get the lights off.'

'No, John, leave them. The crowd love it,' Mick pleaded.
'They're licking each other's pussies live on our stage and the EHO guy is due in any minute. He can close us down tonight. I will lose my fucking job and so will you.'
'Just one more minute, John please,' Mick begged.
As I reached for the lights Mick's face said it all. He hit the lights and the mike like a true professional:
'Come on, Tower. Give the girls a big round of applause. Show them your appreciation.' There were a few boos. Then the crowd erupted into applause and the sultry mood was blown away by the sound of M People.
I got a call on the radio. 'Mr D. from the EHO is on his way up to the balcony to meet you, John.' I legged it up there as quick as I could, meeting him as he came through the door. Mr D. was always trying to catch me out.
'Many in, John?'
It was obvious there was. I ignored his question.
'Sorry I'm late. Has the show finished?' he asked peering down from the balcony onto the stage.
'Yes. It went down really well. You should have come earlier.'
'Look, John. I can't stop. I've got to get home. Tell me. Are those plastic glasses on the dance floor?'
The EHO are notorious killjoys. 'Tell them to get those glasses off the dance floor.'
'In fact have you ever thought of going completely plastic?'
I had after seeing some of the glassings at the Tower. I would have been happy to get rid of them all. But it's not glasses that hurt people, it's people who hurt people.
'I will get it sorted, mate,' I said, paying him the lip service he deserved. It was a close call. I was always getting hassle from the EHO. They would have been a lot happier if the Tower was shut down altogether. It appeared that the more I tried to comply with the environmental health department, the deeper they stuck the blade in and the more they twisted it.
We had come closer to that tonight and although the crowd were enjoying it, it was completely illegal. Strippers at the Tower often got carried away.

One of the most successful professional revue shows at the Tower were the Centurions. They dressed as Roman centurions, sailors, soldiers; all of the fantasy characters that women go daft about. I teamed up with a local radio station: Viking FM. The station wanted their radio jocks to join in the revue show with the Centurion's teaching them how to become strippers. They were then going to perform the Full Monty show. The Tower played host to over three hundred hungry women, no men allowed except for the bouncers and the manager, oh and as it happens Mr D, who always seemed to turn up to these kind of events. The radio link was brilliant; we were advertised all over the region. Radio advertising cost a fortune and we were getting it for free.

Some weeks before I'd had the honour of taking on a new employee at the Tower. Lesa was to become my assistant manager. She was a former holiday rep, a bubbly, crazy girl who loved to be the centre of attention. This enabled me to slink into the background: always a good idea at the Tower! Lesa had settled in well and had got used to the atmosphere of violence. She seemed to ignore it and get on with the main part of her job: interacting with the crowd and geeing up the entertainment. She wasn't afraid of the microphone or the stage, especially when the strip shows were on.

The radio jocks were taken backstage by Lesa to meet the Centurions. She demanded she take them and decided to stay and witness the one thing that aroused her curiosity. How do the male strippers keep it up throughout the show? What with nerves, fear of the crowd, surely it must be difficult. Lesa asked to be shown how the strippers kept it hard. One of the Centurions decided to use one of the radio jocks to demonstrate on. He got a tube and placed it over the jock's manhood then literally pumped him up, filling his manhood with blood. The increase in blood flow made his manhood erect and bigger than it could get naturally – almost twice the size. Whether it was the sight of his manhood growing bigger than he'd seen it before or the fact that blood had drained from his body too quick, the radio jock fainted. One of the strippers took action and tied off his manhood at the base with a piece of soft cotton material. When he came round and stood up his manhood stood proud for all to see. When Lesa told me the story I was in hysterics. Not at the lad fainting, but the fact she witnessed the whole scene. The soft cotton did its trick keeping the radio jock proud for the rest of the show. When it came to the Full Monty there was a gasp from the crowd as the Velcro was ripped off and glares of amazement from his colleagues when he proudly removed his hat.

There was another act that played the Tower stage, funny weird was one way to describe the piss-taking group of mini centurions. They were a dwarf strip act by the name of the Half Monty! It was the first time I'd heard the Tower lot complain. They thought they were being ripped off because they were only half an act!

TABLE TOPS AND TITS

Lap dancing was something new. I hadn't seen a lap dancing show before but I was assured that the show was professional. At the Tower our main job was to enforce the 'no touching' rule (which most adhered to). The men were very respectful of the girls and they had to be; the girls took no shit. They knew how to handle themselves, no pun intended.

The sight of 20 completely naked women gyrating on tables sucking on their own tits and exposing parts of themselves that were normally never seen in public made me nervous. But like a good manager I held myself together and faced up to the job.

Lesa, the ever present assistant manager, helped look after the girls. She would see to their needs and make sure nothing untoward went on in the dressing room, as some of the girls were inclined to have a toke, on a joint or two which was a no-no. Lesa, being the fun loving girl she was, decided in her wisdom to sort me out a gift for, as she put it: being a good manager.

I walked in to the office excited at the prospect of receiving a nice bottle of wine or a gold pen but at the same time I was wary. Lesa was always trying to get me on stage or pull some kind of stunt. I opened the office door to find Lesa standing with three lap dancing girls wearing practically nothing. What they had on wouldn't take much getting off. The girls were strategically placed on and around my office desk. My eyes lit up, then, realising that I was a happily married man dimmed again. 'Lesa, what are you doing?' I said.

'I thought you would like a private dance from the girls.'

'Sorry, Lesa. You will have to get them out of here.'

'There's no charge, John. It's a freebie.' She just didn't get it.

'Sorry, girls, I'd love to but I'm really busy at the moment, perhaps some other time.'

Well I had to let them down easy; I didn't want to hurt their feelings. Besides, I was shitting myself! I rushed out of the office to the main door where I was safest.

I often wonder how many lads would have turned that one down?

DAILY BLAG

The Tower had now become known for its sexy image. The violence was still present but nowhere near what it had been. One Wednesday evening I got a phone call from the Sunday Sport. They said they would like to come to the club to check out the venue for a new feature series they were running. I thought about it for a few seconds then committed myself and the club to the scrutiny of the Sunday Sport. After I put the phone down I felt a strange feeling of trepidation. I cast the thought to the back of my mind and remembered what my Area Manager Steve had said to me once: 'any publicity is good publicity, even if it's negative.'

The following Monday they arrived at the club strip night. I had stopped the full-on amateur strip. I didn't want the local licensing officer or the public health finding out about it. I was a bit worried about the Sunday Sport coming to the club in case they highlighted any problems like drugs or prostitution.
'It will be a giggle, John,' said Mick Spurr my favourite DJ. Mick was always up for a good laugh.
A man arrived at the club with cameras strung over his back and a notepad sticking out of his pocket.
'What's the camera for?' I asked.
'Well it's part of my job, you know, to take pictures.'
'Oh you're a reporter are you?'
'Yes. I'm here to do a feature on the club.'
'Well listen, mate. Go easy on the pictures you take. This is a rough club, you know what I mean? And if you can do me a favour keep any mention of drugs out of the paper. It's a pet hate of the company. Also there are a few dodgy people in here tonight. You might come across the odd pimp or prostitute. I have a licence to look after. Don't print anything too bad will you?' The reporter winked.
'Don't worry; I'll do a nice piece for the club. It might not go in the paper yet and if it does it will only be a small piece,' he said. I got him a pint and he disappeared into the club 'hunting sex' as he put it. I knew he would find it.

I naively thought all would be well. It seemed like he was getting around speaking to lots of different people and taking photos by the dozen. By this time I was feeling pretty relaxed about the whole affair, so much so I wandered around with Mick Spurr offering up different characters for the reporter to speak to. As the night was drawing to a close I met the reporter on the staircase talking to 'Essex' and 'Wessex'.

'Skillen, you wanker.' She pointed to the reporter and said, 'Photo.' The reporter called me and Mick over.

'Hiya, lads. I've had a great time tonight. Got loads of good stuff. Some bird even offered me a blow job. I'm off now. Can I get a quick photo of you two and the girls together?' Mick wrapped his arm round one of the girls and I wrapped mine round the other. The reporter winked once more. As the flash went off the girls grabbed their tops and out popped four of the biggest tits I'd seen since the last lap-dancing night. Mick erupted into laughter. I followed suit. The bastard journalist had set us up. I had that horrible sinking feeling! Before he went he had the last word.

'By the way, great club. Check out Sunday's newspaper. You'll love it!'

On that he slammed the door behind him and disappeared into the night. I feared the worst.

DOUBLE PAGE SPREAD

I couldn't wait to get home to tell Tina about the Sunday Sport reporter. She took it well. I didn't tell her everything. Well I felt that it would be better to wait until the paper came out so she could read for herself what the night had been like. Besides, I didn't want to spoil the surprise of getting a mention in a major newspaper.

Whilst we were in Hull, every so often a member of either of our families used to visit. Mostly it was Spider, my best mate and Gina his wife, Tina's twin sister. But this particular weekend Tina's grandma Clara was visiting. She was a lovely lady, getting on in years who was very chatty and good for a laugh.

It was Sunday morning and I had almost forgotten about the paper. We were taking Tina's grandma to the seaside for a portion of Sullivan's fish and chips. On the way I stopped for petrol. I went inside to pay and my heart turned over and my stomach filled with waves rolling back and forth like the tide. I picked up the Sunday Sport. I turned the next page and nearly fainted. The small piece on the club had turned into a double page spread with the title: 'The Tower nightclub – is this the sexiest club in Britain?' and right in the middle of the piece, yes you guessed it: Mick, two topless babes and me with a wry smile on my face.
I hatched a plan to ease Tina into the situation of her husband, the father of her children spread across the centre page of the Sunday Sport with two random, topless birds. The plan? Let the grandma see it first. If she reacted badly then I had no chance with Tina.
'Look at this!' I said 'It's a piece on the club where I work.' She opened the paper. I bit my lip as I fastened my seat belt into place and started the engine, then sighed with relief as she blurted out.
'Oh, ya bugger, is that you, John?' she laughed hysterically. 'Look, Tina. Your John made the Sunday paper,' she said. Tina looked at the picture. And in a tone I knew sounded disgusted said:
'Oh my God. Who are they, John?'
'Meet Essex and Wessex,' I said proudly. 'Named after the two biggest counties in England.' Tina cracked up laughing, more so because of the infectious laughter of her grandma than the pictures.

If I thought the picture was bad enough the write up was far worse. I could feel myself shrinking in the driver's seat as Tina read it out. The story overflowed with tales of drug dealers, prostitutes and shagging stories: everything that could shut a club down was scribbled across the page for all to see. All I could think about was what would the company say? Would I still have a job the next day?

I decided to ring my Area Manager and told him to get the paper and ring me back. He did and after the shock of seeing one of his clubs hailed as a place of debauchery, he saw the funny side. It turned out the company loved it. It was great promotion for the Tower, 'a little near the mark' as the company director had put it, but great promotion. The club was what it was: the sexiest club in Britain.

REFIT

The refurbishment of the Tower was a nightmare from start to finish and in effect fucked up the whole idea of what a refurbishment was about. It would have been far better to close and re-open with a big party night featuring a great celebrity than try and stay open. The numbers dropped and the complaints went up. I was plagued by the EHO officer who seemed to be there more than I was, especially if we had a male stripper on. I was beginning to wonder about him. The company didn't seem to realise it wasn't the Tower that needed refitting, it was the *clientèle*.

One night the club toilet floors had been layered with a special mixture of chemicals which would become the new non-slip toilet flooring. So the company decided to put in place chemical toilets that you would find on the building site or those you get at festivals and open air concerts. I suppose they actually suited as the club was now a building site.
The club was nearly full. Three hundred people crammed into one room with only one toilet for the gents to use. The night consisted of a few scraps and the ejection of a few punters for pissing up the walls and in the fire escapes. The club was taking less money and it was decided to have only two door staff on duty: another bad move which created another nightmare. In the situation we were in we needed more like ten on duty.
The night was in full swing and the crowd, considering the conditions, were in good spirits. I noticed a lad walking about pissed as a fart. He circled the chemical toilet trying to find his way into it. With a little help from his friends he finally made it through the door. After a couple of minutes his mates circled the toilet, grabbed a corner each and lifted the toilet onto the dance floor. They placed it down carefully so as not to disturb their mate who was obviously taking a shit!
Me and Brian watched, letting the lads have their fun. I had a tear in my eye from laughter. The toilet sat in the middle of the dance floor. The crowd surrounding it danced away ignoring the fact it was there. The lad inside was so pissed he hadn't made any attempt to get out and didn't realise he was on the dance floor. A

few minutes later the door opened and out popped the youth, trousers still down his thighs as he struggled to pull them up, his face a ball of confusion.

His half closed eyes scanned the crowded dance-floor as he tried to come to terms with what was going on. His mates were in hysterics as they pointed at him and sang along to the track playing, 'He takes a whisky drink. He takes a lager drink. He takes a drink to remind him of the good times. He takes a drink to remind him of the bad times. He gets knocked down and he gets up again. You're never going to keep him down.'

The kid ran into the middle of his mates, trousers still hanging off him, and arm in arm they danced away.

After a few short weeks we were fully refurbished and playing host to the same crowd. Nothing changed and we gained a few new customers. The general consensus was that the Tower was now too posh to party in. I got my head together with the Area Manager Steve and we gave the Tower a tweak.

CELEBRITIES

The tweak came in the form of celebrities. They were loved by the Tower crowd, especially the soap stars. They were big business and could easily fill a club. I booked a series of celebrities, ones I thought that the crowd would warm to. It was no good getting the nicey, nice ones. The Tower crowd needed something a bit more that they could relate to. So I went for the bad boys. The guys that played the mean parts and the down-to-earth stars. One of these down to earth stars was Lisa Riley, better known as Mandy Dingle from *Emmerdale*. She went down a storm and the Tower was packed solid the night she appeared.

She went from bar to bar serving as many of the crowd as she could. She was brilliant. Another favourite was Bruce Jones, who played Les Battersby in *Coronation Street*: a real Tower-type lad himself, especially as I asked him to come in character.

The bad boys went down a storm. None other than Paul Usher aka Barry Grant filled the tower. The girls went crazy over him and the lads thought it was great rubbing shoulders with the infamous Liverpool bad boy from *Brookside*. There were a host of other celebrity types, but no one took the Tower more by storm than the great Ross Kemp aka: Grant Mitchell: star of *Eastenders*, *Ultimate Force* and *Front Line Afghanistan*. During these visits I personally took charge of the security for each celebrity. It was a tense time during the visits as the Tower crowd was so unpredictable.

The Tower eventually started to show a better side and there was less violence. The violence appeared to have moved up to George Street, one of Hull's entertainment strips. I knew it wouldn't be long before it returned. I'd been at the Tower for two years. In that time Tina, my wife, had only ever been there twice, once at night to sample the delight which was the Centurions and secondly when we were on a night out at the opening of the Waterfront nightclub. The second time she saw the type of people that used the Tower. Her words, 'Oh my God, John. How can you work here?' summed it up.

For me the Tower was a fun, down-to-earth place to be. What you saw was what you got: real people with real lives, a living soap opera. And as in all soaps the characters change, time moves on and it was time for me to move on. I'd been approached by my old employers, Eric Schofield and Mark Walsh. They made me an offer to join them as General Manager, licensee and Head of Security at one of the best dance venues in the country. I had to make a final decision: do I go or do I stay?

You could never completely stop the violence at the Tower. It was part of the people's lives. I'm sure they would have preferred a quieter time of it. Trouble was, most were born into it with no chance of a better life, or so they thought. Like I said before they were violent people living on the edge. We had the club under control but couldn't relax for a moment. If you did it was kick off time. The club was still successful but it was one of those rare clubs that had to be kept on a tight leash. It required strong management principles with flexibility. It also required a strong security team with a good leader who didn't buckle under the pressure.

I thoroughly enjoyed my time at the Tower: the characters, the constant struggle to keep the peace, the laughs. All in all it was a great experience for me and if I had the chance to do it again, would I? You bet! The following men are my list of the names of who I stood with on the doors. These were the regulars. There are others. They know who they were. I will only give first names to some as I don't know their circumstances. I thank you for your support: Brian, Terry Gilby, Terry F, John F, Big Dave T, Big Dave, Frank, Brian (ex-para), Jim and Glen and Louis, two of the best.

The Tower eventually shut its door a few months after I had left Hull after turning a few replacement managers grey. My next stop: a nightclub situated in the mining town of Coalville, Leicestershire. Another tough town.

NEW START

I had a great two years working and living in Hull. I really didn't want to leave the area. I liked the people of Hull. They were very real characters, full of life. I loved the house I was living in and my wife and family were very happy. I had to say good bye to Sullivan's fish and chips, Nellie's cheap beer with its gas lamps and jazz nights, the weekend drives to the seaside, the lanes I used to run and the friends I made. Tina was extremely happy and moving was not what she wanted. But once I had made her fully aware of the struggle to keep the Towers' licence; the incident reports stacking up on the desk; the never ending cycle of violence, working days and nights and keeping up my training leaving me very little time with my two boys; she came round to the idea of a move.

So when I was approached by my old employers, I negotiated a good wage and instead of five nights and days working, I would be working one night and three afternoons. It was an offer I couldn't refuse. Throw in the moving costs and they had a deal. The leisure company I was working for offered me the same deal and an end of year bonus in the thousands, but they couldn't match the working hours or the environment I was going into.

I worked my notice, said my goodbyes and commuted until I finally sold up and moved back to Loughborough. We bought a new house and settled down to getting it comfortable.

Hull had another problem in 2002. The Observer reported that it was the drugs' capital of the North. And the Japanese built a bigger bridge than the Humber Bridge which up until then was the longest in the world and the boast of Hull city. The tide has turned slightly in the favour of Hull with their football club doing well in the Premiership. I wish them well.

EMPORIUM OF PASSION

'All drugs misuse is worrying, but it is particularly worrying when young people are turning to drugs.'
Keith Hellawell, former government-appointed drugs czar. Between 1999 and 2000 seizures involving ecstasy-type drugs were up by 46%

The Emporium nightclub was situated in Coalville, an ex-mining town near zthe M1 motorway in north west Leicestershire. The club was home to Passion, ranked alongside Sheffield's Gatecrasher, Liverpool's Cream, Birmingham's God's Kitchen, and Bournemouth's Slinky as one of the top five dance venues in the country. The Passion night had an atmosphere like no other club. And I, John Skillen, the lad from the council estate who left school with no qualifications and a criminal record was appointed to run it. I was to become the licensee, general manager and head of security. Whoever says they can't get a job because they're an ex-con ain't trying hard enough!

Running this venue was a massive responsibility. I rode the fear like a surfer rode the waves. The techniques I'd learnt over the years were now helping me face up to greater challenges. A good manager is a problem solver and I'd had years of dealing with problems on a daily basis. The wages and employ of everyone in the venue relied on one night's takings. Any fuck-ups and I would be out on my arse quicker than Thatcher was after bringing in the poll tax.
The venue was extremely popular on the dance circuit which was due to the skills of the two owners and the tireless promotion skills of the office team namely, Barbara and Jason. The club had been originally set up as Crystal's Two, a venue which mirrored Loughborough Crystal's. It never really took off like the Loughborough venue mainly due to the trouble that erupted each and every night it was open; the locals were fight mad.

Kenny Schofield, brother of the owner and lifelong friend of mine, had been running Crystal's Two along with Steve Clifford an ex-para who had been working at Crystal's for a couple of years, a good doorman and a good friend of mine. Ken was one of the toughest lads I knew; he could kick, punch, grapple and he had the bottle to back it up. He would fight anyone. He described the locals to me as being potato heads with very low intelligence and self-esteem. There was also a big community of travellers nearby and Ken could be seen regularly kicking someone's arse up the street. He had a great team to back him: Raddle, Jay B, Saunty, Doug, Sooty, among others but Ken, he could have done the door on his own.

One night he kicked a guy out and he threatened he'd be back. Sure enough, later that evening the guy turned up complete with two lurchers and tried to set them on Ken. Ken was too busy laughing to even bother about it. That for me summed up the mentality of the locals, so when Crystal's in Loughborough had been sold on Mark and Eric poured some money into Crystal's in Coalville. They kept the so-called potato heads and travellers out and the night grew stronger and stronger, all credit to the then promoter Ferry who left the venue as it was beginning to really take off.

Within two years of changing to a dance venue, Passion was nominated as one of the best dance venues in 1999 by the industry magazine Mixmag.

Jason Kinch became the name that would propel the venue forward. He was under constant stress to fill the place and he had to do it on a tight budget. And every DJ that came to the venue needed minding. They were like pop stars and the crowd would want a piece of them. If they could get it!

The Emporium was different to the mainstream clubs in that the over indulgence was less alcoholic and more narcotic. The Emporium was like a maze. Get split up from your mate and you might not bump into him or her again. When the night was over, the floors were strewn with empty paper wraps, discarded joint ends and hundreds of plastic, self-seal bags which previous to the night would have held thousands of pills, wraps and powders.

The atmosphere was amazing; the place throbbed. You couldn't help but dance. It was like you could be sucked into their drug-fuelled world in an instant if you let yourself. There has been an argument raging for years on whether or not certain narcotics are safer than others. Personally I don't think there is an illegal drug that is safe. What I do know is that before the dance scene became awash with the drug ecstasy, violence was always present. In fact, in some of the bigger cities like Manchester and Liverpool gang wars and feuds were normal events. Then, as if someone had waved a big wand, everyone stopped fighting and started loving each other. This was all down to a small pill the size of a headache tablet.

Ecstasy put the clubber into what is known as a luvved-up state. They would sooner give you a big hug than fight you, even if they'd never met you before. The hardest villain became like a puppy on ecstasy. To watch them from the outside in, it would seem they were oblivious to anyone not part of their inner sanctum of euphoria. You could go for a night out and feel safe from some thug attacking you. The drugs were available at a price a school kid could afford and most of the kids at Passion were only just off the playground.

It was an over 18's club but can you tell the difference between a 16-year-old girl and an 18-year-old when they've had a makeover? I've been in the game for over 25 years and I'm good, but it's still hard to tell how old a person is to within a couple of years.

My job was to bring the drugs scene under control. You could never stop it coming into the venue, but controlling it was possible. I had to make sure that I had a door team that was anti-drug, but not too hard-line as that would spoil the scene.

I'd found out the hard way whilst working at Crystal's what being too hard-line could do to a night. Everyone was searched and stopped and we got rid of hundreds of pills, plus two major dealers were threatened, beaten and then kicked out. Word soon spreads and the following week the night was empty and a small fortune was lost. We had to be anti-drug enough not to get involved in the sale of drugs and not to turn a blind eye to its overt use. The drugs had to stay underground where they belonged.

Ken was massively anti-drug. If he caught a dealer they got an unpleasant end to their evening; when one particular dealer was caught, Ken flushed his gear down the toilet followed by the dealer's head. They made him strip naked, threw his clothes out the back door and the naked dealer out of the front. The front of the club was extremely busy and the sight of the dealer running down the street looking like a '70's streaker was a sight to behold. Yep, Ken was hard line and many times if he caught a dealer he gave them a choice: flush their drugs down the pan and fight Ken round the back of the club, or be handed over to the police. They usually chose the latter. When they didn't they got the beating they deserved. Ken re-assured me neither of the owners was involved in drugs. They made too much money from the legitimate side of the business to bother.

Over my first few weeks as manager thousands of pills followed by the heads of the users and dealers were flushed down the toilet. Beatings were dished out on a regular basis to those who got caught to send out a firm message: that the drugs had to be driven back underground. I started by choosing my own security. Those I wasn't happy with were laid off, the others retrained to hand drugs over to the police or to detain drug dealers. It was extremely dangerous if there was no correct procedure in place. Accusations could be made. I contacted the local licensing officer and implemented a drugs box and drug seizure forms that would hold information similar to the system I had implemented in Hull. One thing was made clear to me by the police: only target dealers, not the users. The reason? If we detained everyone we thought was using, the police would not be able to cope with the influx of prisoners. So the drugs safe became an amnesty box. I held one key and the police held the other. Neither party could open the safe without the other being present.

With the new procedure in place anyone caught dealing would be detained and handed over to the police. It was the only way we could do it to protect ourselves and the business from the accusations made by certain people. In the old days detaining someone to hand them over to the police was classed as grassing. I made it quite clear to the doormen who had a problem with detaining someone, that if it was the old days and if we were doing the gangster thing, and they were dealing on our turf then what they would get would be a lot worse than being handed over to the police. So it was far better for all concerned to work with the police. And I had no qualms about it at all. If you were stupid enough to get caught you pay the price. And seeing as we weren't doing the gangster thing they got the other. The venue was now considered by the police to be working with them and the licence was safe as it would ever be.

WHEELERS AND DEALERS

Saturday at Passion was one of the tightest doors in the country; you either dressed right and acted right or you wouldn't get in.
'I'm sorry, love. You can't come in dressed like that. You look like you've been to sleep in those clothes,' said Andrew the door picker.
Andrew was overtly camp. Reason – he was gay and proud of it. Don't get me wrong; he wasn't one of the brash, offensive types. He was a gentleman. In a camp way he had a bit of class. He could spot a decent clubber and an undesirable by the expense of their clothes.
The lad splayed his arms. 'I have been to sleep in them. I've travelled fucking miles to be here tonight. Can't you just let it go this once? This shirt cost me 30 quid.'
Lloyd, one of the bouncers, looked at him as he lifted the rope from the crowd control barriers at the front of the club and beckoned the lad to walk through the middle rope which led back into the street. He lifted the second rope not saying a word.
The kid protested as he walked. 'This is fucking stupid. I've travelled from fucking Wales to be here tonight.' Lloyd stood back completely blanking the kid, his way of not getting drawn into conflict.
Andrew (who dressed immaculately in designer clothes fit for a top model and probably costing more than the kid could earn in a month) turned toward the youth and said, 'Get a life.'
The lad had no reply and walked off. I mean how does a straight guy argue with one so overtly gay? It was great. Andy stopped lots of confrontations by just being himself.
A stilt walker and a fire-eater entertained the crowd as they waited to see if they would make the door. Eyes forced wide open by cocktails of alcohol and drugs and frantically chewing heads darted from side to side as the anticipation added to their excited state.
The smell of chips and fried chicken mingled in the air with the smell of the fuel making it smell like a barbecue. Sound systems boomed out of every car body part and traffic buzzed by the club. A local pulled up in a Fiesta and went for a burn out on his tyres. Rubber smoke filled the air as the smoke drifted off into the square

opposite, covering a group of piss-heads awaiting a taxi. The crowd let out a cheer.

I turned around sharpish after feeling a tug on my trousers. 'Boo!'
I looked behind me to see a four foot dwarf in an alien suit. 'See, you'd have no chance against me. I'd head-butt your kneecaps till you dropped then I'd stamp all over you. We're all the same size when were on the floor.'
I laughed then lifted the rope and jokingly put my boot up his arse. 'And don't come back,' I said. The queue cheered and laughed at the dwarf who walked off threatening lads as he passed them by. It was one of the funniest sights I'd seen since the trouser mugging at the Tower. A dwarf in an alien suit.
Before the crowd began to enter the venue the door team took their positions around the club. The most important area was the search area. Four Security, usually three men and a woman, would search everyone that came through the doors for weapons or drugs. No matter how thorough the search, thousands of pills and powders got brought into the venue. Not surprising really. They can't even stop drugs getting into prisons. What chance did we have? When money can be made people will try any way possible to sell their wares.

The real dealers are the ones that make the big bucks and you never meet these guys. They are far too clever to be involved directly in the sale. The likeliest candidates to get caught were the guys trying to finance their night out, or trying to make a living from the sale of drugs. They buy from the wholesaler then bring the drugs into the area, split them up into smaller lots and sell them on the night. They can bring in as many as 500 pills at a time or bags of wraps. Sometimes these dealers take a chance and employ a host of runners.
I would sometimes position myself in some inconspicuous place and watch the floor.
It would be like a bustling stock market: runners slipping through the crowds going from dealers to users and back again. I'd watch them link up with the main dealers then we'd move in and pull them out. One individual was caught with 500 pills and got three years for his trouble. The new rules for the doormen were in place

and any bouncers caught getting involved in drug dealing would be sacked immediately. The clubbers were becoming more careful about their dance floor dealings. The drugs were now well and truly back underground. The only problem was it was now harder to catch them at it! Catching drug dealers was only a part of the job. The main part was ensuring the safety of everyone in the venue, and making sure they had a great night out! But it was difficult to lose the focus of the drug problem.

ARMOUR PLATED BALLS

No matter how hard you try, drugs will always get smuggled into a club. As I said earlier and it needs saying again, they can't stop drugs getting into prisons so getting them into a club isn't difficult. They will try anything to smuggle them in: inside cigarette packets tucked into a corner of the pocket, in a wallet, in the shoe, in the sock, in handbags or the not so obvious places like under the tongue. Inside a lighter with a false bottom. Inside loose tobacco, inside a cigarette stacked up like sweeties (they remove the tobacco put in the pill, replace the tobacco at the top then put the ciggies back in the packet) or simply in the hand wrapped in cellophane. Others would sneak the gear in deodorant cans or perfume bottles. The most difficult to detect are the men and women who place the pills inside their genitalia. One lad when asked if he had any pills on him dropped his trousers, rolled back his foreskin and revealed a circle of pills wrapped in cellophane. One of the doormen was so disgusted in what the kid did he power slapped him knocking him on his bare arse. They would literally try anything.

We pulled one character on a routine search. He was completely wide eyed and not very comprehensible. He was found to have a small amount of pills on him. Normally he would have signed the pills in the book, posted them in the safe and he'd be on his way out of the club. There was something about this kid that set the alarm bells ringing. He was well built, of army stature and about 25 years old. When he was searched I found an ID card inside his wallet which told me he was a serving member of the famous parachute regiment.
Considering he was a para and out of his head I was accompanied by four other bouncers and took him to the office. He was very arrogant and aggressive. If he kicked off we would have to restrain him without hurting him. I asked him if he had any more drugs on him.
His arrogance shone through once more in his reply. 'Yeah why?' He had a strange stare, his eyes piercing. It was like he was looking beyond me, like I wasn't there. I'd set myself to the right

of him, stripping away his chance of lashing out at me. If he became aggressive I could take him out in a split second. 'Where are they?' I asked.

He shrugged his shoulders and gave me a stare, then dropped his trousers and his pants and stared forward as if he was in some kind of military office. Maybe in his mind he thought he was back at his base. He stood there almost at attention (No, not that type of attention).

I stared at his bollocks long and hard along with the other four bouncers who were also transfixed to the same spot as me. 'Are you all fucking queer?' he asked.

I wasn't but I couldn't take my eyes of his nuts. I hadn't seen anything like it in my life. His knackers were completely covered in what looked liked metal studs, his cock was pierced with a metal ring through his bell-end and strapped around his cock with black tape was a huge bag of pills. I was sent dumb for a minute then burst into hysterical laughter followed by the rest of the lads who were trying to keep a straight face.

I called Monty on the radio: an ex-para regular and a brilliant doorman. He was working the floor that night. I wanted him to see the lad and give us advice on what to do seeing as he was a para. Monty walked into the room.

'Monty, this guy is a para. I think you should see this,' I said trying to maintain a serious tone in my voice.

Monty snatched a glimpse at the lad's knackers. 'In the Paras are you, what regiment?'

The lad spoke out. Monty showed his disgust. 'You ought to be ashamed of yourself. Look at you. You need help you do, mate.' Monty gave him a bollocking (no pun intended) for letting the regiment down. For some reason Monty didn't find the situation very funny at all. As far as Monty was concerned the regiment was the best there was and this guy was belittling everything it stood for. Monty walked out disgusted with what he'd seen. His last words were, 'Hand him over.' We did just that. The police, then the army would deal with him.

There were many drug takers and dealers of varying degrees handed over to the police but sometimes I had another approach. If I found that the user was from a good home who was genuinely caught up in drugs by default i.e. giving to friends or carrying for someone else, they got the benefit of the doubt. We would put the pills in the box and kick them out.

If during the chit-chat that took place they informed us where they bought them or if they gave the whereabouts of the dealers they would be given amnesty. The younger ones, however, were not. They had a choice: ring the police or ring their parents. Most took the route of ringing their parents. I would speak to them on the phone telling them that their son or daughter had been caught in possession with drugs and would they like to come and pick their child up. Some did, some didn't. Those that didn't, their children were handed over. Those that did were allowed to take their child with them and deal with them themselves.

It was far better than a prison sentence.

If anyone got cocky and a few did, they would be dealt with by the iron hand. The door team brought in one lad who was extremely aggressive and a real cocky fucker. I sat him down in a chair. He was flanked by two big bouncers. He couldn't see what was happening behind him so in order to teach him a lesson we played with his mind. I was telling him he was being detained and handed over to the police when I heard an almighty roaring sound. The assistant manager, none other than Notorious Nigel, who was a bit of a nutter, had started up the electric plane and was threatening to remove the kid's scalp.

The plane was brought into an inch of the lad's scalp. Within a couple of minutes the kid was a quivering wreck. When the police arrived to take him in, the drugs in his system coupled with the adrenalin of fear of being scalped, were working so strong he couldn't wait to be arrested and admitted everything to the police. Often there would be threats to kill against us and we had to be seen as being strong.

Drug dealers and users are a diverse bunch in the brightly coloured laser lit world of club land. Characters abound in this glitzy, roller coaster, weekend ride; their professions a broad spectrum of everyday British life. It is shocking to know that uncontrolled and illegal drugs infect our nation. Solicitors, doctors, nurses, police officers, prison officers, soldiers, sailors, accountants, estate agents, engineers, etc. The list could go on, but one that held me in disbelief was an airline pilot in charge of millions of pounds worth of equipment with an extremely trusted position. No area of the

British social system seemed to be clean of drugs. We couldn't in our position trust anyone. Dealers and users have their reason for taking drugs; some do it for pleasure, others the money. And some do it for pure kudos and popularity.

The routine searches turned up most of the drugs. Sometimes we'd catch a dealer and other times they would get away.

THE ONE THAT GOT AWAY

I stood in the Red Room surveying the crowd as it moved in time to the house beats of Parker and Pasquale. The crowd cheered as they handed over to the MYNC Project. Nick Correlli got his head down to the decks with Mark Young and the house beats buzzed. The body heat was intense and smoke filled the room. I left the smooth sound and decided to move on to a cooler climate in the chill-out room: one of the larger of the several rooms at the Emporium.
The room holds around 600 people when full. I liked working at this venue. It made a change from the usual shit holes I've had to endure; all part of the apprenticeship as they say. You work the rough pubs and clubs which in turn give you the experience to able to work the finer establishments; there's no substitute for real experience and loads of it.
There were some weird and wonderful people in the 'Green Room' – the name given to this vast chill-out area. The music was low-key and conversation babbled through the air. Glasses chinked, fluorescent clothes, designer hairstyles, glow sticks, weird piercings, painted faces. Everyone trying to outshine the other and see who was the coolest, was the game being played.
A lot of the kids are pretty sensible about the way they take their gear but there are a percentage who are like the 15-pint lager lout, who try to out drink their mates ending up in oblivion then bragging about it the next day. On the dance scene the same thing occurs; these lunatics who over indulge are known as caners and their youthful arrogance takes away any thought of death or serious injury. There were times when I was summoned by our resident paramedic (yes it was that bad we had a resident paramedic) whose sole purpose was to prevent anyone dying from overdosing on a cocktail of drugs. He saved many, I'm sure of that.
I was present at most situations. I have seen 20 stone body builders turned to quivering mental and physical wrecks, so badly out of it they don't know who they are or where they are. Drugs such as Ketamine and GHB are both very strong tranquillisers. Kids have been recorded as taking cocktails of the following drugs: amphetamine sulphate, cannabis, skunk, Ketamine, GHB, ecstasy,

acid, and alcohol, the latter being freely available as it's legal. I lost count of the amount of unconscious bodies we had to drag from the club to be examined by the paramedic. One youth over indulged and even though the paramedic got to him, administered first aid until the ambulance arrived, which then got him to hospital in record time, he never regained consciousness and died of a massive overdose of ecstasy. The more I saw the pain drugs caused, the more I hated them.

But the youth don't see it like that. I remember one youth telling me one night that he had a drug problem. 'Yeah what's that?' I asked.

'I can't get any,' he said laughing. The clubbers on the scene don't see the dangers in drug abuse. They just don't think it's going to happen to them.

The friends of the youth who died now bring a wreath of flowers and lay it at the back of the club in remembrance of their friend. After they laid the wreath they partied on; eyes wide open, heads in the mist. The flowers are a reminder of being ignorant of the dangers of drugs. The lad was still in his teens. He didn't just destroy his own life but probably that of every life he touched: family, friends. It is very sad. But wherever there is a demand for drugs, there will be a supply and where there is a supply there will be a dealer.

I was approached by a girl who was concerned about a man that was giving away pills by dropping them into people's drinks. I spotted the man going from table to table with a big fuck-off smile on his face. I couldn't believe what I was seeing; the girl was right. The girl disappeared and left me to it, worried about getting seen by the man in case he attacked her or something for informing me of what he was doing. The man wasn't trying to hide what he was doing. Everyone he spoke to he gave a pill and took no money. By the look of him he was on a cocktail of cocaine and ecstasy and the cocaine would fire his aggression up as soon as I approached him. I didn't have time to fetch the bouncers. I had to get control of him first. His eyes were glazed, big and round. He was very muscular and stocky, smartly dressed in pure white clubbing wear. Another youth approached me to confirm what was happening.

'What he's doing is out of order. Are you going to do something about it?'

I was close to the dealer. He turned and caught my gaze. 'Excuse me mate. Can I have a word?' I asked. He'd sussed my intention and his body language changed to one of urgency. Before I could grab him he turned and ran toward the toilets to ditch the gear. The chase was on. I got within grappling distance and wrapped my arms around his arms, pinning them to his waist. I was trying to trap his hands inside his pockets so he couldn't get rid of the gear. I didn't have his arms pinned low enough and he fumbled in the pockets. Then he released his fingers, dropping pills as we struggled. Hundreds of pills bounced on the wooden floor and pinged everywhere. Some of the clubbers scrambled for the pills.

I dropped my head to the side of his body so he couldn't head butt me. He exploded. His strength increased tenfold brought on by the influx of more adrenalin and coupled with the drugs. I drove him forward keeping the momentum for fear of losing my grip. I rammed him head first into the studded wall. The effect this had was to infuriate him further.

He screamed and broke free from my grip just as I was switching to apply a strangle.

I'd lost his head and so had he. He was gone, out the double doors and into the corridor. 'Stop him,' I shouted, but the door staff were caught by surprise and were too late to stop him. I gave chase. 'He's mine,' I said as I ran.

Then he made a mistake. Instead of running out into the car park where he could have outrun me he ran into the fenced off compound at the back of the venue and no way out!

'Don't fucking move,' I shouted. Sometimes this would have the effect of making the person freeze but he took no notice of me and charged forward like a cornered dog, screaming like a wild animal. I let go a palm heel strike which caught him flush on the jaw. Down he went. Notorious Nigel arrived on the scene as the kid hit the deck. The animal jumped up and into Nigel's arms. Notorious went to apply a headlock then pulled back in disgust, clutching his hand to his nose. The animal paused. 'Leave him John. He's shit himself.' Nigel was right. It stank. I moved aside and the animal sprinted away, his white clothes turning brown as he fled. He ran back toward the door and the door staff gave chase into the car park after him.

The white clubbing clothes were now a yellow brown.

He was quickly taken to ground by four burly bouncers who reeled back in disgust as they realised he'd shit himself. One of the four retched and almost puked. The animal ran as the bouncers watched on.

At the door the laughter broke the tension. 'Fucking 'ell, John. What did you do to him?'

'You know, lads. Shit happens,' I said and walked back inside the venue.

From that day on the palm heel became known as the 'shit strike'. Muzz, one of the regular bouncers was highly intrigued by this strike. I refused to tell him, citing that it was a secret of the martial arts' world and only a privileged few knew of the secret strike. Muzz begged me to tell him how to perform it. I said I couldn't tell him anymore. Look what happened to Bruce Lee when he gave away his secrets! Muzz was even more intrigued. I offered Muzz the opportunity to show him the strike using Muzz as the stooge. He refused as did the rest of the doormen.

The shit strike became a legendary strike. A few weeks after the event I was attending a meeting at the Loughborough University trying to drum up some business. At the end of the meeting I stood up and offered my hand to the union representative.

'I won't shake your hand if you don't mind,' he said. Then he asked me outright. 'Is it true you can make someone release their bowels by just touching them?'

I smiled and looked at him for a second then turned to walk away.

'Now that would be telling wouldn't it!'

ABOVE THE LAW

'Strike the shepherd and the sheep will scatter'
The 48 Laws of power - Robert Green

'John, can you come down here?' I hated it when the doormen did that.
I ignored the shout and carried on into the toilet hoping that by the time I'd finished they would have dealt with the situation themselves. I left the door ajar, just in case, while I answered the call of nature. They only really called me down if it was really funny or very serious. I had a feeling it was the latter. I started to feel the butterflies playing games in the pit of my stomach; that nervous feeling that makes you feel like running off and hiding in the corner. It's always there no matter how much training you do. It never goes away.
It strikes me as strange that when I'm on the door facing adversity I don't feel the fear the same as I do when I am called to a scene. It's that extra fear of the unknown. Walking into a situation is far worse than watching it develop then taking action.
I started to take deep nasal breaths slowing down the release of adrenalin, a mix of natural chemicals occurring within the body. I felt nauseous as I finished zipping up my trousers. I had a bad feeling, that intuitive feeling that something is not quite right. When I got that feeling on previous occasions something was usually wrong.
I heard the doorman shout again this time with an urgency in his voice. 'John, you'd better come down. I think it's going to kick-off.' His complexion had paled to a greyish pallor; a sure sign that he was experiencing adrenalin release.
'There's a load of gypsies at the front doors. It looks like they're up for it. They've been refused entry and won't leave the doorway. They're trying to start something. One of them is inside the barriers.' I arrived in the foyer. One of the bouncers was holding the front entrance door shut as if it was going to spring open at any moment.
'What's the problem?' I asked the bouncer holding the door.

'They're after me. I've had lots of run-ins with them over the years.'

Just then the door rattled as heavy boots hit the woodwork. The bouncer pushed the door open ajar. 'Pack the fucker in,' he said with an assertive tone, staring hard at the gypsy.

The gypsy surged forward trying to get his hand into the open door to prise it wide open. The bouncer pulled it shut. It slammed into place. I peered through the nine inch by five inch glass pane. Neatly framed within it was the face of a man that looked like he had been hit with a baseball bat at birth. He was an ugly, rough looking traveller who appeared born to fight and a right handful. Behind I could see his gang; every one of them wearing the same checked type shirt and trousers. I always wondered where they bought them from, a funny thought to have in this situation but that's what happens after dealing with violence for so long. You become desensitised. You find a way of dealing with it and my way was to face it head on regardless of the consequences. This was my club and my rules applied.

The gang numbered eight or so with several others milling around in the background observing the proceedings. These were travellers and there might appear to be eight one minute, but those numbers can quickly swell. The travellers stick together. This bunch were of varying ages, mainly in their 20's and equally rough looking. I could see by their mannerisms and body posture that they looked up to the baseball bat victim and were getting ready to fight if he gave the word. These travellers were of Irish decent and very intimidating people, especially after a drink or two. A lot of people (although they won't admit it) are scared shitless of these nomadic types who will fight at the drop of a hat. You see, they don't harbour the same thoughts of consequences as ordinary people. They get hassle they disappear, move on.

I remember about ten years ago having a run in with a gang of gypsies at Crystal's and a comeback was threatened. One of the door lads I was working with advised me not to mess with the gang as they were bare-knuckle fighters. This I found quite funny! The doorman was obviously scared of the fact they were gypsies and thought he was doing me a favour tipping me off about their

fighting prowess. But he was scaremongering. As soon as he said it I saw doubt appear on the faces of the other two doormen.
I countered his scaremongering and told him that whilst working the door we were all bare-knuckle fighters and had been for years as we never donned the gloves and fought with no rules. The other doormen's faces lit up and the threat of the comeback paled into insignificance.

What the gypsies do have is bottle, they appear fearless. It's the way they are brought up. They can, as my Irish father used to say, 'Fight, fiddle or fuck with the best of them and talk the hind legs of a donkey. And they do believe they are above the law.' There are of course good and bad in all and just because somebody prefers to travel the land and live in a different way to the norm doesn't make them bad. Anyone should be allowed to live how they wish as long as it doesn't hurt or interfere with others and as long as they abide by the law of the land. The hard truth is some don't. I've met some fine travelling people over the years with respectful kind and generous natures and decent morals. Proud people who work hard for a living.

It was obvious to me that this gypsy was pushing for a scrap, otherwise he would have had his fun and gone. He was doing the big man act in front of his clan and setting a bad example for his younger followers.

The boot of the gypsy rained in against the door. Again, the doorman playing in to his hands opened the door. When he did the gypsy tried to wedge his boot between the doorframe and the door. At the same time he would growl at the doorman like some kind of crazy man flinching a fake attack toward him. The doorman slammed the door shut to howls of laughter from the younger travellers. The gypsy turned to his flock and mocked the bouncer. I listened to him revelling in his momentary glory.

'Leave the door shut. Don't let them draw you. The guy's just a cunt. Fucking ignore him,' I said.
'I can't keep the door shut. Two of the lads are out there,' he replied.

'Well what are you doing inside here if they're out there? We're a team. We work together, and stick together.'

The bouncer went quiet. It was obvious his bottle had gone, otherwise he would have dealt with the situation instead of letting it get out of hand. He could have doused the spark of intimidation instead of allowing the situation to take flame. Soon it would become a roaring inferno.

I was surprised at how easily the gypsy had put the lads on the back foot. Between them, they must have had nearly 80 years of door-work experience. I had the feeling they didn't trust each other to go for it together and were divided, unlike the travellers.

The gypsies had been pulling this kind of stunt for years, winding people up. They are born into confrontation. It's in their bones. I remember a simple situation on the door one summer evening. A big lad appeared at the front doors dressed in his traveller wear: steel toecap boots (checklers as they call them), jeans and checked shirt. He was clean and presentable and if the club had been a townie type venue I would have let him in. But he was extremely intimidating and an angry person. I could tell by his arrogant walk and the fact he pushed straight to the front of the queue that he had no respect. I hit him with the words that can be more devastating to a man's night out than a good right hand.

'Sorry, mate, not tonight.'

'Why not?' he replied in a broad travelling accent.

'You're not appropriately dressed.'

'What the fuck does that mean?'

'It means you're not conducive toward the dance scene.'

'You don't like gypsies.'

'Whether or not I like gypsies is irrelevant. You're not appropriately dressed for the night so you can't come in.'

'What am I supposed to wear?'

'Look down the queue. That's how you should dress for this scene.'

'I'm not gonna dress like those eejits.' His speech and body language showed signs he was getting to the point where, if I showed weakness he would explode into violence.

I had placed myself just out of reach of the big lummox. If he was going to go for it I would see it a mile off and get in first. I didn't show any malice toward him and I felt no fear.

'You're just a cunt,' he said.
'You're probably right. Why don't you come back later and we'll discuss it.'
'Fuck you,' he said. His speech was now getting down to single syllables: a danger point; he could attack me at any time.
'And fuck you too,' I countered. A black cloud blocked out the sun and chilled the air.
'You're fucking racist. Racist, do you hear?' he said as he turned and walked off.
I smiled at him. He walked back.
'You're a cunt.' Then walked off again daring anyone in the queue to catch his eye. He turned and gave a perfect impersonation of Arnold Schwarzenegger with an Irish twang to it. 'Oi'll be back.' He never came back and he wasn't prepared to take me on in front of the watching crowd. The reason: he knew I was prepared to scrap it out with him and the difference between me and him was that I was getting paid for it. It was my living. I'd had many a run in over the years and most of them ended the same way: a Mexican stand-off.

Now I knew what the situation was about, the fear seemed to dissipate. I accepted the problem and decided to deal with it. I made a decision to confront the main man myself and have done with the nonsense unfolding before my eyes. It was time to play the game.
The two doormen on duty outside the club doors were inbetween the crowd control barriers which were made up of three steel railings, like those at a pop concert connected by three ropes, creating three entrances. The gypsy had caught the door staff unawares and got inside the middle rope. Normally he would have been kept outside the rope and on the pavement in front of the camera. Where he was standing was off camera: a big mistake on his part. He had no intention of coming into the club. He and his followers were banned from entering the premises because they were known troublemakers. His game was to push the doormen into conflict. The two doormen on the outside were playing the situation down to avoid the inevitable. When you do that it sometimes works, but with travellers you are actually inviting more trouble. These types are looking for a weakness, a flaw in the

armour that they can penetrate. It was time to get control of the situation one way or another. The gang's leader was getting over confident and his gang, ready to move in.

My heart was pounding out the usual warning. I released the door catch and took a deep breath. I couldn't leave the lads out there on their own and I sure wasn't going to let this cunt get the upper hand. He would be bragging about it for months to come and everyone would come along for a pop at the doormen. It was time to do what I got paid to do. Keep the peace.

'Come out of the way,' I said to the doorman holding the door.

'Where you going?' he asked. I just gave him a look and walked out of the door. I was immediately confronted by the gypsy. I didn't have time to feel fear and the adrenalin I was feeling from earlier made me feel sharp. I looked out at his crew. They were a mean looking bunch.

'Excuse me, mate,' I said in a deceptive soft voice. The gypsy turned around. He was fired up and well switched on. He was experienced, I knew that. He immediately lined me up. His breath stank of beer and he smelt of bonfires. I hid my fighting stance from the gypsy. I didn't want him to feel threatened. I wanted to talk him down, give him the opportunity to walk away, face still intact. I didn't hold out much hope. I set myself away from his right hand, placing my foot almost central to his centre line. He would have to adjust his stance to punch me or use his head as weapon.

'There's no need for this, mate. Why don't you step outside of the railings and we'll talk about the situation,' I said. This was what he was waiting for: someone to confront him. Now he could show his flock how tough he really was. I had my own ideas on that one. I adjusted my hidden fighting stance staying well balanced, controlling the distance with my hands just above his. Both palms were open in a kind of pleading fashion like Oliver begging for more food, only I was begging him to take the way out I was offering.

I pressed my left hand fingers into his ribs; not hard but just enough to get his attention. The arrogant bastard immediately smacked my hand away from beneath his right elbow.

'Get your fucking hands off me,' he said.

His hand hit the inside of my left arm, aiding the twisting of my torso to his left triggering my response. He went for it ramming, his head forward attempting to butt me. Before he could connect my right fist landed with an almighty crack on the underside of his jawbone.

I'd pre-empted his head-butt with a powerful right uppercut which travelled no more than a couple of inches. The effect was immediate, for a split second he was motionless and unconscious but still upright. It was as if time was standing still and had to catch up with the speed of the event. There was an eerie silence. I felt like I could walk around the scene freely while everybody else was frozen in the stillness. I felt tall like I was looking down onto the scene. Like a felled tree he reeled backwards in slow motion. First his backside hit the pavement, then a shock wave ran the full length of his body. His shoulders hit next then the head finally whipped in to the concrete. I heard the horrible cracking sound as his head hit the hard surface, finally coming to rest centimetres from the corner of the wall.

Blood oozed from the back of his head forming a puddle; his chest heaved, blood mixed with his breath and formed froth on his lips which bubbled in and out. Then like a rush of water from a burst dam the scene fast forwarded to real time. A chaotic outburst of anger erupted from the gypsy gang. They rattled the railings, threatening to surge forward. I was running on pure instinct now. I exploded into a tirade of abuse as the euphoric chemical induced rage hit my system.

'Come on then, you bastards. I'll have the fucking lot of you,' I screamed. I didn't have any thought of the consequences now. I had no mind. The gypsies ran back and forth like chickens do when the head has been decapitated. They were lost without their leader.

One by one I challenged them. I needed to separate them further so that they could not regroup.

'Do you want a fucking go?' I said shouting aggressively. The gypsies backed off. I knew they wanted to attack but didn't have the bottle to come forward for fear of being beat. Then the gypsies were re-ignited by the cry of one of the gypsy gang.

'You've killed my da, you've killed him.' They started to panic and pulled together once more as a gang.

'Come on, you bastard,' shouted another.

'I'll fucking kill ya,' he said.

I moved toward him and he backed off.

'Come on, you fucker, if you want some you can have some,' I said. I was in the thick of it. Something had to give. Then it came, the gypsy challenge.

'Round the back, come on, round the back.' They had a leader again.

'We'll do this the gypsy way. Me and you, nobody else, not your fucking boys, just me and you. Come on.'

He walked away ripping his shirt from his back. His physique was impressive. He wasn't a huge bloke but he was ripped and his aggression made him look like a fierce opponent.

I could feel the support of the bouncers behind me, but this was now a one-on-one, a match fight for him and me. A matter of honour to him and a matter of winning at all costs for me. I didn't want to push him into a corner but it seemed I already had. As a point of honour you either rise to the challenge and give it your best shot or get out of the game.

I looked around for the first time and realised how many people were watching. The whole square had come alive and they waited for my reply. The rest of the gypsies shouted abuse as their hero waited for me to answer his call to battle.

'Aye go on round the back. Do it the gypsy way,' they shouted. I wasn't going to give him the chance of glorifying himself by refusing the challenge, but by offering me out on a one-to-one he'd stolen the initiative away from me. I had to regain it. I stared at him and felt a quiver on my top lip and a wave roll through my stomach. I was getting another shot of adrenalin, I needed it. The words just rolled of my tongue. Years of real experience came out in every word.

'Fuck round the back. Never mind the gypsy way. We'll do it my way, you fucking tosser. We'll do it here, right now.' I gestured to the pavement.

'We'll do it in front of everyone, so that they can see what a fucking wanker you really are. Come on,' I screamed. Now it was his turn to accept or refute the challenge. The gypsy paused, his brain engaged in an internal battle – he looked confused. I goaded him once more. 'Come on, boy,' I said. 'Let's go.' I stood hands at my sides ready to do battle.

He started to look around him nervously. His body language told me he couldn't risk everyone seeing him for what he really was.

'Not here, I'm not fighting round here,' he said. He started to replace his shirt. 'I might get arrested.' His shirt was now on and his voice had softened. I'd beaten him with verbal.

'Just as I thought, you're just like the rest of them: a fucking wanker,' I said.

'That's it. I'm calling the police.' He got onto his mobile phone. The gang all chanted in unison. 'Call the police, call the police.' I surveyed their faces. Not one would catch my eye.

'Call the police. We'll get the cunt arrested.' It was his way out. I played on it.

'One minute you want to fight, the next you want to ring the police,' I said, making sure the crowd knew that the gypsies had bottled it.

'Fucking call them,' I said. I'd had enough of their playground antics. I ventured back toward the club. It was time to make my exit. I turned to the lads on the door and pointed to the still unconscious gypsy.

'Put him in the recovery position,' I said. The gypsy was still out cold and on his back: a dangerous position. He was still breathing. I thanked heaven for that. I never wanted to hurt him and I felt no malice toward him. Our paths had never crossed before. But for whatever reason he wanted to harm me and I couldn't let that happen. It was hit or be hit. I took one last look at him lying on the floor and realised that it could have been me lying there.

The gang verbally abused the door staff and the police as I slipped quietly away into the night.

I later found out that the police had informed the gypsies that if they wanted to press charges on anyone they had to produce their passports at the police station the next day to prove who they were. None did! It was a fair go and they respected that.

LIFE BEGINS AT FORTY

The millennium had come and gone. None of the predicted global breakdowns of computing systems or disasters had happened, and for me it was just another nightclub party albeit a massive one. We were rammed; 3,000 clubbers danced the night and much of the next day away, supervised and protected by some of the best doormen in the country: big Dave Gillespie, Adam Harrison, Nathan Beeby, Lloyd, Jordan, Booty and others whose tireless efforts are not forgotten.

The year 2000 was a special time for me. I was now 40 years young. I had a beautiful wife and Luke and Thomas: two sons who I adore and would die for. And guess what?
I loved my life with all its ups and downs! I'm very much a family man and when I'm not standing on a nightclub door or in a gym I'm spending time with them. And it was a beautiful time watching my children grow and develop into little gentlemen.

To know real beauty you have to know ugly. 'Ugly' is having a beer mug rammed in your face at 50 miles an hour, or a bottle swiped across the back of your head while you stop some innocent from getting a beating. 'Ugly' is picking bits of glass out of the face of a girl barely 16, scarred for life by some jealous lover who decided to ram a glass in her face. 'Ugly' is having your life taken away from you by a boot or a stamp on the head for jumping the taxi queue. And there is nothing uglier than spending wasted months or years incarcerated in a stinking prison cell banged up for 23 hours a day, eating shit food all for losing control in a moment of madness.
I know you would expect ugly in some third world country, not in our modern society.
But it's here every weekend in a town or city near you. Violence is sickening: the worst type of human trait. One we should all be ashamed of. I know you can blame alcohol and drugs but anger, frustration, jealousy and greed are the real culprits. The alcohol just brings it out and when it comes out, the pain and suffering it causes lasts for generations. And it's not a male macho thing; it's

all walks of life – male, female, young and old. Hatred is bred into the young so when they grow they manifest killing thoughts. In a world with so much beauty why is it so ugly? Even with all of my experiences of the violent kind I can't answer that question. Maybe one day I'll be able to make sense of it!
But as I sit here in the beautiful Majorca sunshine, all that violence is up there with the stars. Tina, my beautiful wife, and her equally gorgeous twin sister Gina, had surprised myself and her husband Ian 'Spider' Reeves with a two-week break in a fabulous villa known as the Villa Can Tanca, near Cala Dor. This rustic farmhouse with its oak beams is set on two levels overlooking spectacular views of the countryside with the sea visible in the distance. The courtyard has its own well, a pool and a purpose-built brick barbecue house with its own oven and outside eating areas.
It has its very own star show visible at night due to the lack of light pollution. The air is full of an array of smells: bougainvillea, hibiscus and cypress trees mingled with the smells of citrus fruits: lemons, oranges and limes coming from the orchard set in the courtyard.
I'm having a quiet moment soaking up the sun, healing my wounds from round after round of judo training and easing the mental pressure from a job that still surprises me after 20-odd years. Back home I own my house and a nice 4x4 Jeep. I have a well-paid job, and plenty of time to spend with my kids.

It could be argued that I made my money out of somebody else's misery and somebody else's pain. Maybe I have, but it's a living I've had to endure for over two decades. I'm good at it, one of the best. It's a job that could easily end me, a job fraught with risk. But it's a job that somebody has to do. I would like to move on, do something different.
Do something I really enjoy like owning my own gym or dojo.
I've had gyms before. I've trained all my life and I've dealt with people all my life. I know I could do it. But it's the money; it's kept me and my family in food and clothed them.
My boys want for nothing.
Geoff Thompson, a friend and a mentor of mine, planted a seed in my head:

'Why don't you open your own gym, John?' he said. 'Maybe you should write a book, become a writer, tell people about your experiences so you can help them become better people by understanding violence.'

Me a writer? I thought. I left school with no education, expelled, thrown out. 'You'll never be any good,' they said and I believed them for a while.

'Maybe I will write a book, but who'd want to read a story about a violent man turning good?' I said.

'It's only fear that will stop you, John. It's fear that stops us all from achieving if you let it.' This was Geoff's final word on the matter and he's right. Fear is what stops us.

The same fear that drives us on to great things. You've either got the bottle or you haven't. The good thing about it is you can learn to face adversity. I remember as a young boy hiding under the covers shaking with fear because I was afraid of the dark. Not once did I realise that under the covers was far darker and once under there I became more afraid. I know now that if I had got out of bed and faced up to the fear of the dark room I would have been fine. Fear of the unknown is a terrible fear but one that can be easily beaten. Go to the fear. Take it on and you will find you are far stronger than that which you face. Go to the fear and make yourself a better person. If I can do it anyone can. Anyone.

The intense heat of the midday sun forces sweat beads to trickle down my brow. As I wipe the sweat away I watch a scrawny goat meander across a chocolate covered field sparsely planted with dried yellow grass and green cacti. The sound of the goat's bell clangs a soft note as it makes its way toward a corner of the field where a farmer cuts, chops and throws the cacti across the path of the mountainous creature. In the distance the sound of a crazy donkey is honking away the peace and calm, the butt of many a holiday joke. My attention is drawn toward the sound of children's infectious laughter as they plunge into the still of the pool. 'Come on, Dad, jump in,' says Luke. My Luke, Thomas and my beautiful nieces, Charlotte and Sophie, await my arrival in the cool of the refreshing pool. I laugh and look around me and realise how lucky I am before I too plunge into its depths.

Money is great. It buys the things we need in life but the most important things to me are love, health and happiness. But remember the more successful you can become the more people you can help.

I've learnt that a society that cares more about recycling than drug addiction or crime and probably spends more on it, doesn't care enough about their fellow man. They wallow in self-pity and negativity and when they do find the time to help or give way to someone on the road or open a door for a lady they expect instant praise for their goodness. And if they don't get it hatred raises its ugly head. There is hope, indeed there is hope. If we all try that much harder to help our fellow man regardless of race, colour or creed and expect no thanks, if we remain positive in our outlook and kill off the negativity that pulls us down, then maybe, just maybe, we can change the world.

In writing this book I have strived to tell it like it is so you can have an insight into the world of violence. I know some of you may scoff at its content and criticise its message but as they say the truth sometimes hurts.

I know this book will help others change like I have and help them to become good people regardless of their past.

The final message I have for you is to be positive. Strive to better yourself. We are here but only once and this life is not a rehearsal. If you've ever wanted do something do it today and do it to the best of your ability. Oh, and be nice.

EPILOGUE

FULL CIRCLE

'All good things come to an end' was an apt cliché that sprung to mind as I negotiated my severance pay. The Emporium had been up for sale for some time and now a buyer had been found; it was once again time for me to move on. But unlike before, I decided to take the more difficult option: face my fears in life and go for a career change, a big, big stride forward. I'd had a dream for a number of years but was too afraid to give up my job and attempt to own my own business. I knew I could do it but I was lounging in a very comfortable situation earning thousands of pounds a year for little effort. Not because I did very little but because I knew my trade so well it felt easy for me and I was too comfortable. It was time for me to go it alone, to step out of the shadows of other businessmen and make my mark on a life less ordinary.
With a few thousand pounds scraped together and a good business plan, I got together with my wife Tina and formed a partnership. With the nerves eating out our insides we approached the bank. It was a short interview and when it was over it had me and Tina wondering what all of the nerves were for. The bank loved the business idea and the plan we'd slaved over. All we had to do now was find a suitable building for the John Skillen Martial Arts and Fitness Centre to be housed in. In the meantime we would run the gym from my garage.
After two months I was earning enough money from personal training at my garage. To supplement my earnings I worked the door of Discoteca, a Loughborough nightclub, on Friday and Saturday nights. Sadly a couple of weeks prior to me taking the job on, a young man lost his life at the hands of another young man. Stabbed to death on the pavement in front to of the club! Two families' lives were changed forever that night. You see, when something as tragic as this happens two lives are lost; one for ever and one for ever living with the consequences of his actions, a tortured, tormented mind and the families of both men, grief-

stricken, living out the rest of their days in pain. It was a sad affair but life goes on.

My brief was to get control of the door and make sure everybody enjoyed the experience that was Discoteca. There I was standing on the front door of a venue freezing cold watching the nightlife wander by. A group of students passed by, falling about, narrowly missing lamp posts and people as they headed for the next bar. It wasn't long before one of the youths bumped into the wrong man. There was a stare, a quick verbal exchanged then the student's head was forced back by a tremendous blow to the jaw thrown from an unseen angle. That familiar crunching sound came next as his head hit the floor and he was out cold. The gang walked on coolly not even caring to look back. There appeared to be no fear among them. The student's mates gathered around him panicking at a loss as to what to do, due to their drunken stupor. I arrived by the student's side the same time as another doorman from a nearby pub and we gave first aid. The ambulance arrived quickly after hearing it was a head injury. The police were even quicker. I took one last look at the bubbles of blood seeping out of his mouth and wandered back to the club doorway un-thanked and deep in thought.
The night was building. It wouldn't be long before the club was heaving with sweat-soaked, perfumed inebriated bodies hell-bent on having a good time. I was approached by two such people. It was still early and they had taken advantage of the cheap early entry.
'Some fucking bitch has stolen my purse,' she shrieked at me as if I was the girl's accomplice. 'I'm going to fucking kill her.' I listened. I'd found out over the years that sometimes it's best to listen, get the facts, let them let off a bit of steam and then give words of wisdom.
'Why don't we go and have a look upstairs? Maybe you've dropped it on the floor. Where have you been since you came in to the club?'
'I've only been in here two fucking minutes. I know who's got it. She's a fucking thief.' She ran up the staircase shoes in hand. 'I'll fucking kill her!'

I picked up my pace and followed her into the ladies' toilet. I walked into a tirade of abuse being swapped from one girl to the other. It was like watching a live version of the *Oprah Winfrey Show*.
'Girls, if you both don't calm down you're going out.'
'I ain't going nowhere until I get my fucking purse, money and cards.' They stood hands on hips ready to scrap it out. Then something unusual happened. One of the girls accused of nicking the purse handed it over.
'I've just found it on the floor,' she said.
'Well, where's the money and the cards?' the other girl asked.
I butted in. 'You're the only people in this club at the moment so one of you must have nicked it.' The victim went ballistic; every Tampax bin in the toilet was tipped up and emptied on to the floor, various credit cards were mixed in among the used tampons that were now lying at my feet. I walked out of the toilet in disgust. Discoteca was a decent club. As I walked out the owner Mickey and his son Santino walked in. They knew the women so I left them to it and made my way down to the front doors. The girls left shortly after.

The night was drawing to a close. I stood with my back to the wall watching a youth sitting in the foyer his face contorted with anger. He looked in pain. I watched him turning a glass in his hand, his grip so tight it threatened to break. I'd seen this look many times before. It was a war face. I approached the lad with caution. I placed my hand on his shoulder; as he looked at my hand, I snatched the glass from his grip and placed it behind me.
'What's the problem, mate?'
'I'll fucking kill him.' His words disturbed me. There was conviction in his voice. At that precise moment he meant what he'd said. I felt sad. I knew it was only the beer talking but it was dangerous talk. I escorted him from the club, then warned his potential victim who was unaware of how close he was to a glass in the face. I guided him out of the back doors of the club. With the possibility of violence all around me I remained aware.

Standing on the door waiting and watching for aggro was the story of my life but I realised I'd come full circle. It was now time for me to move on, time to once again exact change in my life for the better. I decided it was time to start my own business: a fitness centre aimed at martial artists and people struggling to live a healthy life.

'Seek and ye shall find', 'ask and it shall be given', two phrases I now believe in, due to how difficult it was to locate a building at the right price. It came in the guise of a phone call from a friend, Nilesh Lakha, who had an old Victorian-style corner shop, which from the outside looked too small for my needs, so I had never considered it before. I viewed the building which was perfect for our needs, negotiated a lease and that was it. After a long search I had found what I was looking for and proceeded to create the John Skillen Martial Arts and Fitness Centre. It became known as 'The Palace of Positivity', aptly named by my good friend, Andy Mitchell.

Life is now very sweet for me and my family. I live like a king, rich because I have my health and fitness and people around me who love me and I, them: something even money can't buy! I truly am living the dream.

THE GYM

The gym to me is a very special place, very different to the doors of various clubs and pubs; it's where I've learnt the most about myself. It has an almost magical effect on my being, as soon as I enter my special place, regardless of my mood, I can't help but feel good. I breathe in and savour the smell of leather emanating from the heavy bags that hang invitingly from cold black metal brackets. I can hear the sound of clanking and the sharp exhalations of breath as the weights are heaved, pulled and pushed. There's the babble of speech entwined in a cacophony of conversation, various groups discussing the finer points of training or the unfolding of last night's escapades from around the town. There's a kind of music formed from the rhythm of focus pads being struck and the sounds of the treadmill – the runner's feet beating out an almost primal beat, like war drums stirring my senses. The thwacking and thumping sound that is created when a bag is pounded with venom, every punch, kick, elbow or slap relieving the stress of the day, dissipating the frustration and anger that can slowly build within the human psyche until it explodes in a tirade of vehemence against some unsuspecting individual. For me the gym is a lifeline to a calmer disposition, a sanctuary against the stress of modern living, it is indeed a special place. For me and for many others, I'm proud to say.

I remember how demanding the journey to get to this place has been; the months of uncertainty, the hurdles, physical and financial that had to be cleared, the difficult first few months after opening when success and failure were in the balance. By my side, my business partner stood like a pillar of strength, a rock for me to cling to when negativity reared its head. My beautiful and supportive wife, whom I love dearly, gave me the courage to press on, to dare, to create a new career out of an empty building and the power of thought, instead of retreating to the relative safety of doing what I had done for the previous twenty years. I remember a comment given to me by one of my many instructors, when I'd told him I was opening the gym. 'Setting up your own business is tough, it's hard work, but at least no one is trying to bury a glass in your face!' With those words ringing in my ears, I pressed on.

The characters filed in through the doors to get a glimpse of the newest gym in town. They also wanted to converse with me, to discuss training methods. Most though wanted to discuss life, to talk about their situations, their aspirations, their dreams. Me, I love to listen, I love to interact, engage their rhetoric, give advice if I feel they're asking for it. I am continually trying to help those less well informed than myself. Some of the characters are just passing through from other towns, cities or countries, others reside within the local boroughs. I have lost count of how many people I have met.

In complete contrast to working the doors, most of the people I meet at the gym are sober and actually make sense when they talk. Well, most of them are sober. As you might imagine, I've become something of an attraction to those caught up in a darker side of life. These guys feel they have the perfect right to hang around my gym even though they have no intention of joining. Oh, they'll say that's what they want to do, 'one day', but often that day never materialises and some of those who call in asking for help have addictions so powerful they can't survive the rat-run of life they're trapped in.

One such man, who I had known as a fairly normal person before his addiction, had fallen deeper and deeper into the dark pit of pain and soul-torturing self-pity. He was almost comical in the way he displayed his persona, a drunken caricature, almost puppet-like in his movements. Occasionally one or two of the strings seemed to have been cut. How he remained upright is still a mystery to me. I actually liked him, although he was a physical wreck and mentally in a bad place and he knew it. But there was something about his character that gave me hope that maybe one day he could change. Maybe he could still make a better life for himself. His old friends, the ones who knew him before his addiction, and his family, despite the way he acted towards them, hadn't given up on him.
Just as I was taking the last swig from a mug of tea sweetened with honey the gym door opened and there he stood, a slight wobble

unbalancing him, and a plastic bag clutched so tightly in his hand that his knuckles were white. He clung to the bag as if it was his life. Dishevelled, he stood staring at me glassy-eyed; no words left his mouth.

'What do you want?' I asked in a firm manner. He never spoke, instead he approached the counter I was standing behind and placed the carrier bag on top. He smiled a painted smile, and it was then that his breath hit me like strong bleach hits the back of the nasal passages and stays there. Only this wasn't anything like the bacteria-killing chemical, this was the acrid smell of stale beer mingling with the stench of body odour caused by weeks without attending to the daily rituals that most of us take for granted. The painted smile grew bigger and formed a few cracks, his true emotional state showing through. For a second I felt myself being drawn into his world – a world I was too familiar with. I composed myself.

'OK, what you selling?' I asked.

'Don't be like that, John,' he said, sadness in his tone. 'It's nearly Christmas.' At that point I should have asked him to leave, like I'd asked so many before him. But I didn't, I decided to let him have his moment to pitch his wares. He delved into his bag, the painted smile he wore reminding me of a supermarket Santa trying to hide the truth from a suspicious child as he withdrew the ultimate dream gifts. And out they came, bottle after bottle of ladies' designer perfume, men's aftershaves and an array of beauty products. For a moment a part of me wanted to say, 'I'll take the lot, how much?' but I was aware of the bigger picture, so I listened.

'You know how much these are worth don't you, John?' he said, reminding me of an Alan Sugar apprentice struggling with the concept of selling. 'I bet your missus would love this perfume, look!' As he spoke he thrust a bottle of perfume into my hand. I accepted it, but then quickly placed it onto the counter. He finished his spiel; now it was my turn to pitch to him the knowledge I'd acquired through experience. You see, I had figured out that to live a clean life free from the negative side, you have to become a better salesman than those people who try to draw you into their dark seedy world. You have to sell to them behind the smokescreen of the buyer, turn the tables on them so to speak. I began to explain to him the reason why I wouldn't be buying any of his wares.

'Where did you get these from?' I asked.

'They're not nicked!' he proclaimed. I looked him directly in the eye, staring for a moment and trying to see beneath his deceitful facade.

'It's nearly Christmas, right?' I asked.

'Yes,' he replied, a look of bewilderment on his face.

I continued, 'You've just been into Boots the Chemist and stolen all of these goods, all of them costing a fair bit? And when you sell these, you'll probably go back and steal some more, correct?' His expression didn't change. 'Well, let me tell you an imaginary tale.' He listened without comment. 'The manager has been newly appointed after relocating from another area. He has a wife and two young children, all excited to receive gifts from Santa on Christmas Day. He has a mortgage, bills, a car which is on finance – a car that he needs. To enable him to work and to keep his job he has to make sure that his store is in profit. Now, when you stole those items you caused his stocks to be down. As soon as he has a stocktake it will become apparent that all is not well; there'll be a deficit and there won't be any profits. Because of your actions, his job is at risk, he'll probably be dismissed and have to go home and break the news to his wife, the car will have to go back and he'll default on his mortgage. His children won't be able to get the Christmas presents he'd worked so hard for. His wife might even leave him, breaking up the family home, and all of that trauma will be your fault because you thought it was OK to steal, to take something that wasn't yours.'

He stood in silence, head bowed, a tear in his eye, and then quickly gathered his display from the counter, putting each item back into his bag.

'Hang on, I haven't finished yet,' I said. 'Why don't you take the goods back to the store, ask to see the manager and give the perfume back, and then apologise for taking what wasn't yours to take?'

He raised his head and said, 'I can't do that! I might get arrested.'

I laughed. 'You could have been arrested when you stole them and that didn't bother you.'

'Well that's different.'

I smiled and shook my head in disappointment. 'Go on, off you go.'
'So you don't want them then?' he said as he opened the door.
'See you,' I replied. 'And have a good Christmas.' He walked off, a homeless soul, off into the cold light of the day, his neck bent. He left me wondering if he'd ever see the true light or would he too end up in the gutter like so many before him. He hobbled off in the direction of the store, clutching his bag tight to the side of his leg. I felt a tinge of hope; maybe, just maybe, I thought.
Later that day I saw him again, a bottle of strong cider in his hand, surrounded by the anchors that held him firmly to that life, his so-called friends all in the same sorry condition. I made my way round to the dojo and pushed the situation to the back of my mind. What else could I do?
About a year or so later I was hanging around waiting for a client. The gym was buzzing, music blaring out of the speakers, the sounds of joyous exercise everywhere. I heard the door of the gym open and someone ask, 'Is John here?' I made my way over and there was a smart, clean, well-groomed man smelling of aftershave and looking pristine. He stood in silence in almost the same spot as on the day when he'd tried to sell me the stolen perfumes.
'Tell me then,' I said and waited for his reply.
'I did it,' he said, with a look of pride on his face. 'I did what you said; I went into rehab. I've been there for a year and I just wanted to say thank you.' I felt a real sense of joy welling up inside and couldn't help but smile. I went right up to him and gave him a hug.
'Well done, mate, that's absolutely brilliant. I'm so proud of you, keep going strong.'
'Don't worry, John, I'm not sticking around, there's nothing here for me any more. I have to get a new start.' On that he turned and left. I realised from that moment that we should never give up hope; people can be fixed when they are broken. Of course it takes time and expertise, but in troubled times a few kind words can make all the difference. We are never alone!

OLD FRIENDS

Due to my past history, much of it contained within these pages, I was always keeping an eye over my shoulder. The gym was an open door. I never knew who would enter from one day to the next. What I did know was the past has a habit of catching up with you – and mine was about to catch up with me!
The knock on the plate glass window and the man beckoning me outside sent a quiver of adrenalin through me. At first I didn't recognise him, there had been a lot of water under the bridge, a lot of time had passed by. He gestured to me again to come outside; it was then that I recognised my old foe Regan. He was not as tall as I remembered him yet despite his age he looked strong and powerful. I didn't hesitate and ventured outside. I placed myself in a position of distance control and before I could ask what Regan wanted, he said in a hurried tone, 'I didn't want to fight you, it was the others, them bastards.'
I put my arm on his shoulder and looked him in the eye. There was no malice there, just a really sorrowful look. I was taken aback by his manner. I wouldn't have expected this of him; as far as I was concerned we'd sorted this out years ago by staying out of each other's way. Oh I'd seen him occasionally and spoken to him by way of a nod of the head, but never had a conversation with him, let alone discussed past events. My strength of character along with my attitude had changed. I continued to train hard to keep my edge but had made a vow to only fight when someone crossed the line I'd firmly set in front of me. Any violence employed by me would be in self-defence and within the confines of the law. I also understood the power of forgiveness. And that alone gave me a bigger internal strength which shone on the outside. I spoke calmly and with a conciliatory tone in my voice.
'That was years ago. As far as I'm concerned it's finished with.'
I reached my hand out to him; he looked at it for a second then shook it. The ice cold of the situation melted right there and then. The next phrase that left his mouth made me realise that one enemy is too many and a thousand friends too few. Regan asked me if he could join my gym. I was gobsmacked for a moment then

said, 'Of course.' He reached into his pocket and paid for a year's membership there and then in cash.

'Come on,' I said, 'I'll show you around.' And in we went like old friends.

That day underpinned everything that I'd been through so far in my life. And I knew I was living it real. Regan and I became good friends and even though we have a laugh and share a conversation or two there is still that competitive edge between us – he throws down the occasional gauntlet that usually means I have to try and equal his best in the gym! Both Regan and I are the same two people we were back then. But time and experience are great teachers and prove that people can and do change for the better.

THE END

Printed in Great Britain
by Amazon